FASTTRACK

Successful IT Projects

Darren Dalcher and Lindsey Brodie

THOMSON
™

Australia · Canada · Mexico · Singapore · Spain · United Kingdom · United States

THOMSON

Successful IT Projects

Darren Dalcher and Lindsey Brodie

Middlesex
University
PRESS

Series Editor
Walaa Bakry, Middlesex University

Publishing Partner
Middlesex University Press

Publishing Director
John Yates

Commissioning Editor
Gaynor Redvers-Mutton

Managing Editor
Celia Cozens

Production Editor
Amy Blackburn

Manufacturing Manager
Helen Mason

Marketing Manager
Mark Lord

Production Controller
Maeve Healy

Text Design
Design Deluxe, Bath

Cover Design
Matthew Ollive

Typesetter
Keyline Consultancy, Newark

Printer
C&C Offset Printing Co., Ltd, China

ISBN-13: 978-1-84480-699-7
ISBN-10: 1-84480-699-5

**British Library Cataloguing-in-
Publication Data**
A catalogue record for this book is available from the British Library

Disclaimer

The publisher reserves the right to revise this publication and make changes from time to time in its content without notice. While the publisher has taken all reasonable care in the preparation of this book, the publisher makes no representation, express or implied, with regard to the accuracy of the information and cannot accept any legal responsibility or liability for any errors or omissions from the book or the consequences thereof. Products and services that are referred to in this book may be either trademarks and/or registered trademarks of their respective owners. The publisher and author/s make no claim to these trademarks.

Successful IT Projects

Contents

The FastTrack Series

Thomson Learning and Middlesex University Press have collaborated to produce a unique collection of textbooks which cover core, mainstream topics in an undergraduate computing curriculum. FastTrack titles are instructional, syllabus-driven books of high quality and utility. They are:

- **For students**: concise and relevant and written so that you should be able to get 100% value out of 100% of the book at an affordable price
- **For instructors**: classroom tested, written to a tried and trusted pedagogy and market-assessed for mainstream and global syllabus offerings so as to provide you with confidence in the applicability of these books. The resources associated with each title are designed to make delivery of courses straightforward and linked to the text.

FastTrack books can be used for self-study or as directed reading by a tutor. They contain the essential reading necessary to complete a full understanding of the topic. They are augmented by resources and activities, some of which will be delivered online as indicated in the text.

How the series evolved

Rapid growth in communications technology means that learning can become a global activity. In collaboration, Global Campus, Middlesex University and Thomson Learning have produced materials to suit a diverse and innovating discipline and student cohort.

Global Campus at the School of Computing Science, Middlesex University, combines local support and tutors with CD-ROM-based materials and the Internet to enable students and lecturers to work together across the world.

Middlesex University Press is a publishing house committed to providing high-quality, innovative, learning solutions to organisations and individuals. The Press aims to provide leading-edge 'blended learning' solutions to meet the needs of its clients and customers. Partnership working is a major feature of the Press's activities.

Together with Middlesex University Press and Middlesex University's Centre for Learning Development, Global Campus developed FastTrack books using a sound and consistent pedagogic approach. The SCATE pedagogy is a learning framework that builds up as follows:

- **Scope:** Context and the learning outcomes
- **Content:** The bulk of the course: text, illustrations and examples
- **Activity:** Elements which will help students further understand the facts and concepts presented to them in the previous section. Promotes their active participation in their learning and in creating their understanding of the unit content
- **Thinking:** These elements give students the opportunity to reflect and share with their peers their experience of studying each unit. There are *review questions* so that the students can assess their own understanding and progress
- **Extra:** Further online study material and hyperlinks which may be supplemental, remedial or advanced.

Successful IT Projects

This book is written as a complete reference source for the management of IT projects and delivery of results, with additional support and activities for improving student projects.

This book covers:

- An introduction to the topics of project management and IT projects (with a unique focus on both project management and systems development lifecycles)
- Feasibility studies (project proposal and business case)
- Management of change (including deliverables and progress)
- Project planning (activities, schedules and cost estimation)
- Leadership and team-working
- Project quality management (quality control and quality standards)
- Project risk management (risk identification, assessment and mitigation)
- Project evaluation and reflection
- Introduction to PRINCE2.

It also offers help and advice about student projects, with guidance on choosing your project topic, on writing your project report and on dealing with deadline pressures. It also relates the project management theory to student project activities, setting appropriate exercises that will help you with your student project.

The book includes a chapter on research methods, which introduces the research process, and describes the main research methods and data collection methods.

Using this book

There are several devices which will help you in your studies and use of this book. **Activities** usually require you to try out aspects of the material which have just been explained, or invite you to consider something which is about to be discussed. In some cases, a response is provided as part of the text that follows – so it is important to work on the activity before you proceed! Usually, however, a formal answer will be provided at the end of each chapter.

The **time bar** indicates *approximately* how long each activity will take:

 short   < 10 minutes

medium 10-45 minutes

long   > 45 minutes

 Review questions are (usually) short questions for each chapter to check you have remembered the main points of a chapter. They are found at the end of each chapter; feedback is provided at the back of the book. They are a useful practical summary of the content and can be used as a form of revision aid to ensure that you remain competent in each of the areas covered.

About the authors

Darren Dalcher

Darren Dalcher is Professor of Software Project Management at Middlesex University and Visiting Professor of Computer Science at the University of Iceland as well as the founder and Director of the National Centre for Project Management.

Professor Dalcher has written over 200 papers and book chapters on project management and software engineering. He is editor-in-chief of *Software Process Improvement and Practice* and editor of a new series of books on *Advances in Project Management*.

Professor Dalcher is a Fellow of the British Computer Society and the Association for Project Management, and a Member of the Project Management Institute, the Academy of Management, the Institute for Electrical and Electronics Engineers, and the Association for Computing Machinery. He is a Chartered IT Practitioner and a consultant to government departments and industry both in the UK and beyond.

Lindsey Brodie

Lindsey Brodie is a Research Student Tutor at Middlesex University. She worked for ICL (now Fujitsu Siemens Computers) for many years: initially on customer projects in the areas of government, banking and retail, providing technical support for operating systems and writing software for operational support, then in product support of data management software.

Having completed an MSc in Information Systems Design, Lindsey moved into consultancy, working in the areas of user requirements, IT strategy and business processes. More recently, she edited Tom Gilb's book, *Competitive Engineering*. She is currently carrying out doctoral research on impact estimation, which is a quantitative method for investigating the contributions of designs towards meeting requirements.

Lindsey is a Member of the British Computer Society and a Chartered IT Practitioner.

Acknowledgements

This book grew from a module taught at Middlesex University. Thanks are due to the lecturers who have assisted in creating and teaching that module, especially Dr Robert Ettinger and Chris Sadler. Other people have also helped with the writing of this book. Gillian Palmer wrote Chapter 7: 'Leadership and teamworking', and Steven Burbidge contributed the example for PRINCE2 in the Appendix. Walaa Bakry contributed to several chapters, in particular Chapters 3, 4, 5 and 10. Thanks are due to Professor Tony White and Dr. George Dafoulas for reading and commenting on early drafts of the chapters; and to Aboubakr Moteleb and Richard Veryard for their assistance; also to Professor Colin Tully for his support and encouragement.

Visit the accompanying website at **www.thomsonlearning.co.uk/fasttrack** and click through to the appropriate booksite to find further teaching and learning material including:

For Students

- Activities
- Multiple choice questions for each chapter.

For Lecturers

- Downloadable PowerPoint slides.

CHAPTER 1

Introduction to projects and project management

OVERVIEW

This chapter introduces the notion of projects and explains the role of project management in guiding projects to successful completion. It also considers project lifecycles with regard to project management and systems development.

Learning outcomes   At the end of this chapter you should be able to:

- Describe the characteristics of projects

- Outline project management activities and the criteria for successful project management

- Describe in overview the project lifecycle and the different systems development lifecycle approaches.

1.1 Introduction

The aim of this first chapter is to provide an introduction to projects and project management; it consists of three main topics:

- **Project characteristics:** What is a project? What is project management?
- **Project management activities:** What activities are involved in project management? What criteria should be used to judge if a project is a success?
- **Project lifecycles:** What does a project management lifecycle involve? What are the different lifecycle approaches to systems development that can be taken?

1.2 What is a project?

Some of you may have spent some time in industry, maybe on a placement year, and have worked on a project. Most of us have used the term 'project' on some occasion. Words, however, can have different meanings associated with them. Before we proceed any further, let's reflect on the term 'project', and try to determine what it means.

> **Activity 1.1**
>
> **Activity 1.1: What is a project?**
>
> What do you think is meant by the term 'project'? (Please note that it need not relate to computing.)

Definition of 'project'

The Project Management Institute (PMI) in its *Guide to Project Management Body of Knowledge* (PMBOK Guide) defines a project as follows:

> 'A temporary endeavour undertaken to create a unique product, service, or result.'

(PMBOK 2004)

Note some specific aspects of this definition:

- **A project has a definable purpose (to create a product, service, or result):** a project exists to achieve some specific outcome: for example, to improve a business process, create a specific product or achieve a specific skill.

  The purpose of a project is defined by the project requirements (which specify such things as the intended functionality, and the performance and resource requirements)

- **A project represents a unique undertaking:** projects are not routine operational work (that is, the sort of work that is done every day within an organisation to keep it running), and they do not involve achieving something that has been done identically before – else why need a project? A project is a unique undertaking, which is carried out in order to bring about some required beneficial change.

- **A project is a temporary activity:** as well as not being routine work, projects also have limited time spans: that is, a project has a start date and a deadline date for completion. The requirements will state these deadlines!

(Note: don't be confused into thinking that 'temporary' means that all projects are short-lived! Project timescales can be very varied: some projects take days, and others, years.)

Activity 1.2

Can 'baking a cake' be considered a project?

Given the definition of a project, would baking a cake constitute a project? Justify your answer with reference to the PMI definition.

Activity 1.3

Examples of projects

Give a few examples of projects - these do not need to relate to computing.

It is interesting to note that every project is different: unique in its own way. The list of examples given in the feedback to Activity 1.3 has a mixture of old and new, big and small. None of these projects are routine operational work, and all are temporary activities (that is, they have dates or timescales for completion).

You will probably recall some of the circumstances and difficulties surrounding some of the public projects on the list. This emphasises the point that projects are innovative, and can therefore be risky. They may also be surrounded by controversy – some of the items on the list, clearly are. Part of the controversy relates to the different perceptions of different stakeholders and to the lack of clear definition of what these projects were about.

Project characteristics

A project can be described by several characteristics. These include:

- **Stakeholder value:** what is at stake for the organisation/business/participants? Can it be expressed in financial terms? For example, is it business survival or perhaps for competitive advantage, such as entry into a new marketplace?
- **Innovation**: how challenging are the project's performance requirements? Are they state-of-the-art or has something similar already been achieved? Is the technology already known or new?
- **Organisational change:** what degree of change is involved for the organisation? How much will this impact on the way the organisation operates and the way people work? Is the timeframe for the type of change involved realistic?

- **Resource utilisation:** what amount of resource does this project involve? Is it sufficient? Is it likely to be available?
    - **timescales:** how long is this project going to take to complete? Given the amount of work to be carried out, how tight are the deadlines?
    - **financial cost:** how much is this project going to cost? Given the amount of work to be carried out, how reasonable is the financial budget?
    - **resource availability:** are the project resources likely to be available when needed? For example, are staff with the right skills going to be available? Are the financial budgets going to be in place in time? Is the hardware and software required going to be available?
- **Organisational scope:** how much of the organisation is involved? How many different functional areas? How many different organisational levels? How many different departments? Does the scope spread across different countries? How many external organisations are involved and what is the nature of their involvement?

By building up a picture of the project characteristics, such things as the size and complexity of a project can be established. From these characteristics, the risk associated with the project can be assessed. Risk is a consequence of uncertainty and, in the case of a project, it is the risk of the project not meeting its requirements that is of interest. ('Project risk management' is the topic of Chapter 9.)

Activity 1.4: Is this a project?

Select one of the projects from the list of examples given in the feedback to Activity 1.3, or suggest an idea for a potential project, and rate it against the definition of a project and the characteristics of projects discussed above.

Activity 1.4

Remember: projects come in different sizes, and different degrees of change are involved. Many project management texts refer to extremely large projects and mention building skyscrapers and the pyramids. However, projects may be large or small (and more or less challenging) depending on the perspective of whoever needs or leads them and the resources and experience they have on hand.

Remember too that while many projects are business-critical (or personally critical to the people involved), some projects may also be life-critical and represent a potential for loss of life!

You should now have a clear understanding of what is a project. A useful quote for defining projects comes from David Cleland:

> 'A project is a combination of resources pulled together to create something that did not previously exist…'

> *Cleland and Ireland, 2002*

Cleland's sense of project is clearly that a project is something new and different. This agrees well with the PMI definition (quoted earlier) and its focus on temporary and unique. Projects are 'special' precisely because they are different and unique, and unlike anything that takes place on a regular basis or that has taken place before.

1.3 What is project management?

Organised project management as a recognised discipline has been in use for about 100 years. Many of the techniques used in project management were refined during the Second World War. However, many ancient projects (from the Pyramids to the Parthenon, and from the creation of civic amenities to the waging of war) will have necessitated the skills now associated with project management.

There is a clear case for management whenever any task or endeavour is undertaken: any job includes management elements of planning, organising, controlling and monitoring. Effective management leads to better use of resources and improved results. The need for management applies to all tasks – even those in routine environments. However, management is especially needed for projects where the work carried out is unique – and therefore much more unfamiliar and uncertain.

Change management is another factor. Change is inevitable in any organisational environment over time, but the amount of change increases when a project is involved. This is because the purpose of a project is to bring about some required change: the very nature of project work increases the need for management.

It therefore can be said that management is needed in most endeavours, but all the more so for projects!

Sommerville (2006) also makes the point that software project management is an emerging discipline. Software processes are not yet as well understood as, say, engineering processes to build bridges and buildings. In his book he suggests there are difficulties because:

- **The product is intangible:** software … cannot be seen or touched. Software project managers cannot see progress
- **There are no standard software processes:** we still cannot reliably predict when a particular process is likely to cause development problems.
- **Large software projects are often 'one-off' projects:** rapid technological changes in computers and communications can make a manager's experience obsolete.

Definition of 'project management'

The PMI defines project management as follows:

> 'The application of knowledge, skills, tools, and techniques to project activities to meet the project requirements.'(PMBOK 2004)

The Association of Project Management Body of Knowledge (APM BoK) provides the following definition of project management:

> 'Project management is the process by which projects are defined, planned, monitored, controlled and delivered such that the agreed benefits are realised. Projects are unique, transient endeavours undertaken to achieve a desired outcome. Projects bring about change and project management is recognised as the most efficient way of managing such change.'
>
> *APM BoK, 5th edition, 2006*

As Sommerville (2006) states, 'Good management cannot guarantee project success. However, bad management usually results in project failure. The software is delivered late, costs more than originally estimated and fails to meet its requirements.'

Project management activities

Project management is responsible for such things as ensuring the purpose of the project is well defined, estimating resources, recruiting staff, preparing schedules and allocating tasks.

Project management activities can be categorised into process groups as follows (PMBOK 2004):

- **Initiating processes**
- **Planning processes**
- **Executing processes**
- **Monitoring and controlling processes**
- **Closing processes.**

A project is often subdivided into phases. If this is the case, each of these activities will occur within each phase.

- **Initiating processes:** define and authorise the project or a phase
- **Planning processes:** create and maintain a workable scheme to ensure the project or phase carries out all the work required to meet its objectives and scope. The project or phase plan has to include all the tasks, task dependencies, task schedules and resource allocations. The plan has to be updated with actual progress and revised to cater for any changes
- **Executing processes:** co-ordinate people and other resources to carry out the project or phase plan and produce the deliverables of the project. Examples of the types of activity involved are developing the project team, disseminating information, contract administration and procuring required resources
- **Monitoring and controlling processes:** measure and monitor progress against the project or phase plan, taking corrective action when necessary. They also involve managing change control. Reviews are a typical controlling activity
- **Closing processes:** formalise the acceptance of the project or phase, and ensure all relevant documentation is put in place.

Project management knowledge areas

The 'knowledge areas' that project management are concerned with are as follows (PMBOK 2004):

- **Integration management**
- **Scope management**
- **Time management**
- **Cost management**
- **Quality management**
- **Human resources management**
- **Communications management**
- **Risk management**
- **Procurement management.**

You should think of the knowledge areas as specific topics that project management turns its attention to when carrying out its activities. For example, when planning a project, the focus will at one time be on time, and then it will shift to considering cost, and then to considering what is needed in the plan to achieve quality. Each knowledge area has to be specifically planned, executed and controlled. (Future chapters will cover some of these knowledge areas: for example, Chapter 6 covers cost, Chapter 8 covers quality and Chapter 9 covers risk.)

- **Integration management:** this involves the processes required to ensure that the various elements of the project are co-ordinated: that is, to ensure all the elements of the project come together at the right time. One specific concern is co-ordinating changes across the entire project
- **Scope management:** this is concerned with the processes involved in defining what is or what is not included in a project. It ensures the stakeholders all have a common, agreed understanding of the project deliverables and the project processes to achieve them. Choice of project and alignment of a project to the business objectives are included within this. See also Chapter 2
- **Time management:** this is concerned with the project scheduling processes: activity definition, activity sequencing and activity dependencies. It is also concerned with schedule control
- **Cost management:** this is concerned with the projects financial estimating and budgeting. It is also concerned with the value generated by the project. See also Chapter 6, which covers cost estimation
- **Quality management:** this is concerned with ensuring conformance to requirements. It also involves ensuring the requirements are aligned to the needs of the organisation. The appropriate quality standards have to be established, and quality controls have to be put in place. See also Chapter 8
- **Human resources management:** this involves all the aspects of managing people: planning organisational roles and responsibilities, staff acquisition and team development.
- **Communications management:** this is concerned with determining the information and communication needs of all the stakeholders, and ensuring information is collected and disseminated accordingly
- **Risk management:** this is concerned with understanding the risk profile of the project, and taking the relevant actions to identify and control risks. See also Chapter 9
- **Procurement management:** this involves the processes required to acquire goods and services for a project from sources external to the project organization. It involves selection of the goods or services, selection of the suppliers, and contract administration (including obtaining quotations)

1.4 Success criteria for projects

What is successful project management?

So we now understand that project management is about managing change. Let's now consider when we can view project management as 'successful'.

The definition of a project, as discussed earlier in this chapter, identified having a purpose as the starting point for a project. Success for a project must therefore be the achievement of this purpose.

That means the project must meet its requirements. The project must be completed such that it is:

- **Within time**
- **Within budget**
- **At the desired performance level**
- **With acceptable quality**
- **Offering at least the minimum agreed functionality**
- **Utilising the assigned resources effectively and efficiently**
- **Accepted by the client**
- **Used by the intended users**
- **Delivering the promised benefits** (which should ideally exceed the costs).

Activity 1.5

Successful student projects

Take another look at the definition of successful project management, as just presented.

Which of these items also apply to student projects?

Software project failures

The Libra IT system was designed for magistrates' courts and included upgraded infrastructure, office automation facilities, a national casework application and electronic links with other criminal justice agencies. The original 1998 deal for £184m collapsed in 2002, due to implementation problems. Following renegotiation in late 2002, the infrastructure portion alone cost £232m. The total system would now take 8.5 years to develop, be over two years late and cost over £400m. Magistrates (the intended users) complained that the system was not designed to be compatible with other systems operating in Crown and County courts. Moreover, the new system was not compatible with those used by the police, probation, prosecution and other services. The incompatibilities mean that files will sometimes be incomplete and occasionally they will not even be available in court. In an early pilot, this has resulted in continuous delays to some cases and in incorrect information being provided to defence solicitors and the prosecution.

Unfortunately, software project failure is all too common. A major study into IT projects by the British Computer Society (BCS) and the Royal Academy of Engineering reports that research shows IT project success rates to be 'between only 16% and 34%' (Royal Academy of Engineering 2004).

Standish reported that the figure for failed projects in the USA in 1998 was 75 billion dollars (Standish 1998). The amount of money that is being wasted is high, but the problem is not simply a financial one; many of these IT systems impact on people's lives. The failure of the initial London Ambulance System in 1992 demonstrated people's lives actually being put at risk by system failures (Flowers 1996, Yardley 2002).

Look at Table 1.1, 'Factors influencing project failure', drawn up by David Yardley (2002). Yardley considers that the probability of failure is low if only one factor is present, but rises if there are multiple factors throughout the project.

Technical failure	Human failure	Process failure
Lure of the leading edge	Lack of executive support	Absence of any project management methodology
Poor technical design	Lack of leadership	Absence of any systems development methodology
Technical solution to a non-technical problem	Uncommitted project team	Absence of any benefits management methodology
Dependence on software packages to satisfy requirements	Dysfunctional project team	Failure to identify and mitigate project risks
Lack of tools throughout development lifecycle	Failure to manage third parties	Failure to manage requirements
Technology-led development	Lack of a project 'champion'	Lengthy project timescales
	Lack of project ownership	Insufficient testing
	Stakeholder conflict	'Big-bang' approach to computerisation
	Resistance to change	
	Hostile organisational culture	
	Inexperienced project managers	
	Lack of business justification	
	Unclear or ambiguous business priorities	
	Lack of user training	
	Misaligned stakeholder motivation	

Table 1.1: Factors influencing project failure (Yardley 2002, page 303)

Activity 1.6: Factors influencing project failures

Which of the factors in Table 1.1, Factors influencing project failure, will be likely to affect a student project, and how could a student mitigate them?

1.5 Project lifecycles

Lifecycle models

Project management literature refers to a plethora of lifecycles: for example, project lifecycles, product lifecycles, organisational lifecycles, acquisition lifecycles, quality lifecycles, risk management lifecycles, support lifecycles and budget cycles. For any project, a whole variety of different lifecycles can be identified. In this chapter, two types of lifecycle are of specific interest: the project management lifecycle, concerned with managing the project, and the project technical lifecycle, concerned with modifying the system. For systems engineering, the project technical lifecycle is termed the 'systems development lifecycle'.

It is important to note that although lifecycle models are a widely accepted notion, this has resulted in many variants. You will find that different textbooks often present slightly different descriptions of the various models. Terminology also varies.

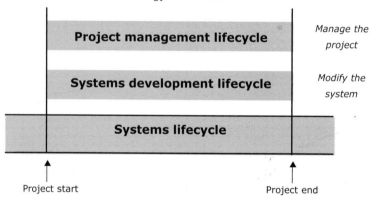

Figure 1.1: The main lifecycles involved in systems engineering projects. Note the 'system' will often be a software product, an information system or some other artefact. It usually has a longer lifetime than the project.

Activity 1.7: Lifecycles and student projects

Which of the lifecycles in Figure 1.1 would need to be considered by a student project? Make a list for each of the three types of lifecycle of the kinds of activities that they involve. (Try to identify at least four specific activities for each of the project management and systems development lifecycles.)

The project management and the systems development lifecycles must be compatible with each other. Information must flow between them, and it needs to occur at the appropriate times. Reviews provide major opportunities for synchronising management and technical lifecycles.

The systems development approach adopted will determine the lifecycles (for example, evolutionary projects will require different project management lifecycles and system development lifecycles from sequential projects).

The project management lifecycle

Most project management lifecycles have four or five phases, but some have ten or more. The basic lifecycle follows a common generic sequence such as the one identified in the APM's Body of Knowledge (APM BoK 2006):

- **Concept**
- **Definition**
- **Implementation**
- **Handover and closeout.**

This sequence focuses somewhat on technical aspects: that is, the construction of some kind of system solution. In fact, the actual management activities concerned are often ongoing across the lifecycle: see 'Project management activities' in Section 1.3 'What is project management?'.

Another point to note is that the generic project management lifecycle, given above, does not support evolutionary systems development. It is more aligned to the sequential model of systems development discussed in the next section.

Systems development lifecycle approaches

There are several different lifecycle models adopted for systems engineering projects. These models are based on a number of different lifecycle approaches, which are concerned with organising the systems engineering work of a project in fundamentally different ways. These approaches include:

- **Sequential:** project work is completed within one monolithic cycle. A project carries out each of the requirements analysis, design, coding, testing and support stages only once. Progress is in a linear fashion with control being passed on to the next sequential stage when the pre-defined milestones are achieved. This approach is resistant to change and the need for corrections and rework
- **Incremental:** the project functionality is divided up into a number of distinct deliverable increments. As each increment is completed, it is delivered to the customer, so the system grows in functionality at each release
- **Prototyping:** a prototype is a learning device; it is a small working model of some part of a system developed with the intent of testing out some ideas and seeing how they work. A prototype can either be thrown away once it has served its purpose, or it can be retained for further use
- **Evolutionary:** the system is allowed to evolve over time: the requirements are not fixed and the intention is to obtain and respond to customer feedback as the system develops. The system develops in small (for example, daily, weekly or monthly) iterative cycles. Each cycle is delivered to the customer and any relevant feedback is used in subsequent cycles. This approach is effective when there is a high degree of change and/or uncertainty involved in a project.

Systems development lifecycle models

There are several well-known lifecycle models used for systems engineering projects; the ones we shall briefly consider include:

- **Waterfall model**
- **Incremental phased delivery**
- **Evolutionary delivery (Evo)**

- **Spiral model**
- **DSDM (dynamic systems development method)**
- **RUP (rational unified process)**
- **XP (extreme programming).**

One main point to note is that the more sequential models such as the waterfall model are now recognised as only being appropriate in project environments where the requirements are well understood in advance and the rate of change in the organisational environment is negligible. Evolutionary approaches are gaining credibility as being far better at delivering successful projects.

It is interesting to note that many student projects end up using the waterfall model. This should only be done once you understand the relative merits and shortfalls of the different approaches and have considered which would be most likely to fit your specific requirements.

The following sections give brief descriptions of each of the lifecycle models listed above.

Waterfall model

The waterfall model, as commonly used, typifies the sequential approach. See Figure 1.2. In practice there is a main sequence of activities working from top to bottom, hence the name 'waterfall'. This sequential model would work best in a stable environment where the requirements were known in advance.

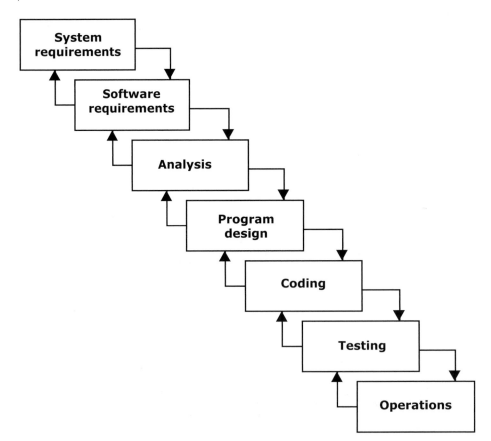

Figure 1.2: The waterfall model (After Royce, Winston 1970)

Winston Royce first described the waterfall model in 1970. It is of note that Royce also outlined in his original paper, five necessary improvements for the approach to work as follows:

- Complete program design before analysis and coding begin
- Maintain current and complete documentation
- Do the job twice if possible
- Plan, control and monitor testing
- Involve the customer.

Unfortunately, the majority of people overlooked these five improvements, even though Royce wrote that without these improvements the basic framework described in the waterfall model is risky and invites failure (Royce, Walker 1998).

Incremental phased delivery

This is a variant on the waterfall model, where system development is divided up into several increments (that is, a series of waterfall developments). The idea is that initial delivery occurs on completion of the first increment, and then subsequent increments further enhance the system as they are delivered (see Figure 1.3). One point of interest is that with additional resource, it is possible to reduce implementation timescales, as increments can be developed in parallel (see Figure 1.4).

The major problem with incremental phased delivery is that there are all the identical problems of using the waterfall model. There is, however, some possibility of using some feedback, and carrying out any required changes, in later increments.

A key issue to determine with incremental phased delivery is at what stages in the process are the requirements specification carried out: a certain amount of requirements specification has to be carried out early to determine the increments.

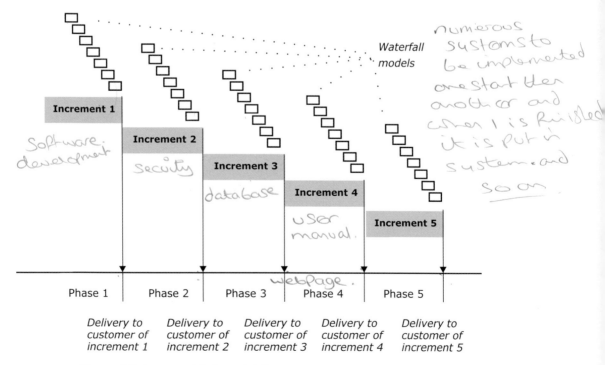

Figure 1.3: Incremental phased delivery

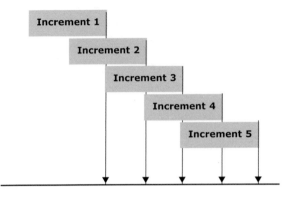

*Delivery to customer on
completion of each increment*

Figure 1.4: The figure shows how timescales for increment deliveries can be
'crashed' by using additional resources (in this example, two separate teams).

Evolutionary delivery (Evo)

First documented in 1976, evolutionary delivery was developed by Tom Gilb based on the
evolutionary methods used by Harlan Mills in the 1960s (Larman 2004). The basis of the
method is the **Plan-Do-Study-Act** cycle devised by Shewhart in the 1920s and used by
Deming (Deming 1986). Evo is included here because it is one of the first evolutionary
approaches (extreme programming developed its evolutionary aspects from this method), and
because it has some practical aspects that very clearly illustrate the evolutionary approach.

The old system is used as the base system and modified. This doesn't mean that revolutionary
change can't be achieved – it simply means that the change process can start very rapidly. The
new system is delivered in a series of steps. Key features include:

- Early and frequent delivery of steps: each step is typically between 2% and 5% of total project
  duration
- Delivery of value: the highest stakeholder value steps are given priority and delivered at the
  earliest possible time
- Use of feedback: feedback is obtained for each step and used to modify requirements and
  future plans as needed.

In Evo (see Figure 1.5), each result cycle represents a step. Within each step, the decision is
made on what to implement next ('the head'), and then any further detailed requirements
analysis and design is carried out and the design is implemented ('the body' – optional
development, optional production and mandatory delivery cycles) (Gilb 2005).

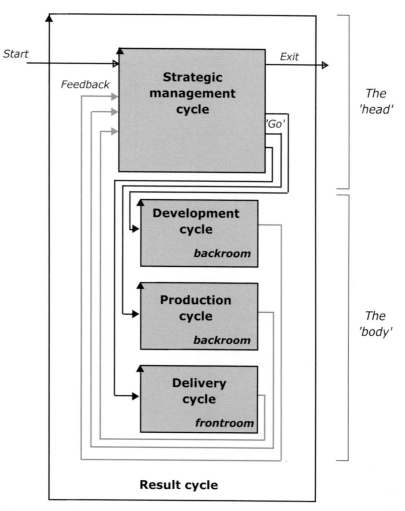

Figure 1.5: The Evo model

The aim is to maintain a constant stream of high-value deliverables from the earliest step. The backroom shows the development and production cycles, which might well take longer than the duration of a step to produce. Ideally, the project manager will have step options in reserve so that any delays are not visible to the customer and the project team is given some flexibility to cater for any unexpected problems (Gilb 2005). See Figure 1.6.

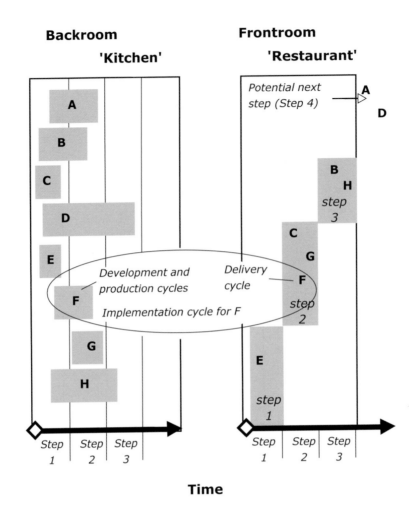

Figure 1.6: The frontroom shows the steps being delivered to the customers.

Spiral model

In 1988, Barry Boehm developed the spiral model. A project starts at the centre of the spiral and proceeds in an iterative spiral outwards. The model is divided into four quadrants:

- **Top left:** objectives are set, alternatives and constraints are identified
- **Top right:** alternatives are evaluated, and risks are identified and resolved
- **Bottom right:** development
- **Bottom left:** planning for the next iteration.

The spiral model uses iterative prototypes as shown in Figure 1.7. Each iteration represents a phase of the development process, such as feasibility, requirements, and design. The explicit treatment of risk is a main feature.

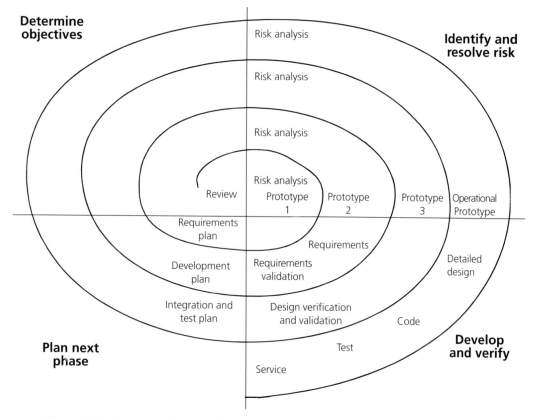

Figure 1.7: Boehm's spiral model. The development process starts in the middle and spirals outwards, producing a series of prototypes (Boehm 1988).

DSDM (dynamic systems development method)

First documented in 1994, DSDM is a rapid application development (RAD) developed in the UK by the DSDM Consortium (Stapleton 2003). The key idea about DSDM is that it time-boxes systems development into specific timescales and allocates specific resources, as opposed to specifying a fixed set of system functionality for each phase.

The DSDM development lifecycle has five phases – see Figure 1.8. The first two are sequential and carried out only once:

- **Feasibility study**
- **Business study.**

The other three phases are iterative and incremental. They are:

- **Functional model iteration**
- **Design and build iteration**
- **Implementation.**

(Note the DSDM lifecycle has seven phases – it includes pre-project and post-project phases together with the five phases of the DSDM development lifecycle.)

A timebox typically is set between two and six weeks. The aim of a timebox is to make something; a timebox is not activity-based. Initially, 'prototypes' are built and these are refined over time to become part of the delivered product. These prototypes are actually partial system components, and they are usually intended to be evolutionary, rather than throwaway.

DSDM recommends four categories of prototype: business, usability, performance and capacity, and capability/design. Often a combination of prototypes will be chosen. The choice of prototype depends on the system feedback required.

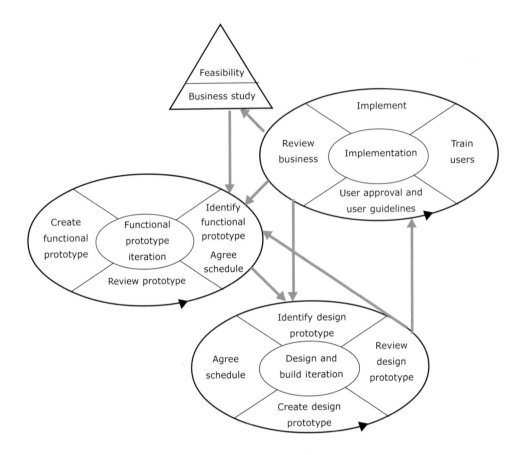

Figure 1.8: DSDM process diagram. The feasibility and business studies have to be completed sequentially, and then the functional prototype iteration, design and build iteration and implementation phases can be carried out. These latter three phases are iterative (Stapleton 2003, page 4).

According to Stapleton, the DSDM framework is based on nine principles:

1 Active user involvement is imperative.

2 DSDM teams must be empowered to make decisions.

3 The focus is on frequent delivery of products.

4 Fitness for business purpose is the essential criterion for acceptance of deliverables.

5 Iterative and incremental development is necessary to converge on an accurate business solution.

6 All changes during development are reversible.

7 Requirements are baselined at a high level.

8 Testing is integrated throughout the lifecycle.

9 A collaborative and co-operative approach between all stakeholders is essential.

RUP (rational unified process)

The rational unified process (RUP) (Kruchten 2000) has been derived from work on the Unified Modelling Language (UML) and the associated Unified Software Development Process (Rumbaugh et al. 1999). It is a process model usually described from three perspectives:

- A dynamic perspective of the phases of the model
- A static perspective showing the process activities
- A practice perspective recommending good practices.

The RUP identifies four distinct phases as follows:

- **Inception:** establish a business case by identifying all the external entities (people and systems) that will interact with the system, and describe these interactions. The system needs to make a significant contribution to the business
- **Elaboration:** understand the system domain and risks, and develop a requirements model, an architectural framework and project development plan
- **Construction:** design, code and test the system. Parts of the system can be developed in parallel and integrated ready for delivery
- **Transition:** deliver the system to the users.

Iteration can occur within each of these phases, with the phase deliverables iteratively being enhanced. Iteration can also occur across the whole set of phases, with the system being delivered in increments.

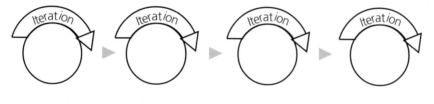

| **Inception** | **Elaboration** | **Construction** | **Transition** |

Figure 1.9: The four phases of the RUP lifecycle model (Kruchten 2000).

There are nine process activities: six core process workflows and three core supporting workflows. The core process workflows are business modelling, requirements, analysis and design, implementation, testing and deployment.

The supporting workflows are configuration and change management, project management and environment (software tools to support software development). These process activities can be used as needed throughout the four phases.

There are six best practices recommended: develop software iteratively, manage requirements, use component-based architectures, visually model software, verify software quality, and control software changes.

XP (extreme programming)

XP or extreme programming (Beck 2000) is the most widely known of the agile methods. Kent Beck coined the name in 1999 to recognise that the method took certain recognised good practice to extremes (for example, iterative development and customer involvement).

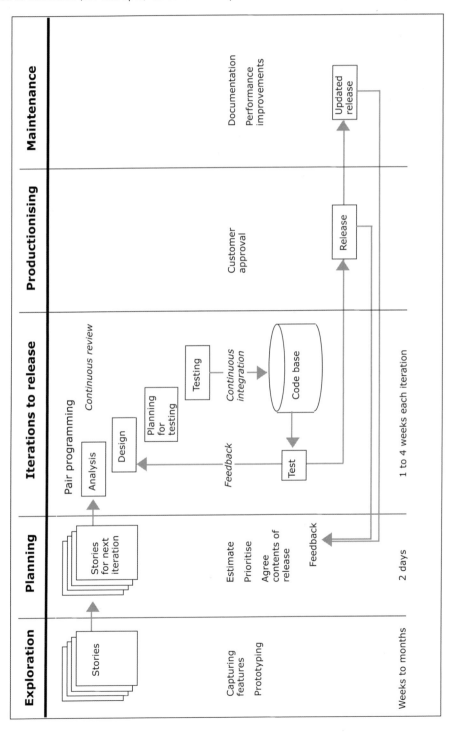

Figure 1.10: The process for extreme programming (Abrahamsson et al. 2002).

Extreme programming involves the following practices:

- Incremental development through small, frequent releases
- The minimal useful sets of functionality that provide high business value are developed for early release
- The first release delivers the essential architecture to support the system
- Requirements description based on customer stories
- Customer involvement through full-time customer in the development team
- Customer in development team is responsible for developing acceptance tests
- People are seen as key, rather than process. Pair programming and collective ownership of system code is promoted. Excessively long hours are seen 'as the exception, not the rule'
- Change is supported by regular system releases of tested code
- Tests are written prior to development
- Code is kept simple by re-factoring and by using simple designs that do not cater for future system changes.

1.6 Summary

This chapter has introduced the topics of projects and project management as follows:

- The terms 'project' and 'project management' have been defined
- Project management activities and knowledge areas as defined in the *Project Management Body of Knowledge* (PMBOK 2004) have been outlined
- Criteria for judging project success has been given, and the topic of software project failure has been discussed
- Project lifecycles have been considered including the project lifecycle phases as described in the APM's *Body of Knowledge* (APM BoK 2006)
- Different systems development lifecycle approaches have been outlined (that is, sequential, incremental, prototyping and evolutionary), and several different systems development lifecycle models have been described.

1.7 Review questions

 Question 1.1
How does a project originate?

 Question 1.2
How does project management differ from line management (that is, routine operational management)?

 Question 1.3
Can you think of a software project that you learnt about in a newspaper or magazine article, or on TV that was either a failure or a success? What reasons were given for the failure/success?

Question 1.4
Thinking about the different systems development lifecycles described in this chapter, can you identify which are iterative and how they incorporate feedback?

answers to review questions are to be found at the back of the book

1.8 Feedback on activities

Activity 1.1: What is a project?

It is likely that you are thinking about a project as involving some special activity. Possibly, you are considering a project as something to do with creating a specific product, building some architectural monument, or perhaps even organising a major event.

These are all instances of projects. But how can we define the term 'project'? Continue reading this chapter, we shall discuss some standard definitions next.

Activity 1.2: Can 'baking a cake' be considered a project?

Baking a cake does not sound that complicated, but let's look at the characteristics of a project.

Is there a definable purpose?	Yes, creating a cake.
Is it a unique undertaking (rather than routine)?	It certainly would be for some!
Is it a temporary activity?	It has a start and a finish (recipes often give timescales).

It would therefore appear that baking a cake is a project: at least for some! For a baker on the other hand, this may be part of their normal work routine (that is, neither unique nor temporary). If this is the case, then it is not really a project. However, if the baker had decided to create a totally new recipe to have a new product to sell, then baking the cake could be part of a 'new cake project'.

Activity 1.3: Examples of projects

Examples can come from various domains. Here are a few:

- composing a symphony
- writing the next Harry Potter book
- building a new bridge
- extending a tube line on an underground rail network
- designing a new electric train
- building the Channel Tunnel between England and France
- building a new water system in a developing country
- building a new theme park (such as Disney World or Legoland)
- building a new civil structure (such as the Millennium Dome in London)
- launching a manned mission to Mars
- opening a new university campus
- cleaning up following Chernobyl
- organising a conference

- building a new runway at an international airport
- scaling Mt. Everest
- hosting the Olympic Games
- organising a charity event
- staging a theatrical production
- planning a wedding
- moving house
- selecting a software package
- redistributing responsibilities within a department
- hosting dinner for twenty relatives
- writing a software component for a new mobile phone
- creating an internet personal banking system for customers
- designing an internet interface for booking holidays.

Activity 1.4: Is this a project?

It is likely that any item on the list will fulfil the characteristics discussed earlier. If not, it is worth considering if you are approaching the project from the right perspective. In some projects there may be multiple stakeholders with different views and perceptions. Whose demands dictate what the project is about? Who defines what is at stake? Who dictates the direction of the project?

Activity 1.5: Successful student projects

- time is a very important constraint!
- cost is not really an issue for a student project, but don't forget that budget can also refer to resources such as a student's time
- desired performance level – as expected from a student at the relevant academic level
- quality as defined in the project requirements
- minimum agreed functionality will be expected
- good use of resources (with rationale) can improve the overall impression
- user acceptance – the system must be viewed as useful and usable in order for it to be considered successful
- deliver promised benefits (or at least explain why they could not be achieved!)
- note that not all projects are successful!
- it is perfectly acceptable for a student project to fail (that is, for the product not to work fully, or not to interact with an essential part of the system, or not to deliver promised benefits) and for the student to still obtain a good mark – as long as there is a good description of what went wrong, and why, and what could be learned from the failure. The project report will also need to explain the rationale for the original choices, and what would be done differently if it had to do it over again (with the benefit of hindsight).

In other words, students need to show that they are capable of learning from the failure, appreciating what went wrong, and discussing fundamental problems and solutions that would overcome them.

Activity 1.6: Factors influencing project failures

The most likely factor to impact is perhaps being 'technology-led', and not seeing the need for project management! 'Lengthy project timescales' is the one not likely to affect a student project!

Notice how the human failure factors outnumber the technology failure factors.

Activity 1.7: Lifecycles and student projects

All of the lifecycles will have to be considered! A student project has to be project-managed and it has to be implemented! The lifecycle stage of the system involved – there always will be a system of some kind – will impact on what the project sets out to achieve!

For project management lifecycle activities, refer back to 'Project management activities' within Section 1.3, 'What is project management?'.

Systems development lifecycle activities cover the project implementation: that is, building the new product that the project is to deliver. For example, this could involve specifying requirements, designing solutions, programming the new code, and integrating the new code into the existing system.

The system lifecycle is concerned with the operational 'real-life' system that the project is aiming to impact. A wide variety of different types of system can be involved. For example, for a project concerned with embedded software for a car, the system concerned would be the car. Alternatively, if a new financial package was being introduced into an organisation, then the 'system' would any information systems, or manual processes of the organisation impacted by the new financial package.

The important point is that you clearly distinguish between the three different types of lifecycle. All are important and need consideration.

1.9 References

Abrahamsson, Pekka, Outi Salo, Jussi Ronkainen and Juhani Warsta, (2002), *Agile Software Development Methods. Review and Analysis*, VTT Publications, Espoo, Finland, ISBN 951 38 6009 4, **www.inf.vtt.fi/pdf/**

Association for Project Management, (2006), *Project Management Body of Knowledge* (5th edition) (APM BoK), ISBN 1 903494 13 3 **www.apm.org.uk/**

Beck, K., (2000), *Extreme Programming Explained: Embrace Change,* Addison-Wesley, ISBN 0201616416.

Boehm, B. W., A spiral model of software development and enhancement, *IEEE Computer*, 1988, 21(5), pages 61-72.

Cleland, D.I. and Ireland L. R., (2002), *Project Management: Strategic Design and Implementation* (4th edition), McGraw-Hill, ISBN 0 07 122969 8.

Deming, W. E., (1986) , *Out of Crisis*, MIT Centre for Advanced Engineering Study (CAES), ISBN 0 911379 01 0.

Flowers, S., (1996), *Software Failure: Management Failure*, Wiley, ISBN 0 47195113 7.

Gilb, Tom, (2005), *Competitive Engineering, A Handbook For Systems Engineering, Requirements Engineering, and Software Engineering Using Planguage*, Elsevier Butterworth-Heinemann, ISBN 0 75066507 6. **www.gilb.com/**

Kruchten, P., (2000), *The Rational Unified Process: An Introduction* (2nd Edition), Addison-Wesley, ISBN 0 201 70710 1.

Larman, C., (2004), *Agile and Iterative Development: A Manager's Guide*, Addison-Wesley, ISBN 0 13 111155 8.

Project Management Institute, (2004), *A Guide to the Project Management Body of Knowledge* (3rd edition) (PMBOK Guide), ISBN 1 93069945 X, **www.pmi.org/** [Last accessed: November 2006].

Royal Academy of Engineering, (2004). *The Challenges of Complex IT Projects*, **www.bcs.org/statements/royal/**

Royce, Walker, (1998). *Software Project Management: A Unified Framework*, Addison-Wesley, ISBN 0 20 130958 0.

Royce, Winston, (1970). *Managing the Development of Large Software Systems: Concepts and Techniques*. Proceedings of IEEE WESCON. August 1970. Originally published by TRW.

Rumbaugh, J., Jacobson, I. and Booch, G., (1999), *The Unified Software Development Process*, Addison-Wesley, ISBN 0 20 157169 2.

Sommerville, Ian, (2006), *Software Engineering* (8th Edition), Addison-Wesley, ISBN 0 32 131379 8.

Standish Group, (1998), *Chaos 1998 Technical Report*, **www.standishgroup.com/sample_research/chaos_1994_1.php** for information about the 1994 report. [Last accessed: November 2006]

Stapleton, J. (Editor), (2003), *DSDM Business Focused Development* (2nd Edition), Addison-Wesley, ISBN 0 321 11224 5.

Yardley, D., (2002), *Successful IT Project Delivery*, Addison-Wesley, ISBN 0 20 175606 4.

CHAPTER 2

Project selection

OVERVIEW

Organisations have to decide which IT projects they are going to invest in. This chapter introduces you to how IT projects are selected and outlines how an IT project proposal is documented in a feasibility study.

Project management's responsibilities include initiating, organising and controlling projects. Managing the system development activities to ensure the systems analysis and design are carried out is one aspect. However, there are additional responsibilities, such as ensuring the project has the correct objectives for the organisation, establishing and negotiating the system scope, and identifying stakeholders and business value. It is these responsibilities we shall discuss in this chapter.

This chapter also discusses how you should go about selecting a project topic for your student project. In addition, there is help on how to set an aim and objectives for your selected project.

Learning outcomes   At the end of this chapter you should be able to:

- Understand how a project must fit (align) with organisational objectives

- Describe the concepts of programme management and project portfolio management

- Explain the project management perspective on specific system analysis components: objectives, scope, stakeholders and stakeholder value

- State the main contents of a feasibility study

- Choose an appropriate student project

- Identify and specify the aim and objectives for a student project.

2.1 Introduction

This chapter consists of three main parts:

- **IT investment:** an overview of how organisations select IT projects
- **Project management's use of specific systems analysis information:** objectives, scope, stakeholders and stakeholder value. This includes discussion on how this information is captured in a feasibility study
- **Choosing a student project:** to help you choose your student project by providing some ideas on how to go about selecting a topic. Further, once you have chosen a topic, how to specify a set of objectives for it.

The theory sections of this chapter should all be borne in mind when selecting your student project: identifying stakeholder value should be a prime consideration.

2.2 IT investment

Organisations have to decide what projects they are going to invest in: they have to determine which changes are mandatory and which changes would be most beneficial.

Reasons for IT Investment

The reasons why organisations invest in IT systems development include:

- **Survival:** for example, reducing costs in an area of the organisation which is operating at a loss
- **Improved efficiency and/or effectiveness:** for example, reducing the time it takes to authorise a customer sale
- **Competitive advantage:** for example, an improved customer interface, which makes it significantly easier for customers to obtain product information and place orders
- **External factors:** for example, a legislative change
- **Changing organisational structure:** for example, mergers, privatisation, outsourcing and internal reorganisation.

The reasons driving change are important to understand, as they set the context for a project. They begin to answer the questions, 'What is at stake if we fail?', 'What are the timescales for this change?' and 'What level of risk can we tolerate?'

How is IT investment managed?

It is quite common within organisations for IT budgets to be set and allocated quarterly or annually. Senior management decide the amount of IT investment and then allocate it to programmes, projects and information systems. Organisational size and structure determine exactly what happens, and who has control of the financial budgets.

It is important you appreciate two organisational mechanisms, which are primarily concerned with IT investment: programme management and project portfolio management.

Programme management

Large organisations will often set up a programme in response to a key 'strategy area', and appoint a programme manager to run it.

A programme is a grouping of projects that together aim to achieve a common set of organisational objectives. The reason programmes exist is to improve the control of investment and co-ordination of effort by bringing related projects together under one programme manager. The programme manager usually has overall control over the projects' budgets.

To give some examples of different scenarios that would most likely call for a programme to be set up:

- If two organisations are to be merged: unification of IT systems, physical relocation of offices, new organisational procedures, creating a new corporate image and other tasks could all result in numerous projects, but they would need to be co-ordinated as a programme

- If there is a need for economies of scale: a common IT infrastructure would allow bulk purchasing of IT equipment and development of expertise for standard products (applications and hardware). It would also enable, where desirable, different departments to share applications. A programme could therefore be set up to co-ordinate and control the rationalising all aspects of the IT infrastructure

- If there is a need for collaboration among different organisations: this is especially the case if some new product is being developed. A programme will be set up to overview and co-ordinate the different projects in the different organisations

- If there is a need to streamline or revamp processes and information systems within a specific area: the projects in such a programme are usually closely linked within a specific organisational process or functional area. For example, all the information systems and projects involved in an organisation's commercial cycle could be managed within a 'Commercial Programme'. Notice how the IT involved would be likely to go across different departments within the organisation.

Adapted from Hughes and Cotterell, 2002

Project portfolio management

Another method used by organisations to manage their IT investment is project portfolio management. A division or strategic business unit (SBU) within an organisation, or perhaps a country-based unit within a multinational organisation, will group all their projects and information systems into a portfolio, and then manage the portfolio. Decisions are then made, usually either quarterly or annually, on which information systems and projects within the portfolio are going to be funded taking into account resource constraints.

These organisational units usually have some autonomy about their IT investment (that is, they have some say in where they choose to allocate their IT budget), even if their IT budget has certain restrictions imposed on it by corporate senior management.

Note project portfolio management is concerned with the ongoing management and development of the IT used by an organisational unit. By contrast, a programme consists of projects with a common set of key objectives.

How are IT budgets allocated?

Within any organisation, there are organisational units (that is, programmes, units responsible for a project portfolio, and others) that have to make IT investment decisions concerning their IT budget: what are they going to fund?

There are several claims on any IT budget, such as:

- Existing information systems need budget for their ongoing operational and maintenance costs
- Existing projects need budget for continued funding to complete agreed work
- Existing information systems will be looking for budget for system improvements
- Existing projects will put in bids for further new development
- There will be project proposals for totally new projects looking for funding.

Some of this funding will probably already have been agreed, but some will not. It is at this point that decisions can be made to retire certain systems, to cease the funding of certain projects, and to invest in specific new developments.

Only when all the essential IT has been allocated budget can attention can be turned to the systems development budgets – what changes should be made to the existing information systems, what new work agreed for existing projects, and what new systems should be considered for development?

For any promising new project proposals, it is a matter of whether to fund feasibility studies and/or to allocate actual project funding. (Given the timescales, money is often earmarked for some specific future projects, on the assumption that their feasibility studies will recommend going ahead with the projects.)

A management committee usually makes the final decisions. The key point is that resources are limited: it is unlikely that organisations can carry out all the IT projects that they would like to. So there has to be some selection process, and only projects that show sufficient promise should be given the go-ahead.

Note that it is always a good idea to understand who holds the 'purse strings' for a project.

2.3 Project management lifecycle processes and proposal selection

Project management lifecycle process

Let's now consider the project management lifecycle processes that are involved in initiating a project. See Figure 2.1, which shows the project management lifecycle and its relationship to the systems development lifecycle.

You can see that setting up a project involves:

- **Selecting a project proposal**
- **Establishing the business case**
- **Commencing the project** ('starting up').

The four main deliverables when setting up a project are as follows:

- **A business case**
- **A project charter** (which can be replaced by a contract or a letter of agreement)
- **A scope statement**
- **An initial project plan**.

Often the business case, the scope statement and outline high-level project plan are documented within a feasibility study.

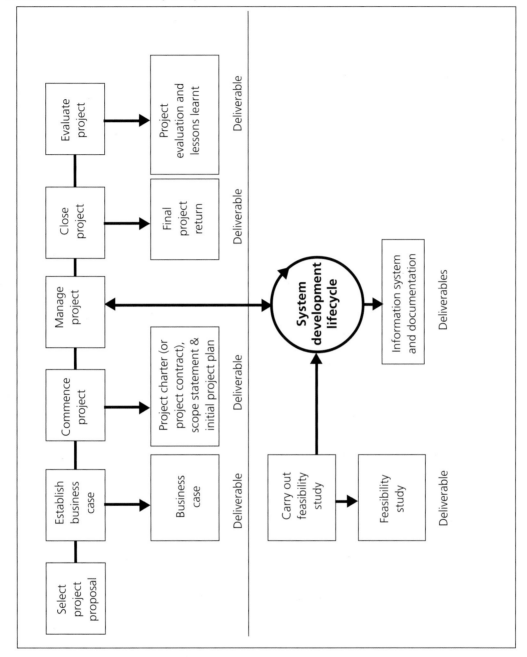

Figure 2.1: The project management lifecycle. (Adapted from Marchewka 2003, Page 26.) A clear distinction is made between establishing the business case and commencing work on the project. The work in establishing the business case can be done within a feasibility study. The feasibility study information forms the initial systems analysis information.

Note that the element 'Manage project' will consist of initiating, planning, executing, controlling and closing the system development phases.

Now let's look at the processes involved in setting up a project in more detail.

Project proposal selection

How do managers initially decide if a project proposal shows any promise?

There are many different ways in which organisations go about deciding which IT projects to select. Prior to a feasibility study, which provides the detailed business case, management is usually concerned about the fit of a project proposal within the organisational strategy (this can also be referred to as the 'alignment' with the organisational strategy/objectives).

Two methods (among others) that can be useful to management at this stage are SWOT analysis and the Balanced Scorecard.

SWOT analysis

SWOT analysis looks at the relationship of an organisation with its external environment. This involves analysing the strengths and weaknesses of an organisation, and then looking at the opportunities and threats facing it from the external environment. The reason for doing this is to try to spot future trends and predict the need for new products and services. If you already have a list of potential projects, you can assess how each project fits with the SWOT analysis (for example, are there any proposed projects that address an identified opportunity?).

Activity 2.1

Carry out a SWOT analysis

Select an organisation, real or imaginary, and carry out a SWOT analysis of it. For example, consider a shop selling CDs and DVDs, or an organisation specialising in designing websites for small companies.

What are their strengths and weaknesses?

What opportunities and threats do they face?

Balanced Scorecard

Robert Kaplan and David Norton (1996) developed this increasingly popular approach in the early 90s. It requires an organisation to identify, and then monitor its achievement against, a combination of financial and other critical measures known as metrics.

The approach balances financial and operational metrics for an organisation across four different perspectives: finance, customer, internal business processes, and organisational learning and growth.

A set of key performance indicators (that is, a set of metrics) has to be developed for each of the four perspectives:

- **Financial perspective:** financial measures are a good indicator of how an organisation is performing: that is, how its strategy, implementation and execution are contributing to the 'bottom line'. They summarise the economic results of actions taken.

  Traditional measures such as return on investment (ROI) and net present value (NPV) are used as well as more recently developed measures, such as economic value-added (EVA).

- **Customer:** this perspective is concerned with how the organisation's performance is viewed through its customers' eyes.

  Measures in this perspective include customer satisfaction, customer retention, new customer acquisition and market share in target segments. Measures that capture what the customer actually wants should also be present: for example, measures that monitor short lead times and on-time delivery, or product innovation

- **Internal business process:** this perspective identifies the critical organisational processes that the organisation must excel at to meet its customer and financial objectives.

  The measures focus on the efficiency and the effectiveness of the critical processes. Measures should be included for both the long-term innovation cycles, and the short-term operational cycles. Measures include quality, response times, cost, and new product introductions

- **Organisational learning and growth:** this perspective is concerned with identifying the infrastructure that an organisation requires to create long-term growth and improvement. The three principal sources involved are seen as people, information systems and organisational procedures. So the measures aim to capture investment in training people, enhancement of information systems, and improvements to procedures. Examples of such measures would be staff retention and information system availability.

By considering metrics across these four different perspectives, the aim of the Balanced Scorecard is to provide a balanced view across an organisation. The greater the impact that a project has on these measures, the better the project is for the organisation (the more aligned it is to the organisational objectives).

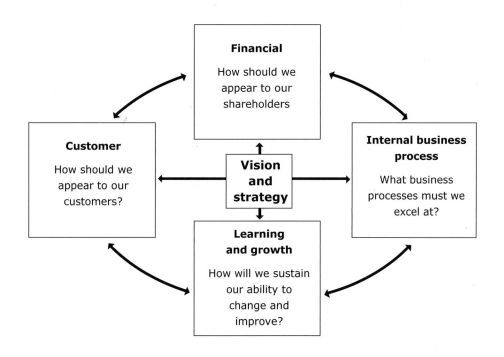

Figure 2.2: The Balanced Scorecard. (Kaplan and Norton 1996).

2.4 Feasibility study

Initiating the feasibility study

The first step, after deciding that a project proposal is worth further investigation, is some kind of feasibility study. A feasibility study is primarily conducted to determine whether a proposed project should go ahead: it includes assessing the business case.

At this stage, it depends on the organisation and the nature of the proposed project exactly what happens. Usually, a project will not get fully underway until the feasibility study has been accepted, and agreement to go ahead with the project (project funding) has been given.

In larger organisations, there can be business consultants specialising in carrying out feasibility studies. In some organisations, project managers carry out feasibility studies with an option of carrying on to be the project manager if the go-ahead is given.

If a project is mandatory (say to meet some new legislation) or considered absolutely essential to the organisation, then a project manager might well be appointed at an early stage to start initiating the project, and they might be responsible for carrying out the feasibility study, which in this case is more about exploring alternative options and identifying issues than obtaining IT investment.

Contents list for a feasibility study

A feasibility study for a project should include the following sections:

- **Perceived need for change of the organisation/product/system (opportunities, problems requiring resolution, and mandatory changes):** this is a list of needs that can be added to as stakeholders are interviewed. Some indication of the value to the organisation/product of each list item should be captured, as this is the basis of stating the benefits in the business case

- **Alignment with organisational strategy/objectives:** the Balanced Scorecard is one approach to identifying the critical objectives for an organisation. Other approaches are to identify and obtain the relevant strategic documents, and/or to ask senior management directly

- **Aim of the proposed project:** a statement of the main purpose of the project – what is it to achieve?

- **Objectives for the proposed project:** the feasibility study should aim to produce a quantitative set of objectives for the product or system to be produced by the project. The following levels should be established:

  - **benchmark levels:** these are the existing levels achieved by a product or system or its current equivalent (there usually is some existing product or functionality that can be used). Competitive information and trend information should also be sought

  - **target levels (success criteria):** the targets provide the success criteria for the project, and once a project is underway, its progress towards meeting these target levels can be measured: for resource, costs can be measured against budget; for time, completion can be measured against deadline; and for benefits, performance improvements can be monitored and stakeholders asked to provide benefit data

- **Analysis of the external environment:** earlier in this chapter, we discussed how SWOT analysis can be used to assess the external environment. A feasibility study will pick up on any earlier work, carry out a more detailed assessment, and formally document what was considered and taken into account

- **Product/system scope:** this should provide an overview of the functionality. It is equally important to state what is outside the scope of the project as what is inside it. If relevant, a statement should also be given about which parts of an organisation are impacted (for example, this project is for the customer services division and excludes any sales division functionality). See also further discussion of *scope* in the later section

- **Overview of any current 'business' process(es) and outline of planned changes:** the focus is on the organisational functionality and explains in greater detail than the topic of the last bullet point (product/system scope) which processes within the organisation the project changes will affect

- **Overview of any relevant current product/system(s) and outline of planned changes:** this is concerned with describing the current state of the specific product or system(s) that are to be updated or replaced

- **Product/system interfaces:** any products or systems that the planned product/system has to interface with need to be identified. Checks will need to be carried out that the interfaces will continue to work as before without any additional changes

- **List of stakeholders:** see discussion in later section

- **Potential benefits and estimated costs of the proposed solutions:** this is about stakeholder value. See discussion in later section

- **Proposed solution(s):** brief description of the proposed solution(s). Alternative solutions/ designs could also be identified

- **Technology considerations:** does the hardware technology already exist? Is the project state-of-the-art? Is the hardware readily available for the project and for the potential users?

- **Staff availability:** are staff with appropriate skills and experience available?

- **Dependencies, issues, assumptions and risks:** any significant factors that impact the project need to be captured here. For example, if your project was to stage the opening ceremony of the Olympics, there would be a dependency that the new stadium was ready, say six months in advance for final testing. You would make an assumption that no major alterations would be made to the planned stadium layout. An example of a potential issue would be if, say, the health and safety guidelines were being updated and could impact your project plans. A risk could be a subsection of the opening ceremony not working well due to a completely new, untried as yet, special effect not working.

  The main point is to capture the factors so that they are taken into consideration: don't get too caught up in exactly how they should be categorised at this stage of the project

- **Outline project plan:** if evolutionary methods are being used, some of the evolutionary deliverables should be identified. Major project deadlines should be specified

- **Summary of financial information**

- **Recommendations:** the final output is a set of recommendations summarising the major conclusions about the project proposal.

A feasibility study can take from a few hours to a few weeks to complete: the level of investment dictates exactly how much effort should be expended. However, a feasibility study should be a relatively rapid survey to establish whether there is sufficient potential to continue to do more detailed work.

Once the feasibility study is completed, there is a go/no go review. The results are presented to management, and a decision has to be made about the IT investment: should the project go ahead?

David Olson (2003) identifies financial criteria, management judgment, or a combination of both as the main selection methods. The different financial criteria used include cost/benefit analysis, net present value (NPV), and payback. Management judgment includes the fit with the business objectives, strategic value, competitive pressure, probability of completion, and satisfaction of legal requirements. Methods involving a combination of both of the other methods include use of checklists, project profiles and multi-criteria decision models.

Identifying the aim of a project

Every project should have one major aim to be accomplished – with several objectives that support the aim. The aim is a global statement for the entire project towards which all the objectives will point. Indeed, finishing the project should entail the successful achievement of the stated aim (or an altered version of it, if project feedback demands change).

> 'It is important that an aim never be defined in terms of activity or methods. It must always relate to how life is better for everyone.'

> *Deming 1993*

We shall return to the subject of objectives in a later section of this chapter.

Identifying the stakeholders

For a given system, the term 'stakeholder' is used for any person or group who will be affected by the system, directly or indirectly. Numerous different types of stakeholder can be involved in a system: for example, end-users, managers, customers, systems administration and even government departments or the public.

One of the tasks during the feasibility study is to draw up the list of stakeholder types and start identifying the key stakeholders. Key stakeholders are the people that have power in influencing the business processes or have detailed knowledge and overviews of how things really work. The stakeholders with power are the ones likely to help implement any changes, so they need to understand and support any proposed changes. The stakeholders with knowledge are useful sources of information, and it is worth getting their opinion on the feasibility of any new ideas.

An important point to note is that organisational charts do not always reflect where power and information are actually located.

Given that systems documentation can be sketchy or out of date, it is important to establish from stakeholders how they perceive the system to be used and to work. Do not be surprised if you get conflicting views from different stakeholder groups.

You need to assess how you are going to obtain representative system information from all the different stakeholder types. You also need to ensure you have access to the relevant stakeholders at the appropriate times.

Establishing the potential benefits: stakeholder value

A project must plan to deliver stakeholder value (potential benefits). Of course, once delivered, it is up to the stakeholders to actually achieve the planned benefits. At the feasibility study stage, communication over stakeholder value is essential because it is stakeholder value that justifies the project. A project manager should pay specific attention to this area:

- Is there sufficient value to go ahead with the project? What are the project costs and what is the ROI? What about NPV calculations? Is this project change mandatory (for example, due to legislation)?

- What could be done to achieve greater value?
- Are there any other projects impacting this value? Or claiming this value already?
- Will the stakeholders actually use this product/system and achieve the planned benefits?
- How will the benefits be measured?

The project costs should cover both the development costs and the ongoing operational costs of running the system. The costs should not exceed the benefits.

Often there are organisational guidelines about the required ROI for IT projects.

Determining the scope

Scope involves identifying what is included in the system, and what is outside the system.

A simple way of looking at scope is to consider the project trade-off triangle:

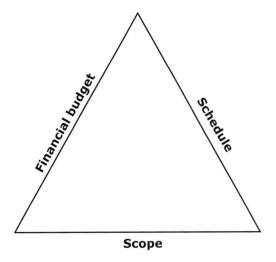

Figure 2.3: A project trade-off triangle for scope, schedule and financial budget

If project scope encompasses 'the work the project has to do', and if there is a fixed schedule (time deadline) and a fixed financial budget, then the only thing that is adjustable (left to trade-off) is the scope – the amount of work to be achieved. Here scope represents everything that is not a deadline or a financial budget. With this definition, acceptable trade-offs include:

- Modifying the **product objectives**
- Modifying the **functionality**
- Modifying the **scale of deployment**.

A key thing to consider when thinking about trade-offs is the impact on stakeholder value.

The scope has to be developed iteratively over the course of the feasibility study (and beyond). A picture has to be built up of the organisational objectives, the product/system objectives, the existing external environment, the existing interfaces, the existing functionality, the existing business processes, and the current perceived needs for change. The context of the proposed change should guide the amount of work that has to be carried out. Initially, nothing is fixed. The business consultant (or project manager) has to take the proposed project outline and investigate.

The scoping process can be carried out while systematically collecting the prescribed system information required for the feasibility study, identifying and interviewing stakeholders, and cross-checking key information.

To give some specific examples of the sort of questions that might need considering:

- Will only financial managers have access to this system or will our customers also be able to view their account information?
- Is this system only UK-wide or will the European organisations also use it?
- Will the expenses system have to obtain all its records of individuals via the employee database?
- Will the sales people automatically be prompted if one of their customers has a major problem logged with customer services?

Positive answers to any of these sorts of question involve considerable extra cost. It is more than simple functionality involved – take, for instance, the deployment costs involved in catering for a European-wide system as opposed to a UK-wide one.

Traditionally, scope was regarded as something that had to be established and frozen. 'Scope creep' is still considered in many textbooks to be something to be avoided. However, it is inevitable that the scope of a project will change over time: for example, the business environment will alter, and the users will change their minds about their requirements as they understand more about the new system. Additional opportunities might well be identified as systems analysts become more knowledgeable about the business and the system interfaces. The essential thing is that any change in scope is managed by the project.

Activity 2.2

Dealing with scope

Figure 2.3 introduces a trade-off triangle showing the relationship between the budget, schedule and scope of a project. Scope includes the range of functionality (or the number of features) that you incorporate in a product. The functionality of your product increases with the number of features.

A successful project is delivered on time, on budget and to specification. Discuss the relationship between the three factors: budget, schedule and scope – limit the scope discussion for this activity to just considering the system functionality. Which of these factors do you control in your student project? What can you do if you are running out of time?

System boundaries and system interfaces

The boundaries and interfaces of a system are key items to establish (as part of the scope) in a feasibility study.

Boundaries might be totally fixed and represent a design constraint, or they might allow modification to achieve some business advantage. For example, if an insurance quote can be prepared and transferred to a customer in seconds rather than hours, then business opportunities begin to be generated. In this case, including considerations of the customer environment within the scope of the project would be advantageous.

Identifying the system interfaces also enables work to start on establishing the main system data requirements. The systems that interface with the project system can also be determined. A picture of the system dependencies begins to develop.

Once you understand the system interfaces, it easier to identify if there are any other projects working within the organisation in the same area.

When interviewing stakeholders, always consider allocating time to discussing the system interfaces and ask for any interface documentation. Draw a diagram of the system interfaces, and ask stakeholders to confirm your diagram is accurate! Alternatively, ask them to draw the diagram for you – this can really help you understand what they are talking about in an interview and can help structure the conversation.

Remember you are trying to establish what is part of the scope of your project and what is not. At the feasibility study stage, you are exploring options, not committing to sorting out any specific problems – unless they have been specifically stated being as part of the project's work to tackle. So, capture a problem, document it, but do not commit to sorting it out prior to some formal agreement that it is within scope!

Communicating with senior management

One final point before we move on from the topic of feasibility study: communication with senior management is vital. You have to understand the level of senior management commitment to your project proposal, and what they understand the project will achieve.

Some strategic information may not be readily accessible to you – after all, it is likely to be competitive information. You need to gain as much understanding as you can from the information that is available, and try to talk to the relevant senior management to determine their views. Preparation, an open mind, good listening skills, and seizing meeting opportunities can be key: senior managers tend not to have much free time in their schedules, but don't be put off; it is far better to seek any clarification that is needed at an early stage.

In some cases, the only option to obtain access to senior management is to use another manager to talk to them and find out the information for you. This can be advantageous if you are not familiar with the corporate culture, but it can also be frustrating not to obtain information directly!

Try to get senior management to agree your project's quantified success criteria. A one-page overview that summarises the key points for the project, and the success criteria is ideal. (Remember to include your name, contact details and the date on the overview page.)

If you come up with new ideas, it is extremely important you discuss them with senior management and check that you are proposing to take the project in a direction that they will support.

Senior management interest is focused on achieving the organisational objectives, and your project is likely to get funding and support if it clearly shows that it contributes towards the key organisational objectives.

2.5 The role of success criteria in projects

Success criteria measure the success of a project and ensure user acceptance. They are typically negotiated prior to the launch of the project and therefore provide a clear and easy way of measuring the achievement and determining if the promises have been fulfilled.

Ideally, you pick up the success criteria as objectives within your project (the project success criteria are likely to form a subset – albeit a very important subset – of the project objectives. See earlier within the feasibility study contents list – target levels under 'Objectives for the project').

Success criteria need to be specific, achievable and measurable – and it should be possible to determine objectively whether they have been achieved. In the modern world of project management, success criteria are often built into contracts to become legally binding. Upon completion, tests are carried out to determine if the criteria have indeed been achieved. If the tests are accepted as having been passed, the clients should accept the project.

You need to take care that you specify your criteria accurately. Consider the following examples of criteria. Are these examples precise and unambiguous enough to be able to ascertain achievement?

- 'At least 80% of users will use the new system'
- 'The new product will generate £350,000 in the first six months'
- 'Average time for data entry will be reduced from 3 minutes to under 2.'

The first example does not specify which system (or part thereof). Furthermore, does this relate to all users? It does not specify the kind of users, or whether a user is someone who uses the full system.

The second example does not tell us when the six-month period begins, or whether the money is expected to be a net gain.

The third example is very vague. What is 'under 2'? More critically, one may also ask under two what? Minutes? Seconds? Hours? Days?

You need to be very careful about defining acceptance criteria. Don't specify success criteria that are dependent on things outside your control.

Detailed, precise success criteria give developers:

- A target to aim at
- The responsibility for ensuring and monitoring that the target will be achieved
- A point of reference
- Proof of agreement that can be used as proof of achievement at the point of delivery.

Determining the objectives

You can view the process of breaking down an aim into a set of objectives as hierarchical decomposition, where the overall aim is broken down into more purposeful objectives. In order for the project aim to be achieved, all objectives must be realised.

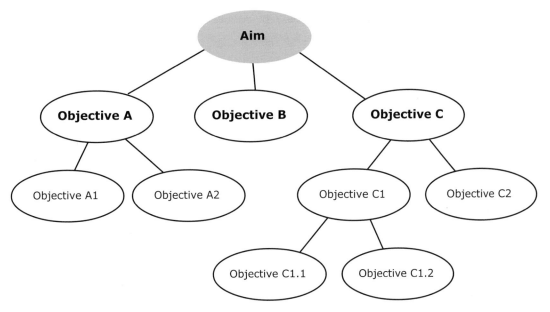

Figure 2.4: An objective hierarchy supporting an aim

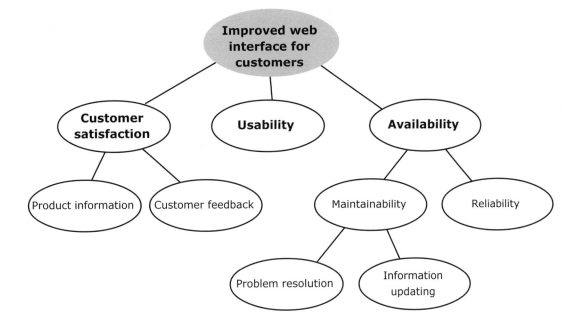

Figure 2.5: An example of an objective hierarchy supporting an aim (only quality requirements are shown here)

2.6 Selecting your student project

It can be useful if you regard a project as 'an investigation designed to find an answer to some question'. The way that you conduct the investigation, and the answer you find, depends largely on the question you are asking. First, we shall investigate how you should go about choosing the 'question' and then, later, how you should specify the aim and objectives of your project.

Choosing your student project topic

There are some lucky students who know from the outset what project they want to do. However, for many students, the decision on which project topic to choose is not at all clear. It is important to get it as 'right' as possible, as it is likely to be difficult to change it – you will have to work on that topic for the duration of the project.

You may not be sure, at the beginning, what kind of project to do. The ideal project is one which:

- Interests you
- Has not been done before
- Enhances your professional and academic standing.

There are a number of routes to finding a suitable project. Frequently, you will be initially urged to look at a list of 'project suggestions'. Many students panic when they don't see any topic that they like on the list. DON'T PANIC! The suggestions are not a restricted menu from which you will be forced to make a choice. There are a number of other options for you to consider:

- Maybe you already have a tentative project idea? If so, it is best to talk to your tutor before you become too fixed on your idea. They will be able to judge whether your idea is feasible or could be made so with a bit of modification. You need to be flexible and willing to take advice (Students tend to propose either overly ambitious projects – or very weak, simplistic, bookwork!). Remember, you will still need to find a supervisor for your project
- Have you had any experience outside the department – for example, vacation work – that could generate a project idea? This scenario may involve an external supervisor as well as an internal one, but many such projects have been successful in the past
- Maybe a member of staff can help you find a topic?
  - have an informal chat with staff members you know, either because you have taken one of their courses, or because they have tutored you. This kind of informal contact generates many projects
  - have a good look at staff research interests. These are another good way to find out the kind of thing they may be interested in supervising, even where there are no previous project suggestions. Mail them and/or ask them if they could put together a project with you in an area of joint interest
- Maybe you could extend the work done by a past student, or do something in a similar area? Look through past projects with topics that interest you
- Maybe you can find a topic of interest in the computer press? Look at articles on current problems and areas of interest.

You should discuss the projects that interest you with your tutor or potential supervisors as soon as possible so that you have plenty of time to think about the best choices for you.

Note that not every project is suitable for every student; some may be specifically tailored to a particular degree (for example, to a BEng or MSc course), and some may only suit students with a very specific set of interests.

If you have your own idea for a student project, it is your responsibility to find a member of staff who both approves of the proposed programme of work, and is willing to supervise it. Your tutor will be happy to help you find a supervisor, but you cannot assume that one can be found in every case.

There are three stages in this process of coming up with your own project idea:

- **Determine your personal set of interests**
- **Develop the area/idea by thinking the problem through in more detail**; one idea usually leads to another and a diagram may help you decide what you need to do, what you do not understand, and the kind of place you want to get to
- After getting this far, you are ready to **see what has been done before** – there is no point repeating work that has already been well covered elsewhere. At this point you should carry out a small-scale feasibility study (which should include some time spent researching in the library). The purpose is to specify the aim of your project and the project's objectives.

Determining your interests

By this stage of your course, you have covered a range of topics and areas. You may also have come across other areas while at work. This means that you are quite familiar with some aspects of computing, and you probably have an awareness of where there are some gaps in your knowledge.

Activity 2.3

Finding a computing topic that interests you

Now let's try to establish what interests you and which areas you want to study further! Write down your answers to the following questions:

1. What was your favourite module during your studies?

2. Was it your favourite – because it was easy? Or interesting?

3. Was there any module that did not go far enough into the subject for you?

4. What pair of modules interested you in combination?

5. Was there a 'gap' between these modules, which you would have liked to see filled?

6. If so, do you know what topics, or what kind of topics, would cover this gap?

There are various ways (some more formal, some less) for mapping the framework of a subject area. The section recommended in Activity 2.4 (taken from Dawson 2005) will introduce you to one or two techniques that can help you.

Activity 2.4

Mapping the research territory

(i) Using your course title as a starting point, make a spider diagram (or a relevance tree or a research territory map) showing how the different parts of your course relate to each other. Draw the diagram on a large piece of paper. You should be prepared to move things about and cross things out as you start refining your ideas.

(ii) Look at the following list of past project titles. Try to match each one against one or more topics in your diagram. Write in the title number close to this (or these) topic(s) and show the links. Extend your spider diagram if you find something that doesn't fit in. It is not important if you cannot match every title, so long as you do the easiest 20 or more titles.

1 Highlighting ambiguities in a requirements specification using natural language processing

2 Implementing security and integrity in a database-web architecture: A taxonomy on the approach

3 An expert system as a precursor of a hybrid intelligent system to minimise manufacturing loss

4 Enhancing search techniques in digital libraries

5 Audio data compression

6 Information systems and organisational structure: a case study of a venture marketing group

7 Genetic algorithms applied to financial engineering

8 How secure are on-line transactions?

9 Cyber-warfare: a current assessment from the United Kingdom

10 Interactive television or the internet? A consumer's choice?

11 Practical evaluation of UNIX security: the vulnerability of a university system to password capture and decryption

12 Software risk management practice: a survey of the techniques used by five successful developers

13 A database design for stock control at a defence company: relating new functional requirements, existing file stores into a new conceptual design

14 Defining the limits of executive information systems at a computer company: evaluating the experience of a sample of actual and reneging users to the prior assessed benefits

15 Designing a security mechanism for an object-oriented database: relating multi-level security strategies to alternative security models

16 Problems of implementing web access to an operational database: a study of critical failure points in providing full transactional access

17 Office automation security at a petroleum company: how to implement critical services in an environment of available technology

18 An empirical evaluation of software complexity measures: can similar metrics be used with different source languages?

19 Approaching the limits of data compression: the trade-off between performance and degree of compression

20 Intelligent assistance for decryption: the development of interactive software tools to aid the decryption process

21 A computer-aided learning system using hypertext: implementing hypertext to achieve claimed benefits

22 Relating financial policy and management reporting at a computer company: solving IT problems of accounting periods by improving management understanding of their own information requirements

23 Survey of attitudes to computing in a local school: how staff attitudes correlate with the expression of developing pupil skills

24 IBM Token Ring networks: a management evaluation – a week in the life of a token ring manager showing how software tools fail

25 The graphical representation of robot blocks world: a demonstrator using MacProlog and a theorem prover to implement plans of arbitrary complexity

26 An investigation of the use of search in artificial intelligence: criteria for developing search strategies demonstrated in LISP

27 Are workstations safe: the relation of actual workstations to ergonomic standards

28 Maintaining data quality in a data warehouse: the analysis of user problems in the management of data feeds

29 Defining service levels for electronic commerce: how to avoid offering a service that cannot be achieved

30 The role of the webmaster: accuracy, integrity and flexibility, and how they relate to consumer behaviour

31 Quality assurance in rapid development: evaluating the structures and measuring resources required

32 Managing security in a large SQL database: an analysis of security incidents over a six-month period

33 Data mining: how users learn to ask the right questions

34 Multimedia courseware development: a study into the deficiencies of conventional courseware development methodologies.

(iii) Now use your answers to the questions about your interests (from Activity 2.3) and the extended spider diagram from above to write down the following:

   (a) The three topics which were the most interesting, or most satisfying, or most relevant to you in your previous studies

   (b) The two topics which you wish had been taken a bit further in the course

   (c) One topic which you hope you never have to deal with again

   (d) The titles of the three past projects you would most like to read

   (e) The title of the past project you are most glad you do not have to do

   (f) The title of the past project that gave you the clearest idea of what the project was about

   (g) The title of the past project that gave you no idea at all of what it was about.

(iv) Finally, place an 'X' on your spider diagram as close as possible to your main area of interest. It can be against an individual topic or midway in between two or more topics. If you cannot decide between two possible places, put Xs in both. If you cannot decide among three, use three Xs (but no more than that). If you know what topic you are interested in, but it doesn't exist on your spider diagram, add it in and link it to the topics already there.

Now you should have a better idea of what you like and dislike about computing. Remember that there is little point in selecting something that you hate or something that you have failed in. If you choose something that you are good at, you are more likely to be motivated and to succeed overall.

The single most important thing at this stage is that you define your project as a question rather than as a topic.

Let's take an example:

Say you have developed an interest in client-server systems. What really interests you in this area? Ignore answers that are regressive – for example, 'it seems important'. It is important, but if that is as far as you can go you might as well just read a textbook on the subject.

You realise (rightly) that there is no point writing a textbook on the theory, but that there may be merit in testing how the theory has been applied, so you formulate your project as a question – 'How effectively do server database management systems (DBMS) manage unreliable clients?' This means you need to think about various relationships within the discipline and figure out which ones are relevant.

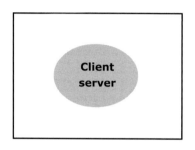

Figure 2.6: Initial simple model of client-server topic

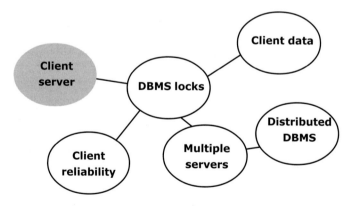

Figure 2.7: Expanded model showing additional topics

You will find that this stage of the work takes a significant amount of effort. Nevertheless, you will find that the clearer you are in what you intend to do and why, the better the report you will produce.

At the beginning, the main problem you will have is vagueness. Even when you are relatively certain about the general area you wish to pursue, you will have difficulty in setting out a concrete proposal and a definite plan of work.

This is natural at the beginning, but you must progress, within two or three weeks, to a definite proposal. You are required to submit a proposal and get official approval from your tutor. At this registration stage, you must have a clear idea about what you want to accomplish.

One approach for defining the problem and developing a clear idea is by progressing 'top-down' as follows:

- Start with your topic and attempt to briefly describe what is known about it
- Describe what current work is being done
- Identify a gap or a problem
- Think about ways of addressing the gap or dealing with the problem.

The following example shows you how the method can work.

Example 1: Starting from the topic

Motivation: I am interested in relational database development methodologies and also object orientation.

1 In the context of Computing, the development of relational databases is a relatively mature and well-established field. Proprietary relational database management systems (RDBMSs) can be purchased from a variety of vendors and there are widely understood methodologies in use by database specialists for developing relational database applications. Companies use relational databases to manage all their operational data: from customer records, to financial asset and stock control. RDBMSs allow companies to store their data as it becomes available and to retrieve that data by means of queries and reports when it is required.

2 Most RDBMSs incorporate mechanisms for guaranteeing the integrity of the data (no single piece of information – for example, a customer's address – is stored more than once in the database; when it is modified, the new information will be accessible to every user who needs it). Ensuring this guarantee at the design stage of an application development, by means of normalisation, is one of the most crucial and time-consuming tasks facing developers who use conventional development methodologies.

3 Since the establishment of the conventional methodologies however, new concepts have emerged in the field of software development methodologies, one of the most prominent of which is object-oriented design (OOD). When an information system is designed using an object-oriented approach (a customer database is an example of an information system), the behaviour of real-world entities (i.e. objects) is simulated within the information system, and this behaviour is encapsulated with the data pertaining to that object. This is such a powerful idea that researchers have begun developing so-called object-oriented databases where object behaviour can be built into the definition of the meta-data.

4 However, it may not be necessary to turn to such experimental systems to gain the benefits of an object-oriented methodology. It is conceivable that the application of OOD techniques to the development of a conventional relational database application will yield advantages, particularly in ensuring data integrity. This is because the modification of data values can be regarded as an aspect of the behaviour of the object to which the data refers (for example, a customer's address belongs to the customer). The proposition that designers will find it more efficient to ensure data integrity by approaching the meta-data from an object-oriented viewpoint is worthy of investigation.

5 In this project, a small-scale database application will be designed using both conventional and object-oriented techniques. During the course of this, particular attention will be paid to evaluating the effort required to develop and document the data integrity mechanisms. Then prototypes of each system will be produced and tested with the same test data designed to check for data integrity. Comparative analysis of figures from both of these phases should make it possible to discern any potential advantages provided by either approach.

In your opinion, does this example provide an adequate definition of the problem and does it follow the four steps highlighted in the list on the previous page?

- Paragraphs 1 and 3 deal with relational databases and object-oriented techniques, respectively. Both need to be described due to the nature of the topic
- Paragraph 2 contains some elaboration but does not really tackle 'work done in the field' in enough detail. Normally some references to research papers and/or software products would be incorporated here to make the work more academic and prove that it is based on other people's work and that you know and can trace the relevant sources
- The gap, or problem, comes in paragraph 5. Note how it ends with a 'proposition'. This is another way of asking a question like 'Could we do away with normalisation if we used OOD?'
- The last paragraph gives a very brief plan of what the author intends to do in the project.

The second approach works 'bottom-up'. It is useful when you have a problem (a question that needs to be resolved) and you need to provide all the other details:

Example 2: Starting from the gap

1 **Motivation:** My company wants me to develop their website. They understand the benefits of having a 'shop window' to attract customers – but don't realise how important it is to have good mechanisms to deal with customers once they have 'come into the shop' – i.e. decided to buy something – and they don't realise how much effort it will take.

2 The Internet has given the world a new method of engaging in commercial activity. Instead of a physical shop for customers to visit to select and buy the goods they want, the World Wide Web offers companies the ability to set up a virtual shop, which they can visit electronically. There are some very good examples of highly successful web-based retail operations: for example, Amazon, a web-based bookseller. Customers who browse the Amazon site are provided with a number of advanced facilities (for instance a 'shopping trolley'), and once customers have made a purchase from Amazon, they will be recognised whenever they revisit the site. These facilities require the development of very sophisticated software, which goes well beyond the basic construction of web pages.

3 Tools exist to help companies to construct the shop window (for example, creating web pages with Microsoft's FrontPage or Macromedia's Dreamweaver). However, once they are interested, customers need information about product ranges and prices before they can make a buying decision. Then they need a mechanism to indicate their requirements (usually filling in a form of some sort). Once this has been received, the company needs to find out if the items are in stock and to work out how to deliver them. Finally, both parties need to establish arrangements for payment and then actually complete the transaction. Developing the functionality which corresponds to the actual shop (i.e. inventory and transaction management as described above) requires technical knowledge of information systems software development and must be done by specialist staff or contracted to specialist companies.

4 This project aims to analyse the website requirements of a typical small company, together with the specification and design processes they need to complete in order that the development can proceed effectively and efficiently. A demonstration website will be produced to show how a fully functional virtual shop can be developed from the actual requirements. In addition, guidelines will be developed to assist future workers in applying information systems development techniques to website developments.

Do you feel that this second example offers a good description of the background, the work being done, the problem and what the author intends to do about it?

- The problem and current work are covered (too) briefly in paragraph 1. The author should have done a bit more work in describing 'advanced facilities' and also said more about the 'sophisticated software' (such as an online database). Once again there is a general lack of references and sources

- The gap, or the problem, is obvious from the 'motivation'. It is more fully described in paragraph 2, which was actually written before paragraph 1.

The author's method of addressing the gap is described in the last paragraph. Note that the project will produce a website but we do not promise that it will be a full (commercial) website for the company. This would involve a lot of repetitive work, which is not very productive from the viewpoint of the project. It also offers 'guidelines' (i.e. the distilled wisdom of the author's experience). This generalises the problem and gives it a more 'academic' aspect.

You cannot solve the problems of the universe. A limited objective carried through systematically, in depth, impresses the examiners; one that covers a wide area superficially does not. Set modest goals, which you can achieve well. Do not attempt too much and do it poorly. If you have serious doubts, then put a few days into investigating the feasibility of your project and your project plans. Remember: it is perfectly acceptable (and good practice in project management) to review the scope of the project as you progress and make adjustments to the scope.

Students tend to wildly underestimate the amount of time needed. Often the work takes two or three times what was expected. Leave yourself an ample margin of time to deal with the unexpected. (Should you find yourself with ample free time at the end of the project, you can always change the scope by adding more functionality ...).

If you choose an idea which, besides having some novel aspects, is founded on areas of computing that you have thoroughly understood beforehand in one or more of your favourite taught modules, your chances of success will be greatly improved.

Activity 2.5

Review your study area

Having read the different examples, try to write an equivalent document for your student project. You could start top-down from a concept or topic or work bottom-up if you already have a problem you are trying to solve. Write something for each of the following four elements:

(i) A brief description of the topic and where it fits into the field

(ii) An account of the current state of work in the topic

(iii) The identification of a 'gap' in the work

(iv) A suggested means of filling the gap.

Selecting a suitable project title

By now you should have quite a good idea about the project that you want to do and what you think you might achieve by doing it. To develop these ideas further and in particular to give your supervisor a chance to judge whether your ideas are likely to produce a satisfactory outcome, you will need to put a bit more structure into the proposal. This can be done by:

- Choosing a descriptive title for your project
- Defining its aim and objectives.

Let's first deal with the selection of an appropriate title that conveys the essence of your project.

What's in a title?

Now consider the following list of different project titles. They are all concerned with a single field of study – the design of communications protocols. See if you can guess what each project is trying to achieve and what the student is likely to be doing.

Project A: Failures in communications protocol designs

Project B: A classification of design errors in communications protocols

Project C: What makes systems safe? An investigation into reliable communications protocol design

Project D: The effect of validation techniques on communications protocol integrity

Project E: Proving 'liveness' in communications protocol designs

Project F: An improved method for detecting design errors in communications protocols

Project G: A tool for automating communications protocol validation

Naming your student project

On the basis of your work on your general area of research, developed in Activity 2.4, can you write down a title for your project?

Once you have a working title, it is worth stopping and reflecting on what the title conveys. In order to do this, follow the procedure given below:

- Write down the title on which you are working
- Underline what you consider to be the most important word(s) in the title. Are these the most important terms related to your project?
- Consider the relationship between the words (i.e. do they reflect what you are trying to say?)
- Finally, look at every single word in isolation. Is it ambiguous? Can it be interpreted in any other way? Are any of the combinations of words in the title confusing or misleading?

Defining your project aim and objectives

Let's move on now and turn our attention to defining the aim and objectives for your project.

In Chapter 1, we stated that a key characteristic of every project was a purpose; a single, definable aim that encompasses and drives the entire project. A project should always have an aim, and a set of supporting objectives. An aim tells us what exactly needs to be achieved. Once you know what the project is about, you can break it down into specific objectives that support the stated aim.

(Later, you can start designing tasks to achieve the objectives. Each task can be decomposed into specific sub-tasks, which is what we need to do when we start planning a project and want to create a work breakdown structure (WBS). We shall pick up on WBS in Chapter 5, 'Project planning I: Activity and schedules'.)

All too often, the aims and objectives that we specify for projects are too vague and imprecise. We can use the SMART method devised by George Doran (Doran 1981) to check out our aims and objectives, and identify such weaknesses.

SMART is an acronym where each letter refers to a simplifying task in the process of elaborating a clear definition:

- **Specific**   Be specific
- **Measurable**   Establish a measurable indicator of progress
- **Assignable**   Make the objectives capable of being assigned to someone for completion
- **Realistic**   State what can realistically be achieved within the budgeted time and resources
- **Time-related**   State the duration (or when the objective should be achieved).

Activity 2.8

Defining a SMART aim

Starting with the aim statement, 'obtain a degree', use the SMART criteria highlighted above to see if you can refine this aim statement and make it a better-defined project.

Defining your student project aim

Now write the aim of your student project.

Once you have written it, try to use the SMART criteria to refine it and make it a more precise statement.

Defining your student project objectives

Now define your project objectives.

2.7 Summary

This chapter has described how project proposals are developed and become IT projects. Specific attention has been given to the project management activities with regards to the required feasibility study information. It is extremely important that a project is the 'right thing' for the organisation to do: that the IT investment is being made in the correct area. It is also important that the project is likely to meet its requirements within deadlines and within financial budgets. The groundwork for all this is put in place at the project proposal and project initiation stages, and forms the foundation for future systems analysis and design to build on.

The chapter has also discussed how you should go about selecting your student project, and set an aim and objectives for it. Hopefully, you can see how some of the theory of this chapter can be applied to your project and it helps you identify an excellent topic!

2.8 Review questions

 Question 2.1

Figure 2.8 shows a contents list for a student project proposal. It can be considered as a cut-down version of a feasibility study.

Student Project Proposal

1. Title
2. Keywords
3. Problem definition
4. Aims
5. Objectives
6. Evidence of requirement
7. Context description
8. Research method
9. Brief product description
10. Deliverables
11. Outcome/product evaluation approach
12. Resources
13. Bibliography
14. Project plan
15. Supervisor's name and signature

Figure 2.8: Contents list for a student project proposal

You will most likely have to complete something similar for your student project. Compare the contents of the student project proposal in Figure 2.8 (or the form you actually have to complete if you have a different one) with the contents list for a feasibility study (given in Section 2.4) and highlight the similarities and the differences. Reflect on the differences.

Who will be responsible for deciding if the topic for your student project is appropriate?

 Question 2.2

Why would 'scope creep' be considered a bad thing?

 Question 2.3

How would evolutionary systems development approaches help with issues concerning scope?

 Question 2.4

Why are the proposed product/system benefits important?

 Question 2.5

What are the benefits of a SMART objective?

2.9 Feedback on activities

Activity 2.1: Carry out a SWOT analysis

If we take a small specialist shop selling CDs and DVDs:

Strengths:
- Strong demand from young people for these products
- Shopping is a popular activity for many
- Specialist music/film advice can be given to shoppers
- Loyal customers.

Weaknesses:
- Doesn't have the bulk-buying power of supermarkets
- One location – dependent on customers visiting it.

Opportunities:
- E-mail: establish e-mail contact with customers
- Lack of product coverage by supermarkets/major retailers: attempt to build specialist customer bases in areas of classical music, world music, classic films, etc
- Could offer better facilities than other retailers: Introduce demonstration listening facilities for customers to sample music
- Lack of specialist advice from other sales outlets on selecting electronics goods: Expand into selling some electronics goods (for example, DVD players).

Threats:
- CD and DVD technology may be overtaken and replaced with something else
- Internet sales from companies such as Amazon, who sell at discount prices
- Downloading music from the Internet
- Economic slowdown.

Activity 2.2: Dealing with scope

The more functionality you want, the more it will cost you and the longer it is likely to take. If you need to deliver the same functionality quicker, it is likely to cost you more, as you will require more people to work on your project. If you have a fixed size team, and you add additional scope, it will take longer and you will need to adjust your delivery timetables.

Which of the factors do you control on your student project? Well, you don't really have much say in term of the schedule as the module has a fixed deadline for submitting your assignment. Cost is not really an issue for a student project. Also, in terms of staff resources, you have no option: there is only a single member of the project team (you) and you should not try to adjust that by looking for help elsewhere! The only other factor is scope. Depending on the time available to you, you may be able to deliver reduced (or enhanced) scope.

If you find yourself running out of time, you may need to consider the overall scope of the project and reduce some of the features you were going to deliver. Keep an eye on your schedule!

We have made your life 'easier' by giving you a fixed deadline. And there is only one of you working on your student project. Look closely at the scope at regular intervals and decide whether adjustments are needed.

Remember: project managers normally have far more variables and parameters to balance!

Activity 2.3: Finding a computing topic that interests you

The main point of these questions is to get you thinking about the modules you have studied and the way you feel about them. In this way you can begin to determine what your own interests are and which directions you might like your project to take.

Activity 2.4: Mapping the research territory

Regardless of the type of diagram, you should try to put something on paper. You should try to look at the topics that you have covered so far in your course. The more of this you can develop on your own, the better your overall grasp of the subject and the better equipped you will be to make sensible decisions about a project topic. However, it may also be useful to discuss your ideas with your friends and your tutors. Remember, however, that ultimately you should be interested in your preferences and what you would like to work on for the next eight months!

Note the different titles and the information each conveys to the reader.

Activity 2.5: Review your study area

The most important thing is to write something down – what your thoughts and ideas are at this moment, divided into the four elements. Number (ii) needs you to do some library reading and/or searching on the web. Numbers (iii) and (iv) might need quite a bit of hard thinking. Give yourself plenty of time to do this.

If you get stuck, re-read the two examples provided in this chapter and try to copy their way of thinking and style of expression.

Activity 2.6: What's in a title?

Project A: A research-based project. The title suggests that the researcher is simply looking for design failures. This might well follow a review format, looking into the literature to collect reports of past failures of communications protocol designs.

Project B: The project seems to be analysing the types of design errors which lead to failures. The approach may involve a survey, which gathers evidence from a carefully selected sample of failed communications systems (or indeed from a set of small case studies of such failures).

Project C: The project seems to be distinguishing between reliable and unreliable systems and trying to answer the question posed in the title. This would probably suggest that the student is using a set of carefully matched case studies to conduct the evaluation.

Project D: Here the researcher is trying to show that using validation techniques makes communications protocol designs more reliable. This suggests that a proof of some kind is needed. The research may involve a laboratory experiment, case studies or action research to give clearer and more positive indications of the sought-after results.

Project E: This project is concerned with formally (i.e. mathematically) proving one of the reliability properties of a communications system and thereby solving a problem.

Project F: Resolving a problem. The researcher is proposing a (new, or in this case, improved) technique for validating a design.

Project G: Novel development. This project is about exploiting the technique (from Project F) to construct a new software tool and to show that it is effective.

Notice how much information can be conveyed by the project's title!

Activity 2.7: Naming your student project

If the answer is 'No', then you need to look closely at what you are trying to achieve and what problem you are addressing. Next, have another look at the list of project titles that appear in Activity 2.6 (as well as the ones provided in Activity 2.4). They are not all perfect titles for the projects they describe, but they may help you by giving words and phrases you can use.

If you still can't come up with the right words, move on to the next area of this chapter and come back to this activity afterwards.

Note that as well as being the first decision in your student project, the title is also likely to be the final decision as it provides a summary of the report. While your project is registered with your given title, you can make minor adjustment to the title when you start the implementation part, and also when you finally submit your project to reflect the direction the work has actually taken.

Activity 2.8: Defining a SMART aim

Applying the SMART criteria, you should ask the following:

Specific: What kind of degree?

Measurable: How do I indicate completion?

Assignable: Can the objective be given to someone (me) for completion?

Realistic: How realistic is it for me to get this degree?

Time-related: When exactly will I graduate? How long is it likely to take?

As a result of these questions, you should revise the aim statement to something like:

'Fulfil the requirement of obtaining a BSc. Honours Degree in Computing Science, from my University, graduating by the end of summer term, 2007'

Note that, being an experienced project manager, you may want to build in a contingency just in case your project takes longer than envisaged.

Activity 2.9: Defining your student project aim

This should be fairly straightforward if you have written a good description of the subject area, the current work already done or known to be in progress in this area, what your project is about and how you intend to accomplish it, because it will have been necessary for you to outline what you intend to achieve, and the project aim is simply a brief statement of the main outcome and approach. To discover these in your study area review, concentrate on the questions about the scope and outcomes of the project that were identified in Activity 2.5.

Don't forget to use SMART to refine your statement and make it more precise, specific, measurable, assignable, and realistic and time-related. This will improve your chances of being able to successfully complete a well-defined, properly understood project.

Activity 2.10: Defining your student project objectives

Make sure that each objective you define relates to the aim you defined earlier. Make sure that each objective is necessary to achieve the aim and that the aim will be achieved when all the individual objectives have been successful completed.

Check your objectives and determine which should be the key project success criteria. It is unlikely you need all the detailed measures specified as success criteria. Try to focus on, say, the top five objectives that will mean the most to your client.

2.10 References

- Dawson, C.W., (2005), *Projects in Computing and Information Systems: A Student's Guide*, Addison-Wesley, ISBN 0 32126355 3.
- Deming, W. E., (1993), *The New Economics for Industry, Government, Education.* MIT Center for Advanced Engineering Study (CAES), Cambridge MA USA-02139, ISBN 0 91137905 3.
- Doran, G.T., (1981), There's a S.M.A.R.T. Way to Write Management Goals and Objectives, *Management Review,* 1981, Issue 11, Volume 70, page 35.
- Hughes, B. & Cotterell, M., (2002), *Software Project Management* (3rd edition), McGraw-Hill, ISBN 0 07 709834 X. NB 4th edition,2005, McGraw-Hill, ISBN 0 07 710989 9.
- Kaplan, R. S. and Norton, D.P., (1996), *The Balanced Scorecard*, Harvard Business School Press, ISBN 0 87584 651 3.
- Marchewka, J. T., (2003), *Information Technology Project Management: Providing Measurable Organizational Value*, Wiley, ISBN 0 47139203 0. NB: 2nd Edition 2006, Wiley, ISBN 0 47171539 5.
- Olson, D. L., (2003), *Introduction to Information Systems Project Management* (2nd Edition), McGraw-Hill, ISBN 0 07282402 6.

CHAPTER 3

Research methods

OVERVIEW

This chapter is about research methods: we consider some aspects of the philosophical assumptions underpinning research approaches, and discuss a number of research methods and a range of data collection methods. The aim is to give an introduction to research design, and to provide information that will assist you with the design of your student project. Even if you are not tackling a research project, there is material in this chapter that is likely to be found useful (for example, the discussion on data collection methods).

Learning outcomes At the end of this chapter you should be able to:

- Outline the different research philosophies (postpositivism, constructivism, advocacy and pragmatism)

- Understand the different research approaches (quantitative, qualitative and mixed methods)

- Describe the different research methods including experiment, survey, case study, action research, narrative, grounded theory and ethnography

- Understand the different data collection methods including sampling, secondary data (documentation, survey and multiple sources), observation, questionnaire and interview

- Select appropriate research methods for a given project.

3.1 Introduction

The aims of this chapter are to enable you to:

- Select an appropriate research method for your project
- Decide how to apply the selected research method to your project.

It's up to you to decide which research methods will fit your project best. This chapter aims to provide sufficient information to help you make this decision – or rather decisions – because it is a series of decisions that you will have to make. To establish your research methods you will need to use your research question to decide:

- A research **approach**
- At least one research **method**
- At least one **data collection method**.

Structure of a research design

Let's first give you an overview of what's involved and then we'll go through the research design process in more detail. See Figure 3.1 for an outline of research design. The first step is to outline your research question (you already considered your research topic in the previous chapter). Your research question drives your decisions and it is likely you will modify your research question and objectives as you further develop your ideas.

You also at this stage have to consider your research philosophy – are you more comfortable with a scientific approach or an approach that is more subjective?

You can then decide your research strategy: your research approach, at least one research method and at least one data collection method. Note: for your student project, given the timescales, you are likely to use only one research method.

From that point you can move to planning your research project (project management planning is the subject of chapters 5 and 6).

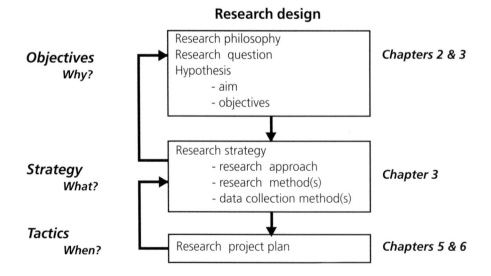

Figure 3.1: An outline of research design

Conceptual framework for the research process

See Figure 3.2, which shows a conceptual framework supporting the research process – it's modified from a diagram by Saunders et al. (2000), the research process 'onion'. This is a very helpful diagram showing how the different elements of the research design 'fit' together. This chapter is structured in much the same way – travelling from the outer 'frame' towards the centre.

(Note you will find if you look at other books on research methods that different authors often use differing terminologies.)

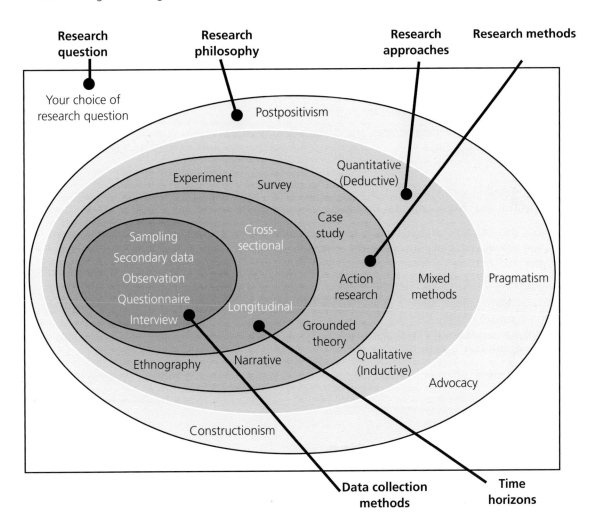

Figure 3.2: The research process 'onion': modified from Saunders et al (2000). One of the alterations was that an outer frame is now added to put the research question in the picture!

3.2 The research process

Let's now look at the process that creates and implements a research design, the research process. The steps in the research process can be set out as follows:

1 Identify your research problem (the **research question**)
2 Define its problem and its boundaries
3 Consider your **research philosophy**
4 Formulate your **aim and objectives**
5 Establish your **research strategy**:
    i. Determine your **research approach**
    ii. Decide on your **research method(s)**
    iii. Decide on your appropriate **data collection method(s)**
6 Produce your **research project plan**
7 Conduct research and gather data (data collection)
8 Analyse the data (data analysis) and evaluate the findings
9 Write up the results.

As you might imagine, the steps are not purely sequential and are likely to involve iteration, repetition and rework cycles taking you back to earlier activities.

Your student project should broadly follow along the lines of this process. Can you see that we have already considered many aspects of steps 1, 2 and 4 in Chapter 2 (section 2.6, 'Selecting your student project'), when we discussed how to identify a project topic, choose a project title and specify an aim and set of objectives?

The research process for your student project is entwined with the systems development and management processes. In this chapter we are providing the information to enable you continue work on these steps and to carry out step 3, 'Consider your research philosophy' and step 5, 'Establish your research strategy'.

Later chapters will cover the topics of planning and writing up (together with evaluating the findings).

3.3 The research question

Let's start by discussing the research question. The way that the research is conducted, and the answer it finds, depends largely on the question being asked. You might remember we have already mentioned in Chapter 2 that it is useful to regard a project as an investigation designed to find an answer to a question. Birley and Moreland (1998) suggest that

> 'A research question is a way of explaining as sharply and pithily as possible to yourself exactly what you are going to research and what you wish to find out.'

A research question needs to be based on a positive statement and it needs to be something that is answered *on the basis of the evidence gathered*. Therefore, you should avoid:

- Value judgements
- Questions for which the evidence can't be obtained
- Statements that presuppose what the answer is.

You might wonder how 'a research question' relates to 'a hypothesis'. A research question drives a research project and a hypothesis drives a scientific investigation. They are essentially very similar. Nevertheless, 'hypothesis' is a narrower concept than 'research question'. A hypothesis is an untested assertion about the relationship between two or more concepts, whereas a research question can apply to a wider range of enquiries.

Often, a research question can be supported by one or more hypotheses. The benefit of having hypotheses as well as a research question is that the hypotheses can serve to qualify or more precisely define the research question. Then your objectives should support your hypotheses. This can be useful when creating your research strategy, as you are better able to judge the likelihood of your solution being appropriate to address your research question.

To give some examples of research questions and hypotheses:

- **Question:** What factors influence successful student projects?
  - Hypothesis: good working knowledge together with use of a project management application is essential
  - Hypothesis: keeping a very detailed journal is beneficial
  - Hypothesis: reducing the amount of learning about new technology is beneficial
- **Question:** Does having a job while studying influence student grades?
  - Hypothesis: students achieving above 70% will work fewer hours during weekdays.

Activity 3.1

Writing a research question

Consider the following ideas for research projects presented by other students. Can you create a potential research question for each idea?

- Student A appreciates that commercial computer systems are vulnerable to attack by hackers and other malicious persons and their software. Accordingly, commercial firms devise security policies that they expect their employees to follow, with the objective of making attacks on the system by outsiders impossible. However, employees frequently don't follow these policies, with the result that the firm remains vulnerable. Student A would like to know why the employees behave in this way

- Student B wants to write an Intelligent Tutoring System that will teach a limited number of topics (concerned with oscillations and waves) to pupils studying for the GCSE Physics exam (part of the exam system used in England and Wales). The system will be called WAVY. And, of course, Student B would like to demonstrate that it works

- Student C is interested in the spectacular rise in popularity of 'virtual world' role-playing games (MMORPGs, or massively multiplayer online role-playing games), as opposed to conventional console-based games. Student C wonders whether this is purely to do with cost, or whether the game-playing experience is in some way superior

- Student D is in touch with a small catering company that hasn't so far computerised any of its business operations. Student D intends to write a database system for this company, and believes that this will solve many of its problems. The company is willing to let her try.

3.4 Research philosophies

Let's now consider the research philosophies. Creswell (2003) identifies four knowledge claims (research philosophies):

- **Postpositivism**: this is the scientific stance: knowledge, in the form of facts, is derived from either observation or experience of real, objective and measurable natural phenomena. Facts can thus be viewed as universal truths, devoid of personal values and social interactions and independent of time and context. An example of research taking this stance would be investigating whether children with higher than average reading skills watched less television. You could write a hypothesis for testing

- **Constructivism**: knowledge is viewed as encompassing beliefs, principles, personal values, preferences, social context and historical background – which are inevitably dynamic, as they change with time and context. The stance is taken that people view the world from their own experiences and perspective, and try to make sense of it. An example of research using this stance would be to carry out unstructured interviews (see later) to find out what issues people had with online shopping for clothes. You don't know in advance what issues people are going to raise, and the relevant values and will emerge from the analysis of your findings

- **Advocacy**: the stance is that constructivism is not sufficient and that there should be 'an action agenda' for change (Creswell 2003). There is an emphasis on working with disadvantaged and marginalised groups and tackling problems in society. There is also an emphasis on collaboration among all the participants involved – hence this research philosophy is sometimes termed 'participatory action'. An example of research taking this stance would be improving the inclusion within schools of children with autism and interviewing local authority administrators, teachers, parents and children

- **Pragmatism**: the stance is that the problem is the most important concept and that more than one philosophical stance can be taken – any research method can be used to contribute to the findings. The focus is on 'what works' (Creswell 2003 quoting Patton). An example of research adopting pragmatism would be to carry out research in the stance of constructivism to determine some hypotheses and then research in the stance of positivism to test out these hypotheses. To give an example, you might wonder why television-viewing ratings were falling. So you could carry out interviews to find out the reasons that people had for not watching a given channel. From the results, you could devise some hypotheses, which you could then test. Maybe you would devise examples of television programme schedules and ask people to select what they would choose to view. Alternatively, you could examine old television programme schedules against viewing figures to see if your hypotheses held. The choice of which methods to mix would depend on exactly what factors your hypotheses involved.

Note some authors use the terms 'positivism', 'interpretive' and 'critical', which can very roughly be mapped to 'postpositivism', 'constructivism' and 'pragmatism' respectively.

So what does this mean for your student project?

You are not going to choose advocacy because there is a need to engage the participants as collaborators and that's not possible within a typical student project. Also, it is unlikely that you would be able to address a problem in society within the timescales of a student project.

Postpositivism is the scientific stance. It is an attractive option for your student project because it allows a deductive approach. You put forward a hypothesis and then you try to disprove it. Constructivism, on the other hand, prefers the hypotheses to emerge out of the data – an inductive approach. The problem with the inductive approach for a student project is the timescales – can you afford the time it takes to do this kind of research, especially when you don't know what is likely to emerge?   Also, what happens if no theory emerges from your data? This approach could put you under added pressure.

Pragmatism allows any stance. It can be said to allow you to adopt stances of both postpositivism and constructivism in your research. The issue once again is timescales – could you cover both in the timescales of a student project?

3.5 Research approaches

The choice of research approach is strongly coupled to the type(s) of data available to the researcher. The most crucial distinction is between two forms of data:

- **Quantitative data:** this consists of measurements in the form of numbers. It may be used to produce mathematical descriptions of the relationships between variables
- **Qualitative data:** this is non-numerical: it consists of descriptions. It is concerned with generating understanding and insight expressed in verbal descriptions.

There are three research approaches taking their names from the type(s) of data involved: quantitative, qualitative and mixed methods.

- **Quantitative research** primarily takes a postpositivist approach and uses research methods such as experiments and surveys to collect quantitative data. Theories are used in a deductive manner – that is, they are found in the literature or proposed by the researcher and then research is devised to test them.

  The quantitative approach maintains that 'causes' determine 'effects'. Problems are reduced to a set of variables and hypotheses are deduced about the relationships among the variables. The hypotheses are then tested to verify whether they hold or can be falsified, by taking measurements of the variables. The validity and reliability of the measurements is an important consideration.

- **Qualitative research** takes a constructivist approach tending to use research methods such as ethnography, grounded theory and case studies to collect qualitative data. Theories are built inductively from the data collected.

  Researchers are concerned with social and cultural phenomena. Social interaction in human activity systems means that actors are forced to negotiate and agree on certain aspects. The resulting emphasis is on the relevant interpretation of knowledge as held by participants in a social activity.

  Such a qualitative perspective relies on words to convey feelings and perceptions, rather than numbers. There is recognition that subjects can express themselves and their feelings, and thereby clarify the social and cultural contexts within which they operate. Meaning, therefore, needs to be 'interpreted' in a process of 'sense making'. Actions thus need to be understood in terms of intentions, which in turn are understood in their original context. Indeed, Kaplan and Maxwell (1994) argue that the goal of understanding a phenomenon from the point of view of the main participants and their particular social, cultural and institutional context is largely lost when the textual data are quantified.

- **Mixed methods research** takes a pragmatic approach and collects both quantitative and qualitative data either simultaneously or sequentially. Creswell (2003) quoting Newman and Benz states that research in more recent times tends not to be so polarised between quantitative and qualitative, but instead falls somewhere between the two. Hence this third research approach, 'mixed methods'.

What does this mean for your student project? Your research approach tends to follow from your research philosophy. However, we said at the start of this topic that there is a strong coupling to the type of data available. You need to look at your research question and hypotheses and think about the different types of data that could be involved. Could you have numeric data? Could you have both numeric and descriptive data?

3.6   Research methods

Let's now introduce a variety of the research methods and discuss some of their notable features. The research methods shall include:

- **Experiment**
- **Survey**
- **Case study**
- **Action research**
- **Implementation research**
- **Grounded theory**
- **Narrative**
- **Ethnography.**

(Note that *implementation research* did not appear in Figure 3.2, but it has been included in the above list. The reason for inclusion here is that implementation research is a common method used in student projects, although it not a common method for researchers at PhD level and so we left it out of the diagram to emphasise this point – the diagram reflects what are more normally considered as research methods.)

Experiment

In natural sciences (which generally means physics, chemistry and their various branches), 'experiment' is a fairly straightforward idea. A scientist, doing things in the conventional way, will come up with a hypothesis that leads to a proposition for a phenomenon (an observable event or 'something that appears or is perceived' (Concise Oxford Dictionary, 1964)), and then look for the phenomenon to see if it's there. An experiment simply means that a scientist proceeds in the following way:

- The scientist determines where the phenomenon is expected to appear or sets up apparatus that will cause the phenomenon to appear (assuming the hypothesis is correct)
- The scientist determines how to observe the phenomenon and this may involve setting up apparatus to make the phenomenon observable
- The scientist looks to see whether the phenomenon really does appear as predicted.

In any branch of social science or technology that involves people interacting with the world around them things are more complicated. This includes us interacting with IT. As we are so complex and so variable in what we think, what we can do, how we behave and so forth, an experiment has to be based on a sufficiently large number of people, to eliminate the effects of individual differences.

What's more, it usually has to be based on the difference between what happens to a group of people who are subjected to some influence (the **experimental subjects**) and what happens to another group of people who aren't subjected to this influence (the **control subjects**).

In addition, it often has to be based on the difference between these two groups of people before they have been influenced (their attitudes, their abilities, or whatever – this is known as the **pre-test**) and the way they are after they have been influenced (this is known as the **post-test**). Finally, one is not just looking for a difference that seems to be caused by this influence: one is looking for a significant difference – one that is so large that it can't be dismissed as a chance variation.

All of this means that it's difficult to perform the sort of experiment that you might want to include in your student project. You really do need to read up on experimental design, and the statistics involved in analysing experimental results, before you get started. Don't assume that simply trying something out (such as a new screen design) on a couple of friends, and noting down what happens, counts as a properly conducted experiment.

But that isn't to say that, with a little care and a little background reading, an IT student can't design and execute a perfectly good experiment. Imagine that you have designed and built a new on-screen help system for a piece of software that hasn't got one, and you want to find out whether users who have the benefit of it really do make fewer errors than users who don't. A well-designed and well-executed experiment would seem to be the best way to find out.

Activity 3.2

Investigating text readability on screen

It's been claimed by Pace (1984) that text displayed on a computer screen in magenta on a green background causes a much higher error rate in reading than text displayed in blue on white.

How would you test this? Provide as many details as you can.

Survey

To conduct a survey is to collect data from a sizeable population, that has something you want to research in common, in order to get a large-scale picture of this population at a certain point in time. This doesn't mean it has to be individuals as such who are surveyed; you can, for instance, survey documentation or organisations (for example, surveying bookshops for their opinions on selling books via the Internet – the bookshops will have to identify their representatives, the people they want to speak on their behalf).

Surveys are used to describe, highlight or measure certain generalised features or trends. It's very likely that you are familiar with surveys; people often get stopped in major cities by pollsters and asked to complete survey questions. Examples of surveys include:

- Opinion polls prior to an election
- Gathering student preferences for academic courses
- Discovering the usage of sporting facilities on your campus
- Satisfaction surveys in your student canteen
- A national census that goes to all the heads of households in a country.

It's generally assumed that surveys are performed using questionnaires, but in fact it's perfectly possible to conduct a survey using a series of interviews or observations, provided the same pieces of information are collected from each person or setting – one notable feature of surveys is that all subjects will be asked the same set of questions.

It's also not true that all surveys have to be mailed or sent by e-mail. Questionnaires can be conducted face to face, interviews can be conducted by telephone, and various electronic media make new forms of questioning possible (for example, video conferencing facilities).

As you can see in the examples indicated, a survey *may* entail contacting every household in a country (in the case of a census). Normally, however, when carrying out a survey the technique of **sampling** is used to collect data from a much smaller number of people. This is possible providing there's good reason to believe that the sample's characteristics are much the same as those of the whole population. Selecting the sample size is an essential part of the survey approach – the validity of the findings depends on using a sample of sufficient size. If you read a textbook on the survey method, you will find mathematical formulae that allow you to calculate the size that the sample must be, given the size of the population of interest and the reliability of the results that is required. Or, rather, the level of *unreliability* that you are prepared to tolerate; the only way to eliminate the unreliability completely is to make your sample as large as the entire population, as in the case of a national census.

Generally, other sampling techniques will also be used to create a reasonable subset of the population that will be contacted for the purposes of the research. Sampling assumes that the trends and patterns observed in the sample population will apply to the population as a whole. There are various sorts of *structured sampling*, in which care is taken to ensure that people of various types, say men and women, rich and poor, young and old – whatever characteristics are reckoned to be important to the research question – appear in the sample in the same proportions that they appear in the population as a whole. And there is a simpler approach: *random sampling*, in which the sample is constructed by the random selection of subjects out of the whole population.

On the face of it, the survey approach is an unpromising basis for an IT project. It doesn't fit very well with the assumption that there is a problem to be solved or a product to be technically evaluated. It's difficult to send out enough questionnaires (or to conduct enough interviews) to get a large-enough sample, bearing in mind that a fair number of the people who you approach will refuse (or forget) to fill in the questionnaire or decline to be interviewed. And, unless one does a careful analysis of the results to reveal concealed relationships between variables in the data, the results of a survey can be trivial and uninteresting.

Nevertheless, a survey can be a valuable component of a project that has other objectives. If you intended to produce some computerised service for other students, it might very well be a good idea to survey a sufficiently large random sample of the students, in order to discover their preferences and requirements – and also what facilities they already have access to. It is also a good basis for determining attitudes to current provision and the general preferences of users or potential users. The alternative would be to use guesswork, or the opinions of one's friends, or someone else's survey (which would almost certainly be out of date); none of these would give you answers that you could rely on to be an accurate reflection of what was required.

Case study

Case study research involves an in-depth analysis of one or more cases of an event, an activity, a process or an individual, in its real-life context over a stated time period. It allows the researcher to focus on the phenomena of interest in great detail.

Case studies are often used in information systems research (Orlikowski & Baroudi, 1991). Data collection methods often used for case studies include observation, documentation and interviews, but other tools can be selected to suit the particular requirements of a case. Case study research needs to be self-contained.

Case studies are ideal for exploring interactions between people and their understanding of a situation (Dalcher, 2003). The richness of the data obtained by multiple means from multiple perspectives provides a real insight into the main issues at play. Case studies are useful in exploring novel situations in real-life settings and in covering different perspectives of the same problem. They do present difficulties in 'controlling' variables (you can't control a real-life workplace) and introducing potential biases (for example, maybe you can only get access to specific organisations, so you don't have a representative sample). Bear in mind that it is tricky to try to generalise from the findings, especially when they only relate to a single case study, leading to doubts about the reliability of any potential conclusions.

If you choose case studies as your research method, you will be expected to clearly explain your choice of case, or cases. You will be expected to explain the applicability of findings from a single case to the entire domain and in what ways your case is representative.

To give some examples:

- If you were researching some aspect of requirements specification, say the specification of metrics, then you might decide to obtain several examples of requirements specification that were currently being worked on from different sources. Each requirements specification and the work you did associated with it (maybe interviewing the author(s) of the requirements specification) would be a 'case'
- You might want to understand how a software application was used and the benefits obtained from its use. Each organisational group implementing the application would form the basis of a case study. You would probably be looking for a selection of organisational groups, say some with similar working practices, and others with different ones. However, there could be other criteria, such as the functionality of the different organisational groups, say finance or customer services. You might sit observing use of the application.

If research is being conducted only on historical information, then the research method is more likely a 'case history' than a 'case study'; for more information, see Dalcher (2003, 2005).

Action research

Action research is distinguished from other research methods by the participation of the researcher in the task being researched. The researcher takes a role in the team carrying out the work being analysed – and can control or influence in some way the changes taking place. This type of research is useful in bridging the gap between research and practice.

Principal characteristics of action research include:

- Makes for practical problem solving as well as expanding scientific knowledge
- Is collaborative and participatory
- Uses feedback from data in an ongoing, cyclical, process
- Seeks to understand complex social situations
- Seeks to understand the processes of change within a social situation.

Action research often starts with small groups and small cycles of planning and implementation – but then can widen to take in the whole community of the organisation in question. It is often described as a series of cycles of action, followed by reflection, leading to further action. The reflective process that takes place leads to decision making by as many of the participants as possible. For action research to be evaluated with any degree of validity, the participants themselves must be involved in the process.

From the foregoing it can be seen that full-scale action research is very unlikely to be a suitable research design for a small student project. This is because:

- You are unlikely to be part of the organisation that is to be researched, and it is unlikely you have enough status to be allowed to set up such a project to manage change
- You will not have enough time to investigate the complexity of the situation and to carry out the different cycles required.

However, there are aspects of action research method that might prove useful to your student project. You can use the open-ended nature of action research to help define the problem to be solved within a practical setting:

- Start with a small group of people and find out what they think is needed, perhaps using a questionnaire or interviews
- Arrange for regular reviews of work in progress, to evaluate the steps and build in minor changes. Record these meetings
- Expect people to learn from their experiences. Note these in your research diary
- Decide on a monitoring procedure and on success criteria for any implementations
- Use the participants to help validate your findings.

Note that unless you are already working on a project and considered as part of the team, it is difficult for action research to be implemented in any effective way.

Examples

Thinking back to the examples given under the case study method, action research would be occurring if the researcher were a member of the project team actively involved in carrying out the specification of requirements; or in the case of the application, if the researcher actually worked in the organisation and used the application on a regular basis. The key thing here is that the researcher would be in a position to influence how requirements were specified or how the application was actually used and could suggest and introduce changes.

Implementation research

Implementation research can, perhaps, be treated as a special sort of action research. The idea is that a practitioner introduces a technological solution into an organisation which has a specified problem, and examines the effectiveness of this solution using rigorous research techniques. In our case, we can assume that the technological solution will involve some form of IT – it might be a new computer system or a new application, for instance.

It is important, in this style of research, that a careful examination of the organisation is made in the early stages of the project in order to establish precisely what the problem is – what exactly the features of the organisation's operations are that need improving. It therefore doesn't quite fit the classic 'scientific' pattern where the research question is known from the start – it is only some time after the start of the project that one is able to pose the question 'Is X a good solution to the problem we have here, namely Y?'

It is essential that the technological innovation be evaluated as a solution to the problem that has been identified. It should be possible to collect quantitative data – or, at the very least, qualitative data – before the innovation, and equivalent data after it; this will allow you to demonstrate that some improvement has – or hasn't – occurred. It is harder, however, to show a statistically significant difference between the two sets of data than it is in the case of an experimental design.

It is also difficult to argue that any findings (about the effectiveness of this particular solution) generalise to *other* settings. If, however, you can locate another setting where a similar solution has been applied and discuss the similarities and differences of the effects in the two settings, it becomes a richer, more useful piece of research.

As with research based on experiments, the evaluation should ideally be based on the outcomes of the intervention, as compared with the outcomes if the intervention hadn't happened. One can't, of course, try it both ways and see, for example, whether a company fares better with a new computer system than without it. What one can do is to compare the period when the company did have use of the new system with an equivalent period in the past when it didn't, and provide evidence that the two periods were in fact equivalent. It is also necessary to investigate alternatives to the solution that you chose, and provide evidence that these alternatives would have been a worse solution, or a better solution, than the one that was in fact chosen. This is the sort of issue that you should cover when you are discussing your findings in your project report.

Grounded theory (GT)

The main philosophy behind grounded theory, as originally created by Glaser and Strauss in 1967, is the *generation of theory from data*. GT is derived from data, systematically gathered and analysed throughout the research process. It is concerned with constructing theory rather than testing theory.

GT research is a process that begins with a set of observations and then moves on to develop theory. In this sense, a researcher does not begin the research process with preconceived theory in mind (Strauss & Corbin, 1998). In addition, the theory derived is from 'real data' rather than 'logico-deductive' speculation (Glaser & Strauss, 1967).

GT provides the researcher with a wider degree of flexibility, because it is generally not restricted by pre-propositions, and therefore the collected data does not have to be forced to 'fit' a certain proposition or theory. GT allows the researcher to derive a hypothesis that 'fits' the data collected in the initial step, and to test it in subsequent steps, in an iterative cycle till theoretical saturation is reached. Research proceeds in a series of inductive and deductive steps.

GT is

> 'grounded in the views of the participants in the study…. Two primary characteristics of this design are the constant comparison of data with emerging categories and theoretical sampling of different groups to maximize the similarities and differences of information' (Creswell, 2003).

Theory is developed and tested by using the data and thence considered as

> 'being grounded in such continual reference to the data.' (Saunders et al, 2000).

Example of a grounded theory approach

You want to investigate students' views about group coursework. You think there might be some issues. You carry out five random unstructured interviews with third-year students. You then transcribe the interviews verbatim and start to categorise the interview material. You identify categories from the data, for example 'OTHER GROUP MEMBERS', 'SELECTION OF GROUPS', 'GROUP MEETINGS' and 'DIVISION OF WORKLOAD'. Then you examine the data collected under each of the categories looking to see if any common themes emerged.

Maybe under 'DIVISION OF WORKLOAD' you would see that there was a recurring theme of some group members not doing their share of the workload… and you might find that was frequently linked to mention of coursework involving programming tasks… so you would begin to build hypotheses ('a testable proposition' (Saunders et al, 2000 quoting Silverman 1993)) about programming tasks in coursework being unpopular or too difficult or too lengthy… and you would look at your data to see if there was any evidence supporting this and any evidence against this, and start to work out your next step to test the theory that you have just derived, and so on.

Narrative

Narrative research is based on the idea that all people are storytellers. Its aim is to capture and investigate experiences as human beings live them in time, in space, in person and in relationships. Those who undertake narrative inquiry need to attend to a 'three-dimensional inquiry space' – the temporal, the spatial and the personal-social. (Wood 2000: quoting Clandinin and Connelly – see **www.aaanet.org/cae/aeq/br/clandinin.htm/**)

The researcher asks one or more individuals to recount stories about their lives. The researcher then rearranges the information into a chronological sequence and then retells the story through a single purposeful narrative – see, for example, Dalcher (2003).

Ethnography

The ethnographic approach is fundamentally that of anthropology (Gill and Johnson, 2002). The researcher studies an intact cultural group in a natural setting over a prolonged period of time by collecting, primarily, observational data (Creswell, 2003 quoting Creswell 1998). The focus is on the manner in which people interact and collaborate in observable and regular ways (Gill and Johnson, 2002).

Given the timescales involved, it is not possible for a student project to adopt this method.

However, an example of this approach would be observing how conflicts are handled on a shop-floor in a factory.

Activity 3.3

Selecting a research method

According to the listed student projects in Activity 3.1:

- Which of the research methods described in this chapter would be the most appropriate for each project?

- Write down your choice and justification in each case.

There is one final point to note before we move on to data collection methods.

The selection of a particular research *method* is not restricted by adopting a certain research *approach* (quantitative, qualitative or mixed methods) – and vice versa. For example, case study research can use mixed (or even be limited to) quantitative evidence (Yin, 2003). Also, a survey can use mixed (or even be limited to) qualitative evidence.

3.7 Data collection methods

There are several trusted and well-used methods for collecting data. If you have done a systems analysis module during your studies, it is very likely that you will have covered most of the relevant methods. Typical methods for gathering data include:

- **Sampling**
- **Secondary data**
  - documentation
  - survey
  - multiple source
- **Observation**
- **Questionnaires**
- **Interviews.**

Generally, you will find that specific methods of data collection tend to be associated with certain research methods. Questionnaires, for example, are often associated with the survey approach, while observation will typically be connected to experiments.

However, it is still up to you, as the researcher, to select the most suitable method for your research method and to make choices about how to implement it: for example, the size of the sample, the number of documents and the time per interview. Your choices will reflect the priorities and constraints of your project. They should also show a clear understanding of the principles of research and you should be able to present a logical argument explaining your decisions. You should not, however, use a data collection method without having a clear idea of:

- What data you need to gather
- What you will do with it once you have gathered it
- Whether this is the best technique for gathering this sort of data.

A data collection exercise can be very expensive in time and effort; time that you spend on it could be at the expense of other aspects of your project work. If you use a survey, or interview, you need to check that the data that you gather could not have been obtained more easily some other way.

Note that data-gathering methods rely on the use of your different senses. The key skills that are required to use them effectively are

- **Listening** (during interviews)
- **Seeing** (observation and once again observing reactions during interviews)
- **Reading** (documentation and questionnaires).

It will also help if you can 'read between the lines' and identify trends and hidden meanings.

Let's now briefly discuss each of these methods for data collection.

Sampling

Sampling occurs when you collect a subset (a sample) of the total population of data that exists. The need for sampling arises when it would be impractical for you to survey an entire population. Time and money are usually thought of as the first constraints, but even if time and money were available, it would not be sensible to proceed to sample an entire population if sampling a subset would give you an answer to an acceptable level of reliability.

There are two main types of sampling technique:

- **Probability** (representative)
- **Non-probability** (judgmental).

(There are numerous subsets of these two main sampling techniques, which it is beyond the scope of this book to describe.) Non-probability sampling is subjective, while probability sampling is based on there being sufficient knowledge to work out the probability of a case being chosen. With probability sampling you have to first determine your sampling frame (a complete list of all the cases you are interested in). From the sampling frame, you choose your sample size; you then decide on your sampling sub-technique and select the sample. Finally, you check the sample is representative of the population (by cross-checking against some other data source for the population). Probability sampling allows you to make statistical inferences and generalise your findings to the entire population.

Secondary data

Saunders et al (2000) identify three main sub-groups of secondary data as follows:

- **Documentation**
- **Survey**
- **Multiple source.**

Key advantages of secondary data are that high-quality data is available, both *cheaply* (maybe not true for commercial data) and *rapidly*. The disadvantage is that the data will have been collected and analysed for a specific purpose, which may well differ from the purpose for which you wish to use it.

Documentation

Documentation can include both written and non-written documents. Examples of written documents include e-mails, letters, books, journals, diaries and organisational documents, such as user manuals. Examples of non-written documents include tape and video recordings, photographs, drawings, films and television programmes.

Document and record searching is often useful in establishing quantitative information about data and procedures. For example, a simple record search can reveal the number of customers or the number of fields per record. It can also highlight the typical number of transactions per record, the forms that need to be filled for a particular task, and the data that needs to be located in order to fill them.

Documentation can also be used to provide qualitative information, for example the reason why a decision was made might be documented.

Document searching is useful because it relies on documents that are already in existence, and so it provides a good introduction to the work, the participants, and the departments and organisations involved. Operating procedures, organisation charts, forms, publicity booklets, job descriptions, statements of company policies and manuals can all be useful in detailing how work processes are supposed to be followed. They provide a background to the organisational setting. It can also be very instructive to compare filled-in documents and forms with organisational procedures dictating how they should be completed. Sampling a set of documents can also be useful for identifying typical mistakes, shortcuts and revised procedures.

Document searching can also be useful in confirming points that have come up during interviews. However, documentation is not always kept up to date. Furthermore, in some situations there is either insufficient documentation – or an overabundance – making it impossible to trace the relevant items. There may also be issues around confidentiality and the release of sensitive documents.

Survey

Survey-based secondary data are usually collected by questionnaires. There are three types of such data (Saunders et al, 2000):

- **Censuses**
- **Continuous and regular surveys**
- **Ad hoc surveys.**

For non-census surveys, you may get access to the aggregated data or the raw data.

Multiple source

Multiple source secondary data is when information is presented that has been compiled from more than one source. Government compilations of industry data are a common form of such data.

Observation

This can be described as the scrutiny and recording of action in natural settings. Detailed observation is, in general, not a very effective way of obtaining the kind of information required for developing computer systems. A new system is likely to change working practice, and observing the details of the old working practices has limited value.

Other major drawbacks are the ease with which people can be antagonised if they are being watched (or even if they think they are). Also there is the fact that behaviour changes if people are being observed – the 'Hawthorne effect', which is the idea that people's productivity is likely to increase if they know they are being observed. It can also be difficult to negotiate agreement from the organisation for you to be present for prolonged periods to observe its operating procedures.

Observation is also very expensive in terms of your time. Furthermore, it does not reliably reveal emotions or feelings, or provide any rationale for particular behaviour patterns.

However, when a special event or a critical time is anticipated, it may be worthwhile observing it to see what kind of special behaviour patterns it stimulates. Observation is direct and focused – it can concentrate on a specific aspect of an organisation's operations and uncover unexpected relationships. It can also provide a check on data gathered by interviews or questionnaires.

For instance, if a respondent claims, in an interview, that they never spend more than half an hour in the morning reading and replying to their e-mail, but observation shows them spending an hour and a half on several successive days, the shortcomings of the data derived from the interview have been laid bare. (But notice how long it took to obtain the true data!)

If you intend to use observation as a technique, you should take care to document the activities thoroughly. You need to decide, in advance,

- The plan for observation
- What you are observing
- The method of recording observations
- How the observations are to be analysed.

Informal observation – simply being present, and 'being observant' – can be very valuable as a way of getting the feel of a particular organisation and the way it is managed. Look for piles of papers, closeness of supervision, frequent interruptions, bad time-keeping, as well as the positive signs of a productive and efficient workplace. This can be done during a visit or on your way to an interview. However, remember to be careful of such subjective information, which can be embarrassing and misleading if it is taken out of context.

Questionnaires

A questionnaire can produce useful data for a project, provided the necessary detailed work is done in advance. Note that questionnaires have been described as the most difficult method of information gathering to use successfully. If you decide to use a questionnaire, then it would be wise to read up on the subject of setting up questionnaire questions and analysing questionnaire data.

Typical reasons why a questionnaire might be used include:

- **Geography:** it might be that the organisation under investigation has branch offices in different parts of the world. You cannot visit them all and it is not feasible to get the people you want to come to you. A questionnaire survey with telephone follow-up could be useful
- **Population:** suppose that there are fifty offices involved. Even if they are close, the actual time required would probably prevent you from having fifty separate meetings
- **Verification:** suppose that you have collected information from what appears to be a typical area. You might wish to confirm that the same results apply to other areas
- **Consultation:** you want to give everyone in the organisation a chance to express their own views or attitudes. However, if some of them don't respond, this won't seriously affect your research
- **Participation:** you want to give everyone in the organisation a feeling that they are involved in the development of the system.

Advantages of questionnaires

- They achieve **wide coverage**
- They are **fast**, in terms of reaching a large or geographically dispersed group
- They are relatively **cheap** to produce and administer to a large group
- They are **standardised**, ensuring identical questions are asked of all subjects
- They can be **anonymous**, if that is desired, which encourages full and honest answers
- They are suitable for **extending** data collection beyond a set of interviews.

Disadvantages of questionnaires

- They need to be carefully designed, and this requires specialist skills
- Their design can be time-consuming
- They are normally subject to poor response rates (a typical return rate is in the region of 10%)
- You can't check or validate the results unless the respondents are named
- You are only analysing the results of those who bothered to return the forms. There might be bias – you cannot assume that they are typical of the whole group (for example, if carrying out an organisational survey are the respondents more likely to be happy or unhappy with the way things are in the organisation?).

Activity 3.4

Designing a questionnaire

Design a questionnaire to find out the user requirements for your software, product or service. Use the following types of response requirements:

1. Yes/no
2. Agree/disagree
3. Make a list
4. Choose from a list
5. A statement
6. Rate in order (where 1 = poor, 2 = good, 3 = very good, 4 = excellent)

Interviews

Interviews are most likely to be used in many student projects; they are a type of meeting used to collect information verbally. As a data-gathering technique, the purpose of an interview is of course for the researcher to gain information. Desirable side effects may be the creation of mutual confidence and trust. In many situations, the first step in dealing with a problem is to interview someone carefully about it. All interviews need to be documented, together with their subsequent analysis.

Whether one actually *transcribes* the interview (that is, makes an accurate record of everything that was said), or simply *records a summary*, is a difficult question. It's not normally possible to make such a transcript while the interview is going on, and transcribing the contents of an audio or video recording is extremely time-consuming. However, a summary or notes, written down during or after the meeting, will inevitably be incomplete.

Interviews are of various types and include:

- **Structured interviews:** there is a list of questions (a script) and all interviewees are asked the same questions. At an extreme, the answers can be pre-coded
- **Semi-structured interviews:** there is a list of questions and topics to discuss but the questions will vary depending on the interviewee and there's some flexibility where the interview conversation is allowed to go
- **Unstructured interviews:** these are informal. There are no set questions, only certain topics that need to be covered. The interview can cover any aspect that the interviewee wants to talk about.

Interviews can be carried out on the basis of:

- **One-to-one,** with one interviewer and one interviewee
- **Group interviews** where 4-6 people meet together with the interviewer to talk about certain topics
- **Focus groups** where a small group is brought together to explore attitudes and perceptions.

Interviews are particularly useful in their openness and flexibility: unlike a questionnaire, they allow the interviewee to broach new topics that the researcher hadn't anticipated, allowing the interviewer to turn to the investigation of new directions and topics as they emerge. They can foster a positive relationship between interviewer and interviewee.

Interviews tend to fail for two reasons:

- Inability or unwillingness to listen
- Inability or unwillingness to establish an open relationship.

Active listening

Remember, an interview is a form of conversation between two parties. Many people who cannot express themselves well in writing may be able to discuss their feelings during a conversation. Listening is an important part of any dialogue. After every interview, you should try to evaluate your own performance. When you discover problems, develop techniques to correct or avoid the triggering situation in the future.

Such warning signs are likely to include situations when:

- What you are saying is more interesting to you than any possible response
- You assume they (or you) know the answer already
- You do not like the speaker
- You do not like what the speaker is saying
- You know the response will be too complex, irrelevant, or totally familiar
- You are distracted
- Listening is inactive and weak.

You are more successful when:

- You like the speaker and she/he has something to say
- There are risks and rewards involved
- You are desperate for the information!

Do not neglect *watching*. Facial expressions, gestures, body posture often say much about what a person really thinks, frequently communicating things that he/she would prefer to conceal. Body language communication is therefore extremely important. Watch out for hand movements, facial expression, eye contact, posture, proxemics (the way space is handled) and body rhythms. Remember that if you record the conversation, many of the non-verbal cues may get missed.

Styles of dress and tone of voice are also important: look and sound interested. Sit in the front part of the seat, leaning slightly forward to show interest. Your own unconscious actions and reactions are great give-aways. Furthermore, remember that honesty is the best policy: make your motives and the reason for the interview clear from the outset.

Many interviews now take place by telephone. However, there is a special problem with the telephone interview where there are no non-verbal cues. As a result, you need to pay special attention to the tone of voice, hesitations and the unexpected – such as sudden changes of subject.

Establishing a relationship

It is important to establish a professional and adequate working relationship between the interviewer and interviewee. This is a very personal factor. You need to be yourself and use your own personality resources carefully to establish the correct balance.

Relationships are established quickly, and normally the first few moments of an interview are critical. Try consciously to get this right, especially at a first meeting. Remember the interviewee has feelings too.

The context of an interview

A work environment can always present a source of difficulties. There can be no general advice. Remember only to meet your brief, not someone else's. Learn the corporate culture and standards and adopt them yourself.

Use the company jargon, not your own. Don't let an interviewee use jargon that you don't know. Stop them and ask as soon as possible without being rude. If you let the matter go, you will find after a time that it becomes impossible to ask without appearing foolish and/or irritating the interviewee. Note: when you are new to an organisation, you will find interviewees tend to be apologetic for using jargon without some explanation.

Always try to make sure you know something of the work of the person you are interviewing, and make sure that the questions you ask are relevant to the person you are speaking to. A senior manager may be excellent on matters of business policy but you would not expect him or her to know how orders are taken in great detail (but he or she may well not be prepared to admit it or not be aware of her/his own ignorance). In any case, you will want to check things with the people actually doing the job.

Watch for signals. If something you have said seems to get an unexpected response, it may be because you have inadvertently hit upon a sensitive subject. You should not feel that the details you pick up on the workplace environment are wasted even if they do not seem to relate directly to your problem. They will help you draft and present reports and help you determine the best ways of convincing people as well as alert you to possible training problems.

Organisation of interviews

There is a wide variation in the degree of formality that occurs during interviews. At one end of the scale you might just be hoping to bump into someone in the corridor – you then find excuses to walk along that corridor. Normally, however, a degree of formality is both a practical necessity (to actually get to see the people you need to see), and is also expected of you (both by the interviewee and whoever you have to report to).

- Select relevant interviewees who can help you to shed a light on the problem. Don't interview people just because they are willing or available; choose them because they are able

- Give notice of the interview. Make an appointment either directly or through a secretary. Always do this carefully; you are not in a position, usually, to insist and this is likely to be your first contact. Remember: first impressions last. It is also a good idea to confirm the *date*, *place*, *time* and *duration* in writing. Always agree on these points over the phone anyway

- Define and make known objectives. Sometimes you may not want to go into detail until the meeting but often you might want to stimulate some preparation on the part of the interviewee. In any case you do need to make known and to some extent agree on the content of the interview. No one likes to meet a stranger completely out of context

- Arrange a mutually convenient date, time and location

- Prepare an agenda that includes the main topics for discussion

- Confirm all agreements made at the interview and confirm further action perhaps as you do it. If you look and act professionally, the chances are your respondents will try to behave the same

- Sort out the seating layout prior to the start of the interview

- Document all interviews carefully as soon as possible after completion. If you need to take notes, get the respondents' agreement but try to keep notes to purely factual details. Interview reports are useful both to you and to those who come after you. They also help keep track of where you got certain information. Use interview reports to record your own thoughts and ideas

- Open and close interviews carefully. Both acts condition responses to a disproportionate extent. *Opening* means that the first thing you say has to hit the right level; you will, therefore, need to sound suitably confident, friendly or deferential. *Closing* involves summarising the main points of agreement for further action and leaving the door open for further discussion in both directions. Do not overstay your welcome!

- Do not prepare a long list of questions you must ask. This leads to rigid interrogation, of less and less relevance the longer it proceeds. What you may find useful is a short list of topics that you think you want to explore. Prepare and then memorise and discard the list.

Barriers to communication

- **Language** is clearly one of the biggest potential barriers – even between native speakers, as many words can mean different things to different people. At some point, one interview out of three will become confusing when the different parties start talking about different things using the same words.

  As well as denotative problems, English words often have multiple and personal connotations. The use of wrongly chosen words develops emotional noise that distracts from the problem in hand

- **Frame of reference:** the lack of a frame of reference is a common difficulty as the two parties frequently have little in common. Both parties need to know what is going on and each must be prepared to share with the other. Give some time to ensuring that you are talking about the same thing from known viewpoints

- **Emotional situation:** this can be very important. If an interviewee is emotionally upset or threatened, this will block more rational communication. What may seem trivial to you can be quite the reverse to someone else. You can generate these emotions easily yourself if you are not careful

- **Stereotyping:** hearing the expected is a frequent problem. We do not hear what people intend to say. We perceive that what they say in the light of our previous experience and expectations. We also ignore things that conflict with what we already know or expect to hear

- **Credibility:** some people are believable and can, therefore, communicate. Others have very low credibility. This is one reason to be professional in your approach. Once you have let someone down, they are not likely to take you seriously again

- **Group behaviour:** if your interview involves more than one interviewee, you will need to prepare for the session. Few people in groups behave as an individual unit, they tend to act in groups. Your interview is also likely to be discussed beyond the interview room walls, both before and after the session.

Questioning

- Watch carefully for the kind of questions you use as each has its time and place. The wrong choice can be disastrous:
  - **open questions** encourage the interviewee to talk. Use open questions especially to open up a subject. Always give the interviewee plenty of chances to speak. Do not expect everyone to be articulate. Carefully keep the interviewee on the subject – but only when you are clear you know what the subject should be
  - **reflective questions** are those that rephrase the interviewee's words. They confirm your interest and attention and generally stimulate further information. Use reflective questions to keep a useful source talking. Formulate these questions as statements (you feel that ..., so you wanted to ...) that ...... summarise and give emphasis
- **Do not guess or press** if reflection brings no response. It is usually a good idea to reflect the positive rather than the negative if this leads discussion in the right direction
- **Use silence:** if there is a pause while the interviewee responds, do not jump in with another question. Give people enough time to sort out their thoughts. A difficult question requires time to answer. Take care. People may need to be rescued if they get stuck, they might be having difficulty working out exactly what information you want or they might simply find the question too difficult to answer accurately
- **Use direct questions:** but not too many and not until you know what you want to ask or until the respondent is in the position to understand the question and why you want to know
- **Avoid leading questions:** do not put words into someone's mouth; you are then heading for a directive approach and you will not gain much from the interview
- **Avoid subjective judgments:** keep to the facts. Whatever happens, do not run down other members of an organisation
- **Expect to be questioned yourself:** the best advice is 'be honest'. If you do not know, say so; if you do know, say so. If you know but do not want to say, say so and explain why. Do not speculate on the unpredictable.

Interview precautions

- Never, ever take sides in any internal dispute
- Do not make promises you cannot keep
- Do not make promises you do not keep.

Conducting the interview

- Be there in good time to arrange seating and prepare recording equipment
- Start by introducing yourself. Explain about the work you are carrying out and what is going to happen to any information. Give reassurances about confidentiality and anonymity
- Start with an easy question to set the correct atmosphere
- Use 'stimulus' material that leads to the subject
- Ask respondents about themselves and their roles that relate to the area of the interview

- Read between the lines and use other clues
- Ask for clarification or explanation where necessary
- Check for inconsistencies
- Keep a suitable level of eye contact
- Offer the interviewee a chance to raise any other issues (and ask you questions)
- Thank her/him for their time and participation.

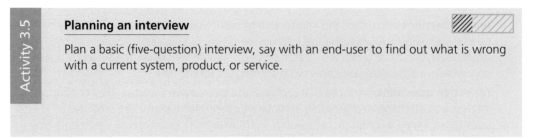

Activity 3.5

Planning an interview

Plan a basic (five-question) interview, say with an end-user to find out what is wrong with a current system, product, or service.

One final point: remember that you can mix the different methods of data collection! You do not have to choose just one method.

3.8 Data collection and analysis

Different types of data

We have already discussed earlier in this chapter that there are two different types of data: quantitative and qualitative. Quantitative data can be obtained from questionnaires, financial reports and measurements of responses in experiments. The data is likely to refer to specific instances in a predetermined sequence of research activities. Detailed analysis of such data will be likely to employ advanced statistical techniques such as regression, variance analysis and estimation.

Qualitative data can be obtained from interviews, observations and questionnaires. The role of the researcher may be different, depending on whether she/he is involved or is acting as an external observer. Ultimately, qualitative methods rely on interpretation based on the observations. Research is likely to focus on more holistic and general problems and be more open to the identification of new directions and twists. As they have less control over the variables that they are studying, qualitative researchers are expected to be more sensitive to the environment and are required to capture additional background information to provide the context for interpreting and making sense. The information can then play a key role in supporting and constructing an emergent understanding. Qualitative data should require some reasoning (for example: What is the data telling me? Does it make sense? Does it contradict other data?).

It is beyond this chapter to go into all the details of data collection and analysis. However, let's discuss a few key points that you need to consider:

- **Longitudinal versus cross-sectional data:** are you going to be able to gather data over a long time period (longitudinal data) or just at one particular time period – a 'snapshot' (cross-sectional). Typically, given its timescales, a student project can only be cross-sectional
- **Access to data:** are you likely to obtain this data? Time, cost and sensitivity should be considered

- **Ethics:** is what you are asking ethical? Does it respect an individual's privacy? Are you concealing information from the participants that they should be aware of – such as the purpose of the research? Have you permission to obtain this information? Are you taking too much of a participant's time? Who owns the research data and findings? Will the results have sufficient anonymity?

- **Confidentiality and trust:** is confidential information sufficiently protected from unauthorised access? Are you taking sufficient measures to ensure you don't breach trust?

Reliability and validity

- **Reliability** is about the consistency of the results. Under the same conditions, will a researcher always make the same observation on different occasions? Will different researchers? For a given measurement, will the same result always be given?

  Reliability can be defined as replicability in case study research. Do you get the same results if you use the same methods with different cases?

- **Validity** is 'concerned with whether the findings are really what they appear to be' (Saunders et al, 2000).

  - **measurement validity:** is the measuring equipment always consistent in its measurement?

  - **internal validity:** is there something inherently wrong in the procedures being used? Is an appropriate interpretation of the results always being made? Could there be respondent selection effects influencing the results? Maturation – could learning be taking place over the research, which impacts the results? History – could something have happened over the course of the research that would have had an impact? Could there have been something extreme about the situation (not the normal conditions) that would mean incorrect results were obtained?

  - **generalisability or external validity:** population validity – can the results be generalised (applied) across the entire population? Ecological validity – can the results be generalised from a specific time, place or event? Triangulation is a measure of generalisability.

    - **triangulation:** Saunders et al (2000) define triangulation as 'the use of different data collection methods within one study in order to ensure that the data are telling you what you think they are telling you.' The idea is that different methods will have different effects, so by using different methods the 'method effect' can be cancelled out. For instance, if you obtain the same information by questionnaire and by unstructured interview then you have triangulation of that finding.

      You should note however that there are different definitions for triangulation. Some people use it in the sense of triangulating their data sources within one data collection method.

- **Bias:** this is a threat to validity and reliability. There can be researcher bias and/or respondent bias.

  - **researcher bias** concerns how the researcher interprets the results – prior experience and knowledge can impact on interpretation

  - **respondent bias** can occur when the respondent gives the responses that they think are wanted rather than the truth. This can be a problem if there is overbearing management and/or job security issues.

When designing your research methods, specific steps can be taken to reduce or eliminate such problems and strengthen your research design. You should investigate the specific issues of the research methods you are intending to use.

3.9 Student projects

Not all student projects are research

It is possible that your student project objectives can be achieved in other ways than research. In this case, your project will still need to have a research element, but it is unlikely that it will be a research investigation in the sense described in this chapter. Such projects would instead include elements such as the application of knowledge, use of techniques gained from student courses and development work which leads to a product of some kind.

The problem-solving nature of student projects

IT student projects are normally 'problem solving'. A student project will normally require you to conduct the following steps:

- **Identify** a problem which has occurred at a particular place and time
- **Propose** a solution
- **Implement** the solution
- **Assess** the result with regard to this particular problem (at this place and time).

Typically, students who are planning an IT project look for a real-world problem to solve. Their intention is to use their skills to come up with a practical solution to this problem.

In practice, you are likely to be faced with a problem for which you will have an idea (an hypothesis or a proposition) about what the solution might be. The natural way to proceed is to implement the solution and to examine the result to see whether or not it satisfies the hypotheses (for example, hypothesis A: XYZ is a good solution to this particular problem) or propositions (for example, proposition B: a framework for IS development exists) that you initially suggested:

- **If the solution fails:** your hypotheses or propositions are presumably wrong
- **If the solution succeeds:** you have some evidence that this is a good solution to this particular problem within the confines of your specific situation.

Notice, however, that you haven't *proved* that this is the best solution to the problem – and you haven't proved that this is a good solution for all problems of this type. Those are two questions that you will want to discuss in your report – you will probably have a section labelled 'discussion' to do just that. You will probably want to consider other possible solutions and reasons for believing that your solution generalises to other similar circumstances – or alternatively discuss why your solution doesn't generalise.

Limitations of timescales and resources

In essence, the process can be viewed as a preliminary study. In other words, as a piece of scientific investigation, it is the first phase in a larger study – the later stages involve trying the same solution out in different settings, to discover the extent to which it does generalise (Does it still work if other people are using it or if it's used in a different sort of organisation?). This would normally entail an extended and prolonged research process.

You should recognise that all you can hope to do (given your limited timescale and resources) is a preliminary study. Provided you are testing a hypothesis about what works in one setting, and provided you make it clear that the question of whether the results generalise to other similar settings remains open, you can claim to have done a useful piece of scientific work.

Activity 3.6

Selecting your own research method

Look at your individual objectives and select a research method that will help you accomplish all the objectives related to research.

Activity 3.7

Identify a data collection method

Once again, take a look at your objectives and at your choice of research method likely to satisfy these objectives and select an appropriate data collection technique.

3.10 Summary

In this chapter, we discussed how to design a research project. To achieve this, we explained the following elements of a research design:

- **Research question**
- **Research philosophy**
- **Research strategy**
  - **research approach**
  - **research method**
  - **data collection method.**

The research question defines the general area and the specific problem within it that you are addressing.

The research philosophy dictates the range of approaches and methods that will be used within the problem context. It shapes your project. Research philosophies discussed included: postpositivism, constructivism, advocacy and pragmatism.

The research approaches (named according to the type of data collected and analysed) included: quantitative, qualitative, and mixed methods.

The research methods, the 'tools' used to conduct the research included: experiment, survey, case study, action research, implementation research, narrative, grounded theory and ethnography.

The data collection methods used to gather the relevant data included: sampling, secondary data (documentation, survey and multiple source), observation, questionnaire and interview.

In the Chapters 5 and 6 we shall consider planning a project (creating and updating a project plan).

3.11 Review questions

 Question 3.1

Which research methods would you be unlikely to use in your student project?

 Question 3.2

Name two research methods that could be used in quantitative research.

 Question 3.3

What are the advantages of interviews over questionnaires?

3.12 Feedback on activities

Activity 3.1: Writing a research question

- Student A's project: the research question is something like 'Why do a significant proportion of the firm's employees fail to follow the firm's security policies?'

- Student B's project: the research question is something like 'Is WAVY a more effective way to teach the topic oscillations and waves to GCSE Physics students than the conventional alternatives?' You might wish to explain the word 'effective' further, by saying something like 'in terms of scores achieved on a standard test'.

- Student C's project: the research question is something like 'What are the relative influences of cost and quality of game-playing experience in purchasing decisions with respect to MMORPGs?'

- Student D's project: the research question is something like 'Will a database system, designed to perform certain of the business operations of this particular company, increase the efficiency of the company's operations?' But notice that the question is vague about what problem or problems are being solved on the company's behalf (low profitability? low customer satisfaction?), and about what aspect or aspects of the company's operations are to be computerised. The research question will need to be rewritten in a more focused form once the company's operations and problems have been analysed.

Activity 3.2: Investigating text readability on screen

The best way of investigating this is by an experiment: a number of subjects read text from a screen, aloud; the experimenter listens and notes down every mistake that the subject makes.

The causal/independent variable will be the screen colours, and the effect/dependent variable will be the number of errors made.

There will be an experimental condition in which the screen colours are magenta on green, and a control condition in which the screen colours are blue on white.

Text size, typeface and complexity of text are extraneous variables that will have to be controlled. Text size and typeface will be controlled by making them the same in both conditions. Complexity will be controlled by using the same text for both conditions, or by using two texts of equivalent complexity – but see below.

It's possible to design the experiment so that the same subjects take part in both the experimental condition and the control condition, but in that case it is essential that they read two different texts, of equivalent difficulty (otherwise they will learn the text, and naturally make fewer mistakes the second time they read it). Half the subjects should read text A in the experimental condition and text B in the control condition; half the subjects should read the text the other way round. The correct statistical test to use is the related version of the t-test.

It's also possible to design the experiment so that different subjects take part in the experimental condition and the control condition. In this case one should choose subjects who have roughly the same reading skill, and allocate them at random to the experimental condition and the control condition. All subjects will read the same text. The correct statistical test to use is the unrelated version of the t-test.

We don't expect you to have got *all* these details for the experiment. But we hope you got at least *some* of the ideas about the dependent and independent variables right.

Activity 3.3: Selecting a research method

- Student A's project: assuming the student can persuade the firm to give him/her access to the staff (and that's quite a large assumption), this should be treated as a case study. It's necessary to study the attitudes of these employees, and their relationship with the organisation in which they work, in some depth. The data collection methods will probably be questionnaires, interviews and the examination of documents

- Student B's project: this should be tackled as an experiment. There should be an experimental group of subjects who are taught a portion of the syllabus using WAVY, and a control group of subjects who are taught the same portion of the syllabus by conventional means. Both groups should be drawn at random from a pool of pupils of the right age, and the improvement in knowledge of the two groups should be measured by testing their knowledge of the subject before and after the teaching session(s). The idea is to find a significant difference between the two improvements in knowledge. Note that it isn't at all easy to organise all of this!

- Student C's project: this should be based on a survey

- Student D's project: this should be based on implementation research.

Activity 3.4: Designing a questionnaire

Each type of question requires different details:

- Yes/no (and agree/disagree) questions are probably the easiest to design (but you may still get 'maybe' as an answer)

- Open-ended questions requiring a statement or opinion take more effort to design carefully (and are likely to remain unanswered)

- Choosing from a list means that you need to find the set of relevant factors or reasons and offer it to the subjects. (Are you excluding answers they are likely to come up with? Are you limiting them to your set?)

- Making a list gets them to do the work of compiling the set of possibilities. It also means that it is truly based on their views and priorities (and not on a set imposed by you)

- Rating in order also assumes that you produce the basic list.

Activity 3.5: Planning an interview

- Start by selecting the most suitable user

- Define the basic area that you need covered

- Highlight any issues that need clarifying

- Devise a set of five questions that will give you the information you require

- Did you remember to include a starter question to set your subject at ease?

- Can you obtain all the information you require in five questions?

- Are your questions ambiguous?

- Do you expect complex answers that will address more than a single topic?

Activity 3.6: Selecting your own research method

At least one of your objectives should have a strong research underpinning and should involve some significant research.

Ask yourself the following questions:

- Is the method appropriate to one of my objectives?   Does it also match the research problem?

- Will the method enable me to arrive at the required type of result?

- What kind of result will it support?

- Have I the experience (or the skills) required to use this method?

- Have I the time to apply it correctly and effectively?

- What are the limitations associated with this method?

- Can I use it exclusively, or do I need to supplement it?

- Is this method better than other methods for my project?

Activity 3.7: Identifying a data collection method

It is possible that more than one data collection method is suitable. Ask yourself:

- Is this data collection method appropriate for my problem?

- Is the method suitable in terms of the research approach?

- Are there any alternative methods that I could use?

- What are the main benefits of using the method I selected?

- What are the drawbacks?

- Would any of the alternatives offer a better balance between benefits or drawbacks?

- Is there any point in combining methods?   Have I time to do that?

- Do I know how to use this method?

- Do I need any special skills?

- What do I need to learn?

- When can I start?

3.13 References

Birley, G.I. and Moreland, N. (1998), *A Practical Guide to Academic Research*, Routledge Falmer

H.W. Fowler & F.G. Fowler, (eds), (1964), *The Concise Oxford Dictionary of Current English* (5th edition), Oxford University Press.

Creswell J., (2003), *Research design: qualitative, quantitative, and mixed methods approaches*, (2nd Edition). Sage Publications, CA, USA

Dalcher D., (2003), Stories and Histories: Case Study research (and Beyond) in Information Systems Failures in *Handbook for Information Systems Research*, Michael Whitman & Amy Woszczynski (eds.), Idea Publishing, Hershey, PA., pp. 305-322.

Dalcher D., (2005), Methods for Understanding IS Failures, *Encyclopaedia of Information Science and Technology*, Volume II, Idea Publishing, Hershey, PA, pp. 1931-1938.

Gill, J. & Johnson, P., (2002), *Research methods for Managers,* (3rd edition), Sage Publications Ltd.

Glaser B. & Strauss A., (1967), *The discovery of grounded theory: strategies for qualitative research*, Aldine De Gruyter, NY: USA

Kaplan B. & Maxwell, J.A., (1994), Qualitative Research Methods for Evaluating Computer Information Systems, in *Evaluating Health Care Information Systems: Methods and Applications*, J.G. Anderson, C.E. Aydin and S.J. Jay (eds.), Thousand Oaks, CA: Sage.

Orlikowski W. & Baroudi J., (1991), Studying Information Technology in Organisations: Research Approaches and Assumptions, *Information Systems Research*, Vol. 2 No.1

Pace, B. K., (1984), Color combinations and contrast reversals on visual display units (pp. 326–330). In Aluisi, M. J., de Groot, S., and Aluisi, E. A. (eds.) *Proceedings of the Human Factors Society* 28th annual meeting, Volume 1.

Saunders, M., Lewis, P. & Thornhill, A., (2000), *Research Methods for Business Students*, 2nd Edition, Financial Times Prentice Hall:Pearson Education

Strauss A. & Corbin J., (1998), *Basics of qualitative research: techniques and procedures for developing grounded theory*, Sage Publications, CA: USA

Yin, R., (2003), *Case Study Research: Designs and Methods*, (3rd edition), Sage Publications, CA: USA

CHAPTER 4

Managing progress and change

OVERVIEW

Project managers have to plan, monitor and control the systems development processes. In Chapter 1, we discussed the project management and systems development lifecycles, and briefly commented on how evolutionary and agile methods were impacting these lifecycles. In this chapter, we pick up from there and look from a project management perspective at some important aspects of monitoring progress and managing change.

Much of the discussion centres on the project deliverables, which are the main outputs of a project as it progresses.

One specific aim of this chapter is to help students identify the main monitoring and controlling tasks that they need to build into their student projects. This is in preparation for project planning which commences in the next chapter,

(Note there is also discussion of verification and validation, V & V. This could have simply been put into Chapter 8, 'Project quality management' under the topic of 'quality control'. However, it is essential that testing and management reviews are built into the project plan and therefore the rationale for them and the discussion about them has been moved into this chapter, and not left until later. Discussion of walkthroughs and inspections is however left until Chapter 8.)

Learning outcomes	At the end of this chapter you should be able to:

- Outline the different types of testing

- Explain some of the issues associated with managing change

- List the main project deliverables

- Discuss configuration management

- Describe two types of management review

- Understand the requirements for a student project report.

4.1 Introduction

In Chapter 1, we discussed the project management process groups. See Figure 4.1, which shows the different groups as defined in the PMI's *Book of Knowledge* (PMBOK 2004).

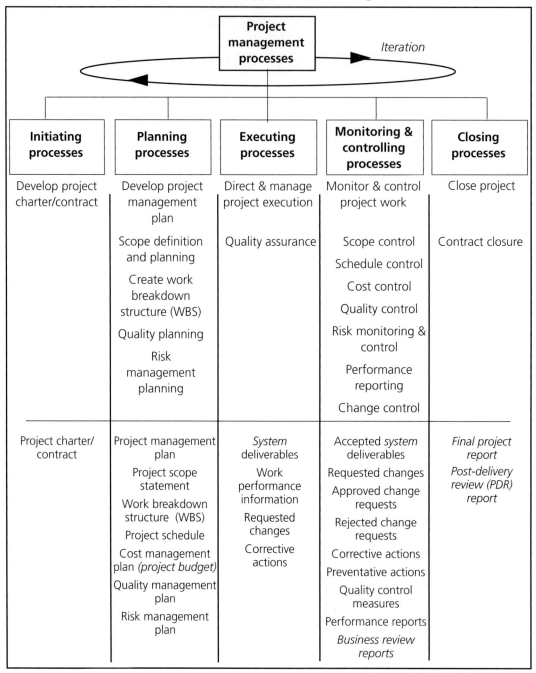

Figure 4.1: The project management process groups (*PMBOK Guide* 2004) are shown with a selection of their processes. Note the processes for the project management knowledge areas of *project human resource management* and *project procurement management* have not been included. The lower part of the figure shows a selection of the deliverables. The italics denote departure from the PMBOK material – additions made to help understanding.

In this chapter we are concerned with parts of the *executing* and the *monitoring and controlling* process groups.

- With regard to the executing process group we are interested in thinking about the project work that is actually being managed – the systems development processes
- For the monitoring and controlling process group we shall mainly be considering change control, some of the processes of quality control, and performance reporting.

We have already considered scope control in Chapter 2, and later chapters will cover aspects of schedule control, cost control, and risk monitoring and control, as well as more on quality control.

The structure of this chapter is as follows:

- Systems development processes
  - requirements specification
  - verification and validation (V & V)
  - testing
  - delivery to operations
- People issues associated with managing change
- Project deliverables
- Configuration management
- Project management reporting
- Management reviews
- Producing a student report.

To explain the rationale behind this structure: the chapter starts by briefly considering the systems development processes and outlining their deliverables. Specific attention is given to quantitative quality requirements specification, testing and delivery to operations. All too often, projects fail to pay sufficient attention to these topics. Certainly, student projects frequently put too little effort into testing.

Having started the discussion about delivery to operations, the chapter then looks at the people issues associated with delivering change and outlines some suggested actions to help. The project deliverables are then discussed, including documentation standards, and following from that the configuration management processes required for change control of the deliverables. The chapter then moves on to look at the relevant project management processes and deliverables, considering project management reporting and management reviews. Finally, following on from the discussion about project deliverables, advice is given on writing a student project report – the main deliverable of a student project.

4.2 Systems development processes

Let's begin by briefly looking at the systems development lifecycle. It's not the intention here to go into all the detailed technical aspects of systems development, but rather to give some pointers about important topics and set the scene for identifying all the project tasks – such a task list will be developed and used in the next chapter when project planning commences.

Figure 4.2 provides an overview of the systems development processes and their associated deliverables. It doesn't really matter which systems development lifecycle model is being used; all these processes will be needed at some point and, further, there is likely to be iteration round these processes during the systems development (unless you are using the waterfall model).

We are going to consider **requirements specification, testing** and **delivery to operations** in a little more depth.

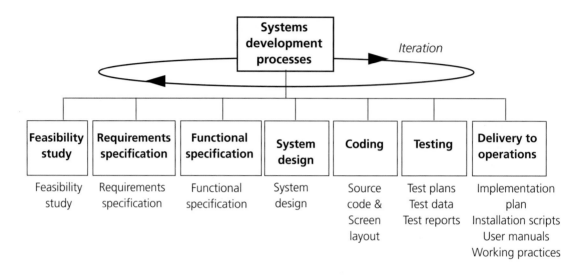

Figure 4.2: Overview of some of the systems development processes showing their deliverables

Requirements specification

The requirements specification process takes over the systems information from the feasibility study and develops it even further. Requirements specification has three sub-processes:

- **Requirements elicitation:** communicating with the stakeholders in order to identify/confirm requirements
- **Requirements analysis:** establishing how the requirements information from the stakeholders 'fits' together
- **Requirements documentation:** capturing the requirements information in a structured way. A requirements management application (for example, Telelogic's DOORS) can be used.

Requirements are often captured as functional requirements and non-functional requirements.

- **Functional requirements** capture the required functionality – what the system is expected to do – and can be documented as functional descriptions or by using use cases
- **Non-functional requirements** express the system properties and constraints. They include the quality requirements (for example, usability, security, availability and maintainability), the workload capacity requirements, quality standards and design constraints. The quality requirements express the project success criteria (see Chapter 2, the section on 'The role of success criteria in projects'). Quality requirements should be measurable.

Examples of specifying requirements

To give some examples of requirements:

From **www.foi.gov.uk/map/gusv4contents.htm**, a generic user requirements specification for public authorities to use for information systems handling the provision of information under the Freedom of Information Act. Here, because this is generic, there are no quality requirements with specific measures attached.

A statement of a functional requirement:

> '**Logging requests & appeals:** requirements associated with the capture of information about applicants, [Ed. Requests for Information] RFIs and appeals. This also includes the effective handling of the RFI including searching for requests by the same applicant, categorising the request against subject lists / taxonomy; searching the public authorities own disclosure log to determine if the information has already been released; and searching for similar requests.'

This functional requirement is then decomposed into its elements and captured. The Logging Application functionality is stated as follows: (Note 'HD' stands for 'highly desirable' and 'E' stands for 'essential'. A third category of 'D', 'desirable', also exists).

Logging Applicants

ID	Description	Priority
F-LA-01	The user shall be provided with a search facility to determine if the applicant already exists in the system. If the applicant already exists, the user may need to update his or her details.	HD
F-LA-02	The system shall allow details of any new applicant making an RFI to be captured. (See Appendix A for recommendations on information that should be recorded)	E

An example from the same specification of non-functional requirements expressing the need for conformance with specific standards:

ID	Description	Priority
N-ST-03	The system shall comply with the UK Government Data Standards Catalogue (GDSC) that specifies standard format and validation rules for those information types indicated in Appendices A, B and C.	E
N-ST-04	The system shall comply with the National Archives' Requirements for Electronic Records Management Systems, 2: Metadata Standard.	HD
N-ST-07	If the system uses an underlying relational database, it must conform to the SQL standard ISO/IEC 9075.	E

Usability

Jakob Nielsen defines 'usability' as consisting of five quality components:

- **Learnability:** how easy is it for users to accomplish basic tasks the first time they encounter the design?
- **Efficiency:** once users have learned the design, how quickly can they perform tasks?
- **Memorability:** when users return to the design after a period of not using it, how easily can they re-establish proficiency?
- **Errors:** how many errors do users make, how severe are these errors, and how easily can they recover from the errors?
- **Satisfaction:** how pleasant is it to use the design?

  (From **www.useit.com/alertbox/20030825.html**)

Usability measures (metrics) include:

- For **effectiveness**:
  - Percentage of tasks completed
  - Ratio of successes to failures
- For **efficiency**:
  - Time to complete a task
  - Time to learn
  - Time spent on errors
  - Percentage or number of errors
  - Frequency of use of help facilities or documentation
- For **satisfaction:**
  - Number of times user expresses frustration or anger
  - Rating scale for usefulness of the product or service
  - Rating scale for satisfaction with functions and features

    (From **www.usabilitymetrics.com/usability-metrics.html/**)

Nielsen also gives some reasons as to why you would want to measure usability (Maybe you can see the direct relevance to project management?):

'In general, usability metrics let you:

- **Track progress between releases.** You cannot fine-tune your methodology unless you know how well you're doing.
- **Assess your competitive position.** Are you better or worse than other companies? Where are you better or worse?
- **Make a stop/go decision before launch.** Is the design good enough to release to an unsuspecting world?
- **Create bonus plans for design managers and higher-level executives.** For example, you can determine bonus amounts for development project leaders based on how many customer-support calls or e-mails their products generated during the year.'

  (From **www.useit.com/alertbox/20010121.html/**)

Specifying a quality requirement using metrics

One issue not addressed in the foregoing example, is how you actually specify a quality requirement using metrics. Gilb (2005) provides the following template (slightly simplified here – only the main parameters are shown):

Tag: <Name of quality requirement>.

Scale: <Scale of measure giving the units of measure>.

Meter: <The method to be used to obtain the measurements>.

Benchmarks:

Past [When, Where, If]: <Past or current level> ← <source of information>.

Record [When, Where, If]: <State-of-the-art level> ← <source of information>.

Trend [When, Where, If]: <Prediction of future rate of change> ← <source of information>.

Targets:

Goal [When, Where, If]: <Planned target level> ← <source of information>.

Stretch [When, Where, If]: <Motivating target level> ← <source of information>.

Wish [When, Where, If]: <'Dream' target level – not budgeted> ← <source of information>.

Constraints:

Fail [When, Where, If]: <Level at which project ceases to be a success> ← <source of information>.

Survival [When, Where, If]: <Level at which project survival starts to be threatened> ← <source of information>.

The main points to notice are as follows:

- One or more current or past **benchmark levels** can be stated
- One or more future **target levels** can be set
- Fail and Survival levels provide information about what levels are not acceptable
- Record (state-of-the-art) and Trend (future forecast) levels provide information about what's going on in the system's environment against which the system levels can be assessed. Any level that approaches or exceeds the current state-of-the-art is likely to be of high cost and high risk
- Stretch and Wish levels show what the customer would like, but these levels are unbudgeted, so are not planned levels
- The origin (source) of all the levels is captured
- Specific levels can be specified for different **[When, Where, If] conditions**. A given level does not have to apply across the entire system.

To give a specific example for a Usability metric concerned with Efficiency:

Tag: Task Completion Time

Scale: The average time it takes in minutes for a defined [User Type: Novice User, Experienced User] to carry out and complete a defined [Task].

Meter: Analysis of the transaction processing journal log.

Past [January 2007, Support Desk, User Type = Experienced User, Task = Entering a customer phone request for support]: 5 ← Support Centre Manager.

Goal [June 2007]: 3 ← Support Centre Manager.

Verification and Validation

Before we move on to discuss testing, let's consider verification and validation (V & V). Testing is one of the main approaches to achieving V & V, which aims to address the following questions (Boehm 1981):

- For **Verification** *(from the Latin, veritas, 'truth')*:

  Are we building the product right?

  Does the product correspond with its specification?
- For **Validation** *(from the Latin, valere, 'to be worth')*:

  Are we building the right product?

  Is the product fit for 'its operational mission'.

To give an example, a beautifully built bungalow may not please the client who wanted a three-storey house…. Here, the product is built right, but it is the wrong product.

Note: there is a definition problem regarding the terms, 'verification' and 'validation':

> 'Some people believe that all testing is verification and that validation is conducted when requirements are reviewed and approved, and later, by the user when the system is operational. Other people view unit and integration testing … as verification and higher-order testing … as validation.' (Pressman 2005)

When reading textbooks, you need to take this into consideration. However, both verification and validation – regardless of how they are defined – are integral to the quality control of a product.

Verification

Taking Boehm's definition, verification is process-oriented. It focuses on whether the correct processes and procedures were followed by the project to ensure the product/system meets its specified requirements. *Is the product/system built right?*

Verification demands that the standards and metrics are clearly defined. This is so that it is possible to establish whether the product/system conforms to the required standards, and whether the product/system achieves the specified metrics.

Verification is also concerned with whether the product/system meets its specified requirements. Does the product/system produced match its specification? (Note this is not the same as is the product/system the right thing for the organisation.)

Verification methods include:

- **Unit testing, interface testing, function testing and system testing**. See later in this section
- **Management progress reviews**, which check project progress against plan. The project can be reviewed to ensure it meets scope, schedule, budget and quality requirements. See later in this chapter
- **Technical reviews** (also known as peer reviews) involve checking conformance to standards (for example, walkthroughs and inspections). These are discussed in Chapter 8, 'Project quality management'.

Another way of expressing what verification is about is 'Have the developers produced what they were told to?'

Validation

Is the product/system which has been produced the right thing for the business?

Validation is a product-orientated process to determine if the product/system meets customer expectations and ensures the system performs as required by the organisation. In other words, 'Is this what the users really want?' Validation methods include:

- **User acceptance testing.** See later in this section
- **Management business reviews.** See later in this chapter.

Testing

Testing comprises a collection of different testing types or strategies. You will find that textbooks differ slightly in their description of the types of testing. The different types of testing include (see Figure 4.3):

- **Unit testing** (also known as component testing) is carried out on a system component, such as a module of code. It is concerned with the internal program logic and data
- **Integration testing** is concerned with the interfacing among system components. Are the components compatible with each other? The system architecture is the framework controlling what tasks the components have to carry out, and how the components interface
- **Function testing** checks that the system performs according to its design specification. It checks that the functionality works as specified
- **Systems testing** finds out if the system performs as required in its operating environment with regards to aspects such as recovery, security, workload capacity (stress), and performance
- **User acceptance testing** can be carried out by the users just before handover to establish that the system meets their acceptance criteria
- **Field testing** (also known as field trialling) can also be carried out. This is when a product is handed over to the users to trial on their sites. The product is closely monitored and priority given to fixing any installation issues, documentation issues, or product faults found. If a product passes its field trial, then it is ready to go on general release.

The term *regression testing* is also often referred to, especially 'system regression testing'. This is more an approach to testing than a type of testing. In fact, regression testing could be applied in any of the different types of testing given above. Regression testing involves setting up a comprehensive set of tests to check that a product is continuing to work as it has previously been tested to do (and as it should). This set of regression tests is then run through at specific stages to check that any more recent changes introduced into the product have not also impacted other aspects of the product that had previously tested as correct – hence the term 'regression' meaning 'going back'.

Ultimately the amount of testing carried out will depend on how critical the system is, the contract acceptance criteria, and the systems development lifecycle methods being used. It is beyond this chapter to discuss the testing processes in detail. However, testing is one of the key activities in ensuring the quality of a product/system. You should build testing into a project plan right from the start of a project and you should develop the test plans as you develop a system.

In your student project, you do not have additional resources. However, in industry, it is usual to have testing experts. One advantage of having different people involved in the testing process is that they offer different perspectives and can 'stand back' from the system, allowing them to identify additional issues.

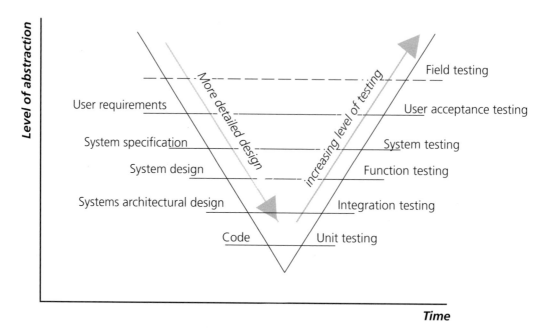

Figure 4.3: The V-process model

Delivery to operations

Handover (delivery) of system software into operational use has to be supported by the following documentation (termed 'release documentation'):

- Description of the delivery including change control information
- An installation script
- User manual
- Changes to working practices.

Preparing the software and the release documentation takes considerable effort. As the handover is a more formal step, getting some aspect of it wrong, reflects badly on the project team. If the project team are more remote, it can also be difficult and costly to detect the problem. Always leave sufficient time for preparing the handover and consider having a member of the project team on site with the end-users in the early days to sort out any problems. Dry-running the handover to a field trial can be helpful.

Working with end-users

Requirements specification, testing and delivery to operations all involve working with the end-users at some point. When working with end-users, project managers and systems developers need to take into account a number of things. These include:

- **Authorisation:** is there authorisation in place to use the end-users' time?
- **Security:** is there any confidential data involved?
- **Work pressure:** how busy are the end-users? Are they busy all day? Week? Month? Year? What amount of time do they need to answer a query?

- **More than one attempt:** has enough time been left to retry if this fails – several times?
- **Daily work pattern:** what hours do they work?
- **Dress code:** what do they wear – smart casual or suits?
- **Culture:** what is the business culture?
- **IT experience:** how much IT experience do the end-users have?
- **Jargon:** do they have a glossary of terminology? Note that IT terminology should be kept to a minimum
- **Access to the building:** what are the restrictions over building access?
- **Risk:** what is the risk to the organisation if this fails? Is there a fallback (a contingency plan) in place? How soon could the fallback be used?
- **Existing work practices:** how does the new system fit with existing work practices? How does the user manual fit with existing documentation?
- **Compatibility:** what existing hardware and software is in place? Is it what you expect?
- **Real data:** has the end-user handed over any real data for testing purposes? (Real data and test data can diverge….)
- **Parallel running:** could this system run in parallel with the old system? What are the dangers of doing this?

4.3 People issues associated with managing change

'Change management' is a term used in several different ways. It can be used to refer to:

- **The people issues** associated with change (for example, end-user resistance to change)
- **Configuration management** and the change control procedures
- **Organisational change** associated with business process re-engineering (BPR)
- **Managing change** associated with the handover and installation of new software into an organisation.

Whenever the term is used, care has to be taken to consider exactly what is meant. In this section, it is the first interpretation we are going to discuss. The second interpretation, involving configuration management and change control, is explained later in this chapter. The third, change associated with BPR is a strategic consideration and part of business planning – it's not considered any further in this book. The fourth, we discussed briefly in the previous section on 'Delivery to operations'.

People issues associated with change

Imagine someone walked into your room now and announced that from next week you would have to use a different word processor for writing your documents. What would be your reaction? How would you feel about the matter if you also knew you had to hand in a report during that week? You would likely feel put under pressure and be irritated, or at least concerned, about how much extra work on top of your existing workload was going to be involved in learning to use the new word processor. You would start asking questions:

- What if you got stuck with problems over how to achieve some of the mandatory formatting for your report?
- Could you just continue using the old word processor?
- What benefits would you get from the new word processor that would make it worthwhile?
- How much effort are you going to have to make to learn about the new word processor?

Of course, you might like the challenge of using a new application. Many IT people are used to fairly constant change and would perhaps feel they could cope. However, such acceptance is unlikely from people with less IT knowledge. Instead, they are likely to resist the change. They can resist in several ways including:

- Continuing to use the old system
- Switching over and then switching back
- Switching over but deliberately seeking to draw out any problems by not co-operating.

The problem starts in many cases because the IT management, designers and developers pay too little attention to considering and managing the end-users' perspectives. A systems development project team will be mainly comprised of technical staff, whose main concern is writing and testing the code. Handover to the customer can be an afterthought. Certainly, detailed consideration of the end-users' work practices during systems development is not common. One reason for this is the time and effort it would take to understand the end-user environment.

Yet it is the end-users that are meant to achieve the benefit from using the system – and if an end-user doesn't use the system then there is less benefit gained. Solutions to reduce or remove resistance include:

- Find a business champion for the project
- Include line workers in design and development activities
- Keep communicating about the project's progress
- Keep reiterating the business reasons for the project
- Provide adequate education and training.

> Source: (Marchewka (2006) quoting Leslie Jaye Goff, Change Management, *Computerworld*, February 14, 2000,
> **www.computerworld.com/news/2000/story/0,11280,41308,00.html**

Agile methods seek to involve the customer continuously throughout the project to improve the exchange of knowledge and ensure good communication.

4.4 Project deliverables

Let's now turn our attention to the deliverables. A deliverable can be defined as any tangible output that is produced by a project. Deliverables include project plans, specifications, reports and software. Some deliverables will be internal and only used within the project, while others will be external and will be distributed to customers and others outside the project.

The key points to be made about deliverables include:

- Deliverables belong to either the project management or the systems engineering lifecycles
- There are many different types of deliverables to consider!
- Deliverables often have to conform to content and document layout standards
- Deliverables are often held as models (that is, not simple documents), and updated using automated tools
- Evolutionary methods have changed the way we produce project deliverables: deliverables are now developed in an evolutionary manner
- Systems documentation is costly to produce and yet essential to the systems development lifecycle

- Deliverables have to be distributed to the relevant people
- The security and backup requirements of deliverables have to be considered
- Deliverables have to be under appropriate change control.

We shall discuss most of these points in more detail later in this chapter.

Overview of the different types of deliverable

Let's consider the different deliverables produced by a project. One useful way to gain an understanding of project deliverables is by thinking about who is producing them – is it the project management or the systems development team? See Figure 4.4 (adapted slightly from Walker Royce's), which clearly separates the systems development project deliverables (artefacts, or 'artifacts' using US spelling) from the project management deliverables. If you think back to the discussion in Chapter 1 of the distinction between the project management and the systems development lifecycles (Figure 1.1), maybe you can see a similar mapping here?

It is also worth noting that Walker Royce places emphasis on project documentation being captured in models and updated using automated tools, not necessarily being held as simple documents.

Management set	
Planning artifacts	**Operational artifacts**
1. Work breakdown structure	5. Release descriptions
2. Business case	6. Status assessments
3. Release specifications	7. Software changes
4. Software development plan	8. Deployment documents
	9. Environment (tools, etc.)

Systems development set			
Requirements set	**Design set**	**Implementation set**	**Deployment set**
1 Vision documents	1 Design model(s)	1 Source code	1 User deliverables
2 Requirements model(s)	2 Test model	2 Test files and data	2 Executable software
	3 Software architecture description		3 Installation scripts

Figure 4.4: Overview of the artifact sets for a project. *Adapted from Royce (1998)*

Note Walker Royce uses the term 'artifacts' instead of 'deliverables'. Note also the distinction between management and systems development deliverables. Note also the further distinction between management planning and management operational deliverables.)

Now look at Table 4.1. This table doesn't make the distinction between management and systems development documentation that Walker Royce did, nor does it so explicitly state that information is captured in other ways than as simple documents. However, it provides an extremely useful checklist of deliverables. In addition, it raises questions about standards, authorisation and resources.

Deliverable	Structure	Standards	Approval Needed By	People Resources Required
Business case	Document	Organisational standards and IT standards	Sponsor	Business consultant and/or project manager, & sponsor
Project charter & project plan	Document	IT standards: project plans	Sponsor	Project manager
Technology & organisational assessment	Document	IT standards	Project manager & sponsor	Project manager & sponsor & users
Requirements specification	Document	IT standards: requirement specification	Sponsor & project manager	Systems analyst & sponsor & users
Functional specification	Document	IT standards:	Sponsor & project manager	Design team
User interface	Prototype	User interface guidelines	Sponsor	Design team & users
Physical and technical design	Document	IT standards: design	Project manager & systems architect	Design team
Testing plan	Document	IT standards: testing	Project manager & testing manager	Testers
Testing results	Document	IT standards: testing	Project manager & testing manager	Testers
Change management & implementation plan	Document	User standards & IT standards	Sponsor & project manager	Systems analyst & project manager & users
User manuals	Document	User standards & IT standards	Sponsor	Documentation writers
Training plan	Training class	Training standards	Sponsor	Trainers
Final project report	Document	IT standards	Sponsor	Project manager & sponsor
Project evaluations & lessons learnt	Document	IT standards	Project manager & IT management	Project team

Table 4.1: System documentation and specific other deliverables

Source: Adapted from (Marchewka 2006), whose original inspiration was Graham McLeod and Derek Smith, *Managing Information Technology Projects*, San Francisco: Boyd & Fraser, 1996, pages 51-52. Further information about the software tools required was also outlined in Jack Marchewka's table.

Activity 4.1

Trialling a prototype

Imagine you are working on a project team and have developed a prototype user interface. You want some users to try it out for you. Consider how you would go about arranging for this to take place and how you would conduct the user testing of the prototype. Draw up a plan of the tasks for both arranging and conducting the testing. Specific steps to consider include:

- Establish the stakeholders involved in this testing

- Consider how you would make arrangements for the testing to take place

- Think about what you would need to supply for testing to take place

- Consider how you would conduct the testing

- Consider how you would capture the test results (think back to the data-gathering methods discussed in Chapter 3, 'Research methods')

- Consider the different means of communication that you would use (for example, reports, meetings, e-mails, presentations, phone calls and test scripts).

Activity 4.2

Test evaluation criteria

Now take another look at your proposal for testing the prototype user interface from Activity 4.1. Suggest the evaluation criteria you would use to determine the success of the prototype user interface.

Standards for documentation

Many organisations have documentation standards. These standards set out the types of document/artefact that should be produced and their specific contents (often detailed in templates). It is worthwhile obtaining such standards and templates as early as possible and using them when producing any project documentation. This saves a great deal of later work conforming to these standards, and it means that you can be sure you have considered all the required content. We'll look at a specific standard for document change control in the next section, 'Configuration management'.

The project methodology will also be likely to impose certain standards. The IT standards might well simply defer to the project methodology standards.

See Figure 4.5 for an example of a document template, which specifies the information that must be entered when specifying a function requirement. Use of such a template ensures all the relevant information is captured (or at least you know if it is missing) and structures the information – once you are familiar with the template structure, you know exactly where you are going to find a specific type of information.

Template for Function Requirement Specification <with hints>

Tag: <Tag name for the function>.

Type: <Function Requirement Specification>.

============ **Basic Information** =====================================

Version: <Date and/or other version number>.

Status: <{Draft, SQC Exited, Approved, Rejected}>.

Quality Level: <Maximum remaining major defects/page, sample size, date>.

Owner: <Name the role/email/person responsible for changes and updates to this specification>.

Stakeholders: <Name any stakeholders with an interest in this specification>.

Gist: <Give a 5- to 20-word summary of the nature of this function>.

Description: <Give a detailed, unambiguous description of the function, or a tag reference to some place where it is detailed. Remember to include definitions of any local terms>.

============ **Relationships** ==

Supra-functions: <List tag of function/mission, which this function is a part of. A hierarchy of tags, such as A.B.C, is even more illuminating>.

Sub-functions: <List the tags of any immediate sub-functions (that is, the next level down), of this function>.

Is Impacted By: <List the tags of any design ideas or Evo steps delivering, or capable of delivering, this functionality>.

Linked To: <List names or tags of any other system specifications, which this function is related to that are in addition to the above links>.

============ **Measurement** ===

Test: <Refer to tags of any test plan or/and test cases, which deal with this function>.

============ **Priority and Risk Management** ==============================

Rationale: < Justify the existence of this function. Why is this function necessary? >.

Value: <Name [Stakeholder, time, place, event>]: <Quantify, or express in words, the value claimed as a result of delivering the function requirement>.

Assumptions: <Specify, or refer to tags of any assumptions in connection with this function, which could cause problems if they were not true, or later became invalid>.

Dependencies: <Using text or tags, name anything, which is dependent on this function in any significant way, or which this function itself, is dependent on in any significant way>.

Risks: <List or refer to tags of anything, which could cause malfunction, delay, or negative impacts on plans, requirements and expected results>.

Priority: <Name, using tags, any system elements, which this function can clearly be done after or must clearly be done before. Give any relevant reasons>.

Issues: <State any known issues>.

============ **Specific Budgets** =======================================

Financial Budget: <Refer to the allocated money for planning and implementation (which includes test) of this function>.

Figure 4.5: An example of a template. This template is for a function requirement specification. It has been slightly modified and simplified from Gilb (2005).

You also need to consider whether it is just the IT standards that you need to take into account. Users can have specific standards you need to consider – for example, maybe they already have a 'working practices manual'. While you would not want to constrain an excellent new system design by making it 'fit' with existing working practices, integration in some form is necessary, and you need to consider these requirements – otherwise there will be some delays, and quite likely problems to sort out, at the time of any system handovers. For example, what happens when your user documentation has a new course of action required to handle, say, inputting a specific type of order data which is already documented in the users' existing manual with the old procedure?

The impact of evolutionary methods

It is important to understand how the deliverables are developed. Under the Waterfall model the system deliverables were produced in a sequence and not updated after release, but this no longer tends to be the case. Walker Royce (Royce, Walker 1998) makes the point that:

> 'Over the past 20 years, the software industry has matured, and has transitioned the management process to be iterative. ….. Recurring themes from successful projects demonstrate that the software artifacts develop together with balanced levels of detail. Artifacts do not evolve in a one-way linear progression from requirements to design to implementation to deployment. Choices about implementation and deployment affect the way in which the requirements are stated and the way in which design proceeds. Information and decisions flow in various ways among artifacts. The purpose of a good development process is to remove inappropriate, premature constraints on the design and to accommodate the real engineering constraints. …..The primary difference from the conventional approach is that within each life-cycle phase, the workflow activities do not progress in a simple linear way, nor does artifact building proceed monotonically from one artifact to another. Instead the focus of activities sweeps across artifacts repeatedly, incrementally enriching the entire system description and the process with the lessons learned…'

'Light' documentation

Attempts have also been made to move documentation in another direction in recent years. One of the main features of agile methods is their insistence on 'light' documentation. Given the large volumes of system documentation that had to be produced under such lifecycles as the Waterfall model – long before any working system was visible - it is easy to be swayed towards this idea. However, there are other issues involved – writing something down can often assist you to better understand a subject – you realise you have missed something out, or not considered some dependency, or some other issue. It also gives others a baseline or a starting point for discussing or reflecting on that particular aspect. Without sufficient documentation, communication and discussion of ideas and plans becomes severely limited. At a later stage, systems maintenance becomes extremely difficult, thereby increasing costs and risks. So the question is really, what is the appropriate level of documentation? There is no easy answer to this; ultimately it will depend on the project.

Provision of information

One of the aims of the project lifecycle processes (both the project management and the systems development lifecycle processes) is to capture and communicate good practice. As we have already seen, specific project documentation is demanded, and it has to be written to the relevant standards.

However, it is one thing to produce the project documentation, but you have also to consider the provision of the information to the stakeholders: who needs access to what information, when will they need it, and how are you doing to provide it to them? The needs of all the stakeholders have to be considered: for example, senior management, the systems analysts, the suppliers, systems support, and the users.

A project needs to specifically plan what documentation it is going to produce and where it is going to hold the information. Who has access to what information is another consideration. Adequate backup facilities also need to be in place to safeguard the information.

For your student project assignment, it is mandatory that you produce systems documentation. It is best to capture your thoughts or events while they are still fresh in your mind. Documenting at a later stage can lead to things being left out because they have been forgotten. You may also run out of time (or momentum) if all the writing is left to the end. So start writing up your documents as soon as information becomes available. It will make the final writing up that much easier and you will be in better control of your assignment. It will help you identify any questions that you need to ask, and you will also have a better understanding of your project's progress. You can always revise things. Evolve your documentation – try to keep it in a deliverable state. Get other people to read your drafts and give you feedback.

4.5 Configuration management

Deliverables and documents undergo various changes, not least when corrections are made and improvements are added. Configuration management is the use of standard procedures to keep track of deliverables and their status. It provides a framework for holding information about a deliverable that can include:

- **Deliverable name**
- **Authorisation status**
- **Authorisation authority**
- **Author/originator**
- **Date last modified**
- **Quality level**
- **Version number**
- **Variant number**
- **Readership**
- **Configuration control** ('build') information
- **Change control information** (List of changes applied with dates).   The change control information for each change includes:
  - change request identifier
  - change request status
  - change request originator
  - date change request received
  - reason for change request
  - date change was raised
  - details of change
  - filename containing code for change (if applicable).

Standard for document change control

Each document under change control should have the following information maintained:

- **Document title:** the formal name by which the document is known
- **Document filename:** refer to your organisational standard for format – the filename must have a specific format that enables it to be easily identified
- **Document storage:** the deliverable file must be stored in a specific place, which has appropriate access security and backup protection
- **Author's name:** so you know who to send/give comments to, and who did the work
- **Version:** usually an indication of major revisions (VV) and subsequent updates (UU) given as VV.UU as in Version 1.2. Alternatively, date may suffice
- **Date last modified:** depending on convention, for example: YYYY-MM-DD
- **Status:** 'Draft', 'Inspected', 'Authorised'… or whatever set is considered useful
- **Authorised by:** so you know who takes responsibility and what level of authority is involved
- **Changes:** every time you update the document you must update this section with brief notes, so that readers know the major changes that have been made and do not have to read the entire document again. You'll find it also helps you keep track of your changes too!

Authorisation status and quality level

A deliverable will pass through a number of stages as it is developed (by adding enhancements and/or correcting errors) from initial outline, to draft version, to completed release version. At various points the quality level of the deliverable will be assessed and the quality level information captured. It is then up to the authorisation authority, that is, the relevant management or technical authority, to authorise status changes (say, from 'draft' to 'approved for release') based on the quality level information.

The authorisation status (often simply termed 'status') of a deliverable is the key to understanding how any subsequent changes to it should be processed and how the deliverable can be used. See 'Change control' on the next page.

Version and variant control

As a deliverable evolves, several different versions of it will be produced. Version control ensures that each version of the deliverable is uniquely identified using a version number and that its place in the evolution of the deliverable can be established. It is especially important to know which version should be being used at a specific time. (For example, there could be a released version of software being used by customers, there could be a version being updated with some new as yet untested features, and there will be backup versions.)

If more than one person is working on the same deliverable then, version control at a lower level might also be needed to help avoid losing work, or introducing duplicated or conflicting material.

Variant control is needed when there is more than one variant of a deliverable. For example, say English and a Spanish version of the same website material. Variants need to be kept aligned.

Configuration control

Configuration control keeps track of each of the individual software components of a deliverable, and records the details of the software components of the different 'build' versions. This helps ensure that the right components are assembled and that the right versions are in use, and aids any later tracking. For example, the details and results of system regression testing could be linked to a particular build version.

Change control

Once a deliverable has reached a status that involves it being 'under change control', it becomes important to keep a record of any changes that are made. Then if problems are detected, there is a means of backtracking to establish exactly what has changed.

When at 'draft', or for software, 'under construction' status, updating of a deliverable can be carried out on an informal basis. However, once a deliverable reaches a formal acceptance state, there must be a procedure for any updates that includes their formal acceptance (that is, a proposed change has to be formally agreed prior to being carried out and then once the change has been done, the deliverable must be successfully tested and authorised for release). For example, say some software on general release has several reported faults. The software producer will collect together a list of all the known faults and all the outstanding change requests and decide which faults are going to be corrected and which change requests are to be carried out. The customers might also be involved in this decision making. Once decided, the software producer writes the appropriate fixes and actions the approved change requests. Once the software has been updated with the fixes and the changes, a new software version is created with a status of say, 'untested'. Only when the system regression tests have run successfully can this version's status be updated to 'system regression tested'. There will probably be a management review meeting to review the results and consider changing the status to 'general release' where it will replace the current version of the software.

Change control register

All changes requested are input as change requests into a change control register. The status of each change request is maintained. Likely status settings include 'submitted', 'accepted', 'rejected', 'scheduled' and 'completed'. Other data, such as originator, submitted date, reasons for change, urgency and authorised by, will also be kept.

4.6 Project management reporting

We have already seen that projects are steeped with change which requires monitoring and managing. Let's now consider the deliverables and methods used by management to monitor and control a project: project reports and management reviews. We shall start with project management reporting.

Project management reporting or, more simply, project reporting (termed 'performance reporting' in Figure 4.1), is a routine activity and tends to fall into the following categories:

- **Status reports** describe the state of a project at a specific point in time. How does the project stand in relation to its objectives for scope, time and cost? Earned-value management (EVM) described in Chapter 6, on cost management, is an example of a method used for status reporting

- **Progress reports** describe what a project has accomplished over a set period of time. Usually there is comparison against the tasks in the project plan

- **Forecast reports** predict the future status or progress of a project based on past trends. When is the project likely to be completed and how much is it likely to cost?

If we look back at Figure 4.4 and Table 4.1, we see that project reporting only features as 'status assessments' and 'final project report'. It's not clear why project reports are not given more prominence, but take care not to exclude considering them when producing your student project plan!

Project reports document the project's progress towards its objectives, and the progress in completing the tasks on the project plan to schedule and within budget.

A project plan is produced as a result of the project planning. It includes consideration of the planned project schedule and the planned financial budget. Production of a project plan is discussed in the next two chapters.

4.7 Management reviews

Managers need visibility to understand the current status of deliverables and the work that needs to be done. Management reviews are meetings that focus on specific project deliverables, milestones or phases. The purpose is usually to ensure that work has been completed to the relevant standards, to review the outcomes and to decide what the way forward should be. A review meeting can also present an opportunity to discuss major issues and decide what actions to take about them. Often a formal review will force stakeholders to declare their position on an issue.

There are two types of management review:

- **Progress reviews:** a progress review compares a project's actual progress to its planned progress. The project manager is usually responsible for presenting a progress report. Any issues and problems that the project needs to resolve are considered, and any corrective actions are put in place. (For example, maybe resources need to be adjusted, or a key decision holding up the project pursued.) Progress reviews tend to take place at regular intervals, say weekly or monthly. Due to the fact they are more routine, they tend not to be quite as important as business reviews
- **Business reviews:** a business review should check that the project is doing the 'right thing' for the organisation: in other words, that the product or system being produced meets the requirements and is still correct in terms of the overall organisational objectives and the current external environment.

Business reviews are often held at key contractual points (often linked with key deliverables) and should occur at the end of every phase or step cycle of a project. They are key decision points (gates) for a project and they make the go/no-go decisions for the future of the project. Release of payment or budget is involved, so such a review is the time to consider the likelihood of project success. Kerzner (2003) identifies that increasingly in project reviews there is more pressure on projects to justify their claim on resources, and a greater willingness of senior management to cancel projects if they can see a better use for the resources elsewhere. Business reviews are sometimes known as 'phase exits', 'end-of-phase reviews', 'go/no-go reviews' or, even 'kill points'.

(As well as management reviews, there are also peer reviews. Peer reviews are technical reviews and they are discussed later in Chapter 8; they include walkthroughs and inspections.)

The impact of evolutionary approaches

Under the traditional waterfall model, a project review is held at the end of each lifecycle phase. However, waterfall lifecycle phases typically take months to complete and often the only checks demanded are that the relevant systems documentation is authorised, and then the next phase of the lifecycle commences. Little feedback from the completed phase is catered for as the project work was completely specified right at the start of the project; the project simply moves onto the next phase.

Under an incremental lifecycle model, a project review is held at the end of each increment. Each increment typically lasts several months; so, as in the case of waterfall, a few major reviews are held. One major difference though is that there is far more visibility about what the project has, or has not, delivered.

Evolutionary approaches change the nature of project reviews: rather than there being a few very major project reviews, numerous more frequent project reviews are required. This has several effects: management involvement with the project is increased, but lower-level management can take project responsibility. This is because the direction of the project has to be considered at the end of every delivery cycle: how successful was the step we have just delivered, and what are we going to do next? As there is a track record of the project delivering value to the user, the risk of the project being cancelled is considerably reduced.

Further, when using evolutionary approaches, the amount of project financial budget and project scheduled-time being considered at each review is much smaller, and as a result the level of management responsibility can, again, be much lower. In fact, the project team management can be more empowered to make review decisions. Given the increased visibility of the progress of the project and the more frequent reviews, project reports can also become 'lighter'.

Format of a review

Two specific communication skills, writing reports and giving presentations, are key to project reviews. A report is usually prepared prior to a review and circulated to the review attendees. This report typically is written to a specified template and often the technical experts have to submit written statements about specific aspects of the project. For example, they have to answer such questions as the likelihood of the systems architecture delivering the required performance requirements or, the estimated future reliability of the system. There is usually a fixed agenda set in advance for a review. The project manager and other senior members of the project team are required to give presentations and be 'grilled', with questions put to them at the review meeting by more senior management.

Project management take review meetings very seriously. Given the go/no-go nature of review meetings at major milestones, a project manager's presentation can be key as to whether a project continues or gets cancelled. As a result, a great deal of work can go into preparing for such a project review with practice run-throughs to rehearse presentations and answers to likely questions!

Selecting a management review format

Think about the student project that you are working on and select the most suitable format(s) for management reviews. When and how often would you hold your reviews? Who would you invite?

4.8 Student reports

Don't get confused between student project reports and project management reports – both are sometimes termed as 'project reports'. Consider the context; in this section, references to 'project reports' are to 'student project reports'. Your student project report is more than simply a project management report as you are systems developer as well as project manager (and maybe other roles!) for your student project.

Now let's look at student report writing. The main deliverable of your student project is your project report which will be submitted at the end of the project. In this section, we shall consider the planning and structuring of student reports, writing styles and how to create a strong written argument. We will also outline the principles of critical evaluation and cover the issue of plagiarism.

The ability to write documents in a well-structured intelligent way is perhaps one of the most basic, and yet most important, skills a student can learn at university. As part of your studies, you are expected to produce reports in an academic style: that is, written argument that is backed up by suitable references.

Why is writing documents so important?

Why does technical writing matter so much for your student project? Large-scale software projects are about building something comparable in complexity to an aeroplane. To accomplish this, a team of specialists is needed and no one person can possibly know all the details of the design and construction. Likewise, using and maintaining such a system, once it has been built, needs the same detailed knowledge. Nobody can know everything about the system, so the people, who know a given sub-system, must be the ones to document it. You might as well accept that, if you are going to work in the IT industry, all your creative ideas and all your technical wizardry are going to have to be communicated to others in writing. This is the only way that they will be able to understand your work sufficiently well to judge its worth, and, ultimately, to use it. This is the main reason that so much importance is given to your student project report.

The purpose of a student project report

Report writing is a practice that is a common occurrence in both universities and the workplace. A report is a way of feeding back information about a project, an event or the implications of a new system. It is used for the analysis of data or situations. Reports look at what went right, and what went wrong, with a project.

Your student project will culminate in the submission of a report on your work. A project report is an extremely important aspect of a project. It serves to show what you have achieved and should demonstrate that:

- You understand the wider context of IT, by relating your choice of project, and the approach you take, to existing products or to research
- You can apply the theoretical and practical techniques taught in the course to the problem you are addressing, and that you understand their relevance to the wider world of IT
- You are capable of objectively criticising your own work and making constructive suggestions for improvements, or further work based on your experiences so far
- As an IT professional, you can explain your thinking and working processes clearly and concisely to third parties who may not be experts in the field in which you are working.

The quality of your project report matters because at least one of the people marking your project will not have followed the project throughout: they will rely heavily on the report to judge your work. Also, if at the end of the day, your overall degree marks put you on a boundary between two classifications, the final outcome can be influenced significantly by the quality of your project. In addition, you should appreciate that the external examiners, who play a crucial role in the final recommendation, have only the report by which to judge your project performance. The same applies to projects, which are put forward for a project prize or for professional accreditation.

Many students underestimate the importance of the report and make the mistake of thinking that top marks can be achieved simply for producing a good product. This is fundamentally not the case and many projects have been graded well below their potential because of an indifferent or poor write-up. In order to get the balance right, you should consider that there are two aims of the project: to produce a good report and to produce the artefacts (that is, the software, hardware, theory and other things) that you develop during the project. Don't make the mistake of leaving the write-up to the last minute. Ideally, you should produce the bulk of the report as you go along and use the last week or two to bring it together into a coherent document.

The physical layout and formatting of the report is also important, and yet is very often neglected. A tidy, well laid-out and consistently formatted document makes for easier reading and is suggestive of a careful and professional attitude towards its preparation. Remember also that quantity does not automatically guarantee quality. Projects need to be concise, clear and readable. This is the basis for assessing them – not a page count.

Some layout instructions for student reports

Nowadays, all documents that are to be read by others are expected to be word-processed. Documents need to be well written and also well presented.

Before word- processing any report, you need to determine if there are any special instructions regarding the document layout that need to be applied. In particular, you need to establish if there are any document standards that you need to follow. For instance, when writing papers for conference proceedings, a specific recommended template for document layout is usually provided and has to be adhered to. Student project reports usually don't have to conform to such a specific template. For example, here is a set of instructions on document layout that have been applied to student project reports:

- **Word processing:** your project report must be word-processed
- **Paper size/paper colour/printing instructions:** the project report must be printed single-sided on white A4 paper
- **Word count:** the overall length of the individual report should not exceed 10,000 words (excluding appendices)
- **Margins**: margins should be 4cm wide on the left-hand side (to allow for binding) and 2cm wide on the other three sides
- **Pagination:** page numbers should begin on the first page of the main report, following the acknowledgements. Page numbers should be placed at the top of each page
- **Spacing:** single or one-and-a-half spacing is acceptable
- **Headings:** chapters and sections should always begin on a new page. Subsections should be differentiated from the main text by extra spacing: their titles should be in capitals. Minor subheadings should be underlined and should have only initial capitals.

Activity 4.4

Investigating a document layout

You will require computer access for this activity.

Have a look at the manuscript instructions provided by INCOSE (the International Council for Systems Engineering) for its annual international symposium. Using your Internet browser, go to the 2006 INCOSE international symposium website at **www.incose.org/symp2006/**

In the left-hand panel on that web page you will find 'Manuscript Instructions/ Template'. Click on this and the template instructions will be downloaded as an MS Word file (**Manuscript_Template_2006.doc**). Look at the layout instructions in this file.

When considering the layout of the contents of a report, your aim is for your reader to be able to concentrate on what you are saying (that is, your words) without any distractions caused by the layout. Therefore, keep the content layout simple and consistent.

In addition to the layout instructions already given, here are a few more simple guidelines to help achieve this:

- Don't end a page with a heading or subheading
- Ensure that lists are aligned using correct indentation
- Don't let the last word of a paragraph end on a separate page (instead, insert a page break to ensure at least one complete line appears on the following page)
- Make sure that all your table captions are consistent (with the same justification and font size and type)
- The final thing you should do before printing off or sending off a document should be to check its page layout.

Report structure

In an important sense, the structure of any document – the nature and extent of the different sections, and the order in which they appear – represents the design of the document. A good document structure will take into account the purpose of the document and its target readership. When writing a report, you are not being asked to write a textbook, but to competently conduct a piece of work for an informed readership. In the case of your project document, its primary purpose is to report on your project, and its primary audience is your examiners. Many project reports are far too long and lack purpose.

A student project report is a combination of status, progress and forecasting reports. However, by its nature, a student project report has also to have considerable elements of specification within it – this will not typically be the case in industry project reporting (unless there are specific technical issues that need consideration during the review).

To satisfy your readers – the examiners – you should be aiming for:

- **Continuity:** so that your material is ordered both so as to demonstrate the development of your work and to develop the reader's understanding
- **Completeness:** so that you give as full account of your work as is necessary and (especially) that nothing significant is left out. Put simply, the report must tell a story – a full story, and an interesting one.

Unlike an essay, a report contains headings and subheadings that support the storyline. Each subheading may be further divided into subsections or subdivisions. Each section and subsection is numbered and relates to the 'design' of the story.

To develop and improve the continuity of a report, it is necessary to pay more attention to the fine structure of your document – to how the individual chapters within the main body of your report are designed. If these are thought out beforehand, in outline or even just as subheadings, then at least you will know where you are going as you write. For each subsection in your outline plan, try to begin with a more general idea (or a broad picture) and then develop your argument (or focus) towards the more detailed points or areas you want to consider. This follows the maxim 'Move from the general to the particular', which is also useful when you finally come to write the paragraphs.

The main sections

Any report that you are developing will be divided into sections. Here we shall discuss the specific requirements for your project reports. Typically, the sections supporting the general flow of the story of your project should include:

- **Title page:** state the title, your full name, the qualification for which the work is being submitted, the university name and the date of submission.
- **Abstract:** a synopsis of your work, which gives a flavour of the work and encourages busy researchers to read on: a brief informative summary of about 250 words normally written as the last item in your project when everything else is already known (so that it can encapsulate what the project is actually about). The abstract summarises the content of your report, the scope of the work, the research methodology used, and the main findings or conclusions.
- **Acknowledgements:** this section provides acknowledgements of help from supervisors, other members of staff, colleagues who helped and any other relevant people. Where access to facilities, resources or individuals was provided, this must be mentioned and the relevant providers thanked. Don't forget to give credit to any individuals who may have commented on early drafts of your work and to helpful librarians and technicians.
- **Table of contents:** this table gives the full headings of all chapters (and the sections within them) with the appropriate page numbers. It should also list the appendices in similar fashion. Page numbers should be right-margin aligned.
- **List of figures:** if any figures appear in the text, this list will provide the number and name of each, together with the relevant page numbers. Note that sometimes this may be split into a List of Figures and a List of Tables (if the report contains many tables in addition to diagrams and charts). Number your figures consistently using either sequential numbering (for example, Figure 1, Figure 2 and Figure 3) or numbering within chapter (for example, Figure 1.1, Figure 1.2, Figure 2.1, Figure 2.2, Figure 2.3 and Figure 4.1). Tables should be numbered separately from figures (for example, Table 1, and Table 2 or Table 1.1 and Table 1.2)
- **Abbreviation list:** if you have used any abbreviations (for example, abbreviations of components, methodologies or different sections within an organisation) within the text, you should list them in this section for easy reference (just before the main report).

- **Introduction:** the introduction contains a brief outline of the topic as a whole. The aim and objectives of the report are then stated. What is the purpose of the report and what did it set out to investigate? There should be no indication of the author's own personal stance on the topic. The statement 'the impact of the proposed M39 to the East Dublin region' is more appropriate than 'the M39 will damage all the wild life in the area'. The second statement may be the conclusion of the report or indeed the findings of the report, but it cannot be the objective.

  The introduction is probably the first chapter that you will write as it sets out the work. It is probably also the last chapter that you will rewrite to reflect the changes that have taken place in the work

- **Method consideration:** explaining your choice of method

- **The context:** this section examines the organisational context of the project. For example, was the investigation carried out by a well-financed, well-resourced multinational organisation, or carried out by a local group concerned about the environment? These factors may affect the information gathered. A group from a multinational organisation may have talked to businesses, but found local residents unco-operative. They therefore would be unable to give a clear idea of local feeling towards the proposed road. On the other hand, a lack of money may affect the report of the small local group. They might not be able to carry out large-scale surveys. They may rely on the generosity of others to gather scientific information and ecological studies

- **Literature review:** review of previous research highlighting useful work on which you can build. Even a project focusing on a particular organisation will benefit from a literature review! If your project is more practical, this chapter should focus on the context that you are operating within, typical applications, alternatives tools and development approaches and how they have been used in practice or on alternative systems and what they do or do not achieve

- **Research design** (also known as research methods or methodology. This section is only needed for research-oriented reports): This section should include general research approaches, the information or data you need, methods for obtaining it, sample sizes and techniques for collecting and analysing the data. Note:

  Practical problem-solving projects may also feed in the structure of the lifecycle to take full account of the phases and activities that have taken place. This may replace the research design chapter (or sit alongside it).

  Remember that you need to relate your choice of method to the objectives and be discriminating in your choice. This will apply equally to research methods and development tools and processes.

  You could also add, or replace, sections to explain the various stages of the development lifecycle of your product

- **Results:** your data and findings

- **Evaluation:** discussion and analysis of the results with the aim of either validating or refuting the results. Here the collected information is evaluated to determine what conjectures can be deduced from it. All information is brought together and analysed and an evaluation is made

- **Summary and conclusion:** the final section summarises the project as a whole, outlines the main findings and lists the recommendations of the project. The summary should include what you set out to achieve, how you went about it and what you ended up doing. The conclusion section is also likely to include any limitations on the interpretation and recommendations for future work to be carried out in this area. The project planning should also be described and critically evaluated in light of actual events. If certain aspects were compromised as a result, you should explain why the decision was made and what impact it had on the project.

Any omissions or scope reduction will contribute to additional further work, which can be recommended. Don't forget to comment and retrospectively evaluate both the product and the process used.

In this way you will get a chance to explore what you have learned and how you would do it differently next time. Note that this section may be split into two sections or even more – it depends on the number and type of comments that you have to make

- **Appendices:** additional material which did not make it into the main sections, but which is relevant to the report should appear as separate appendices. Such material should be self-explanatory or can be referred to from within the report itself. The appendices can also include material, which contained too much detail or was too lengthy for the main report. For example, you should aim to include lengthy items such as program code, raw data, text of questionnaires and detailed statistical analysis as separate appendices. This will enable the examiners to read them separately from the report

- **References:** a complete list of all the works mentioned in the text (and possibly in the appendices). Full bibliographical details are needed for each entry. If you feel there is a need for a brief bibliography that lists key books, papers and articles that you have not referenced, you may add a bibliography

- **Index:** not normally required for student project reports.

Activity 4.5

Creating a document structure

Try creating a title page and a table of contents for your project. Use the report structure just presented in this chapter to help you.

Prepare:

- A title page

- A draft table of contents.

Remember, before starting to write a document, you should always determine what document standards and/or document templates apply.

Some organisations will have both document layout standards and specific document structures for specific types of document – there may or may not be document templates available for use. For example, a feasibility study might have to contain certain standard sections, and would fail quality control checks unless it contained these sections.

Structuring an argument

Notice how any story flows from one section to the next in order to form a cohesive storyline. The core of any report is the argument (the storyline) it presents. The argument must be clearly defined and well presented. Without a clearly defined argument the material in the project report becomes little more than a list of unrelated ideas and facts, which serve little purpose. All information in your report should go some way towards proving the main argument in the essay is correct.

The structure of an argument has a number of different sections. Each section contains information vital to structuring your argument, and the sections should link together to make a unified storyline. It is not only reports written for university assignments that are structured this way. If you read any material written by academics in journals or books, it will also follow the same basic structure.

In practice, it is a good idea to provide a brief summary (no more than a paragraph or two) at the end of each main section, highlighting the main points covered, and perhaps giving some introductory links to the next (or subsequent) section(s).

Style

The style of writing refers to:

- The *manner* in which you address your reader
- The *skill* with which you express your ideas.

To do the former effectively it helps to keep the reader in mind at all times when you are writing and to maintain consistency, that is, adopt a policy for the form of address and stick to it. To do the latter you need to be clear about what particular ideas you are trying to convey at any given point in the 'story' and then apply your skill to communicating (just) those ideas. Organise your ideas (with brief notes if necessary) carefully before you start writing, so that the storyline develops in a controlled way as you write.

Linking

A report should flow easily from one sentence to the next, and from one paragraph to the next. The ideas and arguments should be written in a well-thought-out, logical way. Sometimes when reading back over a report that you have written, it might not flow as well as you hoped. Using a few key words and phrases to link or join the sentences and paragraphs together can make all the difference. Examples of some phrases that are used commonly to create transitions are 'for example', 'however', 'on the other hand', 'in contrast', 'looking at it from another point of view', and 'furthermore'.

Avoiding common pitfalls

Here are a few of the common phrases you should avoid using in a report.

- **I and me:** you should never use 'I' or refer to the first person in your report. Sentences such as 'In my opinion' or 'I think' or 'When I did' are not appropriate in an academic report. The person marking your essay is not interested in your opinion or what you did or how you feel. What they are interested in is the argument you put across and how you support that argument. You therefore need to use the third person, to eliminate any personal bias
- **'It is obvious':** when writing an essay, nothing should be stated as 'obvious'. Though it may appear obvious to you, it may not be obvious to everyone. For example, 'the link between poor education and drug abuse is obvious'. This sentence tells you very little
- **Generalisation:** many generalisations made are untrue and have little basis. They offer your arguments little in the way of evidence and should be avoided at all costs. Examples of generalisations are 'all women know how to iron shirts' or 'all men like football'.

Diagrams

'A picture is worth a thousand words.' Tables and figures form an important part of a report as they can often provide information in a more comprehensive or concise manner than can be presented by the written word. This is usually when there is a lot of data to present, or when complex structural information is being given (for example, a database design).

Using diagrams also breaks the text, making it easier for the reader to assimilate the information you are trying to convey and hence remain responsive to your message.

Citation and referencing

References give credit to other authors whose ideas and findings you use in your work. On the one hand, your project report must give an account of your original work: on the other, you need to show that your work rests on and contributes to the body of knowledge in your chosen topic. The purpose of referencing your work is to enable your readers to trace the sources that have influenced you for the purposes of support, verification, or simply for further exploration. Citation is the mechanism you use to separate your own work from those who have published beforehand.

In the main body of a report, whenever you refer to someone else's work, you refer to it by the surname of the author and the year of publication. Optionally, you could give the chapter or page number for the specific text being referenced.

Then, at the back of the project report, the references section should give the name of the author, the name of the book or paper, the name of the journal if a paper is being referenced, the year of publication and the publisher. In addition, further information can also be needed to specifically identify where to find a paper, such as the month of publication, the volume, and the page references for the start and end of the paper.

For example, you may have, in the text of the report:

> Wrigley et al. (1991) have shown that life expectancy was also increasing for ordinary adult Englishmen, especially for the rural 'stayers' who formed the core of England's reconstituted families.

Then in the *Reference* section:

> Wrigley, E.A., Davies, R.S., Oeppen, J.E. and Schofield, R.S. (1991), *English population history from family reconstitution 1580 – 1837*, Cambridge: Cambridge University Press.

Note the reference list should contain only those references you specifically use in the body of the report: no more and no less.

Whenever you quote directly from a source, you should also give a reference for the quote, the page number and make it clear that it is a quote by placing it in quotes or indenting it. For example:

> As Rheingold (1995) states, 'By the early 1980s, the bureaucratic and financial demands of running ARPANET had outgrown ARPA.' (p 81).

Academically, it is crucial to get your references correct. Marks will be deducted if you don't. Make sure you know which standard referencing format you should be using in your student project report. The Harvard format is commonly used.

Activity 4.6

Review some references and citations

Take a look at the way several of your textbooks handle references. Do they use the Harvard format? Can you find examples of the following types of referencing?

A citation of a book

A citation of a journal paper

A citation with two authors

A citation with three or more authors

A citation for a website.

Activity 4.7

Find out about Harvard referencing

You will require computer access for this activity.

Go to the Middlesex University library resources website at **www.lr.mdx.ac.uk/**

Now, on the left-hand menu under 'Web Helpdesk', select 'Documentation'. Scroll down some way to 'Study Skills' and select 'Referencing and Citation: Health and Social Sciences'. Look also at 'Referencing and Citation: Arts & Humanities'.

Also, input 'Harvard referencing' into a search engine. There are several good university library documents discussing referencing. You will probably find it useful to look at two or three such documents. All have slightly different approaches and it's a question of finding the one that you find most helpful.

Do not quote more than one or two sentences from another source. If you want to refer to a large piece of someone else's work you should summarise it in your own words (and reference it correctly). Always remember that if you quote large chunks of other people's work without referencing it correctly, your work will be reported for plagiarism.

Plagiarism

Plagiarism is using words and ideas from another text without acknowledgement and without referencing correctly where the information came from. Often, plagiarised sections in student project reports stand out because they are written in a different style to the rest of the report. Your tutor or the person marking your report will be familiar with the main texts in the subject area you are writing about. They will also be aware of the main arguments and theories, so trying to pass something off as your own work is not that easy. Copying another student's work is also plagiarism.

Avoiding plagiarism

If you are using quotes or text from another author, make sure you reference it correctly. Ideas can also be plagiarised, so these need to be referenced as well.

When summarising from books or journal articles, make sure that they are written in your own words if you are going to use them in your essay. Read over your summary and check that the phrases and sentences are structured differently from the original text. Use your own examples. Some information that is well known and agreed upon does not need to be referenced, for example 'London is the capital of England' or 'smoking is bad for your health'.

The penalty for plagiarism can be high, so if in doubt add a reference. If you are unsure about the format for a reference, ask your local seminar tutor for help.

Evaluation of writing

Prior to completing a piece of writing, the author will sit back and review the text. He or she will ensure it flows easily from one topic to the next. They will make sure all the relevant sections are intact and that the main objective is met. This is a process of evaluation. Whether you are evaluating your own work or someone else's, the same rules apply. When a document is evaluated, its strong and weak points are noted. The validity of the text is examined, as is its relativity to the reader.

If you understand the basic principles of good essay and report writing, you should be able to adequately evaluate a piece of writing. When evaluating a piece of writing, you should look specifically at the following areas:

- **The structure:** earlier we highlighted the structure for the project reports. When reading a document make sure that all chapters and sections are present, and that they contain the appropriate information

- **The objectives:** the aim and objectives of the report need to be clearly stated, and they should be fulfilled. If the writer was attempting to answer a question, then an adequate answer should be given

- **The evidence:** the writer should make appropriate use of the evidence given, and should explain the relevance of a quote or reference if it is not obvious. The evidence should be from a reliable source. The more you study an area, the more familiar you will become with the main authors or publishers in this area.

  References to the Internet are not always reliable, as information on the Internet does not always have to be true or of any benefit. Consider how reputable each website is likely to be – will its papers and articles have been peer-reviewed?

  You should also check the accuracy of the evidence given. If the writer refers to another study, you should read that as well. It is not unheard of for authors to misuse a study for their own benefit. The inclusion of counter-arguments should make the evidence for the argument seem stronger. Finally, the evidence should be presented in a logical manner

- **The quality of writing:** the way a document is written to a large extent reflects the quality of it. If the author has spent time collecting and organising their information into a coherent argument, they will want to present it in a well-written manner appropriate to their overall objective.

  When reading the sentences, you should make sure they make sense; read them a second time if they do not. Ask yourself if they all follow on logically from one to the next. Look for any spelling and grammatical mistakes and assess whether or not the style is appropriate for the text.

  If you are reading a published piece of work, the quality of writing should not really be relevant. If it has been published you can assume it has reached a certain standard. However, you may want to look at the style of writing.

Remember that all documents need editing. It is through the final editing process that the document will obtain its final form. However, writers and authors are rarely satisfied with the final article and will always think of other examples or phrases that could have been used. Do not miss deadlines because you are not completely satisfied with the final result; you never will be. Hand in your project when it is due.

4.9 Summary

Management of both progress and change is essential for project success. A project manager must understand what system deliverables are to be produced, how quality control is to be carried out and what change control must be in place. Further, a project manager must understand how the system deliverables 'fit' into operational use and manage their deployment to end-users.

As a result of reading this chapter you should be able to make a start on a list of deliverables and tasks for your student project. You should know to look for documentation standards and to consider quality control and change control for all your deliverables. You should understand the importance and purpose of producing project management reports and of carrying out management reviews. You should also have a better understanding of the change management issues associated with delivery to operations and user resistance to change.

You have also been given advice and guidance on how to structure and write your student project report. The next step is to move onto planning your project, which we shall start in the next chapter.

4.10 Review questions

 Question 4.1

What management reporting is relevant for a student project?

 Question 4.2

What are the advantages of being provided with a standard contents template for a report?

 Question 4.3

What impact will an evolutionary systems development lifecycle compared to a waterfall model systems development lifecycle have on testing?

 Question 4.4

What configuration management have you seen practised or have you used?

 Question 4.5

Activity 4.1 involved testing a user interface prototype, what systems development lifecycle model would that suggest was being used?

4.11 Feedback on activities

Activity 4.1: Trialling a prototype

You need to arrange for some time (that is, some work-hours) from the users. Assuming you are going to test your prototype initially on only one group of users, you need to obtain the relevant user manager's agreement. As users are involved, you also first need your project manager's approval and maybe his or her involvement. It depends on your relationship with the users – do you know who they are, how to contact them and what their workload currently looks like? Do you know their manager? The most likely thing is that you communicate your requirements to your project manager and he or she will liaise with the user management on your behalf.

- Draw up a draft plan (Written Plan)

- Talk to your project manager. Do you need other members of the project team to help you? (Meeting)

- Amend your draft plan and give to your project manager.

Assuming given the go-ahead, names of users, location, user contact and a date and time:

- Phone the user contact to check they understand what is happening. Give them your contact details. (Verbal Conversation)

- Agree to send them an e-mail of the details and maybe arrange a meeting at the user site to go through exactly what hardware and software you will require and the information the users will have to supply. What skill level should the users be? Do you want them to supply test data? What instructions will the users need? How much help are the users likely to need? (E-mail. Maybe Meeting)

- Expand your initial plan with a detailed test script to support the prototype testing (Written Test Script)

- Try your test script out on other members of the project team. Brief any members of the project team who are going to help you out on the user site. (Verbal Conversation)

- Set up the prototype in advance and test it works on user site. (Verbal Conversation)

- Explain to the users what you want them to do (Brief Presentation)

- Conduct the prototype testing and help out the users as needed (Verbal Conversation and Written Note Taking)

- Obtain feedback from the users. Consider whether you need to record user comments. (Completed Written Test Scripts and Verbal Conversation. Maybe Recorded Feedback on Cassette.)

- Thank the users and their manager (Verbal Conversation and maybe E-mail)

- Write up your findings and talk to your project manager about how the testing went (Written Report and maybe, Meeting)

Can you see that there is quite a lot to think about, and quite a lot of communication involved in even a simple prototyping testing activity? Can you also see how a checklist of things to consider when arranging user prototype testing could help you?

The aim of Activity 4.1 was to give you some idea of the amount of communication and effort involved in project work, especially when customer staff are involved. This activity only involved a small number of stakeholders. Think of all the activities across an entire project: writing systems documentation, interviewing users, presenting to user groups, reporting to management in meetings, negotiating with client management for budget, writing progress reports, revising user working practices, providing telephone technical support, giving system demonstrations, delivering training to users, updating website information, and many others.

Activity 4.2: Test evaluation criteria

You need to make sure that the criteria are measurable (that is, that they are clearly understood and unambiguous).

Try to answer the following questions:

- Are your criteria objective?

- Can they be measured?

- Are your evaluation criteria good enough to prove that you have achieved what you set out to do?

If the answer to any of the questions is 'No', you will need to revise the criteria accordingly.

When testing a prototype user interface, you would be interested in the total number of reported defects by severity and by defect type (severity depends on the impact on the organisation of the defect occurring). You would set or be given the maximum number of defects by severity, and perhaps the maximum number of defects by type, that would be acceptable. These numbers would have to relate to the kind and amount of testing being carried out. You would most likely have a testing script that outlined the testing to be carried out.

Activity 4.3: Selecting a management review format

Management reviews include routine progress reviews and end-of-phase/stage/step business reviews. So these are the two different types of management review you should be considering planning for your student project.

You need to decide when you are going to hold the different types of management review. You need also to consider who should attend the different reviews.

In terms of stakeholders for your student project, you should be able to identify two or three, maybe more: say yourself, your supervisor and your client manager. If you select formal management reviews to mark the end of a phase/stage/step, you need to allow time for them.

Think about the amount of planning that is required for each type of meeting. You should also take into account the type of input you need to produce for the meeting and the type of output that you need from the meeting.

Ask yourself: Do you need to have someone running the session? Will people talk to each other? Do you have time for preparation?

Although reviews take considerable effort, there are significant rewards. By producing the reports, you are helping document your project, which undoubtedly will make the final writing-up easier. You are also going to get feedback about whether your project is progressing well, and whether you have forgotten anything. There is also the chance to raise issues in a more formal way. Remember to produce review reports capturing the key review outcomes.

Activity 4.4: Investigating a document layout

This INCOSE manuscript instructions/template document is written to the same standards that it is trying to instruct on. As it suggests, you can simply write your material into a copy of the document and pick up the correct styles from it. Notice that when you have this document open, if you go to the style menu – usually in the MS Word formatting toolbar on the left-hand side towards the top of the screen, then you can see all the styles that the document is using, for example, 'Title', 'Heading 1' and 'Body'.

It saves a great deal of time if you write your documents from the beginning using the correct document layout. Using a good document layout as you write helps you organise and structure your report – you think about names for headings and subheadings and you can see exactly how much you have written. You can also find your material quickly because it is in the appropriate section.

Activity 4.5: Creating a document structure

The title page must follow contain the information below:

- Title
- Author
- Author's student ID number
- Date
- Supervisor.

Your table of contents should reveal the structure of your report. Include all the sections mentioned in the theory that are going to be relevant to your project.

For the 'main body' include numbers and draft titles for all the sections you are planning to write, in the order in which they will appear. Where it would be helpful, include section subheadings, or a sentence or two to describe the intended contents.

For example, the structure suggested in the book, *Project Research in Information Systems*, T. Cornford and S. Smithson could produce a Table of Contents as given in Figure 4.5.

Chapter 1: Introduction

   (Scope of project, Rationale, 'Map' of succeeding chapters)

Chapter 2: Project Definition

   2.1 Objectives

   2.2 Methods Used

Chapter 3: Literature Survey

Chapter 4: Work Undertaken

Chapter 5: Data Collected

   (Put the 'raw' data in here)

Chapter 6: Analysis and Discussion

Chapter 7: Conclusion

   7.1 Summary

   7.2 Evaluation

Figure 4.5: An initial table of contents for a student project

If you are doing a practical problem-solving project, you may find it useful to change the order of Chapters 2 and 3 above, since it can be easier to define what you are trying to accomplish once all the issues discussed in the literature survey have been dealt with.

Try to think of things you may want to put into the appendices. Label your appendices A, B, etc. and try to give each of them a draft title. (You can always add or remove these later if you change your mind.)

Activity 4.6: Review some references and citations

You should easily find such examples. Look at the references in this book to start with, but also look at some of your other textbooks or look at some textbooks in a library, for example Marchewka (2006).

Activity 4.7: Find out about Harvard referencing

There is no specific feedback for this activity.

4.12 References

Boehm, B., (1981), *Software Engineering Economics*, Prentice Hall PTR, ISBN 0 13822122 7. See also **http://sunset.usc.edu/index.html**

Gilb, T., (2005), *Competitive Engineering: A Handbook for Systems Engineering, Requirements Engineering and Software Engineering using Planguage*, Elsevier Butterworth-Heinemann, ISBN 0 750 66507 6

Kerzner, H., (2003), *Project management: a systems approach to planning, scheduling and controlling* (Eighth Edition), Wiley, ISBN 0 471 22577 0

Marchewka, J. T. (2006), *Information Technology Project Management: Providing Measurable Organizational Value* (2nd Edition), Wiley, ISBN 0 471 71539 5

Pressman, R. S., (2005), *Software Engineering: A Practitioner's Approach* (6th edition), McGraw-Hill, ISBN 0 07 123840 9. Note (5th Edition published in 2000 is also referenced, ISBN 0 07 709677 0)

Project Management Institute, (2004), *A Guide to the Project Management Body of Knowledge* (3rd edition) (PMBOK Guide), ISBN 1 93069945 X, ISBN13 978193069945 8. **www.pmi.org/** [Last accessed: November 2006].

Royce, Walker, (1998), *Software Project Management: A Unified Framework*, Addison-Wesley, ISBN 0 201 30958 0

CHAPTER 5

Project planning I: activities & schedules

OVERVIEW

As part of a project proposal it is necessary to produce an outline project plan for the systems implementation (including the systems development and project delivery). Once project funding has been agreed, a more detailed, initial project plan will be drawn up and this will then be further developed over the course of the project.

A project plan will normally identify the different tasks or activities which are to be accomplished, together with some estimate of how long each task is likely to take and an outline of what each task is expected to produce. It also presents this task information linked together into a schedule showing the task dependencies and the order in which it is planned to carry out the work. From the schedule, a project manager can see when the various project components (the 'deliverables') are to be ready. Later, as the project plan is carried out, project progress can be measured against the schedule. In addition, the impact of any changes to the project plan can be understood and scheduled in appropriately.

This chapter describes the project planning process. It discusses all the aspects of planning outlined above with the exception of cost estimation, which is described in the next chapter, 'Project planning II: cost management'. Note that a project plan can in some organisations include more information than the project scheduling and budgeting information. Additional components could include information on adherence to industry standards and organisational policies and guidelines. By convention the term 'activity' is used for 'activity network' and so has been used in this chapter. An 'activity' is the same concept as 'task'. There are several points in the chapter where this has been emphasised, but readers should bear this in mind while reading this chapter and not get confused by the terms!

Learning outcomes	At the end of this chapter you should be able to:

- Produce a work breakdown structure (WBS)

- Construct a project activity network diagram

- Analyse a project's critical path

- Discuss the use of project management applications.

5.1   Introduction

This chapter starts by outlining the project planning process. It then describes this process in greater detail, explaining such concepts as work breakdown structure, milestone, activity network, task dependency and critical path. The chapter also considers project management applications and discusses Gantt charts.

With regards to its relationship to the Project Management Institute's (PMI's) definitions (*PMBOK Guide* 2004), this chapter corresponds to part of project integration management (the 'develop project management plan' process), part of project scope management (the 'create WBS' process) and all of the project time management processes. The PMI's project time management process comprises the following sub-processes:

- **Activity definition:** identifying and describing the activities (tasks)
- **Activity sequencing:** identifying dependencies among the activities (tasks)
- **Activity resource estimation:** describing the resources required to carry out the activities (tasks)
- **Activity duration estimation:** estimating the time to complete the activities (tasks)
- **Schedule development:** combining the activity (task) information (that is, definitions, sequencing, resources required and duration) into a schedule
- **Schedule control:** measuring and monitoring the project's performance against schedule, and also updating the schedule with any required changes.

In addition, there is an overlap with the PMI's project cost management process when discussing a project's budget. However, cost management processes are mainly covered in the next chapter, *Project planning II: cost management*. Some overlap between the two chapters is to be expected as during the planning process there is going to be iteration occurring between scheduling and budgeting.

5.2   Planning

Planning is the essential prerequisite for controlling a project. It facilitates project action and enables estimation, budgeting, scheduling and resource allocation.

A project plan needs to tell the project manager what should happen, when and in what order, and at what cost. It helps the project manager of a project to calculate how much effort, and therefore how many people, will be needed to complete each phase of the project in a given period of time – once that information is known, then the project's budget can be calculated (total project cost and cost against time). It also enables the project manager to know what everybody should be doing at any particular point in time during the project and to track the project's progress against schedule. When changes are needed, it enables the project manager to better assess the impacts of the changes and to re-plan the schedule accordingly.

This can be thought about in terms of the project trade-off triangle – see Table 5.1.

Requirements of the project plan	Project trade-off triangle	Main concepts discussed in the planning chapters
What	Scope	Tasks (activities) & work breakdown structure (WBS)
When & what order	Time or schedule	Schedule
What cost	Money or financial budget	Budget

Table 5.1: How the project trade-off triangle maps to the main concepts of this chapter

The project planning process

The project planning process can be outlined as follows:

1 Develop a statement of work (SOW)

2 Identify the project tasks

3 Create a WBS

4 Identify the milestones

5 Estimate effort/duration of each task

6 Identify the resources required for each task

7 Create the project schedule

- establish the task dependencies
- identify the critical path
- examine the task scheduling
- allocate resources
- set project time data
- establish project completion date
- establish cost schedule
- get customer approval and project team members' agreement to the schedule.

We'll discuss this planning process in greater detail in the following sections.

Note: if incremental or evolutionary/agile methods are being used then this planning process is going to be repeated many times during the course of the project (project completion time becoming increment/step completion time). In addition, such projects are also likely to have an initial high-level project plan sketching out what is intended. This has to be prepared to the level of detail that senior management can understand the business case and are prepared to allocate initial funding and provisional future funding. Further detailed planning will occur as the project is carried out.

This is a form of *rolling wave planning*, which means that you do not construct a detailed project plan at the project's inception but a 'skeleton' plan, which identifies the key stages of your project. Your project planning is thus performed 'on the fly' as your project progresses. You make decisions as to where you are actually heading and what work you will have to perform in the following stage of your project as you complete previous stages. Thus, your planning detail ebbs and flows as your project progresses.

5.3 Develop a statement of work

A statement of work (SOW) provides a detailed description of the project work that needs to be completed. It should be formally agreed with the client. It becomes a reference for the project as to what exactly they should be working on. A SOW relates to scope – it describes part of the scope of the project. If incremental or evolutionary/agile methods are being used, then a series of SOWs will be developed as the project work is carried out.

Note: the term 'statement of work' (SOW) is not used by all organisations to describe project work descriptions – use of the term can be restricted to only being used when contracts are put out to subcontractor tender.

5.4 Identify the project tasks

In starting to plan a project, the first thing is to list all the tasks (activities) that need to be done before the project can be finished.

Working out the list of tasks that need to be completed will later allow you to:

- Estimate the effort, duration, resources and cost required to complete the project
- Identify milestones
- Sequence and schedule the tasks.

It is worth taking time over this initial planning activity, as an accurate and thorough list of tasks will make the rest of the planning activity easier. With a thorough list of tasks, you have a better chance of including everything necessary to complete the project. Also, if you do remember something else later on, you stand a better chance of fitting it in before the final project deadline (because you will have a better understanding of the outstanding tasks).

In writing your initial list of tasks, the list will probably be quite abstract and generic. There are several approaches to producing an initial task list:

- Using **lifecycles** (for example, systems development and project management lifecycles)
- Using **functional specialisation**
- Using the **project objectives**
- Using **project deliverables**
- Using **past project information.**

Using lifecycles

From your knowledge of different systems development lifecycles you should be able to come up with a list of tasks that looks something like this (*Note that in this example* feasibility study *and* functional specification *have been omitted. Note also these tasks will have to be iterated through several times if you are using incremental or evolutionary delivery.*):

- Requirements specification
- System design
- Coding
- Testing
- Delivery to operations.

However, this list omits tasks that are not within the scope of systems development; for example, management lifecycle processes such as planning, and monitoring and controlling are missing. These also need to be factored into the workload of the project – and estimated, controlled and monitored.

Further thought about what happens over the course of a project's lifecycle can identify other likely main tasks including 'project documentation' and 'training users'. These, together with the management lifecycle additions, would give us the following slightly longer list:

- Planning
- Requirements specification
- System design
- Coding
- Testing
- Delivery to operations
- Project documentation
- Training users
- Monitoring and controlling.

Note that the different tasks (activities) do not necessarily have to happen in the given sequence, nor as discrete elements that do not overlap in time: for example, 'monitoring and controlling' should occur throughout the project.

Using functional specialisation

Starting with generic systems development and management lifecycles (as we have done in the example in the previous paragraphs) is likely to lead to missing out tasks that are specific to a particular project. An alternative approach to address this problem is to conduct the task breakdown on the basis of functional specialities. You can use *organisational roles* and *knowledge areas* to help you identify additional specific tasks.

- **Organisational roles:** for example, if you were building a house and needed different groups of experts, you could try to divide the tasks according to the different functional specialities. You could end up with a major branch dedicated to all the activities done by carpenters, another to plumbers, and another for surveyors, and so on. The focus in this case is not on precise timing and when tasks take place but rather on responsibility for the tasks: who 'owns' and completes each task. The carpenter could have some tasks that take place in the early stages of the project, as well as some tasks that come at the very end of the project
- **Knowledge areas:** we discussed the different project management knowledge areas in Chapter 1. They include such topics as project quality management, project integration management and project risk management. For example, if you considered project quality management, you might identify that a 'quality assurance' task needs adding to the task list that we were developing earlier in this section.

Using the project objectives

A third approach is to begin with each of your objectives for the project and to break each one down into its constituent parts, until you have all the tasks needed to successfully complete that objective. There are many advantages in following this approach as you maintain your focus on one objective at a time.

Using the project deliverables

From your knowledge of the different systems development lifecycles, you should be able to identify the necessary technical outputs (products/deliverables). However, for those tasks that are not covered by the systems development lifecycle, such as planning, monitoring and controlling, quality assurance, project documentation and training users, you will probably need to think more carefully. To give some examples, 'monitoring and controlling' deliverables are likely to include the contract, stage approval criteria and management progress reports. 'Quality assurance' products may include inspection reports, and user acceptance sign-offs and completed quality review forms. 'Training users' will require some form of documentation, such as online training manuals or paper documentation for a trainer to work from.

Using past project information

Yet another approach – assuming the information is available and relevant – is to look at old project plans and project feedback (that is, past experience: what actually happened) for similar projects. You can modify the given task lists to better suit your project. A major benefit of this approach is that (assuming the project documentation has been kept up to date) you know these task lists have been used for 'real' work.

Whichever task decomposition approach you adopt for your student project, you need to be consistent when you present your project plan (for example, you don't want to mix and match task breakdown by objective with task breakdown by organisational role – it would lead to overlaps). However, during the actual planning process (especially if you do not have much planning experience) it might be useful to briefly use *all* the approaches to check you have considered all aspects and issues, and to try to gain some additional insights.

The important thing is to ensure that you have listed all the key tasks and covered the scope of the project. For example, if the interface is an important part of the system being developed, you might want to have 'interface design' and 'software design' as two separate tasks, rather than simply having the more general task of 'system design'.

At this stage in the planning, it is acceptable to have the kind of high-level list of tasks shown above. Such a list will be broken down further when the WBS is developed, as described in the following section. You might find even at this stage that you have to start introducing hierarchical structure into your task list. This is fine; it is much better that you capture the detail as you think of it. And in fact, building a hierarchical structure is exactly what is needed (as we shall see in the next section).

Activity 5.1

Identify the project tasks

To get you to think about project planning in general terms, rather than focusing on the management of IT projects, the activities in this chapter require you to start preparing a project plan for a project to organise a party or family gathering.

To start this, write down a list of what you consider are the key tasks for organising a party or family gathering.

In order to identify additional tasks, try using the different approaches for identifying tasks. To recap, these approaches were as follows:

- Using lifecycles (for example, systems development and project management lifecycles) *In this activity, you'll be thinking about the lifecycle of planning a party!*

.../cont

- Using functional specialisation (organisational role and knowledge area)

- Using the project objectives

- Using the project deliverables

- Using past project information.

5.5 Create a work breakdown structure

A work breakdown structure (WBS) provides a breakdown of the project tasks in a hierarchical tree structure. The WBS for a project aims to identify all the tasks that need to be done to complete the project. It is a hierarchical structure where the smaller sub-tasks at a lower level in the hierarchy contribute to the completion of a larger task at a higher level.

A project manager uses a WBS for a project to establish the schedules and budgets for the accomplishment of the project work. To achieve this, the project manager has to estimate the amount of effort to be expended for each task, assign responsibility for each task to an identified organisational role and also provide information about the dependencies among the tasks. Project managers tend to view the WBS as the most important element of the project plan because it provides a framework for understanding the project.

An additional advantage of using a WBS is that many project management applications (such as MS Project) can restructure the WBS information: once the basic information for the WBS has been entered into them, they can then generate other charts (for example, a Gantt chart which we shall discuss later in this chapter).

Drawing up a WBS

To build a WBS, it is useful to start with a list of initial tasks (we discussed how to build such a list in the previous section). To obtain a hierarchical tree structure, each task has to be decomposed into lower-level sub-tasks. In turn, some of these sub-tasks may need further decomposition. This decomposition will continue until all the sub-tasks have been identified at their lowest level (that is, to the level where it is not appropriate or impossible to further decompose the sub-task). The aim is to get to a level where it is possible to estimate the effort required to complete the sub-task and where the sub-task can be assigned to one organisational role. This is known as a work package.

A general rule of thumb is that you should continue to break your project down into activities that take no less than 5% of your project's total duration. For example, there is little point in identifying activities that will take you less than a week to complete in a six-month project. If you do, you will be likely to waste time planning and controlling your project at too low a level and trying to keep your plan up to date as things change.

You must ensure that the tasks in the WBS are not repeated and do not overlap. If this happens, then you may be duplicating effort or your WBS may be incorrect.

A typical six-level WBS would consist of the following levels:

1 **Total programme** (that is, a collection of linked projects)
2 **Project**
3 **Task**
4 **Sub-task**
5 **Work package**
6 **Effort.**

The following information is needed to describe each work package:

- What work needs to be done
- Who is responsible for carrying out the work
- What deliverables and milestones will result
- Dependencies on other tasks
- Effort/duration (or start and completion dates)
- How the work is to be carried out (methods to be used)
- The hardware, software and tools required
- Any special skills required.

Once the project work is understood at this sort of level of detail it becomes easy to work bottom-up from each of the work packages and get the resource requirements, the number of people needed and even the costs needed to complete each activity. By working bottom-up it becomes possible to obtain the overall time effort and cost estimates for the entire project. The WBS has been adapted by many organisations to supply a cost breakdown structure (CBS), a risk breakdown structure (RBS) or a product breakdown structure (PBS), and can also help to create an organisation breakdown structure (OBS), required to underpin a project.

Based on your understanding of the different lifecycle approaches, you should be able to break down main tasks into smaller sub-tasks. Assume the following project tasks have been chosen: requirements specification, system design, coding, testing and delivery to operations. The requirements specification phase could be further subdivided into requirements capture and requirements analysis. The requirements capture phase could then be further subdivided into tasks such as interviews, observation and documentation. Testing could also be subdivided. The resulting WBS diagram for the project tasks should look like Figure 5.1.

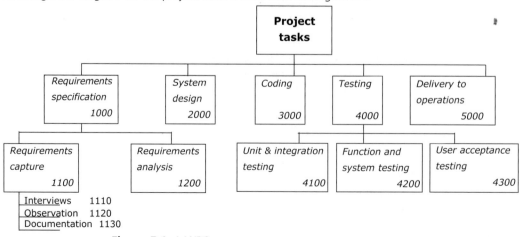

Figure 5.1: A WBS

As you can see the breakdown begins with a **project box**, or in this case a box explaining that this is the breakdown of the project tasks. It is then broken down into the main project tasks. The requirements specification task was then broken down further into two tasks, which are shown in the diagram. One of these tasks, requirements capture, is further broken down into three tasks. In addition, testing is broken down into three tasks.

We can refer to each box as a **node** in the diagram. The project box is sometimes referred to as the **root node**. Here is some other useful terminology for you:

- **Task:** a task is any node other than the root node
- **Sub-task:** a sub-task is any node that has a task as its parent
- **Terminal node:** a terminal node is any task that does not have any sub-tasks defined for it.

Note in Figure 5.1 the convention used to identify the lowest level of the WBS: the tasks are not drawn as boxes, but as lines. The fact that other terminal nodes are still drawn as boxes indicates they might still be decomposed further.

Another convention for identifying the lowest level tasks of the WBS is to place an underscore at the end of the task name, for example 'Documentation_'.

Numbering a WBS

One additional feature in Figure 5.1, that we have not discussed so far, is the numbering notation. Once you have completed the initial decomposition, you should start numbering your boxes. This is considered to be essential good practice because it provides a unique reference to each node (which is useful when you use the tasks elsewhere or when you refer to the diagram again in your subsequent cost calculations). It is very important to use a consistent approach for numbering tasks. As you can see in Figure 5.1, we have started by numbering the planning task or activity as 1000 and proceeded to number other tasks *at that level* as 2000, 3000, 4000, 5000, etc.

This enables us to go down a level and use 1100 and 1300 for the sub-tasks within the requirements specification task. Then 1110, 1120 and 1130 for the sub-tasks within requirements capture. If you were presented with a task numbered 1127, you would know that it has something to do with observation (1120), which takes place as part of the requirements capture task (1100), which is part of the requirements specification task (1000).

Remember to allow plenty of scope for potential tasks. Using 1000, 2000, 3000, etc. leaves plenty of free space for adding new tasks. (An alternative method of numbering is to refer to requirements specification as task 1.0 and then to system design as task 2.0. Requirements capture would then become task 1.1, and so on.)

Some organisations refrain from using diagrammatic notations for the WBS and simply rely on using the numbers and the names in outline format. The same WBS as in Figure 5.1 would therefore become:

> 1000 Requirements specification
>> 1100 Requirements capture
>>> 1110 Interviews
>>> 1120 Observation
>>> 1130 Documentation
>> 1200 Requirements analysis
> 2000 System design

3000 Coding

4000 Testing

    4100 Unit & integration testing

    4200 Function & system testing

    4300 User acceptance testing

5000 Delivery to operations

Generally, it is recommended that you use a more pictorial notation, as it allows you to gain a good grasp of the project task structure by simply analysing the diagram.

As you can see, the WBS provides a useful picture of the tasks that need to be completed within a project. The diagram gives the project manager the ability to uniquely identify each task or activity and to observe how all the tasks fit together.

It is likely that you will need a number of attempts on paper until you can refine a WBS. This is normal. Project managers draw many versions of diagrams until they are satisfied with the outcome. Do take the time to make sure that you have included all the tasks.

Purposes of a WBS

A good WBS is likely to be straightforward and easy to comprehend with familiar task names. It will have independent and measurable lowest-level sub-tasks.

A good WBS helps the project manager to do the following:

- Gain an overview of the total project
- Perform detailed task planning
- Group related tasks
- Allocate tasks to particular organisational roles
- Estimate the required effort and time
- Estimate the costs associated with each lowest-level sub-task
- Estimate the overall budget
- Allocate resources
- Link objectives to resources
- Track time, cost, responsibilities and performance
- Obtain the basis for producing other forms of diagrams.

Activity 5.2

Create a WBS

In Activity 5.1, you produced a list of tasks for a project to organise a party. Now break this down to produce a WBS that is composed of several levels (at least three levels). Do not worry if you do not manage to break down all the tasks to this level of detail, but try to do it for at least some of them.

5.6 Identify the milestones

Once a WBS has been produced for a project, there is a structured list of all the tasks that need to be completed. Looking at these identified tasks, there will be certain tasks concerned with producing a deliverable, which significantly contributes to the project's progress – for example, the completion of the system design task, which produces the system design documentation, or the conclusion of the user acceptance testing, which produces a user acceptance testing report. We refer to the completion of such tasks as 'milestones' in a project. Milestones are events rather than tasks; they occur after a task has successfully completed. By identifying the milestones, you will be able to monitor and measure your progress towards completing a project.

Some milestones can be described as 'formal' and others as 'informal'. Informal milestones are internal to the project team – that is, only the project team recognises them as significant. Formal milestones involve the customer and tend to require sign-off. Project funding is often tied to milestone achievement and there can be bonuses or penalties involved depending on whether a milestone is reached 'on schedule'.

Activity 5.3

Identify the milestones

What do you think are the key milestones for the party project? Identify them and state the deliverables that you expect on reaching each of them.

5.7 Estimate effort/duration of each task

A project manager has to calculate the amount of effort required to complete a project. The usual way to do this is to take a bottom-up approach and calculate the required effort task by task. Effort is measured in person-time units, say, person-hours or person-days. Therefore, 'effort' is also referred to as 'task duration' or simply 'duration'. This refers to the amount of time that is needed to complete a particular task. It is not the same as elapsed time for a task, which measures the amount of time that elapses between starting a task and finishing it.

You can draw up an effort estimation table (EET) using your WBS. See Table 5.2.

Task	Effort/Duration (Days)	Accumulated Effort
Project ABC		9+2+3+5+1=20
Requirements specification		2+7=9
Requirements capture		3+2+2=7
Interviews_	3	3
Observation_	2	2
Documentation_	2	2
Requirements analysis_	2	2
System design_	2	2
Coding_	3	3
Testing		2+2+1= 5
Unit & integration testing_	2	2
Function & system testing_	2	2
User acceptance testing_	1	1
Delivery to operations_	1	1

Table 5.2: An effort estimation table

5.8 Identify the resources required for each task

In order to estimate the *task schedule*, the *cost schedule* and the *total project budget*, account has to be taken of the *type* of resources needed, the *quantity* of resources needed and *resource availability*. From a description of a task, the types of resources can be identified. From its estimated effort, the quantity of resources to complete the task can be calculated. From this resource requirement information, the costs can be determined if the rates of pay for the different roles are known. Resource availability can also become a factor if scarce resources are required.

Let's just clarify what is meant by the term 'resources'. A project's resources include any people, equipment, facilities, services and materials that a project needs to utilise in order to carry out the project tasks. For example, software and hardware, books, office space and cars assigned to the project are all resources. The project team members (the project management, the technical project team members and any administrative staff) are usually the key resources required for a project.

In the next section, we are going to consider the resource allocation of the project team members. Note there might be situations where some of the other types of resource have also to be allocated and scheduled because they impose some resource constraints; for example, a specialist piece of test hardware equipment might have to be scheduled as it might be needed at several locations – but could only be in one place at any one time.

5.9 Create the project schedule

We are now at the stage when we can start to assemble the tasks into a schedule. We shall discuss how to achieve this in this section.

Establishing task dependencies

Some tasks are independent – they have to be done, but it does not matter very much when you start them or in what order they are done. Others are interdependent. By this, we mean that you cannot begin one until you have finished one or more preceding tasks. For example, if you look at Figure 5.1, the task 'Requirements analysis' should probably only start after 'Requirements capture' has been completed. Therefore, there needs to be some sequencing of the various tasks. This can be documented in what is referred to as an 'activity network'.

Activity network diagrams

An activity network diagram shows the sequencing relationships among tasks. Project managers use activity networks to schedule multiple tasks simultaneously and to calculate the risks and other effects of any delays, which may occur in any given task.

There are two types of activity network diagrams:

- **Activity-on-Node (AoN)** diagrams
- **Activity-on-Arrow (AoA)** diagrams.

We will explore both types of network diagram. Let's first discuss AoN diagrams; we'll return to discuss AoA later.

Activity-on-Node diagrams

Activity-on-Node (AoN) diagrams attempt to represent the project schedule by mapping the different activities or tasks and their relationships. Each activity or task appears in a box (called a node) as shown in Figure 5.2.

- In the centre of the box, the task name is written.
- In the top left-hand corner, you write the earliest possible start day.
- In the bottom left-hand corner, you write the latest possible start day.
- In the top right-hand corner, you write the expected duration of the task.
- Finally, in the bottom right-hand corner, you write what is called the 'slack'.

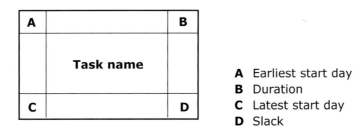

Figure 5.2: A Node in an Activity-on-Node diagram

You start at the beginning of your task list and you are only interested in the lowest-level tasks (that is, the tasks that have no other task beneath them – note that these tasks can be at differing levels of the WBS). The first task should be one, which does not depend on any task being completed beforehand, such as 'Interviews' in the WBS we looked at earlier (see Figure 5.1). This first task is referred to as the starting node.

You then continue through your task list, creating a node for each task. When you come across a task that cannot be started until another task has been completed, you link those tasks together with an arrow. For example, you might consider you cannot begin a 'Literature review' until a 'Literature search' has been completed. See Figure 5.3, which shows how you would then link these two task nodes.

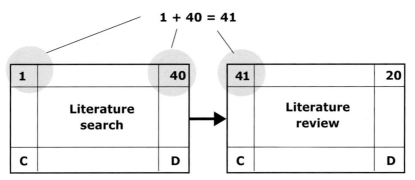

Figure 5.3: Linked nodes

Can you see, in Figure 5.3, how linking the boxes together helps you to establish what should be entered for the subsequent node in its top left-hand box, which represents its start date? If your 'Literature search' begins on Day 1 and is expected to take 40 days, then the subsequent 'Literature review' cannot begin until Day 41. You can continue like this, adding the A and B of each node to calculate the A of the next node until all the tasks in that sequence of related tasks have been added to the network.

Note that the entries for A, B, C and D in Figure 5.2 are the number of project days rather than actual dates. This is because you are only concerned with the project working days, and you don't include weekends and public holidays. In industry, projects typically work a five-day week! Remember also that employees have time allocated for their holidays, training and other non-project tasks.

When you come across a task that is not dependent on the completion of any other tasks beforehand, you can start to create a new sequence. Its Earliest Start Day must be Day 1, just as with the 'Literature search' in Figure 5.3.

We say that a task has multiple dependencies if two or more tasks in separate sequences must be completed before that particular task can be started. In that case, it should have arrows linking it to all the tasks on which it is dependent. Its Earliest Start Day is the largest number that you get when you add the Earliest Start Day and Duration for each of the tasks on which it is dependent. For example, in Figure 5.4 you see that 'Coding' is dependent on 'System design' *and* 'Interface design'. Just looking at 'System design', the Earliest Start Day for 'Coding' is 70 (60+10). Just looking at 'Interface design', the Earliest Start Day for 'Coding' is 65 (60+5). We take the larger of these two totals (because both tasks have to be completed before this task can commence), so the Earliest Start Day for 'Coding' is in fact Day 70.

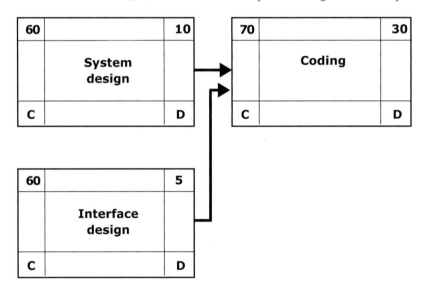

Figure 5.4: Multiple dependencies

You can continue adding nodes in this way until all the tasks appear on the network. When you come to a milestone, enter it on the network inside a circle (see Figure 5.5).

Milestones do not have any duration, so any nodes following a milestone should have an Earliest Start Day based on the completion day for the latest node before the milestone.

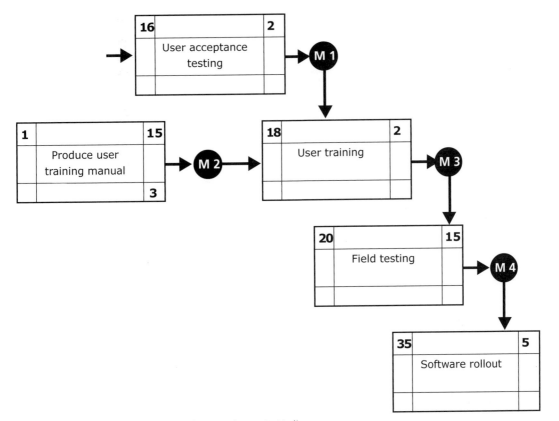

Figure 5.5: Depicting a milestone in an AoN diagram

So far, we have only been completing the top left-hand box and the top right-hand box for each node. The bottom left-hand corner, used for recording the Latest Possible Start Day, we have left blank. Similarly, the bottom right-hand corner, used for recording the 'slack', has also been left blank.

To calculate the Latest Possible Start Day and the slack for each node, we have to start by working backwards from the last node in the network. Make the latest possible start day for this node equal to the Earliest Possible Start Day. You can then work backwards through the network, calculating the Latest Possible Start Day by subtracting the duration of the node from the Latest Possible Start Day of the succeeding node (see Figure 5.6).

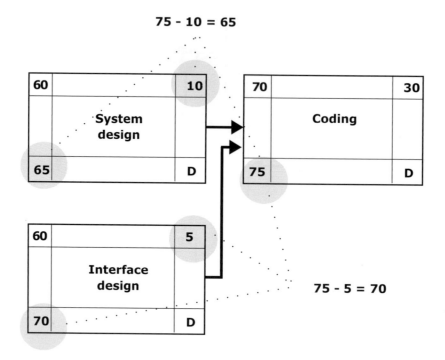

Figure 5.6: Calculating the *Latest Start Day*

The 'slack' value recorded in the bottom right-hand corner refers to the number of days that that particular task can 'slip' – the number of days it can be delayed in starting or the number of extra days that can be spent on that task without the overall deadline for the project being affected. The slack for each node is calculated by subtracting the Earliest Possible Start Day for that node from the Latest Possible Start Day for that node (see Figure 5.7).

We stated at the beginning of this section that project managers use activity networks to manage multiple tasks simultaneously and to calculate the risks and other effects of delays, which occur in any given task. If you are doing a project on your own, it is not really possible to do several tasks simultaneously, although you may chose to swap between several tasks. If your progress on one task is blocked, or if you finish a task earlier than expected, you can start working on another one, which is scheduled for later, provided that any earlier dependencies have been resolved.

Note that some books use a variation of the Activity-on-Node network called Precedence Charts (or Dependency Charts) where more sophisticated types of dependencies are allowed between the start and finishing dates of the various activities.

It is also worth noting that some AoN notations may include more information in the basic node box.

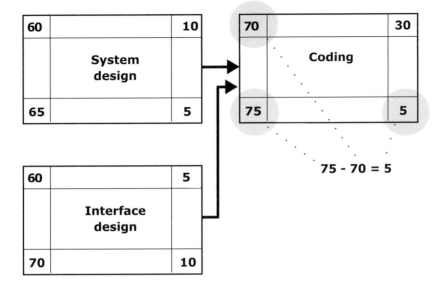

Figure 5.7: Calculating the 'slack'

Create an AoN diagram

Create an Activity-on-Network (AoN) diagram for the example party project you started earlier.

Start by creating nodes for each task, sequence them and enter the Earliest Possible Start Day and the duration. Once you have completed the network, work backwards to calculate the Latest Possible Start Day and the slack for each node. You can either draw your AoN diagram by hand or use a computer application to produce it.

Activity-on-Arrow diagrams

Now let's discuss the other type of activity network diagram, the Activity-on-Arrow (AoA) diagram.

In Activity-on-Arrow (AoA) diagrams, the roles of the node and the arrow are reversed so that the arrow represents the activity that is taking place and the node provides the linking point between activities. Each activity starts and finishes at a node.

Each node represents an event, a point of zero time duration, which signifies the completion of all the activities leading into that node and the start of all activities spanning out from that node.

A node (represented here as a circle) has three sectors:

- The left sector is a unique node identifier
- The top right sector gives the finishing time for the previous activities and therefore also the start time (E) for the following activity

- The bottom right sector contains the latest finish time (L) of the activities terminating in that node and the latest start time for any activities beginning with this node (when there is any slack available).

Where there is no slack, the top and bottom figures are likely to be identical. See figure 5.8 for an example of an AoA node. Note that all the times for E and L are calculated in days.

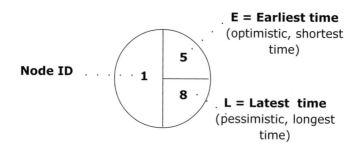

Figure 5.8: An example of an AoA Node

Activities are the straight lines connecting the circles (nodes). An activity is depicted by drawing a named arrow connecting two nodes (used as the start and end points for the activity). Activities have a duration, which is typically depicted below the line (see Figure 5.9).

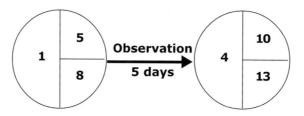

Figure 5.9: An example of an AoA diagram

Once you start adding activities linked through nodes, you begin to form chains (see Figure 5.10. Note that the earliest time and latest time information has been omitted from this and subsequent AoA diagrams).

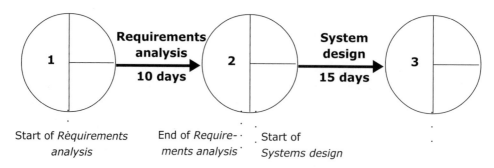

Figure 5.10: An example of an AoA chain

Activities follow one another to form task sequences. One of the most common patterns is branching. This occurs when the completion of one activity is followed by the beginning of two others. As shown in Figure 5.11, activities B and C can only begin following the completion of activity A.

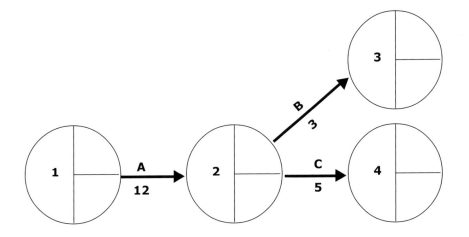

Figure 5.11: Branching

Another common pattern is that of merging, or joining. In merging, the start of one task depends upon the completion of all predecessor activities. In our example, Figure 5.12, F can only begin once both D and E have been completed.

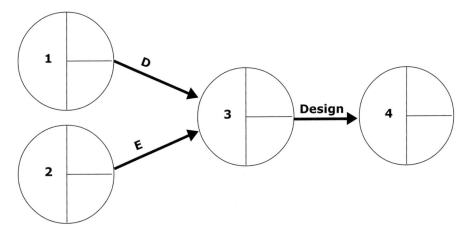

Figure 5.12: Merging

In AoA diagrams, the flow progresses from left to right. Nodes are also numbered from left to right and from top to bottom. (The convention is that an activity arrow must always go from a lower-numbered sending node to a higher-numbered receiving node – the arrow head being at the higher numbered node.) Each activity can be identified by its name or by a unique pair of nodes between which it resides. So in Figure 5.12 the activity F can also be identified as 3-4 (as it resides between node 3 and node 4). This implies that any two nodes can only have a single activity between them. Note that the two nodes between which an activity resides must be numbered in ascending order. This means that activities 1-3 or 7-15 are acceptable but you could not have an activity going down in numeric order, such as 4-3.

When two activities take place in parallel, you will need to distinguish between them by creating a dummy node so that each can be uniquely identified. A good example of such a situation in a computing context could be if, following a detailed design, you had the activities of develop hardware and develop software running in parallel and you had to uniquely identify them. Dummy activities are shown as discontinuous arrows indicating a dependency without duration, because they do not consume real time and resources. They are particularly useful for distinguishing between two activities that occur in parallel, but may also be used to improve sequencing of tasks or to tidy up the logic of AoA network diagrams. An example is shown in Figure 5.13.

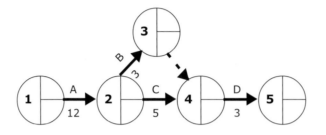

Figure 5.13: Dummy nodes

In Figure 5.13, activities B and C both begin after the completion of activity A. Activity D depends on the completion of both B and C. In order to distinguish between the two activities, which would otherwise both be identified as 2-4, we drew an additional node (3) with a dummy activity connecting it to 4. We now have two unique activities 2-3 (activity B) and 2-4 (activity C). Adding the dummy activity preserves the basic logic of the diagram.

The sequencing of tasks takes into account the components that need to be completed before the next task can begin. For example, a sequential lifecycle, such as the waterfall model, would have direct dependencies between activities, connecting each activity to its predecessor.

Multiple starts and finishes

As a matter of convention, multiple starts ought to be avoided to avoid confusion. We use a unique starting node by adding a start node numbered zero, with dummy activities to all the nodes that can start immediately. Similarly, it is accepted convention to ensure that there is a single final termination node. In this case the final end node is used – you do not create a new end node. See Figure 5.14.

Dangles

Dangling events are nodes appearing without at least one preceding activity and one succeeding activity. They contradict the overall logic of the network and must be corrected. If you are faced with such a situation, you may use dummy activities to correct dangles.

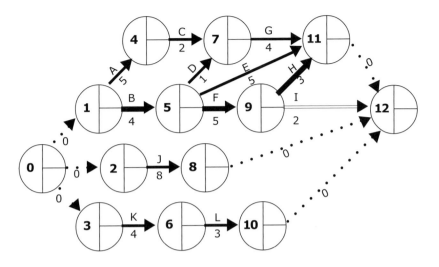

Figure 5.14: Shows the convention for having a unique start node and a single termination node

Create an AoA diagram

Create an Activity-on-Arrow (AoA) diagram for the party project. You can either draw your AoA diagram by hand or use a computer application to produce it.

Identify the critical path

One of the most beneficial aspects of activity networks, from a manager's perspective, is that they allow us to identify critical paths. Any task on the critical path, which becomes delayed will result in a delay for the whole project (unless additional effort is now used to try to reduce the duration of other tasks on that path). The critical path represents the longest sequential chain of activities, which determines the minimum time to delivery. It is one of the most crucial concepts in project management, as it has a great impact on the overall project.

Activities that are not on the critical path can be delayed (a little) according to how much slack they have without affecting the overall duration of the project.

Establishing the critical path for AoN diagrams

So, how do activity networks help us to identify the critical path for a project? The description of AoN diagrams earlier in this chapter left out an important final stage. On an AoN diagram, any two connected nodes with zero slack should be joined with a double-lined arrow, as shown in Figure 5.15. When you develop the AoN diagram for your project, you will find that there is at least one path from the beginning node to the final milestone that is entirely connected by double-lined arrows. This is the project's critical path.

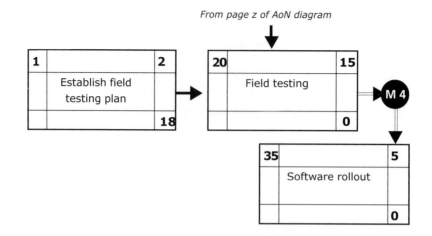

Figure 5.15: How a critical path is represented in an AoN diagram. Double arrows show the critical path.

Establishing the critical path for AoA diagrams

To use AoA diagrams to calculate the critical path, we need to calculate the duration of each possible path through the network and determine which is the longest path from beginning to completion. The longest path is the critical path.

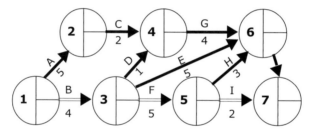

Figure 5.16: An example of an AoA showing information to enable calculation of the critical path

For example, if we wanted to identify the critical path for the AoA diagram in Figure 5.16, the first step would be to list the different paths and to calculate their overall path duration by adding up the duration of each activity on that path. This would give us the following table:

Path	Duration
A, C, G	11
B, D, G	9
B, E	9
B, F, H	12
B, F, I, (Dummy)	11

Table 5.3: Path duration table for Figure 5.16

The critical path is the path B—F—H as this path takes the longest to complete. It affects the overall completion date for the project, as any delay to activities along this path will delay the entire project. We can identify the critical path on the diagram as shown in Figure 5.17.

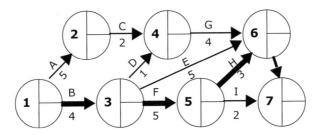

Figure 5.17: The AoA diagram with the critical path identified

Note the network is not subject to resource constraints. The final duration does not make any assumptions about the availability of resources. Even if only one person is available, non-dependent tasks should be drawn in parallel. You, therefore, are assuming that any number of people will be available to complete the tasks. In other words, the network diagram is logical and not a physical tool. We shall handle resource constraints later in this section when we discuss resource allocation.

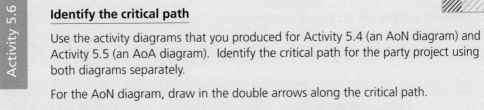

Activity 5.6

Identify the critical path

Use the activity diagrams that you produced for Activity 5.4 (an AoN diagram) and Activity 5.5 (an AoA diagram). Identify the critical path for the party project using both diagrams separately.

For the AoN diagram, draw in the double arrows along the critical path.

For the AoA diagram, you should create a table like Table 5.3.

Examine the task scheduling

Once you have the initial critical path, you can examine the activity network to see if you can make any improvements. If any contractual dates were threatened, you would certainly be looking to see if there was anything you could do. Questions you can consider include:

- Can any activities/tasks be eliminated?
- Would software reuse or components off-the-shelf (COTS) help?
- Are the estimates for the task durations reasonable?
- Is there a reasonable balance in the distribution of time among the project tasks? For example, how does your time distribution match with industry recommendations for time distribution? What percentage of the project time is, say, being spent on requirements?
- Could some tasks be run concurrently?

In addition, you must look at the critical path and ask:

- Where are the risks in the critical path and the activity network generally?

There are probably certain tasks that you can identify that you will have to monitor more closely: for example, you are more uncertain of the accuracy of your estimated task duration, you are not certain that the project has sufficient experience to complete the task 'on-time' or you know the task is attempting something new that might not work as you expect.

You might decide to build in some extra time. This could be done by scheduling differently or by adding in extra time as contingency. If the consequences of not meeting a deadline on time are large and costly, then it is worth planning some 'breathing space'.

You should make any adjustments, but take care to make only reasonable ones (tasks must be capable of completion in their allocated timescales and no essential tasks must be cut), and then re-examine the critical path. You will probably iterate making adjustments and re-examining the critical path a few times. Remember to check the critical path is still the same set of tasks, as your adjustments could have altered it.

Allocate resources

The next step is to allocate the resources to the tasks. As we discussed earlier, typically this means assigning the project team members. So we need to look at each task in turn and identify a project team member with the appropriate skills to be responsible for it. Only when you have taken into account resource allocation and understood staff availability will you be able to determine your project's total duration.

Let's illustrate this by an example. Let's assume for simplicity that work is allocated in whole days (not hours) and that the staff work whole days. We'll ignore calendar time for the time being and just work with durations.

Say you had a list of tasks, task durations and task precedence information about a project as shown in Table 5.4.

Task	Task ident	Resource required	Task duration	Task precedence	Earliest Start Day	Latest Start Day	Slack
Requirements specification	R	Systems Analyst	5	-	1	1	0
System design	SD	System Designer	3	After R	6	6	0
Interface design	ID	Interface Designer	1	After SD	9	9	0
Test design	TD	Test Designer	2	After SD	9	13	4
SQL	SQL	SQL Programmer	2	After SD	9	13	4
Application coding	C	Programmer	5	After ID	10	10	0
Unit testing	T1	Tester	1	After C	15	15	0
System testing	T2	Tester	1	After T1	16	16	0
User acceptance testing	T3	Tester & User	1	After T2	17	17	0
User manual	M	Writer	4	After ID	10	14	4
Delivery	D	Programmer & Systems Support	2	After T3	18 *	18	0

Table 5.4: Precedence table showing tasks, duration and precedence information

For the entire project, this would result in a resource loading chart over time in days as shown in Figure 5.18.

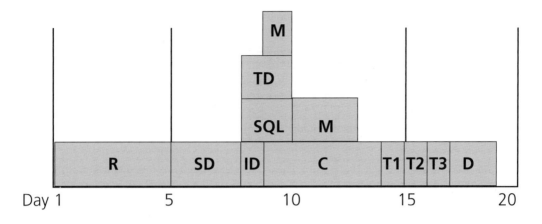

Figure 5.18: Total resource loading chart for the project

Figure 5.18 fails to take into account the different skills needed. However, what we can say from this resource loading chart, is that it looks as if two staff would suffice – providing they had the appropriate skills needed. Say you had two project team members: Omar who was able to write the user requirements, do some SQL coding, carry out the testing and write the user manual, and Jane who was able to design, write the code required, and install it on the customer site. That would give the possibility of resource allocation as shown in Figure 5.19.

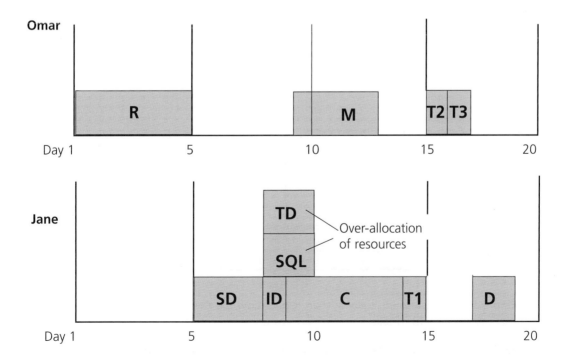

Figure 5.19: Initial resource loading chart for each team member showing resource over-allocation for Jane

At this point you need to consider resource over-allocation or under-allocation. Under-allocation might mean you were at times paying for staff who had no allocated work.

Over-allocation occurs when any resource is assigned more work than they have project hours to do it. Note that this is not a matter of being assigned to more than one task at any one time. For example, you can be carrying out your literature survey and doing some initial program design, and you can interchange from working on one to working on the other. That's fine. The over-allocation problem occurs when in a given week you have 20 hours allocated to the literature survey, 30 hours allocated to the program design and you have specified a working week of only 37 hours. The extra 13 hours of time for this work has to be found somewhere. In this example, you can see that Jane is clearly over-allocated – she can't do three tasks at once! (Remember the earlier assumption, we made to allocate tasks in whole days.)

Now you have to look to see if there is any slack in the task schedule so you can smooth the resource allocation. For Jane's tasks there is no slack for system design (SD), interface design (ID) and application coding (C). There is some slack for testing design (TD) and SQL (SQL). However, clearly Jane can't do these extra tasks and it's no good considering swapping these tasks with ID as ID is only of one day's duration. So let's look at Omar's tasks. Writing the user manual (M) has some slack, but insufficient to allow Omar to schedule both testing design (TD) and writing the SQL (SQL). However, thinking about the task of writing the user manual, it could be started earlier – there is nothing to stop the writing of the introduction and design of the layout once the requirements are known. So you would adjust your task start date or split the task into two parts, one with an earlier start day of Day 8. This would give the situation shown in Figure 5.20.

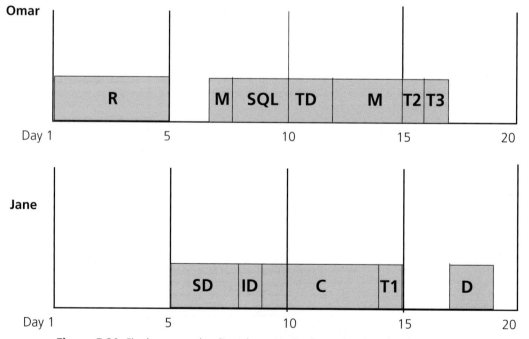

Figure 5.20: Final resource loading chart. Notice how the days for the task of writing the user manual have been split.

Note that what we have done in this example is to keep the total project duration fixed – the project still ends after the same number of days – and we have tried to utilise the slack time. Fortunately, we could smooth the resources here without bringing in extra resources.

The APM defines **resource smoothing** as the

> '...scheduling of activities, within the limits of their float, so that fluctuations in individual resource requirements are minimised. (In smoothing, as opposed to resource levelling, the project completion date may not be delayed.)' (**www.apm.org.uk/RtoT.asp/**)

The alternative approach would be to adjust the project duration – alter the project completion time if need be – and just schedule people against their availability.

The Association of Project Management (APM) defines **resource levelling** as the

> '... scheduling of activities so that predetermined resource levels are never exceeded. Note: this may cause the minimum overall or specified project duration to be exceeded.' (**www.apm.org.uk/RtoT.asp/**)

For a student project, there is a fixed deadline for project completion and so resource smoothing is the appropriate method to use.

Set project time data (start date and weekly hours for resources)

In order to be able to map the schedule onto calendar time you need to set the project start date and the weekly hours or days that the project team members work, say 37.5 hours or 5 days respectively. You will probably have to adjust for some staff for part-time allocation to work on the project (say three days out of the five days a week).

For simplicity it can be assumed that a month consists of exactly four weeks and there are no breaks in the project for holidays. However, in reality, holidays, sickness, or other work can often occur and need to be considered when forming project plans.

(*Note: if you are using a project management application, such as MS Project, you will enter this time data at an earlier point in the planning process.*)

Establish project completion date

At this point you have (or you can work out) your estimated project completion date. This date needs to be compared to any expected or contractual project completion date (if there are several staged contractual dates then you will have to examine each of them in turn). If your estimated completion date means the project is to be completed too late, then you need to consider:

- Could extra resources help? (For example, extra programming staff?)
- Could some tasks be shortened if more experienced staff were used?
- Would it improve matters if there were better technology to help staff?

Make any adjustments you think appropriate and then examine the revised estimated project completion date. (For your individual student project you can't add extra project team members!)

If you are not happy with the project completion date, then you are going to have to redefine your project (expanding or reducing its scope) and then re-plan it. Such change requires negotiation with your customer (or, if a student project, with your supervisor).

Establish cost schedule

Once you know the task schedule, you can work out what resources you need and when. For example, you will know how many project staff you need and which weeks you will need them. (You will have to consider how you are going to handle any contingency, say if tasks overrun. You might have in-built some contingency already into your schedule.) If you know the resources, then you can work out the costs involved and see how they vary over time. This enables you to draw up a cost schedule. We'll return to the subject of project costs in the next chapter.

Get customer approval and project team members' agreement to the schedule

If you are happy with the project completion date, then the next step is to discuss your task and cost schedules, and total project budget with the appropriate customer staff. Are they happy with the schedules or can they see any problems with them? Is the total budget OK? Once you have checked with the customer and all is well, then you need to discuss the task schedule individually with each of your project team members. It is an important step to get their agreement in advance to their workload and they might spot problems you have overlooked. (Of course you can also discuss any major concerns you have with the project team earlier as you are planning the schedule! A formal meeting to explain what you have finally decided is still essential.)

5.10 Gantt charts

Creating a Gantt chart using MS Project is an excellent way of presenting your project plans. Gantt charts are simple to understand and easy to construct. Because of this, they are used by most project managers. Gantt charts are similar to activity networks in that they attempt to represent a project in diagrammatical form. However, while activity networks show explicitly the relationships among tasks, Gantt charts show explicitly the durations of activities and identify instances where tasks are performed simultaneously – Gantt charts plot the activities/tasks against calendar dates. A further benefit is that 'adjusted Gantt charts' can show project progress – we'll discuss this later.

Figure 5.21 shows an example of a Gantt chart, which represents the WBS shown in Figure 5.1.

- Durations have been estimated and input, and several milestones have been identified (see diamond shapes)
- The task boxes show the task durations against calendar time
- The thick black lines with downward pointing arrowheads are summary tasks that are shown unexpanded. The arrows between task boxes show dependencies
- Only one person is working on this project, hence there is no scheduled parallel working.

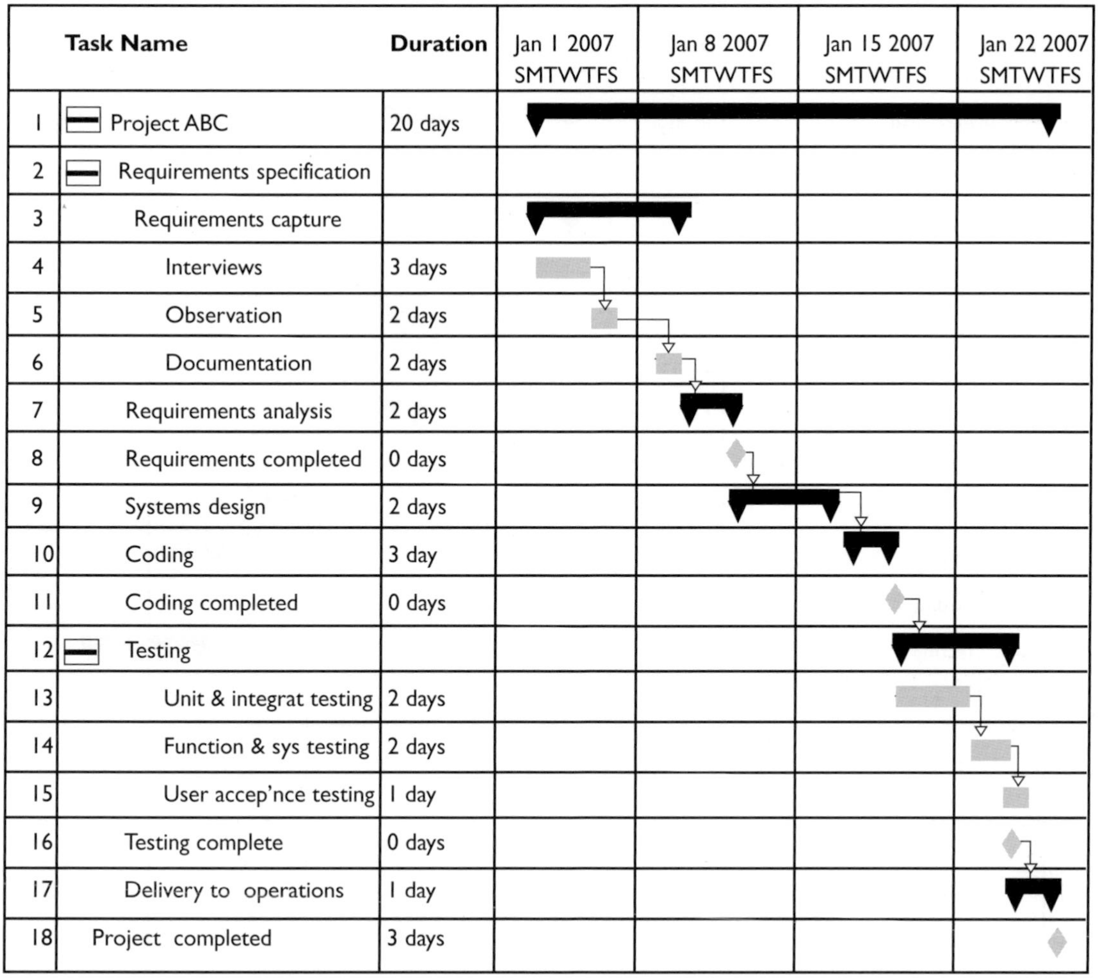

Task Name	Duration	Jan 1 2007 SMTWTFS	Jan 8 2007 SMTWTFS	Jan 15 2007 SMTWTFS	Jan 22 2007 SMTWTFS
1 Project ABC	20 days				
2 Requirements specification					
3 Requirements capture					
4 Interviews	3 days				
5 Observation	2 days				
6 Documentation	2 days				
7 Requirements analysis	2 days				
8 Requirements completed	0 days				
9 Systems design	2 days				
10 Coding	3 day				
11 Coding completed	0 days				
12 Testing					
13 Unit & integrat testing	2 days				
14 Function & sys testing	2 days				
15 User accep'nce testing	1 day				
16 Testing complete	0 days				
17 Delivery to operations	1 day				
18 Project completed	3 days				

Figure 5.21: Example of a Gantt chart

If information is input on a regular basis about project progress (percentage completed) then applications such as MS Project can display the completed amounts in the task boxes by shading in the appropriate proportion of each task box. This is best shown when activities have been completed as there can be no doubt that the activity is 100% complete. Such a chart, as shown in Figure 5.22, is known as an adjusted Gantt chart. You can then check if you are on schedule or not. (Note that you can also create time-scaled network diagrams for a similar purpose.)

Why don't you try creating a Gantt chart using MS Project? You could use the information given in Table 5.4 to get started.

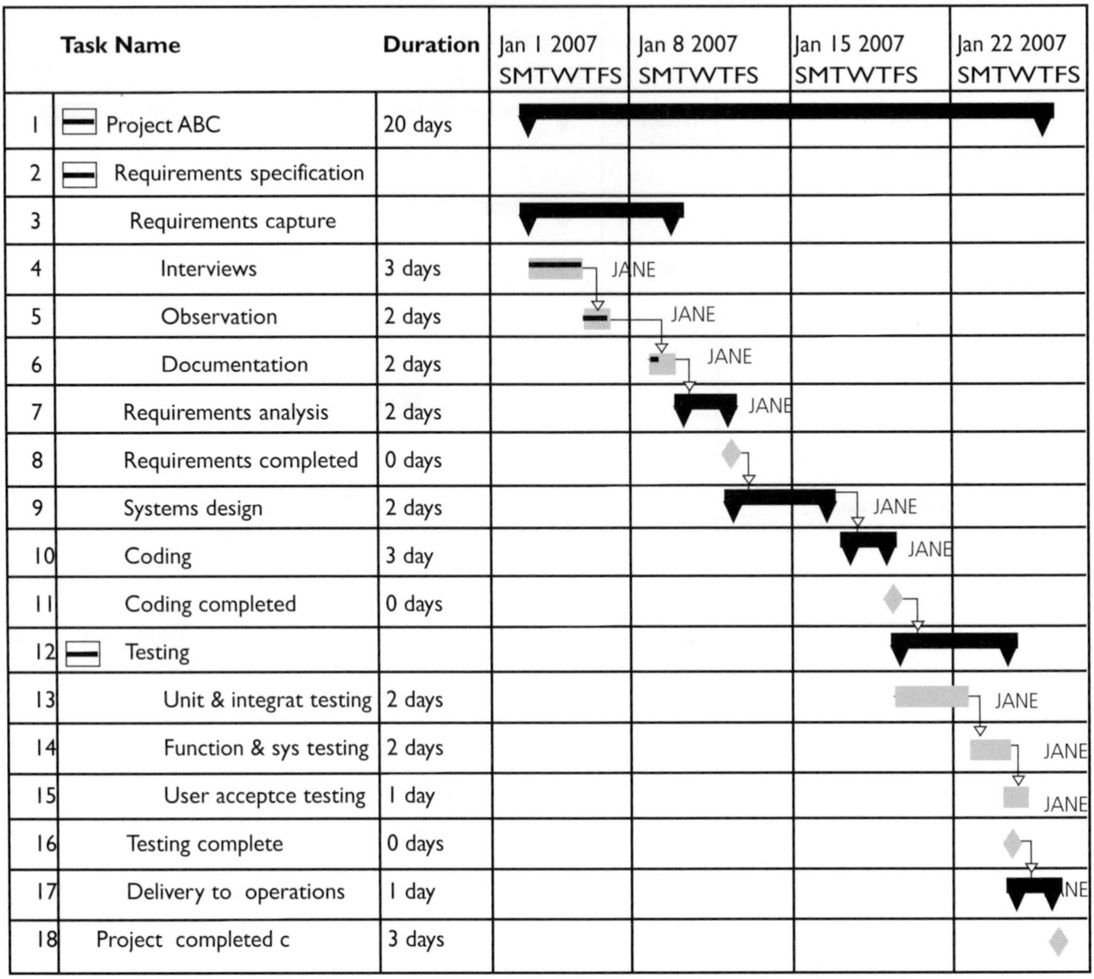

	Task Name	Duration	Jan 1 2007 SMTWTFS	Jan 8 2007 SMTWTFS	Jan 15 2007 SMTWTFS	Jan 22 2007 SMTWTFS
1	Project ABC	20 days				
2	Requirements specification					
3	Requirements capture					
4	Interviews	3 days	JANE			
5	Observation	2 days	JANE			
6	Documentation	2 days	JANE			
7	Requirements analysis	2 days	JANE			
8	Requirements completed	0 days				
9	Systems design	2 days		JANE		
10	Coding	3 day		JANE		
11	Coding completed	0 days				
12	Testing					
13	Unit & integrat testing	2 days			JANE	
14	Function & sys testing	2 days			JANE	
15	User acceptce testing	1 day			JANE	
16	Testing complete	0 days				
17	Delivery to operations	1 day				NE
18	Project completed c	3 days				

Figure 5.22: Adjusted Gantt chart showing project progress – after six days' work, the documentation task is half completed – the project is 'on track'. Note also the resource allocation of one project team member – Jane.

5.11 Use of project planning tools and project management applications

We discuss three project planning tools in this book: Gantt charts, activity networks (both described in this chapter) and cost estimation (described in the next chapter, 'Project planning II: cost management'). In this section, we are going to 'take some time out' from project planning and think about some background theory: we consider why it is that we use such planning tools.

To begin with, it is useful to think about the different information that different planning tools provide us with, or allow us to represent. This is summarised in Table 5.5.

Planning tool	Project scheduling information
Gantt chart	Task breakdowns; duration; start date; finish date; dependencies between tasks; milestones
Activity networks	Dependencies between tasks; earliest possible start date, latest possible start date; duration; slack; critical path
Cost estimation	Number of days' effort and cost required for each task

Table 5.5: Planning tools and project scheduling information

To summarise the benefits of each of these planning tools:

- **Gantt charts** allow us to calculate the duration of projects, to track their progress, and provide an easy-to-understand representation of what needs to be done and when
- **Activity networks** help us to identify dependencies between tasks, identify a project's critical path, and identify tasks where there is any slack. Table 5.6 lists the uses and advantages of using AoN and AoA network diagrams
- **Cost estimation** allows us to work out how many people-hours (the effort) a project will take, in turn allowing managers to calculate the number of people required for a project to be completed on time. From the effort information, the cost can be calculated by using the appropriate payment rates.

AoN network diagrams	AoA network diagrams
Uses: - Is used more typically in computing - Is utilised in project management software applications *Advantages:* - All the required information about an activity appears in one box - Allows a greater variety of links and various types of dependencies (for example finish-to-start lag) - Does not require dummy activities (and so keeps the number of activities to the real number)	*Uses:* - Is used in engineering and construction *Advantages:* - There's a logical resemblance to a bar chart - Events are explicitly shown - Easier to check calculations manually - Easier to find critical path - Can be adjusted to show passage of time - Better at representing relationships with multiple precedents - Dummy activities can be used to simplify complex project interactions

Table 5.6: Uses and advantages of AoN and AoA network diagrams.

In many cases, the planning tool itself does not provide us with the information, but it provides us with a structure to think about the information and to calculate some of the information. For example, with activity networks, you have to work out for yourself where there are dependencies among tasks, and the tool provides you with a way of representing that information. You also have to work out for yourself the duration of each task and the initial start date for the project. Once you have done that, the representation helps you to work out the Earliest Possible Start Date for later tasks, the Latest Possible Start Dates, and the slack.

Project management applications automating these tools can provide considerable support to help you with your project planning. For example, when you were developing your activity networks by hand, you had to calculate all the information yourself. In contrast, if you use, say

MS Project (to produce a Gantt chart), the application calculates a lot of the information for you, such as the start dates and finish dates for tasks. The benefit of such an application becomes even more apparent when you have to make changes: an application can cascade the impact of a change throughout your plan and make the necessary updates to the project information. This not only saves you time, it allows you to input 'what if' ideas and to get rapid feedback about the consequences.

5.12 Planning your student project

You should now be ready to start planning your student project. To recap on the planning process given at the start of this chapter:

- Develop a statement of work (SOW)
- Identify the project tasks
- Create a WBS
- Identify the milestones
- Estimate effort/duration of each task
- Identify the resources required for each task
- Create the project schedule:
  - establish task dependencies
  - identify the critical path
  - examine the task scheduling
  - allocate resources
  - set project time data
  - establish project completion date
  - establish the cost schedule
  - get customer approval and project team members' agreement to the schedule.

It is probably best to start off using pencil and paper and list out your tasks. At some stage, you will want to start inputting your plan into a project management application, such as MS Project. It depends on your preferences, but it can really help initially if you have organised your thoughts and have a clear outline diagram of how you want at least the higher levels of your WBS to look. Once you have created your WBS, the argument for using a project management application becomes much stronger: it will save you time.

One approach that you could adopt is to work through the activities given in this chapter again, but this time carrying them out for your student project rather than the party project.

You should be able to show all the deliverables of the planning process in your project plan: the SOW, a WBS, the estimated effort required for each task, the milestones, the schedule showing task dependencies and the critical path. You might want to delay estimating durations for tasks involving writing software until after reading the next chapter. You can't work out your critical path(s) until you have all the durations. Below, you will see some 'rough and ready' guidelines for estimating durations. Note for a student project there will be an ultimate deadline date for completion already set!

Rough and ready guidelines for estimating task duration in student projects

- Budget ½ day (about 4.5 hours) to read each journal paper or chapter of a book or report. You will still have to guess how many of these your literature review will need

- Budget about 1 day to write and debug every 50 lines of code. You will still need to guess how many lines of code you will need to produce in total (this depends on the type of coding you are doing and the level of the language)

- Budget ½ a day for every 1-hour interview you plan to conduct, since you need time beforehand to prepare for the interview, and time afterwards to write up your notes

- Budget 2 days for every presentation you are planning to give since you need time to prepare the materials and to practise the presentation

- Budget 1 day for every 500 words you are planning to write. This is because everything you write will need careful editing, and the inclusion of diagrams and creating and checking references always takes longer than you expect

- Double the initial time you estimate for any design tasks since you may only spot design errors when the design is nearly complete and you must leave yourself time to go back and correct the design diagrams

- Remember always to build in some time after a major deliverable (for example, the requirements specification) so that you can make any corrections that arise out of the review for the deliverable

- Remember to leave some regular time for project management:
    - measuring project progress against the plan
    - adjusting the plan
    - recording events and decisions
    - making progress reports

- If you are producing a product, double your initial estimate of the time taken for testing, since if one of your tests fails you will need to spend time getting things going right again

- Product testing and the evaluation of your project as a whole should be kept as separate tasks. (If you are not producing a product, then the evaluation of your project is even more important. Budget extra time to develop thorough and recognisable evaluation criteria to measure your project against.)

- Don't forget to allow time for your supervisor to read the report and to make recommendations for changes, corrections and rework which you will have to make prior to submission.

You will also need to work out your working week. You should take the number of nominal hours of learning time, say 18 hours, and assess how you plan to spread those hours over the week. You will need to schedule some time, say an extra two hours, for meetings with your colleagues, your supervisor and your tutor. Table 5.7 gives an example of typical weekly effort.

Such a work schedule will leave you some extra time at the weekend as contingency in case you fall behind.

You must schedule some time each week specifically for project management. This includes reviewing project progress against the plan and making adjustments to the plan. It may also include documenting particular events, accomplishments and decisions and communicating with your supervisor.

Weekday	Work allocated	Time allocated (hours)
Monday	Working at home	3
Tuesday	Working at home	3
Wednesday	2 hours' tutorial 2 hours' work in library	4
Thursday	On customer site	4
Friday	Spend evening with wife & kids	0
Saturday	Working at home	4
Sunday	1 hour's project management 1 hour's work at home	2
		20

Table 5.7: Typical weekly effort

If your project is going to involve data gathering 'in the field' (that is, getting facts and figures from people working on specific, real tasks) or otherwise interacting with people in an organisation, this will probably need to be done during working hours. You need to make sure that you are going to be able to commit yourself to these tasks when the time comes for them to be done.

Don't budget every working hour for the project. You won't be able to avoid your work and family commitments, and budgeting to do so will give you an unreasonable idea about how much you can actually do on your project.

Because you have a plan, you know what you should be doing at any time, and you will receive early warnings if you begin to fall behind.

You will use your time most effectively if you work steadily and try to stick to the plan. Even if you do this, it is likely that unforeseen events will delay you and some of your effort estimates may be unrealistic, so it is important that you revisit your plan every now and again, and adjust it to reflect the current situation. Try to keep a record of your progress. You could record progress in the form of a **project diary**. Here you can note the dates:

- When you accomplished a task or achieved a milestone
- When you hit a particular problem (and what that problem was)
- When you made a crucial decision or altered the plan
- When you contacted your supervisor.

You can also make a note of future events such as:

- When an interview has been arranged for
- When a milestone is due.

This record can be extremely useful when you come to write your project up and it becomes necessary for you to account for your time. As an alternative to a diary, you can use the annotation feature (*Task Notes*) in MS Project to keep your records. It is up to you.

Remember to stay in touch with your classmates and tutors, it is easy to lose your sense of perspective when you are doing a project, and having a few friends who have an idea about what you are trying to do can help to 'keep your feet on the ground'.

The six rules for project success:

- **Work steadily**
- **Try to stick to the plan**
- **Update your plan occasionally**
- **Keep a record of your progress and other project events**
- **Stay in touch**
- **Keep your tutor informed.**

5.13 Summary

This chapter has discussed the planning process: how you go about identifying tasks, creating a WBS, and scheduling the tasks. It has also described how you establish a project completion date and how you identify a project's critical path. It has also outlined how this planning information can be presented in a Gantt chart.

The link between a WBS and the project budget has also been mentioned. In the next chapter, the second part of project planning, we discuss project costs and describe cost estimation: how you can estimate the amount of effort to develop software.

5.14 Review questions

 **Question 5.1**

What are the difficulties in identifying the project tasks for a software engineering project?

 **Question 5.2**

What are the benefits of producing a Gantt chart?

 Question 5.3

What are the benefits of using a package such as MS Project to produce a Gantt chart?

 Question 5.4

What do you think are the benefits of identifying project milestones?

 Question 5.5

When you create your Gantt chart in MS Project, what do you think would happen if you did not link dependent tasks, and instead just manually adjusted the start dates for each task to represent this?

 Question 5.6

What do you consider to be the benefits of AoA diagrams?

 Question 5.7

Why do you think that it is important to identify your project's critical path?

 Question 5.8

Does a critical path identify all the critical activities?

Question 5.9

Who decides the schedule of project activities and their durations?

5.15 Feedback on activities

Activity 5.1: Identify the project tasks

There are lots of possible tasks that you might have written down for this. Here is a potential list:

- Decide date
- Decide location
- Invite guests
- Decorate location
- Prepare food & drink
- Hold party.

Activity 5.2: Create a WBS

A possible simple WBS for the party project would look like this:

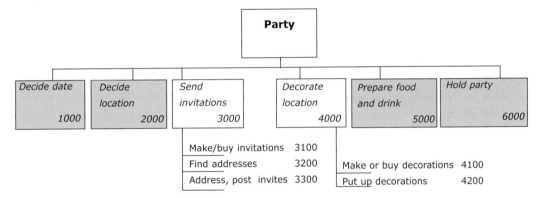

Figure 5.23: Possible simple WBS for a party. Lowest levels on the WBS have shaded boxes.

Party
1000 Decide date_
2000 Decide location _
3000 Send invitations
    3100 Make or buy invitations_
    3200 Find addresses_
    3300 Address and post invitations_
4000 Decorate location
    4100 Make or purchase decorations_
    4200 Put up decorations_
5000 Prepare food & drink_
6000 Hold party_

This WBS could be expanded into slightly more detail as follows:

Expanded Party

1000 Decide date
    1100 Check diary_
    1200 Check date is okay with other people_

2000 Decide location
    2100 Think of possible locations_
    2200 Work out benefits and limitations of different locations_
    2300 Make a choice_

3000 Invite guests
    3100 Decide guests to invite_
    3200 Send invitations
        3210 Make or buy invitations_
        3220 Find addresses_
        3230 Address and post invitations_

4000 Decorate location
    4100 Make or purchase decorations_
    4200 Put up decorations_

5000 Prepare refreshments
    5100 Prepare food
        5110 Decide on which food_
        5120 Find recipe_
        5130 Purchase ingredients_
        5140 Make food_
        5150 Set out food_
    5200 Prepare drinks
        5210 Decide on which drinks_
        5220 Purchase paper/plastic cups_
        5230 Pour drinks_

6000 Hold party
    6100 Welcome guests_
    6200 Invite guests to have refreshments
        6210 Serve drinks_
        6220 Serve food_
    6300 Check guests are happy_
    6400 Say goodbye to guests_
    6500 Clear up after party
        6510 Clear up drinks_
        6520 Clear up food_
        6530 Take down decorations_

7000 Manage party budget_

Hopefully, you can see that the additional detail could help improve the planning of the party. A more thorough task list helps identify the resource requirements. Note that it helps to use verbs at the start of each task name (as in 'Manage party budget'). Sometimes at the higher levels of the WBS hierarchy the use of such verbs is not possible. However, you should always aim to use verbs at the lower levels of the WBS.

Activity 5.3: Identify the milestones

Milestones are important events that allow you to measure the progress of your project. Milestones could be the completion dates for any of the major tasks of your project. Note that milestones are not tasks. For the party project, the following milestones could be chosen (To avoid having a great deal of detail, we'll use the initial shorter list of party tasks):

Party

1000 Decide date <>

> *Milestone: Event = Party date is identified. Milestone date = Party day - 45*
>
> *Deliverable = List of people who can attend on chosen date*

2000 Decide location <>

> *Milestone: Event = Location is identified. Milestone date = Party day - 35*
>
> *Deliverable = Contract for hire of location / Written agreement concerning use of location*

3000 Send invitations

  3100 Make or buy invitations

  3200 Find addresses

  3300 Address and post invitations <>

> *Milestone: Event = Guests invited. Milestone date = Party day - 30*
>
> *Deliverables = List of people invited and posted invitations*

4000 Decorate location

  4100 Make or purchase decorations

  4200 Put up decorations <>

> *Milestone: Event = Decorations ready. Milestone date = Party day - 1*
>
> *Deliverables = Notification that decorations are put up*

5000 Prepare food & drink <>

> *Milestone: Event = Food and drink ready. Milestone date = Party day - 1*
>
> *Deliverables = Notification that food is ready.*

6000 Hold party

> *Milestone: Event = Party completed. Milestone date = Party day*
>
> *Deliverables = List of people who attended, feedback from guests and your feedback (reflections on what went well and what you would change the next time).*

Don't get confused between the date of the party and the milestone date when you have decided the date of the party!

Activity 5.4: Create an AoN diagram

An AoN diagram for the initial list of party tasks may look something like this:

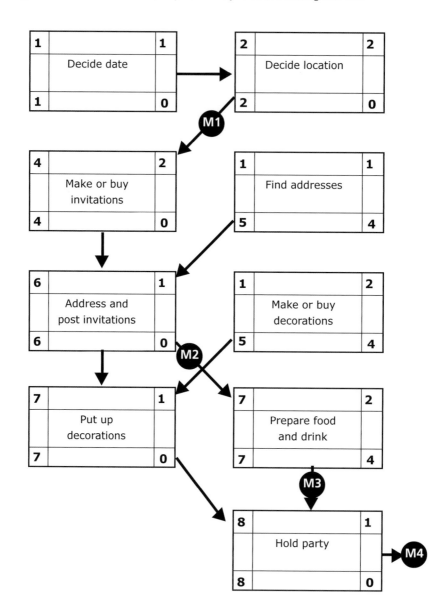

Figure 5.24: Task dependencies

What is interesting with this example is that, although it initially seems like a very simple project, with a straightforward sequence, in fact there are different ways that the tasks could be sequenced.

Note that all the lower level tasks of the hierarchical structure appear in Figure 5.19. Look back to the shaded boxes in Figure 5.18 to observe this. Note also that figures have been estimated and input for the Earliest Start Day, Duration, Latest Start Day and Slack.

Activity 5.5: Create an AoA diagram

A simplified AoA diagram for the party project should look something like this:

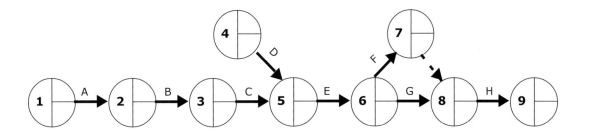

Figure 5.25: An AoA diagram showing the solution for Activity 5.5

Activity A (1-2): Decide date (1 day)

Activity B (2-3): Decide location (2 days)

Activity C (3-5): Make/buy invitations (2 days)

Activity D (4-5): Find addresses (1 day)

Activity E (5-6): Address & post invitations (1 day)

Activity F (6-7): Put up decorations (1 day)

Activity G (6-8): Prepare food & drink (1 day)

Activity H (8-9): Hold party (1 day)

Activity 5.6: Identify the critical path

Based on the example AoN diagram given in the feedback to Activity 5.4, the following critical path can be established:

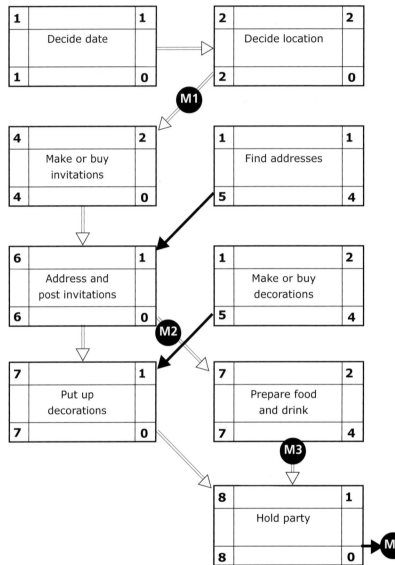

Figure 5.26: Feedback showing solution for *Activity 5.6: Identify the critical path* for the AoN diagram of the party project. The double arrows identify the critical path.

Based on the example AoA diagram given in the feedback to Activity 5.5, the following table can be produced:

Path	Duration
A, B, C, E, G, H	8
A, B, C, E, F, H	8
D, E, F, H	4
D, E, G, H	4

Table 5.8: Table showing solution based on AoA diagram for activity 5.6: Identify critical path

In this example, there is no single critical path, because paths A-B-C-E-G-H and A-B-C-E-F-H are equally long. Any delay to activities along either of these paths will delay the entire project.

CHAPTER 6

Project planning II: cost management

OVERVIEW

Cost management is a key component of project management. Successful projects pay particular attention to the issues of cost management in the early stages of the project, establishing cost estimations and determining that the potential project benefits outweigh the likely project costs.

Following on from Chapter 5, which discussed work breakdown structures (WBS) and scheduling, this chapter forms the second part of project planning and introduces the topics of cost estimation and cost control. Ideally, cost estimation (this chapter) and scheduling (Chapter 5) should be done in parallel with iteration between the two processes occurring as appropriate.

Learning outcomes	At the end of this chapter you should be able to:

- Understand the place of cost management within project management

- Outline a process for cost estimation

- Describe COCOMO II and other methods used for cost estimation

- Explain the use of earned value management (EVM) for cost control.

6.1   Introduction

In this chapter we discuss the importance of cost management to the stakeholders and describe the processes involved, paying specific attention to cost estimation and cost control. Various methods of carrying out cost estimation are introduced including the COCOMO II method. For helping to achieve cost control, earned value management (EVM) is described.

6.2   The importance of cost management

Background to cost management

Software is generally a means to some 'end'. The value of software depends on its delivering enough benefit within an organisation to justify the costs of developing and operating the software. If costs soar, any potential benefit is eroded.

Many large business and public sector organisations are highly dependent on IT, with system costs representing a significant part of their total expenditure. These organisations are faced with many needs and opportunities for spending additional resources on systems. As a result, the planning, monitoring and control of systems development costs is an ongoing, major concern for the management.

For smaller organisations, bearing the costs of any systems development may have an even more critical impact on their finances (because any system costs are likely to represent a much greater percentage of the organisation's annual expenditure than is the case for a larger organisation). Therefore, whatever the size of an organisation, cost management is an important element of project management.

Purpose of cost management

The purpose of cost management varies at the different stages of a project:

- At the planning stage, cost management is focused on ensuring that projects are only undertaken when they are 'viable' (that is, there is a reasonable prospect that the benefits will outweigh the costs). Cost management puts in place a budget (usually expressed as a set of cost constraints) for each project. (In other words, planning is concerned with cost estimation and cost budgeting)

- At the execution stage, cost management is focused on keeping the project within its budget (within its agreed cost constraints), while maintaining an appropriate balance among costs and other management concerns, such as quality and timescales. (In other words, cost control.)

Cost management is also the subject of special attention at project reviews. It depends on the type of review exactly what management investigate in detail, but the project costs and progress against the project plans always form a key part (see Chapter 4).

6.3 Software costs

Now let's consider the costs associated with software. The total cost of developing, maintaining and operating software can be broken down into several components:

- The **direct costs** of developing and maintaining the software include:
  - creating and updating the software requirements and design specifications
  - carrying out the coding and testing
  - ensuring software quality (for example, reviews, inspections and further testing)
  - carrying out software maintenance, including both bug-fixing and minor enhancements
  - purchasing bought-in software artefacts (for example, packages, templates and components)
  - project management.

- The **indirect costs** of developing and maintaining the software include:
  - the development and test platforms (hardware, system software, and software tooling)
  - the communications and collaboration platforms (for example, e-mail and intranets) used for the development process
  - office space and administrative facilities.

- The **costs of operating** the software after delivery (the operating costs) include:
  - the operating platform (hardware and system software)
  - software costs (for the developed software)
  - installation and upgrading costs
  - training costs
  - user costs (for example, time spent on data entry or search)
  - quality costs (for example, business costs incurred as a result of incorrect or unreliable software).

The importance of these different cost components varies from project to project. Capers Jones (2005) reports that, for smaller projects, it is generally the software development effort that is the major cost, while for large projects it is typically fixing the software bugs and producing the documentation that tend to dominate the costs. A smaller project is defined in this case as one with less than 1,000 function points (equivalent to 125,000 C statements), while a large project is one with over 10,000 function points (equivalent to 1,250,000 C statements). Function points will be explained later in this chapter.

Activity 6.1

Investigate costs

For your student project or maybe some coursework or a report you have recently written or are currently working on, write out a list of all the activities that had to be completed (look at the WBS or the contents list for help with this). Now against this activity list, list the resources that were needed and the amount of your time required. Now think about any major changes that have occurred in planning this work or as you were carrying out the work – how did they impact on your work in terms of effort involved? Assume an hourly rate for your effort and calculate the costs of the different activities. Now consider how the costs vary/varied over time.

Stakeholders and costs

As we have seen, there are many different components to software cost. One question worth considering is who pays these costs? A project has many different stakeholders, and the level of the various costs and their distribution will differ depending on the nature of the project.

See Figure 6.1, which shows a relationship between a project (the software producer) and a set of software users (software consumers). This kind of relationship can apply either to separately managed units within one organisation or to separate organisations.

Where a software project involves several organisations, the distribution of cost will be an important aspect of the commercial/contractual negotiations among the organisations. Even if a project is completely within a single organisation, there typically will be similar negotiation among the divisions and/or the different departments, though no formal contracts are needed in this situation.

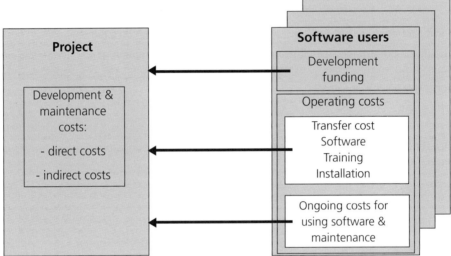

Figure 6.1: Relationship regarding costs between a software development project and its users

To give an example showing the importance of understanding the complete picture of the distribution of the costs: imagine you were the manager of a department with responsibility for, say, 100 PCs. You purchase all the hardware using your departmental budget. A project manager from the systems development department then tells you the system requirements for the planned new software his project is developing and you suddenly realise it will mean replacing all your PCs in six months' time when the new application is rolled out. Nobody realised this was the case: the software developers were told everyone had higher specification PCs so nobody checked across all the users. Also nobody told you the full implications of the new software and you assumed it would run on your existing hardware – you were not told about the new features in sufficient detail. You have no budget for replacing the PCs. So who pays? Things have gone wrong here because of poor communication between the two departments – ideally all the stakeholders would have understood the impact of the project at the planning stage and the cost of the new hardware would have been factored in. In this case, it is not obvious who exactly pays (though it's likely to hit some budget within the user organisation) and it's up to more senior management to sort out!

Questions along the following lines need answering: How important is it that this department uses the new software this year? What's the impact on the maintenance budget of supporting the old software for another year? What's going to happen over training? Has the project created this problem by altering the agreed design?

It is also important to realise that cost transactions do not always occur at cost price (that is, the cost it actually took to develop or purchase). There is often some difference, either a markup to make some profit or a markdown to promote sales. Going back to Figure 6.1, it shows the project received some development funding upfront. Any such upfront funding will be taken into account in the transfer price when the software is delivered. The users will initially be able to approach the project for maintenance; once the project disbands this will no longer be the case and maintenance responsibilities will transfer elsewhere.

Managing project funding

Certain stakeholders (the project sponsors) fund a project – that is, they agree to provide money at agreed times to the project. The project manager then allocates the funding – according to the project plans and the budget – within the project to meet the project costs. As we have already discussed (the PC example), it is important for all stakeholders to know where the cost responsibilities lie (what is inside the project budget, and what is additional). The project manager has ultimate responsibility for the project budget, but other stakeholders may have the power to decide how certain aspects of the project funding are spent by imposing constraints. In order to ensure that funding is allocated to the project as planned, a project manager needs to:

- Produce credible plans showing funding requirements
- Ensure stakeholders are not surprised with major changes to plans or costs
- Keep stakeholders informed of progress at regular intervals
- Alert stakeholders to any difficulties as early as possible, preferably with suggested options for overcoming these difficulties and the impact of each option on the total cost of the project.

Where a contract is appropriate, a project manager needs to ensure that:

- Financial commitments by various stakeholders are clearly stated
- Appropriate measures for dealing with non-payment by any of the stakeholders are clearly articulated
- Where payments are dependent on certain deliverables, those deliverables are well defined with responsibility and procedure for approving them clearly stated.

In many cases, software projects take more than one financial year to complete. This introduces an element of risk to the project budget, which needs to be specifically managed, particularly if some stakeholders allocate their share of the funding annually, based on their annual financial planning. If some of the stakeholders have a financial problem during the course of the project, they may decide to reduce their contribution or abandon the project altogether. Similarly, if part of a project is delayed it may push certain costs into a different financial year, causing potential difficulties in the necessary allocation of funds. Good communication needs to be established with the stakeholder representatives to ensure the project management is alerted to any problems that stakeholders are facing which may have a financial impact on the project and to alert stakeholders to project issues and delays which may impact project funding. Reviews can play a key part in getting formal stakeholder agreements to release funds.

6.4 The cost management process

This section looks at the processes of cost management. The main processes of cost management are as follows:

- **Cost estimation**
- **Cost budgeting**
- **Cost control.**

This decomposition into three sub-processes follows the Project Management Institute's (PMI's) definition of project cost management (*PMBOK Guide* 2004). See Figure 6.2.

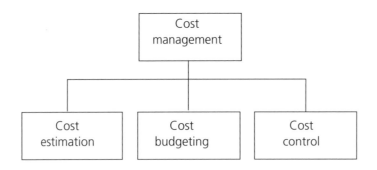

Figure 6.2: Overview of cost management processes

To put these cost management processes into a wider project context, see Figure 6.3, which shows how the feasibility study, contract negotiation and project monitoring processes fit with them. Note: project scheduling is not included here. See also Figure 6.8 towards the end of the chapter.

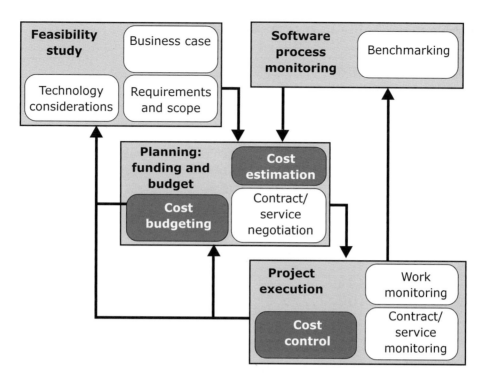

Figure 6.3: Overview showing the wider context into which cost management fits

6.5   Cost estimation

A common approach for estimating software costs is to start by estimating the quantity of software that will be required to satisfy a given set of requirements. Software quantity is sometimes termed 'software volume' but it is usually referred to as 'software size'.

Once we have an estimate of the software size of the required software, we can estimate the amount of effort required to produce it. This assumes we understand the software tasks required to produce the software, and we know the rate at which software is produced when these tasks are carried out. Once we have an estimate for the amount of effort, we can calculate the estimated financial cost assuming we know the cost rate for the task. An outline of this procedure is shown in Figure 6.4 (see also Figure 6.8 later in this chapter for greater detail).

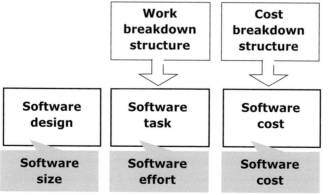

Figure 6.4: Outline of a typical cost estimation procedure

Let's now examine this cost estimation process in more detail.

Step 1: Software size

There are two basic ways of measuring software size used for cost estimation purposes: metrics based on the code size and metrics based on some aspect related to the required functionality.

Metrics based on code size

The simplest and most obvious way to measure the quantity of software is to count the lines of code or instructions: a large system has more lines of code than a small system.

Of course you can only actually count the lines of code once they are written, but we'll come back to this later!

Counting the lines is not as simple as it sounds. Even within a single programming language, there are different ways of counting lines of code. See Table 6.1.

Source lines of code (SLOC)	Only source lines that are delivered as part of the product are included – test drivers and other support software is excluded
	Source lines are created by the project staff – code created by applications generators is excluded
	One SLOC is one logical line of code. Declarations are counted as SLOC. Comments are not counted as SLOC
Delivered source instructions (DSI)	The major difference between DSI and SLOC is that a single source line of code may be several physical lines. For example, an 'if-then-else' statement would be counted as one SLOC, but might be counted as several DSI.

Table 6.1: Counting 'lines of code'

In general terms, it doesn't matter very much which way you count the lines of code – as long as you do it consistently and as long as your methods/applications are set up to interpret your input data correctly (i.e. they know what type of counting metric you are using, say SLOC).

One thing to remember is that you are trying to estimate the work to be done by the project team, so if project time is to be expended on some activity then it needs to be counted.

Metrics based on functionality

There are several difficulties with code-based metrics. Firstly, they cannot be easily compared or aggregated across different programming languages. Secondly, they don't apply very well to new software development paradigms, especially those where a significant amount of development effort is not directly focused on the production of code, but on the production of models (from which code is automatically generated), or the reuse and integration of existing artefacts.

For this reason, alternative software size metrication systems have been proposed based on certain aspects of functionality, which are supposedly free from at least some of these difficulties. The best known of these metrication systems is function points, which was originally developed by Allan Albrecht at IBM, and is now maintained by the International

Function Point User Group (IFPUG 2005) and subject to an ISO standard. Other such metrics include object points (known as application points in COCOMO) and use case points. All are based on counting things at a higher level of abstraction (as shown in Table 6.2). As we shall see later in the explanation of function point analysis, the counts are usually weighted before being added together to produce a total point score for a piece of software (say, a software module).

One of the main benefits of counting based on functionality is that the information required to carry out the counting is available earlier in the software development lifecycle – in order to directly estimate lines of code requires more detailed design information.

Type of functionality-based metric	What sorts of things get counted?
Function points	Inputs, outputs, files and inquiries
Object points/application points	Screens, reports and modules
Use case points	Use cases

Table 6.2: Software size for metrics based on functionality

Function point analysis

Let's look at how function point analysis is carried out.

To calculate the total number of function points in a software module, you start by identifying all the instances of the following function types going to be present in the software:

- Internal logical files: any file created or updated by the software
- External interface files: any file only read by the software
- External inputs: a process allowing data to enter the software, for example an input screen
- External outputs: a process allowing data to exit the software, for example a report or display screen
- External inquiries: reads data from internal and external files with no updating.

Then according to its function type, each instance is assessed to determine its complexity (low, average or high). Under each function type, the instances can then be summed according to complexity; for example, for external inputs you might have 5 of low complexity, 7 of average complexity and 10 of high complexity. Each of the resulting summed values then needs to be weighted by multiplying it by its appropriate weight. You can either use a standard function type/complexity table of weights (see Table 6.3 with values from 3 to 15) or you can choose to use your own organisation's values based on experience.

Function type	Complexity weight		
	Low	Average	High
Internal logical files	7	10	15
External interface files	5	7	10
External inputs	3	4	6
External outputs	4	5	7
External inquiries	3	4	6

Table 6.3: Complexity weights for the different function types

By totalling all the weighted values, the total unadjusted function points (UFPs) value for the software can be obtained.

For the example just given for external inputs, where the complexity weights are Low = 3, Average = 4 and High = 6, the calculation would be as follows:

$$(5 \times 3) + (7 \times 4) + (10 \times 6) = 15 + 28 + 60 = 103.$$

This would then have to be added to the totals for the other function types to get the UFP.

The UFP value is used by the COCOMO II method (see next section).

The standard function point procedure is to further adjust the unadjusted function point (UFP) count by calculating a value adjustment factor (VAF) for the software project. The VAF aims to assess the overall complexity of the project.

VAF is calculated by assessing the degree of influence of each of 14 system characteristics (such as multiple sites, end-user efficiency and reusability) using a scale of 0 to 5 for each one. The resulting set of 14 degrees of influence are added together to give a total degrees of influence (TDI) value. Then VAF can be calculated as follows: VAF = (TDI x 0.01) + 0.65

By multiplying together VAF and UFP, you get the total function point value (FP).

$$FP = VAF \times UFP$$

Once you have the FP value, you can calculate the development estimates. There are two ways of doing this:

- Productivity rates
- Conversion rates to lines of code.

For productivity, you can transform FP into a measure of the amount of time if you know the rate at which function points can be coded. For example, if the estimated function point value is 300 and the corresponding productivity metric is 6 FP/person-month, then

$$\text{Effort} = 300/60 = 50 \text{ person-months.}$$

You can then multiply this figure by the cost of one person-month to arrive at the total financial cost of development.

Note that the productivity metric (in this case, 6FP/person-month) can only be obtained from experience by organisations capturing their local productivity rates from past projects.

You can obtain an estimate of the lines of code (size) from the function point value if you know the conversion rate from function points to lines of code. The rate varies according to the programming language being used; see Table 6.4. For example, for C++ the average SLOC per unadjusted function point is 55. Standard tables are available showing the conversion rates for the different programming languages. An alternative is for organisations to calibrate their own values.

Programming language	Average number of SLOC per unadjusted function point (UFP)
C++	55
Java	53
Visual Basic 5.0	29
Fourth Generation Language	20
HTML 3.0	15

Table 6.4: Some examples of conversion rates from unadjusted function points (UFP) to SLOC for different programming languages (Boehm et al 2000c quoting figures from Jones 1996)

Application points and use case points

Application points (renamed from object points to avoid confusion with object-orientated terms), are used by COCOMO II within its application composition model, which deals with software developed using prototyping and reuse. The issue was that a higher-level method than function points was required. The application points method counts the number of screens, reports and third-generation language (3GL) modules. It is similar to function points in using complexity weights. It then adjusts for reuse. In addition, Boehm et al have added rating scales to adjust according to a project's productivity (Boehm et al 2000c).

Use case points are still relatively new. Boehm et al (2000c) report that

> 'experience so far with use case points is that they still have a very wide range of interpretation, which makes it difficult for them to be used confidently as a sizing metric outside a relatively uniform group of applications and practitioners.'

Step 2: Software effort

At first sight, calculation of effort appears to be an exercise in elementary arithmetic:

> 'If 2 pretzel makers can make 444 pretzels in 6 hours, how long does it take 5 pretzel makers to make 88 pretzels?' (Enzensberger 2006)

Software productivity is usually thought of as a ratio between the quantity of software produced (using any appropriate size metric) and the effort taken to produce it.

Therefore, if you think you know the level of software productivity that can be attained in a given context, then you can determine the required effort by dividing the required software size by the expected productivity.

Units of effort

Effort is almost always expressed in standard units of time per person – thus person-hours, person-days, person-weeks, person-months or person-years. For some purposes, we want to calculate effort in fairly small units (person-hours).

Some resources (possibly including subcontractors) are costed by the hour. Other resources (possibility including full-time employees) are assigned to a project for extended periods, and must be costed by the week or month. Large projects often need to use larger units of measure, say weeks or months or even years.

Note, don't get confused between *effort* and *elapsed time*! A software module might be estimated to take ten person-hours, but it might take one week of elapsed time (because the programmer is also working on something else at the same time).

Hours of work

How many hours of real work does someone do in a month? Do we have to take away holidays, sick days, lunch, non-project tasks, meetings, travelling to meetings, and other unproductive time; do we have to add in overtime (paid/unpaid) and thinking time?

Each organisation may have a different notion of what counts as 'productive time'. And each organisation may have a different notion of which roles/tasks count as productive (for example, how costs for managers and administrators are included can vary). People within the same organisation may interpret these rules differently, and complete their timesheets in diverse fashions.

To simplify this, we generally have to assume a standard number of hours in a person-month. For example, COCOMO II (discussed later in this chapter) is based on a person-month of 152 hours (38-hour weeks) – but you can vary this if appropriate.

People productivity

However, even if you know the average number of hours a person works, there are still problems over estimating effort accurately:

- Some people work steadily, while others have bursts of highly productive time
- Some people have higher productivity than others
- Experts in a task are more productive than novices
- People have different characteristic levels of sickness and absenteeism.

Difficulty/complexity of the task

Then you have to look at the task being carried out: some lines of code take more effort than others.

Using multiple categories

In short, not every line of code is the same and not every hour's labour is the same. However, we can, if we want, make an assumption that we can produce good-enough calculations using averages in the estimation process.

If we want to make the calculations more accurate, then we can try subdividing effort into multiple categories. Thus developers can be divided into trainee, standard, skilled and expert, and software can be divided into simple, medium and complex. You can divide into as many categories as you can cope with – but this additional complexity may not produce any improvement in accuracy:

- Smaller categories may lack statistical significance – if you don't have much historical data for each category, the averages will be less stable/reliable
- The categorisation itself may be imperfect, and may change dynamically (a line of code may become more complex because of an interaction with something else; a developer may become more skilled as the project progresses).

Further complexity – not simple arithmetic

There is in fact even further complexity to deal with. *The Mythical Man-Month* is the name of a classic book on software projects by Fred Brooks Jr (Brooks 1995; originally published in 1974). His 'myth' is the notion that software effort obeys simple arithmetic: addition and multiplication. The fact is that estimating effort when you put people and tasks 'together' requires slightly more difficult maths, referred to as an 'algebra'.

Software projects experience a diseconomy of scale. A 10,000-line project will take more effort than 10 projects of 1,000 lines each. This is because of various factors, such as on a larger project more effort is spent on communication and organisation, rather than on technical work. For loosely coupled software projects (for example, component-based development), less co-ordination may be required, and this might reduce the diseconomy of scale.

Algorithmic approaches

In order to estimate more accurately the nonlinear increase of effort as a result of the increase of project size, algorithmic models use an exponential component in their formula. For example:

Effort = C x M^e

... where **C** is a constant representing a complexity figure based on data from past projects, and where **M** is a metric indicating the size of project; this could be line of code, effort or a function point.

The exponent **e** is also a constant, which is close to 1 and represents the non-linear increase of effort for large projects.

This type of model is called *single variable model*. The earlier version of COCOMO (COCOMO 81) is an example of such a model. In addition, there are multivariable models, such as COCOMO II, which we shall discuss in more detail later.

Other approaches than algorithmic

Other approaches than algorithmic also exist; for example, expert opinion. We shall consider these alternative methods in more detail later when we discuss the different methods for cost estimation.

Step 3: Software cost

Once we know the amount of effort required, we can convert it into cost. In simple calculations, the standard unit of effort is associated with a standard cost. So multiplying the amount of effort by its standard cost gives you the total cost for the software. However, once again, even this calculation is not so simple:

- People are on different pay scales (for example, a programmer will be on a different pay scale to a project manager) with different expenses (for example, they may travel different distances)
- The same job can be paid at a different rate depending on industry and location (for example, a programmer in Wales will earn less than a programmer in London)
- New recruits typically incur a high start-up cost in support and training.

However, if we assume that the more highly skilled and productive developers are also the more expensive, then variation in cost may be set against variation in productivity, to some degree.

6.6 Methods for cost estimation

Having discussed the basics of the cost estimation process, let's now consider the different methods that can be used for cost estimation. We have already briefly mentioned one of these methods, COCOMO.

It's important to understand the different methods, especially as there is a general recommendation to use more than one method when carrying out cost estimation. This is because the different methods have different strengths and weaknesses. By reviewing the results from more than one method, better estimates will be achieved.

Figure 6.5 shows an overview of the different techniques that can be used for software cost estimation. It also gives some examples of the methods that use the different techniques. We shall only discuss some of these methods here – marked in bold. For further details read the online Boehm et al paper (Boehm et al 2000a).

Some of the methods, such as Wideband Delphi, are 'top-down' processes and others, such as (work breakdown structure) WBS-based costing are 'bottom-up'.

Sometimes cost estimation doesn't actually translate into the price charged.

'Priced to win' refers to the situation where the price (the 'cost' to the customer) is set to a value the customer is known to want to see or is deliberately reduced to make a bid more competitively priced. The idea is that winning the business is the key thing. This is often used to establish a foothold in a new sector or to form a new relationship with the contracting organisation (or simply to keep the workforce in employment).

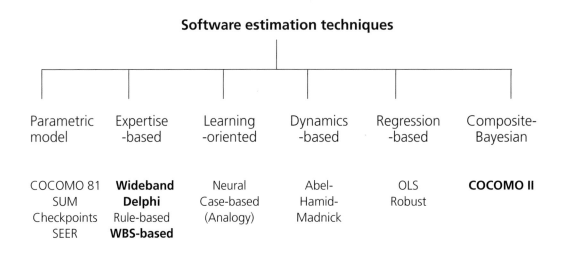

Figure 6.5: The different types of software estimation techniques and examples of methods that use them (very slightly modified from Boehm et al 2000a)

Another scenario is where there is a fixed cost already in place and the system is deliberately designed to come in at that cost. A slight variation on this occurs when using evolutionary or agile methods: it can suit a project using such methods to work under a fixed overall budget. The project doesn't worry too much about cost estimation as such, it just aims to deliver as much stakeholder value as early as possible in a series of deliveries.

When the money runs out, then the project stops – given it has focused on delivering the solutions with the highest value/development cost ratios, the project knows it has done the best it could with the project budget.

Wideband Delphi

Wideband Delphi is a specific example of expertise-based cost estimation. It is an iterative estimation technique involving several experts. Originally introduced by Barry Boehm in the 1970s, it has spawned several variants. The basic principle is to bring several experts together on an issue and try to reach a consensus. The managers and systems developers are asked to estimate the module and system sizes based on their experience of previous development and on any additional data provided. The key difference with Wideband Delphi is that the experts are allowed to discuss the tabulated results of their estimates with each other (traditional Delphi techniques don't allow such discussion). When the experts comprise the actual development team, the resulting estimates are more likely to get the team's buy-in than would apparently random numbers 'raining down from above'. This is very roughly how it works:

- The project manager defines what is to be estimated, the units of measure, and the assumptions. He or she gathers data for similar tasks or projects if available — for example, data from previous iterations or a previous project – and then selects participants
- All the participants are briefed on the procedure and goals, and given any available data
- The participants develop their own estimate (each one on his or her own), preferably not interacting with each other
- The project manager gathers all the data, tabulates it in a spreadsheet, and compares the numbers
- All participants meet again. If the numbers match, then fine; you have a likely estimate. If the numbers are widely scattered, it is interesting to discuss with participants the thinking behind them. When one team member explains his or her assumptions, others might point out some important parameter that was forgotten, some new risk that has arisen, and so on
- The participants are then given a chance to adjust their estimate based on the discussion
- Iteration of the project manager tabulating the data, meetings reviewing and discussing the tabulated data and the participants setting their own estimates continue until sufficient consensus is reached
- The new numbers become the working estimate.

As the phase or iteration unrolls, actual data is collected for these tasks. When it is time to do another estimate (for example, for the next iteration), participants consult the previous estimates and actuals to help them adjust for their natural optimism or pessimism.

There are plenty of variants and refinements, as you can imagine. It can be done very informally, using e-mail or simply walking from cubicle to cubicle with a notepad to discuss planning hypotheses with the people whose estimates varied widely. You can also take a more formal approach, using templates and tools to compute ranges and uncertainties, or even Monte Carlo simulations to generate a probability distribution of possible estimate outcomes, based on the final estimate values (Wiegers 2000).

WBS-based costing

WBS-based costing is sometimes also known (slightly misleadingly) as activity-based costing (ABC) or, even, as bottom-up costing. It derives its name from the use of the work breakdown structure (WBS). Each component at the bottom level of the WBS branches is individually costed and then all the costs are added together using the structure of the WBS. So the final estimate grows from the bottom of the WBS – hence 'bottom-up'.

There are in fact two types of WBS that can be drawn up for a project: a product WBS and a process WBS. So costs can be assembled both by the product modules and by the types of process being carried out (for example design, coding and testing). 'Process' can also be termed here as 'task' or 'activity', and so it is the process-related costs that give rise to the name 'activity-based costing'. The process-related effort estimation can also help a project manager understand the numbers of the different types of personnel required for the project team by areas of expertise (for example, one systems architect, one business analyst and four programmers). This structure also forms the basis for capturing actual cost breakdown information by process for the project, which enables calculation, for example, of the percentage of the project budget spent on testing.

WBS-based costing takes a great deal of effort, but estimates are based on a detailed understanding of the work involved. One problem is a tendency 'to overlook many of the system level costs (integration, configuration management, quality assurance, project management) associated with software development' (Boehm 1981). The result is underestimation of the costs. In addition, Boehm (1981) gives a percentage range of between 30 to 50% for incidental project activities associated with producing the product (such as 'reading, reviewing, meeting and fixing' defects). He also suggests a further 30 to 50% is likely to be spent on incidental non-project activities (for example, training) – though these last percentages are based on a 1960s workplace and things might well have changed since then!

COCOMO II

COCOMO stands for *constructive cost model*. It is a well-known non-proprietary model developed by Barry W. Boehm (1981) for use in both software cost and schedule estimation. It is a parametric (or algorithmic) model, which was calibrated by collecting data from a large number of software projects.

The original version introduced in 1981 now tends to be known as COCOMO 81 and has been largely superceded by COCOMO II. COCOMO 81 was designed for software developed using the Waterfall model, whereas COCOMO II has been specifically designed to cater for 'evolutionary, incremental, and spiral models' (Boehm et al 2000b). COCOMO II also caters for new techniques, such as very high-level languages (VHLLs), commercial off-the-shelf (COTS) and reuse. COCOMO II achieves this flexibility through use of various extension models:

- **COPSEMO:** phase schedule and effort estimation
- **CORADMO:** rapid application development estimation
- **COCOTS:** COTS integration estimation
- **COQUALMO:** quality estimation (concerned with defect introduction and defect removal)
- **COPROMO:** productivity estimation
- **Expert COCOMO:** risk assessment.
  (Boehm et al 2000c)

COCOMO II has three basic models to cater for giving estimates at the different stages of development. These models are as follows:

- **Application composition:** this caters for projects developed by prototyping using application composition methods. Typical utilisation will occur during the early phases of the project but the model will support prototyping at any stage in the project lifecycle. As discussed earlier, it uses application points

- **Early design:** this is 'used at the early stages of a software project when very little may be known about the size of the product to be developed, the nature of the target platform, the nature of the personnel to be involved in the project, or the detailed specification of the process to be used'. It uses KSLOC or unadjusted function points (UFPs) for sizing and a coarse-grained set of seven cost drivers. It also uses five scale factors – which are also used in the post-architecture model

- **Post architecture:** 'this stage involves the actual development and maintenance of a software product.' The model has the same granularity as COCOMO 81. It 'uses source instructions and/or function points for sizing with modifiers for reuse and software breakage; a set of seventeen multiplicative cost drivers; and a set of five factors determining the project's scaling factor'.

(Boehm et al 2000c)

Cost drivers capture software development characteristics that affect the effort required to complete the project. A cost driver can be said to drive the cost. Each cost driver has a qualitative rating level, called an effort multiplier (EM), expressing its impact. Rating levels range from extra low to extra high, and are converted into numbers; see Tables 6.5 and 6.6. Each EM has a nominal value of 1.0. If the impact is to cause more effort, then its value is above 1.0; if it reduces effort, then its value is lower than 1.0.

Baseline effort constants: A = 2.94; B = 0.91							
Baseline schedule constants: C = 3.67; D = 0.28							
Cost driver	**Extra low**	**Very low**	**Low**	**Nominal**	**High**	**Very high**	**Extra high**
RCPX Product reliability & complexity	0.49	0.60	0.83	1.00	1.33	1.91	2.72
RUSE Reusability			0.95	1.00	1.07	1.15	1.24
PDIF Platform difficulty			0.87	1.00	1.29	1.81	2.61
PERS Personnel capability	2.12	1.62	1.26	1.00	0.83	0.63	0.50
PREX Personnel experience	1.59	1.33	1.12	1.00	0.87	0.74	0.62
FCIL Facilities		1.43	1.30	1.10	1.00	0.87	0.73	0.62
SCED Required development schedule		1.43	1.14	1.00	1.00	1.00	

Table 6.5: COCOMO II. Early design calibrated values for cost drivers (Boehm et al 2000c)

Baseline effort constants: A = 2.94; B = 0.91
Baseline schedule constants: C = 3.67; D = 0.28

Cost driver	Very low	Low	Nom- inal	High	Very high	Extra high
Product						
RELY Required software reliability	0.82	0.92	1.00	1.10	1.26	
DATA Database size		0.90	1.00	1.14	1.28	
CPLX Product complexity	0.73	0.87	1.00	1.17	1.34	1.74
RUSE Required reusability		0.95	1.00	1.07	1.15	1.24
DOCU Documentation	0.81	0.91	1.00	1.11	1.23	
Platform						
TIME Execution time constraint			1.00	1.11	1.29	1.63
STOR Main storage constraint			1.00	1.05	1.17	1.46
PVOL Platform volatility		0.87	1.00	1.15	1.30	
Personnel						
ACAP Analyst capability	1.42	1.19	1.00	0.85	0.71	
PCAP Programmer capability	1.34	1.15	1.00	0.88	0.76	
PCON Personnel continuity	1.29	1.12	1.00	0.90	0.81	
APEX Applications experience	1.22	1.10	1.00	0.88	0.81	
PLEX Platform experience	1.19	1.09	1.00	0.91	0.85	
LTEX Language & tool experience	1.20	1.09	1.00	0.91	0.84	
Project						
TOOL Software tools	1.17	1.09	1.00	0.90	0.78	
SITE Multisite development	1.22	1.09	1.00	0.93	0.86	0.80
SCED Development schedule	1.43	1.14	1.00	1.00	1.00	

Table 6.6: COCOMO II.2000 **post-architecture** calibrated values for cost drivers (Boehm et al 2000c).

Note: SCED (the last EM in the table) operates at the overall project level and does not vary from module to module, so only is used in the schedule calculations.

The **scale factors** (or scale drivers) deal with the diseconomies of scale, and are some of the most important factors contributing to a project's duration and cost. In the COCOMO II model, this diseconomy of scale is represented by an effort equation with an exponent greater than 1.

The five scale factors are as follows:

- **Precedentedness**
- **Development / flexibility**
- **Architecture / risk resolution**
- **Team cohesion**
- **Process maturity.**

See Table 6.7, which shows the scale factors used in both the early-design and post-architecture models.

Scale factor	Very low	Low	Nom- inal	High	Very high	Extra high
PREC Precedentedness	6.20	4.96	3.72	2.48	1.24	0.00
FLEX Development / flexibility	5.07	4.05	3.04	2.03	1.01	0.00
RESL Architecture / risk resolution	7.07	5.65	4.24	2.83	1.41	0.00
TEAM Team cohesion	5.48	4.38	3.29	2.19	1.10	0.00
PMAT Process maturity	7.80	6.24	4.68	3.12	1.56	0.00

Table 6.7: COCOMO II.2000 calibrated values for scale factors (Boehm et al 2000c)

The COCOMO II tables all show the values calibrated by the COCOMO II developers using data from numerous projects. While this data can be used by default, each organisation should calibrate its own cost drivers and scale factors to their local conditions. This can only be done after historical project data has been collected by an organisation.

Using the appropriate cost drivers and scale factors, the COCOMO II.2000 equations can be used to calculate first effort, and then schedule. The COCOMO early-design and post-architecture models (not the application composition model which uses a different equation) convert an estimate of software size into an estimate of effort, using the following **effort equation**:

$$\text{Effort} = A \times EAF \times (KSLOC)^E$$

where

Effort is measured in person-months (PM)

A is a productivity constant and is calibrated to 2.94 for COCOMO II.2000

KSLOC is an estimate of software project size, measured in thousands of SLOC

EAF is the effort adjustment factor derived from the EM values of the cost drivers. How many EMs there are depends on which model is being used. EAF is calculated by multiplying the EMs together

E is an exponent derived from the five scale factors.

$E = B + (0.01 \times \text{sum of the scale factors})$

where B is calibrated to 0.91 for COCOMO II.2000

As an example, consider a project with an EAF of 1.46, and a normal scale driver, resulting in an exponent, E, of 1.0997. Assuming that the project is projected to consist of 7,500 source lines of code, then the person-months of effort required to complete it is calculated as follows:

$$\textbf{Effort = 2.94 x (1.46) x (7.5)}^{1.0997} \textbf{ = 39.3 person-months}$$

Then the COCOMO II schedule equation can be used to predict the number of months required to complete the software project. The value for effort calculated using the effort equation has to be fed in. The schedule equation is as follows:

Duration = C x (Effort)^{SE}

where

Effort is the effort from the COCOMO II.2000 effort equation

C is a constant and is calibrated to 3.67 for COCOMO II.2000

SE is the schedule equation exponent derived from the five scale factors.

Continuing the example, and substituting the exponent of 0.3179 that is calculated from the scale drivers, yields an estimate of just under a year, and an average staffing of between 3 and 4 people.

Duration: 11.8 months

Effort: 39.3 person-months

People: 3.3

Schedule trade-offs: *time versus money*

- **Effort affects schedule**. The more effort for the project, the longer it will take. Adding people to a late project often just makes it later
- And **schedule affects effort**. A project developed on an accelerated schedule will require more effort than a project developed on its optimum schedule.

COCOMO has a way of calculating the trade-off between duration and effort. Above, we had a project that had an estimated effort of 39.4 months, which could be completed by 3 or 4 people in just under a year. This is the optimal schedule.

But suppose we wanted to finish this project in 75% of the optimum schedule. In COCOMO, we would set the required development schedule factor to very low, giving an effort multiplier of 1.43. As the figures show, the accelerated schedule calls for a much larger team putting in a greater total effort over a more intense period.

	Optimal	Accelerated
Duration	11.8 months	8.9 months
Effort	39.3	56.3
People	3.3	6.4

6.7 Cost estimation tools

Let's now look very briefly at some of the tools available to help with cost estimation.

Capers Jones (2005) lists the set of estimating tools as including COCOMO II, CoStar, CostModeler, CostXpert, KnowledgePlan, PRICE S, SEER, SLIM, and SoftCost. There are websites for many of these tools.

Capers Jones lists the features of such tools as follows:

Major features:

- Sizing logic for specifications, source code, and test cases
- Phase-level, activity-level, and task level estimation
- Adjustments for specific work periods, holidays, vacations, and overtime
- Adjustments for local salaries and burden rates
- Adjustments for various software projects such as military, systems, commercial, etc.
- Support for function point metrics, lines of code (LOC) metrics, or both
- Support for backfiring or conversion between LOC and function points
- Support for both new projects and maintenance and enhancement projects.

More advanced features of some tools include the following:

- Quality and reliability estimation
- Risk and value analysis
- Return on investment
- Sharing of data with project management tools
- Measurement models for collecting historical data
- Cost and time-to-complete estimates mixing historical data with projected data
- Support for software process assessments
- Statistical analysis of multiple projects and portfolio analysis
- Currency conversion for dealing with overseas projects.

Some of the available **adjustment factors** include the following:

- Staff experience with similar projects
- Client experience with similar projects
- Type of software to be produced
- Size of software project
- Size of deliverable items (documents, test cases, etc.)
- Requirements methods used
- Review and inspection methods used
- Design methods used
- Programming languages used
- Reusable materials available
- Testing methods used
- Paid overtime
- Unpaid overtime.

Capers Jones reports that in a study of 50 projects in the 5,000 function point range comparing manual with automated estimating, the automated estimating was more accurate (with 22 projects being estimated to within 10% of actual results and 24 being conservatively estimated to within 10-25% of actual results). His findings were as follows:

> 'For large projects, automated estimates are more successful than manual estimates in terms of accuracy and usefulness. In descending order, the costs of large projects include defect removal, production of paper documents, coding, project management, and dealing with new requirements that appear during the development cycle. In addition, successful estimates for large projects must be adjusted to match specific development processes, to match the experience of the development team, and to match the results of the programming languages and tool sets that are to be utilized. Simple manual estimates cannot encompass all of the adjustments associated with large projects.'

Capers Jones also makes the point that cost estimation tools were developed separately at first from project management tools with activity scheduling capabilities. He refers to this in his conclusion about the current state (in 2005) of cost estimating tools:

> 'The commercial software estimating tools are far from perfect and they can be wrong, too. But automated estimates often outperform human estimates in terms of accuracy, and always in terms of speed and cost effectiveness. However, no method of estimation is totally error-free. The current best practice for software cost estimation is to use a combination of software cost estimating tools coupled with software project management tools, under the careful guidance of experienced software project managers and estimating specialists.' *Capers Jones (2005).*

Activity 6.2: Look at a website for a cost estimation tool

Look at a website for a cost estimation tool: CoStar, CostModeler, CostXpert, KnowledgePlan, PRICE S, SEER, SLIM, and SoftCost.

Assess the similarity between the tool and the methods discussed in this chapter.

What advantages does the tool offer over COCOMO II?

Is the tool suitable to a particular environment or project context?

6.8   Software costs – the learning loop

Learning about costs

Learning takes place both within a single project and through projects sharing their data.

As a project progresses, the level of uncertainty and risk should be reduced. Cost estimates should get more accurate, as shown in Figure 6.6.

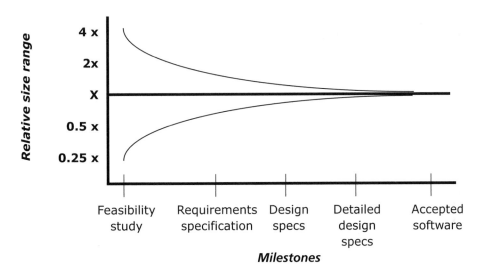

Figure 6.6: Estimate accuracy improves during the project. Accuracy of software size and cost estimates may be out by a factor of 4 in the early stages. COCOMO II uses the estimation ranges shown in the diagram. (Boehm et al 2000c)

Estimates (of time, cost, effort) occur at any point in the software development process. These estimates are often highly inaccurate in the early stages of a project, and should converge to near-total accuracy by the end of the project (when the costs should be known).

Cost estimation accuracy depends on experience with similar projects in the past. Cost estimation algorithms may initially be imported from other benchmark organisations; experienced project managers carry a set of learned expectations from previous projects. These are refined and calibrated with every project, and should therefore become more accurate over time, provided the software development approach remains stable.

Metrication within organisations

The approach which a particular organisation takes to the metrication of its software development processes depends on the ethos within which the organisation operates. At one extreme, software process data may be routinely gathered as part of the every day management control activities. This, for example, was a normal practice in the Japanese software factories in the eighties. At the other end, an organisation may only gather data about certain aspects of the development process in response to a perceived need (for example, cost estimation, quality improvement and productivity enhancement).

Cost metrics are predictive tools, which use past experience to predict the cost of future projects. Some cost metrics are based on a single factor, which is the most important factor that significantly affects the cost of a project (for example, size of software program and effort spent by software developers). Other metrics are technology-specific using quantitative data from a past project in a specific software development environment (for example object-oriented programming, a specific database development environment, or a certain operating system environment).

Mature organisations tend to have a comprehensive metrication programme that not only deals with cost estimation but also with establishing a baseline against which software productivity and quality improvements are measured.

Historical data

By far the best tool a project manager can use to estimate a project, phase, iteration, or simple activity is historical data. The most basic approach is to record at the different stages of a project, the effort, duration, and size estimates as well as the estimating processes and assumptions, and then track actual results against these estimates so estimation can be improved in the future.

Calibration

An off-the-shelf estimation model/tool may produce a 'good enough' estimate for most organisations but, in an ideal world, you would tune it to match your organisation's history. And that's the hard part: collecting data describing completed projects (for example, size, effort, duration and cost drivers). You'll need at least half a dozen data points to start obtaining reasonable results.

Use of feedback

By tracking actual results against estimates, it is possible to gauge the accuracy of past estimates. This allows the margin of error in estimates to be accommodated in current plans, and reduced in future plans.

In a well-managed software organisation, the estimates from projects will become more accurate over time, and this is not just because of the increased quantity of historical data. It is also because the cost management data is used to improve performance, and to reduce the variability of performance.

A feedback loop, in which productivity correctly influences cost structures, should generate several benefits:

- Incentive for individuals and teams to improve productivity
- Reduced variation of the productivity/cost ratio
- Greater management visibility and control of productivity and cost.

6.9 Cost control

Software cost estimates are used to set target financial budgets for completion of project tasks. Project monitoring then tracks actual expenditure against planned expenditure, and actual progress against planned progress. Funding is released to the project in a controlled way.

Decision makers need a high-level view of project status, plus the metrics and trend information for the project. Managers can then, for example, know when the project has met 90 per cent of its requirements, or when there are too many unfixed defects. With the right metrics, they can formulate more accurate cost and schedule profiles. Mid-course adjustments can be taken if necessary to reduce budget and schedule risk. In addition, the trend information improves the schedule and progress predictions.

Earned-value management

For years, government agencies (especially in the USA) and many public sector organisations have used earned-value management (EVM) to help plan, monitor and control projects. EVM establishes a project's progress against its milestones of agreed-upon planned value (PV), or budget. (Note that the concept of 'value' here is not the same thing as 'stakeholder value', which is concerned with potential organisational benefits being delivered. Here 'value' is linked to achievement of the planned, scheduled work defined in terms of costs.)

Earned value (EV) provides an objective measurement of how much work has been accomplished on a project. Using the earned value process, the management team can readily compare how much work has actually been completed against the amount of work planned to have been accomplished. EVM thus provides an integrated approach for planning, cost collection and performance measurement against defined baselines..

First, all work is planned, budgeted, and scheduled in time-phased PV increments constituting a performance measurement baseline (PMB). (This typically relies on having a clearly defined work breakdown structure which defines the work and is used as the basis for deriving the budget against which performance and achievement will be measured.)

As work is performed, it is 'earned', giving rise to EV. EV is calculated in exactly the same way as the PV was calculated. Comparing the EV with the PV compares the value of work accomplished with the value of work planned. EV – PV gives the schedule variance figure (SV).

In addition, the actual costs (AC) incurred are compared to the earned value to establish the cost variance (CV), that is, EV – AC = CV.

See Figure 6.7 which shows a graph of a project's planned and actual progress measured in monetary units against time. The plots for PV, EV and AC are shown.

Originally, EVM information was provided after the fact to support payment and related administration, but over the last twenty years there has been a demand to have visibility about variances as early as possible in the process. EVM shows deviations from baselined plans. It is particularly useful for identifying the consumption of float (slack) not showing on the critical path of the project. One obvious benefit is that the project's future progress can be extrapolated from its past work. If that throws up any problems, then they can be addressed early and alternative projections can be derived showing the impact of the identified problems. Given that EVM provides a measure of performance to date, it further enables the prediction of future performance and the derivation of the estimated cost to complete the project based on observed trends and variances.

This section has only given a brief introduction to EVM and not all the calculations that can be performed have been discussed. See the National Aeronautics and Space Administration (NASA) EVM website (NASA EVM 2006) for further information.

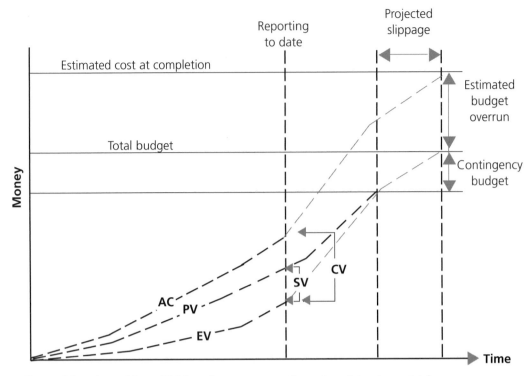

Figure 6.7: Adapted from 'EVM performance reporting – key data elements' from 'Overview' web page on NASA EVM website (NASA EVM 2006)

6.10 Estimating cost for student projects

You may be asking yourself how to relate the topics in this chapter to your project ; financial cost is, after all, not a major factor in most student projects, as typically:

- A student does not have to seek funding for their student project or submit payment requests
- Any hardware or software used is usually already in place, so there are no additional costs
- Student projects have only one project member, who doesn't demand a salary
- Student projects, due to the resources available and the deadlines imposed, are fairly small.

However, there are some significant lessons to be learnt, with estimation of effort the most important. Your project plan should have a work breakdown structure (WBS) and you should be able to apply 'learning from experience' to your work. For instance, if you have several software modules to write, try to estimate each of their sizes. This could be done for other project activities such as writing up. Record the amount of time you put into each of your different project activities and use the data to adjust your estimates. You are then calibrating your productivity rates for the different activities.

Use an *earned-value* management approach: plot your actual progress against your planned progress. If you identify delays, you can try to stipulate if the trend will continue and delay all other activities (in which case you need to re-calibrate all your estimates to take account of the reason for the delays), or whether you simply need to add the total delayed period to the overall duration. If the time available continues to shrink, you may need to reconsider the scope of the project (eg fewer modules or features, delivering less content or more prototypes).

If you are being too ambitious about the size of your project, then remember the discussion earlier about size and diseconomy of scale. It is better to have a design that can evolve: plan to deliver something smaller, which can be grown, later, in stages as time allows.

6.11 **Summary**

In this chapter, we have discussed the cost management process; see Figure 6.8 for an overview. The three cost management processes are outlined: cost estimation, cost budgeting and cost control. The cost management sub-processes are highlighted using shaded boxes. Within cost estimation, the three steps (sub-processes) are identified (Step 1, Step 2 and Step 3). Note how the WBS-related and schedule-related processes fit with the cost management processes.

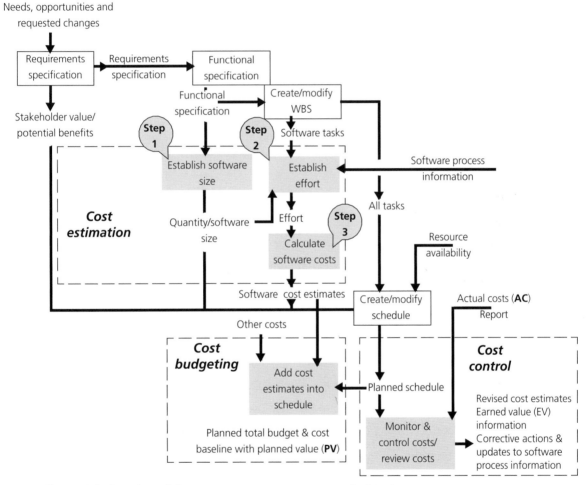

Figure 6.8: Overview of the cost management process and related processes

We have shown how cost estimates can be derived from determining the software size and the amount of effort required. Under the topic of establishing software size, we looked at counting lines of code and function points. For the topic of effort, we considered the issue of productivity rates being affected in complex ways by various different factors. This was further developed when we looked later on at the equations for COCOMO II and saw the influences of cost drivers and scale factors. Changing software development processes have lead to the development of the enhanced COCOMO II.

We also discussed some alternative methods to COCOMO II methods: Wideband Delphi, and WBS-based costing. Finally, we turned to the topics of software estimation tools and organisational learning through collecting data from past projects and considered methods of keeping track of cost and progress.

6.12 Review questions

 Question 6.1

What do you think would happen if there was no concern for costs, and no mechanism for controlling costs? Would this ever be a good thing? Can you identify any software organisations where cost management is not a determining factor in software project management?

 Question 6.2

Identify what happens when a manager is responsible for some elements of software costs, and not others. Can you think of any examples where this applies?

Question 6.3

What would you expect to happen when software size metrics are used to calculate and reward developer productivity? How might this affect cost estimation?

Question 6.4

Why is counting lines of code in a consistent manner important?

Question 6.5

Why do you think contractors might have mixed feelings about earned value management (EVM)?

Question 6.6

What would happen to your costs if a customer demanded much higher software quality levels – say approaching state-of-the-art reliability?

6.13 Feedback on activities

Activity 6.1: Investigate costs

The main aim of this activity was to get you thinking about how a cost estimates are drawn up – and also to consider how the costs are distributed. Look back to the section on software costs to check if you have forgotten any costs. For example, have you included estimates for time spent by users evaluating your design? Have you allowed sufficient testing time?

Now consider how it would have helped you if you had been able to look at historical data from past projects while doing your cost estimation. You would have had examples that you could adapt and you would be able to assess your figures against other projects. It would have saved you thinking time and you would have been reassured that your plans contained the right content and that the time allocations for specific activities were reasonable.

Activity 6.2: Look at a website for a cost estimation tool

Hopefully, you found an interesting website for a cost estimation tool. Did you find the features that Capers Jones described?

6.14 References

Boehm, B. (1981), *Software Engineering Economics*, Prentice Hall PTR, ISBN 0 13 822122 7. See also **http://sunset.usc.edu/index.html**

Boehm, Barry, Chris Abts and Sunita Chulani, (2000a), *Software Development Cost Estimation Approaches – A Survey*, **http://sunset.usc.edu/index.html** Select 'Publications', then '2000', then USC-CSE-2000-505 [Last Accessed: December 2006].

Boehm, Barry, Dr. Ellis Horowitz, Dr. Raymond Madachy and Chris Abts, (2000b), Future Trends, Implications in Cost Estimation Models, *CrossTalk*, April 2000, **http://sunset.usc.edu/index.html** Select 'Publications', then '2000', then USC-CSE-2000-530 [Last Accessed: December 2006].

Boehm, Barry W., Chris Abts, A. Winsor Brown, Sunita Chulani, Bradford K. Clark, Ellis Horowitz, Ray Madachy, Donald Reifer and Bert Steece, (2000c) *Software Cost Estimation with COCOMO II*, Prentice Hall PTR, ISBN 0 13 026692 2.

Brooks, F. Jr., (1995), *The Mythical Man-Month and Other Essays on Software Engineering*, Addison-Wesley, ISBN 0 20 183595 9. Originally published in 1974.

Enzensberger, H.M. (2006), *The Number Devil*, Granta Books, ISBN 1 86207828 9.

International Function Point User Group. See the official website of the International Function Point User Group at **www.ifpug.org** [Last Accessed: December 2005].

Jones, Capers (2005), Software Cost Estimating Methods for Large Projects, *CrossTalk* April 2005

National Aeronautics and Space Administration (NASA) (2006), *Earned Value Management (EVM)*. See website at **http://evm.nasa.gov/overview.html** [Last Accessed: December 2006].

Project Management Institute (2004), *A Guide to the Project Management Body of Knowledge (3rd edition) (PMBOK Guide)*, ISBN 1 93069945 X, ISBN13 9781930699458. **www.pmi.org** [Last accessed: November 2006].

Sommerville, Ian (2007), *Software Engineering* (8th Edition), Addison-Wesley, ISBN 0 321 31379 8.

Wiegers, K.(2000), 'Stop Promising Miracles', *Software Development*, February 2000. See **www.processimpact.com/articles/delphi.html** [Last Accessed: December 2005].

CHAPTER 7

Leadership and teamworking

OVERVIEW

No matter how good your project's objectives, schedules and budgets, it is typically your management and the membership of the project team that will make the difference between success and failure. This chapter discusses project leadership and project teams. It also considers some of the ethical and cultural issues that may affect a project and how they are best handled.

Learning outcomes	At the end of this chapter you should be able to:

- Discuss the importance of people factors in projects

- Explain the role of an effective project leader in an IT project

- Identify and explain the key factors in creating positive teamwork

- Discuss some ethical and cultural issues relevant to projects.

Several of the activities in this chapter do not have feedback, as the issues revolve around your own personal feelings and interactions; there is frequently not a 'right' answer, but it is vitally important that you consider and are aware of the issues in question.

7.1 People make the difference

There is a growing body of evidence that successful projects prioritise people. One study refers to the four critical project success factors (CSFs) as the four COMs: 'comfort, competence, commitment and communication' (Nguyen et al, 2004). It is of note that all these four factors are perceived in *human* rather than *process* terms. Look back to Yardley's table in Chapter 1 (Table 1.1) and read through the list of perceived human factors influencing project failure. Notice how the list of human factors is longer than the lists for technology and process factors.

The original Standish Group's *CHAOS Report* (1994) states that nearly 30 per cent of project success is attributable to user involvement and executive support. More recent writers (such as Melymuka (1997), Markus – for a starting point, see Markus and Cornelis (2000) – and Yardley (2002)) all emphasise the importance of communication.

Key consultancy firms, such as Thomsett International and Bartlett, provide tools that emphasise the importance of finding the right people and of having good communication within the team. Markus (2002) states:

> '…it is not likely that IS professionals are as well placed as organizational executives to manage the full spectrum of IT-related risks. I hasten to add, however, the IS professionals are essential partners in the effective management of IT-related risk.'

All these sources admit that project management tools and methodologies can be used but, at the end of the day, they all conclude that it is the people factors that make or break the project.

Activity 7.1

Project success criteria

Review the project success criteria given below (and repeated from Chapter 1); consider how attention to the four COMS (comfort, competence, commitment and communication) may help ensure success. The success criteria were as follows:

The project must be completed such that it is:

- Within time

- Within budget

- At the desired performance level

- Of acceptable quality

- Offering at least the minimum agreed functionality

- Utilising the assigned resources effectively and efficiently

- Accepted by the client

- Used by the intended users

- Delivering the promised benefits (which should ideally exceed the costs).

7.2 What is teamwork?

Projects are normally conducted in teams. Teams are defined in inclusive terms: you are identified as *belonging to a team*. Also teams, once established, assume an identity of their own and may change their mode of operation as the project unfolds in relation to a wider organisation where the team is seen as somehow exclusive, set apart. Defining teamwork, therefore, needs to take each of these perspectives into account.

Team membership

To understand teamwork, first think about what makes 'a team'. A team is more than a group of individuals; project teams are usually considered to have:

- **A shared goal**
- **Commitment to each other within the project**
- **Willingness to learn.**

These are all *values*. Values have to be developed, made explicit, nurtured and rewarded.

Activity 7.2

Team values

Take a few minutes to think about these three values and what they mean to you.

- Have you ever been a member of a team with a shared goal?

- If you were/have been part of a larger team, what do you think would be/was your commitment to the other team members?

- If someone had a better (or different) idea about how to manage part of the project , how do you think you would/did you react?

To these values, teams also need to add *skills*. Peter Scholtes (1996) identifies the following as being important to good teamwork:

- Expertise in the subject at hand
- Knowing how to work as a team
- Planning
- Conduct of good meetings
- Ability to manage logistics and details
- Gathering of useful data
- Effective analysis of the data
- Communication of the results and implementation of changes.

Activity 7.3

Personal team skills

In which order would you place your own ability in each of these skills? Consider them in relation to any projects you have undertaken in any aspect of your life. (In this instance, 'project' could be any team activity, such as sports, drama or planning a holiday). Where are your skill strengths? And weaknesses?

One team, several modes

In teamwork, values and skills are brought together within an operational environment to be applied in one or more ways to suit the project. Team members may work on different parts of the same task consecutively or simultaneously. They may work on separate tasks consecutively or simultaneously. They may be geographically dispersed with asynchronous communications – or all in the same location with constant discussions. There may be periods of time when team members work independently of each other before group meetings, where ideas and results can then be shared – and a consensus arrived at leading to future work as a group.

There are those, such as Thompson (2006), who consider that true teamwork can only be achieved if work shows both a division of labour and concurrency. He calls subdivided tasks with no concurrency, 'groupwork'; and tasks where individuals all do the same thing at the same time (for example, project brainstorming sessions), 'crowdwork' (ibid). It may, however, be reasonable to consider both of these as types of teamwork, provided the values and overarching organisational structures for each of the activities is the same. The 'team' factor comes from the individuals identifying with each other and working to a common end.

The organisational interface

These team values and skills, important as they are, do not operate in a vacuum. They are set within organisations or communities and may be created within one department, across many, or across several otherwise unconnected organisations. Understanding this interface, its effect on team values and operational constraints, is vital to effective project teamwork. A project team may also have to interact not just with normal organisation structures but with a project board or steering committee (a higher-level group of managers – see later).

Effect on team values

In many organisations, the strength of personal identification with the team and its values is what frequently differentiates project teams in research and development (R&D) or software/ hardware development departments (where team members frequently work with each other) from cross-functional project teams brought together – perhaps to serve a particular requirement or to launch a particular product. Here, the team members may have little or no prior knowledge of the other team members.

Handy (1978) calls organisations that frequently create teams from different departments or specialisms, 'matrix organisations'. These teams are often less coherent than those in more fixed, 'functional', structures because the participants will have loyalties to any departmental teams which are ongoing – and which may well take preference. The project team in this case will find it has 'representatives' from relevant departments and those departmental divisions may surface in such non-productive behaviours as 'Marketing' blaming 'Production' for late delivery and 'Production' retaliating by blaming 'Marketing' for overpromising. To overcome these original loyalties, and to forge a new cross-functional team that stands united within and against the whole of the rest of the organisation, requires adept leadership and good political skills. A key to succeeding in this environment is in fostering and maintaining a project spirit.

Still more complex is the creation of inter-organisational project teams; for example, customer-supplier product development and deployment teams or international research project teams (see later). In such cases, the same principles apply and effective teamwork is only achieved if values are genuinely shared; but the contextual barriers and political rivalries frequently take considerable time to overcome.

Effect on project operations

All teams are likely to operate under very explicit organisational constraints, such as budgets, contracts, deadlines and methods to be used. Constraints may, of course, have both positive as well as negative effects. A contract that stipulates weekly meetings of all the key stakeholders is imposing a constraint that, all else being well, should allow discussion of difficulties and ensure customer buy-in to the eventual product.

Activity 7.4

Project constraints

Take a minute now to create a list of the constraints you have seen, or could anticipate, being applied to projects. Decide whether, on balance, these may be positive or negative in their effects.

Project boards

In large or inter-organisational projects there is often a project board or steering committee to which the project team will report. The composition of this board will usually have a strong business management bias, so stakeholders not directly involved in the daily project work are likely to form most of the membership. There may be representatives from finance, marketing and HR, The line manager of the project leader might often attend. The project leader will not have a seat on the project board but will be required to present reports in person.

This separation between the project team and the project board can seem frustrating but the two groups are there for very different purposes.

- **The project team:** this body is there to attain the project goals as approved by the project board. Sometimes the project board defines these goals and hands them to the project team; at others the project board outlines the goal for the team to fully define and the board then approves the refined version

- **The project board:** there to ensure wider business goals are met, to respond to external influences, to oversee internal resource usage and to provide project governance. A powerful project board can be very supportive of the project team if more resources are needed and the business case is justifiable – but a project board may also decide to close an otherwise successful project if business priorities change.

A note on training and development

In terms of pure single-project delivery, there is a case for selecting teams where every member is optimally skilled, so there is no need for training and development. Within organisations or in constantly reforming cross-organisational projects, however, project teams are often seen as place where existing skills can be developed or new skills learned. Line managers may 'lend' staff for precisely that reason. Staff may be attracted to the project because they want something new. Both for the sake of the organisation, which needs to be seen to develop its people if it is to recruit, and for more selfish reasons if you wish to recruit people to future projects in which you have a say, your project needs to factor this in to team selection, role assignment and team-working.

7.3 Project manager or project leader?

Depending upon where you work, you may find team members called 'project manager' or 'project leader' or you may have both titles in use – and still perceive that the real power rests with someone else entirely. In many instances the team is free to find its own terminology but not in others, such as PRINCE2 (Projects IN Controlled Environments, typically used in the UK public sector – see Appendix) regulated projects. Whatever the case, there are three key roles that need to be adopted by one or more people. Where more than one person is involved, each must know which of the three roles is theirs and be clear about how it interacts with the others. The roles are:

- **Champion**
- **Leader**
- **Manager.**

- **The champion** is the person who promotes the team within the client organisation. The champion is employed by the client organisation and is usually in a reasonably senior position. The champion's role may be within the department; across the company liaising with, for example, sales or HR; or at national and international level, for example lobbying government departments or locating European funding. The champion will therefore have good presentation and negotiation skills. The champion may not have technical subject expertise and in major projects is frequently appointed by the board after the project has been broadly agreed. This sometimes seem strange, or even threatening, to those new to project work but their value to the team is in their ability to take care of the business 'noise'. When the project work is complete, it is the champion who will make certain that the customer is expecting its arrival and is ready to receive it, and it is the champion who will enthuse the customer to use the system

- **The leader** is the person within the team who has the overall vision and can communicate that in ways that inspire others to reach the overall goal. This does not mean that all Leaders lay out the vision explicitly; some facilitative leaders choose to 'lead from behind' and facilitate actions without broadcasting their involvement or 'requirements'. This is particularly true of highly skilled professional teams where the leader may be the one who summarises and focuses discussions, ensuring that all experts are heard and the best solution agreed. In less experienced teams, however, the leader may be more obviously directional, explaining the overall goal and the constraints, suggesting a working methodology that others might then be invited to challenge or improve but nonetheless giving a base on which to build. These leaders and, to a lesser extent, facilitative ones, have the most opportunities for also being coaching leaders. They may not have the unidirectional zeal of a visionary leader but they can take an idea and use it to help others along their chosen professional paths – and help even if that path is sometimes rather obscure to the novice team member

- **The manager** is the person responsible for logistics and administration. In projects being run according to PRINCE2 or European Union (EU) requirements, or other large projects that need to prove compliance to industry standards such as SCORM (Shareable Content Object Reference Model) or W3C (World Wide Web Consortium – for interoperability), the project manager may not have development expertise and may even be seconded to the project from a department with a title such as 'contracting' or 'technical administration' or 'central projects'. The more complex the project, the less likely it is that this role includes management of personnel in the sense of having line management responsibility. They will, however, monitor progress, issue forms and expect everything to be completed to deadlines that are on the schedules that they maintain. They will often locate, and have delegated authority for, purchasing resources – even though they may not have direct budget control. They are often the least flexible members of the team and need to be highly disciplined, detail conscious, and dispassionate in maintaining records and working through the inevitable conflicts and crises.

From this discussion, it should be clear why highly effective teams, especially on complex projects, usually have both a designated project manager and a project leader (sometimes called a project director). The reason is that the two roles often require different skill sets: being both a 'lead from the front' visionary and a dispassionate chaser of detail is not easy!

7.4 Specialist roles

In order to set the project budget, project managers will usually (but not always) be able to list the specialist skills that the team must assemble. If available, reference to similar project schedules will assist. The tasks will typically fall into three main phases:

- **Project scoping**
- **Project development**
- **Project handover**

– and a project manager will need to identify the specialisms needed for each in order to phase the financing appropriately. The following types of staff will be needed:

- At the **scoping** stage:
  - business analysts, requirements analysts, market researchers, report writers
- At the **development** stage:
  - accessibility experts; programmers (in various languages); database designers, developers and administrators; graphic designers; logistics managers; project managers; software testers; systems architects; web designers, programmers and site builders; support technicians; user-interface specialists; user-testing specialists
- At the **handover** stage:
  - business analysts; project managers; publicists; report writers; technical writers; writers of user guides.

7.5 Shaping the project team

There is a wide range of factors affecting who is assigned to a project team and to the roles within it. These include:

- **Organisational culture**
- **Business sector(s) in which the project is taking place**
- **Leadership style**
- **Timelines**
- **Desired secondary outcomes**
- **Regulation compliance demands**
- **Available resources**
- **Anticipated team dynamics.**

We'll discuss each of these in a little more detail.

Influence of organisational culture

Organisational culture is usually defined as 'the way we do things round here'. Think, for example, of the differences driving the design of the online customer interfaces for the Inland Revenue (personal tax) and for a supermarket order-and-delivery service. The first, however friendly it is meant to appear, is primarily about compliance, getting tax returns in on time with each of the questions answered fully and accurately. It is essential that those details are read only by authorised personnel and that resulting tax demands are sent only to the person identified by a unique code. The purpose of the supermarket interface, however, is to entice the customer: the customer could choose to go to the store, or to another store, or not shop at all that week. When you get to the end of the Fruit and Vegetables section, the program will not refuse to move on to Drinks just because you did not order any carrots. The system might, however, remind you when you go to the 'checkout' that you normally order carrots and give you the option to add some if you want. If the supermarket forgets to put aubergines on the website, no real harm is done beyond some lost sales that may, in any case, be offset by substitute sales. If the Inland Revenue forgets to include a box for 'other earned income', the tax assessment will be wrong and may continue to affect future assessments for other years.

Edgar Schein (1980), one of the leading academics in the field of organisational culture, lists seven key areas in which the culture may manifest itself:

- **Language:** the way in which members of a group use vocal sounds or written signs to convey meaning, for example company jargon
- **Use of symbols:** any object or event that conveys meaning usually by representing something else, for example a badge, a uniform, a logo and parking spaces
- **Ceremonies:** a ceremony can be described as a system of rites – elaborate and dramatic activities – connected with an event, usually with an audience, such as graduation ceremonies
- **Customs:** events that happen on a regular basis almost without any thought being taken as to whether they should occur, for example monthly meetings or weekly management reports
- **Methods of problem solving:** what shared basic assumptions are 'taken for granted' and contribute to the problem-solving methods, which becomes part of an organisation's culture and taught to new staff – 'the way we do things round here'? For example, 'all new customers know very little'.
- **Use of tools or technology:** cultural values influence the way in which tools are created and used
- **Design of work settings:** for example, positioning of desks, size of offices and type of building.

Activity 7.5

Organisational culture

1. Take a few minutes to think about and write down some of the key differences in organisational culture between the country's tax office (HM Revenue and Customs, in the UK) and a supermarket's online systems using Schein's categories.

2. Now think about the main organisational culture in which any project within your experience has taken place and list its key characteristics using the same headings.

It is perhaps worth noting that in his advice to leaders, Schein (2004) observes that leaders cannot control cultures – but may be controlled by them. Knowing the culture within which you are working is therefore vital to project management success.

Business sector influence

The business sectors in which projects are based have a considerable influence upon the way in which project teams are assembled.

- **In higher education at national and international level**, for example, it is usual for main team members to have met and worked together informally on research or to have met as junior members in funding bids before they come together in real project teams
- **In IT consultancy firms**, the project teams will be assembled by senior managers picking from an available skillset and that team will then have to integrate, to some extent with existing post-holders in the client firm and, perhaps, with some co-opted members, the selection of whom they may or may not be able to influence
- **In major construction projects**, it is likely that all team members will be interviewed and assessed against a set of clear job specifications and personality profiles and then subjected to pre-organised team-building activities
- **In small software development enterprises**, of course, the team may be whoever is in the office plus the most likely candidate sourced from searching existing lists of contacts in personal address books.

Influence of leadership style

Outside rigidly structured organisations such as the UK Civil Service, it is common for leadership style to have a very strong influence on team composition. The *US Army Handbook* (1973) is just one of many sources to identify three styles of leadership:

- **Authoritarian leadership** is good for coaching and often for short 'crisis' projects
- **Participative styles** suit those teams which are reasonably skilled and where the leader's experience or technical ability is accepted on an equal footing with some of the others
- **Delegative styles** suit teams that are highly skilled and just need co-ordination and support. Where the delegatively led team is too large or the business risks are too high for real teamwork to be accorded shared team accountability, the leader is still the one who will primarily be held to account.

Influence of timelines

Timelines can be inelastic (university assessments, customer contracts) or relatively elastic (research projects). Each has its merits but never confuse the two!

Influence of desired secondary outcomes

Strange though it may sound, the main goal of the project that has just been entrusted to your care might not be the only one, or even the most important one. Many an IT/IS project has ended in misery for the team because they produced the best possible technological solution but nobody ever said 'thank you'. Why not? Well, the business goal was to cultivate a relationship with the client and do something altogether bigger and more interesting.

Activity 7.6

It's not just the end result..

Take a moment to consider why Student A has an assignment solution that does not work, but may get better marks than Student B, whose solution works perfectly?

Influence of regulations

Regulation compliance is one of the strongest determining factors in team selection. Many project management programs and systems have pre-assigned and unalterable role descriptors.

The main advantages of this are that they:

- Ensure good governance by, say, separating auditing from management and development from testing
- Provide a framework for working in multi-organisation teams
- Provide clear, recorded, task boundaries so that staff changeover is less disruptive
- Remind people to allocate tasks that might otherwise be forgotten at the budget stage (e.g. support technician or translator)
- Raise the profile of success criteria (e.g. conformance to accessibility guidelines) that may sometimes be forgotten in the excitement of highly creative projects.

At other times, the influence of regulations can be less benign – especially in small projects or those that utilise many experts. In small projects which need fast completion times, more experienced team leaders may be able swiftly to assign multiple roles to each available individual and work the system efficiently; but there are also occasions when you may need to seek official sanction for running a non-compliant project and that in itself may use up much of your available timeslot. In expert projects, it can be the nomenclature or the forms, or both, that cause the problems as people would rather work in their own 'expert' fashions.

Faced with this, you have two swift options and one that takes rather longer:

- Find a project manager who can disguise the paperwork and activate great people skills
- Work with someone possibly less able but more tolerant of the paperwork
- Spend time team-building, sharing expertise and then, once the comfort level is high enough, make the issue of the required manner of directing 'this team's obvious expertise' a shared challenge. Some expert teams have been known to rotate role designations. Others bring in their own support teams as a non-project cost as this frees up their time to do other things (their opportunity cost).

Influence of resource availability

It is a rare team where all the first-choice members are available for the intended duration of the project. Compromises will have to be made based on ensuring customer satisfaction and delivery of the expected products.

Activity 7.7

Making compromises

Look again at the accepted success criteria and rank them according to where you believe *compromises* can best be made:

a) Within time

b) Within budget

c) At the desired performance level

d) With acceptable quality

e) Offering at least the minimum agreed functionality

f) While utilising the assigned resources effectively and efficiently

g) So that the system is accepted by the client

h) Used by the intended users

i) To deliver the promised benefits (which should ideally exceed the costs).

Influence of team dynamics

Temperament clashes and personal working styles can have profound effects on the way teams work together. The major consulting firms invest heavily in training, to enable staff to adapt and work well in whatever team they are assigned to. However, difficulties can still arise. No matter how large or small the team, a basic understanding of personality and team roles will help. Skilled team leaders consider the likely overall (human and task) contribution of team members when assembling teams.

Work carried out by Meredith Belbin (1981) over three decades has led to a number of versions of his much-used 'team roles' questionnaires and other diagnostic tools such as the Management Team Role-indicator (MTR-i) have similar role descriptions. For teams to be successful, you need people in each role (with people playing multiple roles where necessary). In software projects, you may, as you have already seen, have an abundance of specialists but, from among them or in addition to them, you also need to find:

- **Resource investigators** – to find people, processes, existing code, facilities, etc
- **Co-ordinators** – to ensure smooth communications and workflow
- **Teamworkers –** to help others and plug the gaps
- **Monitor/evaluators** – for the reality checks
- **Shapers** – to take ideas and develop them enough for others to complete
- **Completer-finishers** – to ensure all the detail is done
- **Plants** – to 'plant' creative ideas
- **Implementers** – to turn designs into products.

Activity 7.8

Team roles

1. Consider the list of roles defined by Belbin (and listed above) in relation to a favourite sports team or band: who fills which roles (remembering that one person can fulfil more than one role)?

2. Now think of all the teams you belong to. Which roles do you most often occupy? Have you changed your preference for a role as you have become older or more experienced?

One of the most common mistakes that even experienced team leaders make is to remember people as successful in only one role and select them for that role in the next project. This can lead to a wide range of difficulties. At its simplest, it may prevent a team member from gaining skills. It may also lead to friction if one team member, for example, thinks it is their role to shape the project but others, less well known, are equally or better skilled at achieving that.

7.6 Customers in project teams

As was discussed in Chapter 1, evolutionary and agile methods are demanding more customer involvement. The rapid pace of technological change means that customers are frequently unsure of all the ways in which they want to use new products and so projects develop in a series of small steps, with customer feedback being fed immediately into the decision making about the next step.

External customer teams

Ideally, as has just been seen, a project team is one cohesive unit, regardless of the number of organisations from which it is drawn. In reality, those within the team who are part of an external customer organisation will be subject to similar but totally separate pressures from the supplier organisation. They will have their own project champion/sponsor, their own career structures, their own finance departments, their own inter-departmental rivalries and their own customer bases with ever-changing demands. All of these are stakeholders in the project. Obviously, the longer the project, the more time is available for any of these to cause difficulties – so confidence in the team, both within it and around it, needs to be actively developed. This is usually managed through two means:

- **Quick wins**
- **Active customer relationship management**.

Activity 7.9

Quick wins

Which project lifecycles are best suited to providing quick wins for the customer and why?

Customer relationship management (CRM)

In projects where the external customer is well known, a wide range of historical influences come into play in any new project. This can be both positive (strong goodwill from previous working relationships, knowledge of likely pressure points) and problematic. Consider the following list:

- Do the opposite numbers (e.g. project leaders, sponsors, software developers, systems integrators) know and respect each other?
- Do they like each other?
- Do they acknowledge each other and communicate with one another?
- Does a junior member from the supplier organisation have a better working relationship with the customer's leader than the two leaders have between themselves?
- Have the internal reporting structures changed on either side?
- Have the quality control systems changed on either side?
- Has everyone got the latest versions of order forms, sign-off sheets, logos, etc?
- Are all contact addresses the same as last time? (And has anyone changed their name?)
- Who has been promoted and so may expect a more senior project role?
- What strengths and weaknesses do you anticipate?
- If you have used 'single point of contact' in the past, did it work?
- What history is attached to meeting attendance? Who is likely to be there? Who is likely to change times/locations and why?
- Which business pressures should you factor in to project planning (e.g. different accounting periods, sales conferences)
- Did any specialist, non-technical skills contribute to success last time and are those skills available this time (e.g. speakers of other languages)?

CRM in action

Pause for a moment to consider any projects or teams in which you have been involved – even if only as a customer. Have you observed any of the above factors having an effect on the development of the project and its final deliverables?

Active customer management requires both pre-emptive planning and also, as projects become less predictable (with waterfall models less likely than, say, extreme models), it requires agile CRM.

Agile CRM

This relatively new perspective of interrelating with customers applies whether the project occurs in one organisation or many. Its use means the project team as a whole can respond rapidly to changes in the wider environment; but to do that, it needs effective communication systems. Key to this is usually some form of centralised project tracking system, perhaps with different levels of access for team members and for other stakeholders such as people in other departments who may wish to adopt the eventual product. This system is frequently web-based, to allow simple access for remote workers. A team using agile CRM will also have integrated telephony, e-mail, messaging and, perhaps, voice recognition; no one needs be out of contact and unaware of project developments. The technology, however, is only part of the solution: people, both within the team and the other stakeholders need to use it. Several EU projects, for example, have cited use of project websites as measures of project communication – but individuals then reverted to using a variety of formal and personal e-mail addresses because that is the way they are used to working. Buy-in to the technology comes from understanding the benefits, which include human interaction functionality that allows a wide variety of people to ask questions, flag changes and escalate potential issues for rapid discussion by all the relevant parties.

7.7 Meetings and reports

Managing project progress, staff development, customer interfaces, the demands of other stakeholders and reporting to the project board require a considerable amount of communication. Much of this communication will be handled through meetings, but written reports will of course also be necessary.

Meetings

The main advantages of meetings are that they:

- Save a speaker's time (communication is one-to-many)
- Can allow discussion
- Ensure everyone present is told the same thing at the same time
- Provide incentives for people to complete work before having to report in public
- Provide coaching opportunities
- Can be minuted to provide a record of progress.

On the downside, poor meeting management means that meetings can take over your life. Before calling a meeting you should:

- Have a purpose and an agenda
- Know who needs to attend (as opposed to who wants to attend)
- Check attendees are available
- Check attendees will have sufficient time to prepare, if that is necessary
- If minutes are needed, ensure someone is available to take them in the appropriate format.

Meeting modes

The format of the meeting you call should match its purpose.

- **Coaching sessions**, for example, may be spur-of-the-moment interventions at someone's desk or pre-booked in a quiet room
- **Work-group meetings** may be Voice over Internet phone (VOIP) (with or without webcams) or in a meeting room or, to build team spirit, over a meal in a local restaurant
- **Review meetings** are most likely to be formal face-to-face meetings, with those unable to attend connected over a video link.

Despite the ease with which many communicate using e-mail or instant messaging systems, formal meetings are usually helped by visual contact: it is easier to gauge others' attention to the subject and how they are reacting to what is being said.

The advent of frequent remote and intercontinental working means that some of the most important meetings for team morale and closure, those celebrating successes or commiserating with failures, are particularly tricky to organise. They just do not work as well online; and for the head office staff to have a party and the remote workers not to be included is counter-productive. Alternatives to the meeting are often used, for example couriering small gifts to everyone on the same day, preferably synchronising the hour of delivery.

Cultural differences in meetings

Why do projects have formal meetings? In multinational projects, the answer may not be as obvious as at first appears. The French, for example, tend to have meetings to (re)present the ideas and decisions that have already been agreed in less formal pre-meetings which may not include all those who consider themselves interested parties. The British and the Scandinavians, however, will call a formal meeting to reach those decisions. It follows that if you have both sets of expectations in the same room, considerable miscommunication can occur. Working as a team requires cultural sensitivity.

You also have to take account of cultural differences over approaches to conflict, arguments and shouting. Members of some cultures are faster than other cultures to lose their tempers – and some are faster than others to forgive. Even the way people report that they have found an error can vary considerably – some cultures will make a lot of 'noise' about the issue and magnify it, almost out of proportion, whereas other cultures will only report it quietly: if you were not paying full attention and did not notice the cues, you could miss the point. Some cultures place immense importance on politeness and following etiquette, whereas others are not so concerned. Some cultures will not accept women with equality. Gestures can also mean different things in different cultures. See also later in this chapter.

It is not just cultural differences. Different people within the same culture can, of course, have different views. For example, some people take offence at people pointing fingers at them, others don't. Some people get very upset if their name is misspelt or mispronounced.

Written reports

Many public sector and externally funded projects will impose their own requirements for formal written reports covering such topics as development progress, resource usage and ongoing risk assessment. Assembling the data for these will fall to the project manager, even if the report is written by the project leader. In many instances, the project manager will have some discretion about how this data is collected. Methods include:

- Online forms viewable by all the project team
- Forms submitted by e-mail
- Simple e-mailed data
- Project manager discussion and form filling.

That last method is particularly useful where key personnel are too busy, unable or unwilling to fill in the forms themselves. It is also useful where the sender has an incomplete grasp of the language in which the report has to be filed.

A project leader *may* have total discretion over what written reports are necessary;   the aim should be to have the minimum number of reports conducive to keeping the key stakeholders informed – in a manner that lets them take corrective or supporting action. For example, weekly timesheets will certainly be needed for contracted staff in order for them to get paid, so they will go to the project manager and then on to the finance office – but who else may need them? If the project is working with sub-budgets devolved to workgroups, then the workgroup leader will need a copy; but decisions have to be made whether the form goes initially to the workgroup leader or to the project manager, and what the processing time would be at each stage, to ensure that the accounts department is able to authorise timely payment of the contractor.

Projects with project boards will all require formal reports at regular intervals, usually with about one week's gap between the sending of the report and the meeting at which it will be discussed. When writing these formal reports, you need to keep in mind the composition of the board: it is highly likely that some members will not understand the technical detail of your project (although others certainly will, and they have the power to ask difficult questions). Many of the board will be interested in use of resources and ensuring progress is 'on schedule' to meet the agreed project goals; but how do you define 'on schedule' in an iterative rational unified process project or a Dynamic Systems Development Method (DSDM) one, which is still searching for the accurate business solution? Report writing needs communication and political skills as well as a sound grasp of the project reality.

In all cases, however, reports need to be comprehensible. This may seem obvious but many a project has suffered from allowing reports to be written by people with poor writing skills or an insufficient grasp of the language in which it is written. Sometimes, project managers are too embarrassed to tell specialists (possibly, but not always, working in a second language) that, while people can understand them in meetings, their written language is too hard to follow. At other times, a project is required to report in several languages, with the host country making the translations into the other language. People have been known to do this with the aid of the online translation program Babel and some assistance from a secretary. The end result is a document which can be very difficult for native speakers to read – and incomprehensible to any speakers of third languages. Use the professional translator's rule: for official documents, only translate into your own language. This may mean you need to add translators to your list of project specialists, but better that, than to have the project board reject the report and close down the project.

7.8 Ethics

There are three main areas in project management where ethics related to people factors and relationships tend to surface as a subject to be formally addressed:

- **Human interaction**
- **Payments**
- **Intellectual property rights.**

Human interaction

In many cases, ethical behaviour towards others will be codified either by law or by professional organisations so, as a last resort, these can be invoked in order to control cases of harassment, bullying and unfair treatment. If the whole project takes place under the jurisdiction of one country, only one set of employment laws will apply; international projects may, however, involve a number of ways of 'normal' working, and referring to the contract to find out which law takes precedence is unlikely to be an effective way forward. The project needs to establish its own culture within the legal framework as early as possible. This may include accepting:

- Different working hours
- Multilingual working
- Working alongside people you would not work with in your own organisation.

Activity 7.11

Working with the team

Why can it sometimes be difficult for people to accept other team members as professionals? Think of as many reasons as you can.

Payments

When is it acceptable to give someone involved in a project some money? In many organisations, the only acceptable answer is when it is their contracted salary. But what about contracted bonuses? If acceptance testing for a particular stage is not quite complete but the project manager agrees it is 'almost' complete, can stage bonuses be paid?

Activity 7.12

Paying a bonus

1. Your team will finish acceptance testing two days late on a three-month stage of a project – a stage which was expected to be challenging. If you finish the testing *within* the three-month stage, team members are entitled to a month's extra pay. There are six more stages planned for the project. Do you tell the accountant the testing is on time and authorise the bonus payment?

2. Your international, multi-organisation team is similarly going to be two days late on a three-month project stage. Team members from your own organisation will not get any bonuses until the end of the project – but a spokesman for the team members from a different national participant says that they *will* be paid bonuses at the end of every stage by their employer. However, if they do not deliver the stage on time, they will be replaced. What do you do?

There are, of course, other payment possibilities both to suppliers and to customers at every level from the chief executive to the report writer. In many cases, the giving or taking of 'kick-backs' or 'commissions' is forbidden by the employee's organisation. In some organisations this is so strictly applied that even accepting a cup of coffee in a café is unacceptable and can lead to disciplinary action. In other cases, the tradition of more major payments is so widespread that refusing can give offence and lead to cancellation of the project. Simple guidelines are:

- Know your own organisation's policies
- Find out what your customer's rules are on accepting/receiving hospitality
- If necessary, explain your company's policies – ideally, at the outset – and stick to them
- In potentially awkward situations, have a witness and meet on company property.

Intellectual property rights (IPR)

It is not surprising that in successful projects you can often find many people who claim to be the person responsible – but most listeners will realise it was a team effort. More difficult is the person who claims that a part of, say, the code is 'theirs'. They may well have written it and be justly proud of its elegance and fitness for purpose but it is very unlikely that it 'belongs' to them. It may not even belong to their employer because the contract may stipulate that all newly created code belongs to the customer. That code could then give the customer a major market advantage over other customers of yours.

Activity 7.13	**IPR**
	You are on a supplier's project team and you can create a piece of code that fits the customer needs – but you know it would also work in various applications for other customers.
	What do you do?

Indeed, the whole area of 'know-how' and ownership is complicated but usually subject to specific legislation; as a project manager, you may have to balance a duty to develop people, a duty to let them earn a living and a duty to guard property developed within the project. What, for example, is your attitude to key project personnel who leave immediately the project is over and go to work for the customer or for a rival organisation? Are there any safeguards against this in your organisation and, if so, can they be enforced?

7.9 Working as a team

Great project teams will be innovative because projects 'represent a unique undertaking' (as stated in Chapter 1) but the overall perception of them will be of fluent, harmonious work with effective transfer from one team-member to another, one stage to another. Project scoping, scheduling and resourcing have their roles in achieving this but the key ingredients are:

- Communication
- Support – encouraging, explaining things, checking all is well and being accessible
- Conflict handling.

You saw earlier that individuals may have preferences for team roles such as 'shaper' or 'completer/finisher'. You also saw that agile CRM promotes open and rapid communication to ensure customer satisfaction. You may not be surprised that a detail-conscious completer/finisher is less likely to enjoy the flood of ideas that can be unleashed by agile CRM than is the shaper. You will also have all the questions of divided loyalties, power struggles and ordinary personality clashes that mean you need to find some way of working together productively.

Communicating

In a small team of peers with similar ages and backgrounds you may be able to set the ground rules for this very easily during a working lunch or even by setting an agenda item for your first formal meeting. In larger or more disparate teams, the project leader will need to take the initiative to set the tone. Informal or semi-formal discussions can certainly help but you will need to be careful to find out if anyone has religious or family reasons for not wanting to attend, say, a pub get together at 4pm on a Friday. Very large or inexperienced teams may need more formal help from suitably qualified members of the HR department or from an outside consultant. The core message of the team-building should be that people have all been selected from diverse backgrounds for their individual skills or ability to contribute to the required project outcomes and that everyone has the right to have their own preferences, provided they respect and work constructively with the preferences of others.

Activity 7.14

Getting to know you

Gather with two or three other people with the same specialism as you but from different childhood backgrounds. Start a (friendly!) discussion about whether they think you all have more in common with each other than you individually have in common with people of your backgrounds.

There are many tools used by the professionals to start discussions about communication differences and even more 'introductions' to them or copies of them available on the Web. In some cases, years of research is reduced to one-page summaries and the danger is that people are categorised according to what is gleaned from these. As starters for intelligent adult discussions that may break down barriers and help communications, there are some good sources on the Internet but that is all they are: conversation starters.

In international teams, the work of Hofstede and the later work by Trompenaars on cultural differences in the work place is often used. The two sets of factors they have identified as being linked to culture are different and a selection of project-management-related issues drawn from their separate works includes such topics as preferences for:

- **Group decisions or individual decisions** (Trompenaars): *does a group function as a group or do individuals within it express their individual opinions? Is an individual expected to make a decision or must it be a group decision?*

- **Equality or hierarchy** (Trompenaars): *should all people have equal rights or should some individuals have more power?*

- **Long-term or short-term perspectives** (Hofstede): *what is the 'time horizon'? Long-term orientated societies favour thrift whereas short-term societies value reciprocation of gifts and favours*

- **Uncertainty avoidance or uncertainty tolerance** (Hofstede): *to what extent is anxiety dealt with by avoiding uncertainty? Are there rules and structures in place to avoid uncertainty?*

- **Achieved status versus ascribed status** (Trompenaars): *does status have to be won or is it given?*
- **Time as sequence and time as synchronisation** (Trompenaars): *are things done one at a time or are several things done at once?*

Some concepts such as time as synchronisation will not be immediately obvious.

National cultures

We discussed cultural differences in meetings earlier in this chapter. Let's now explore the differences in national culture in slightly more detail. When working with international teams, the work of Hofstede, and the later work by Trompenaars and Hampden-Turner, on national culture are often used. These works identify two different sets of dimensions for national culture, which overlap slightly. Let's now look at these dimensions:

- **Power or equality** (Hofstede)

  Do the less powerful people in a society expect others to possess more power and if so, how much more power? Do individuals have equal rights? Scandinavian and Germanic-speaking countries view themselves as having more equality.

- **Achieved status or ascribed status** (Trompenaars and Hampden-Turner)

  Does status have to be won or is it given?

- **Individualism or collectivism** (Hofstede / Trompenaars and Hampden-Turner)

  Does an individual act on their own – or do they belong to a group and act as a member of that group? Does a group function as a group – or do individuals within it express their individual opinions? Is an individual expected to make a decision – or must it be a group decision? USA culture was found to be more individualistic than that of other countries.

- **Specific or diffuse** (Trompenaars and Hampden-Turner)

  How involved do people get?

- **Universalism or particularism** (Trompenaars and Hampden-Turner)

  What is more important – rules or relationships? A universalist society will set what it sees as the correct rules and then try to get everyone to conform to them. A particularist society believes that the circumstances are more important than rules. The UK is an universalist society

- **Uncertainty avoidance or uncertainty tolerance** (Hofstede)

  To what extent is anxiety dealt with by avoiding uncertainty and ambiguity? Are there rules and structures in place to avoid uncertainty? Japanese and Mediterranean cultures tend to avoid uncertainty and prefer society to be much more structured

- **Neutral or affective** (Trompenaars and Hampden-Turner)

  Is there an attempt to control the environment – or is the environment worked with?

- **Long-term or short-term perspectives** (Hofstede / Trompenaars and Hampden-Turner)

  What is the 'time horizon'? Is importance attached to the future or to the past and the present? Long-term orientated societies favour thrift, whereas short-term cultures are more concerned with fulfilling social obligations and saving one's 'face'. East Asian cultures (such as China and Japan) tend to be long-term orientated

- **Time as sequence or time as synchronisation** (Trompenaars and Hampden-Turner)

  Are things done one at a time (sequentially) or are several things done at once?

- **Masculinity or femininity** (Hofstede)

  Does the culture place value on typically male-orientated characteristics (such as ambition, assertiveness and acquiring wealth) or female-orientated characteristics (such as concern for relationships and caring)? Japan emerges as the most masculine, with the USA and UK being fairly masculine. Nordic countries are the most feminine. Note that Hofstede identifies that there is a wide variation on going from country to country in the values held by males: in some countries the males are closer to holding the 'female' values than in others.

- **Neutral or affective** (Trompenaars and Hampden-Turner)

  Are emotions displayed?

People from high uncertainty avoidance cultures (for example Austria) will favour regulated projects, with supporting paperwork; people from cultures with a greater tolerance for unpredictability (for example Spain) may prefer informal emails to filling in the forms. People with long-term perspectives (for example North Koreans) will build relationships slowly and only if they fit their view of life, whereas people with short-term perspectives act for the moment – which can make them great project team members – until the next bright idea catches their attention.   People, who ascribe status (usually to older people or people from a particular caste) are less ready to acknowledge the expertise of the young.

Perhaps the most interesting attribute for project management, however, is the distinction between people who see time as *sequential* with one task happening after another (most Americans) and those who see time as *synchronous* with tasks happening in parallel (many Asians).

See Hofstede's website for further detail on his five dimensions of culture (**http://feweb.uvt.nl/ center/hofstede/page3.htm/** [Last accessed: February 2007]).

Personality types

In inexperienced teams, a discussion tool that is often used to help communication is the Myers-Briggs (Personality) Type Indicator (see **www.myersbriggs.org/my-mbti-personality-type/mbti-basics/**) which assesses people against four pairs of descriptive factors:

- Extravert/introvert
- Feeling/thinking
- Perceptive/judgmental
- Sensing/intuitive.

By working out the dominant preference in each pair, people are assigned to one of 16 distinct 'types' that is then discussed in the context in which the person is living/working.

These 16 types are what cause people to say, for example, 'I'm an INTJ' (Introverted, iNtuitive, Thinking, Judgmental) or 'I'm an EFSP' (Extraverted, Feeling, Sensing, Perceptive). There are precise definitions of each of these terms and an MBTI-qualified practitioner will give considerable feedback – but there can still be value in acknowledging that people think and react differently. Some people need space to think (so may dislike instant messaging and agile CRM) whereas others work more on perceptions and hunches that are fed by having as broad a range of inputs as possible.

However, you can probably identify people so busy reacting to new ideas that they never seem to turn any of them into action leading to products. Inexperienced teams can benefit from discussing these differences, just so that they can help each other work more comfortably and help the project team achieve all its success criteria. It is important to understand that there is no 'correct' style – there is no right or wrong answer to any of the questions. What is important in a team is to have – ideally – a balance of the different types or, at worst, an understanding of the different team members' types.   There is, for example, no value in giving a very introvert individual a highly extravert task.

Activity 7.15

Your personality style

How would you feel if you were asked to work in each of these ways? Willing, enthusiastic, unwilling, reluctant...?

1. Reporting in person to a project leader daily

2. Completing an online project progress report daily

3. Reporting to a team once a week in a conference call

4. Given an overall aim and told how you and your team get there is your business as long as it is done by a set date

5. Given a complete project and quality control manual and a predefined project specification.

The preferred style of communication is also sometimes examined when setting up teams and, again, this can be carried out either very simply or through individual analysis and discussion. For normal computing project management purposes, there are three main communication preferences:

- **Visual:** this includes the use of charts and diagrams
- **Auditory:** this centres on speeches, telephone calls, face-to-face meetings
- **Kinaesthetic:** this relates to physical movement and gestures.

You can probably think of people – family, friends or colleagues – who say, *'Don't write me an essay, just draw it'* ; or others who, no matter how often they are told, *'Just give me a call'*, will write a careful and detailed e-mail. Worse, this group may not communicate at all – they do not want to break the rules (by writing an e-mail, for example) but feel uncomfortable using the telephone, as it leaves no audit trail of the content of the conversation.

There are also cultural influences in this mix. For example, in presentations, Americans tend to start with the diagram of the solution and subsequent slides are used to explain aspects of the thinking – if this is called for. The British, on the other hand, tend to start with the problem, work through the thinking and end with the solution. Using the 'wrong' approach (culturally speaking) can ensure your project proposals or reports are not taken as seriously as they should be – and it can therefore be a career-limiting move. Discussing these preferences and, if necessary, establishing compromise procedures, is one of the easiest ways to ensure projects start on a communicative footing.

Support

In the discussion of team roles there was mention of 'teamworker' as a support role – but effective project managers are usually *also* teamworkers, and so are most of the rest of the team. The project leader who, as we saw, may also be the project manager, will usually be responsible for making sure discussions about team roles and communications take place; he or she will ensure that those who feel threatened or under pressure to act in a way they find difficult are given the help they need – either through coaching or mentoring, or by having a quiet word with other members of the team to see if some accommodation can be made for particular likes or dislikes. This, of course, needs to be fair to others and proportionate to the project need: managing IS/IT projects may sometimes feel like running a nursery school but, at the end of the day, meeting the project requirements are what you are being paid to deliver.

Conflict handling

A project without an argument (or several) is probably not a project at all but an operational task. However, there is a difference between a constructive, professional argument and project team warfare. If the project timescale is short and you have to use two individuals who, for some reason, just clash then you may have to take them aside and tell them both that they should limit direct communication with each other – and that all decisions have to be approved by you. This is, obviously, untenable for the long term, so you need to look at possible causes for the tension rather than at the dispute itself.

- **Everyday tensions** are also likely to have a discoverable cause: perhaps a young specialist has queried an older specialist's decision, so the older person feels threatened? Perhaps the project manager's note on Monday, *'Report was due on my desk at 9 so make sure it is with me by 5, please'*, has really annoyed the developers battling to get the product ready for testing to begin at the end of the week. Perhaps it is something as seemingly insignificant as one member who never makes the coffee. Whatever it is, it may take time and effort to find the real answer; in complex (and ideal) cases, you could consider drafting in someone from the HR department to get to the bottom of things, but this may not always be an option

- **Professional disagreements** should be dealt with by respecting the expertise of those involved. If a meeting between the parties (with you or someone else as a neutral observer and referee) cannot resolve the issue, then the parties should agree to formal presentation of their ideas to a wider group of peers, assembled for the occasion. In rare cases where that is not possible, try to run with both ideas in parallel for a while – although budgetary constraints may mean the team has to choose one approach and, in extreme cases, risk losing the expert whose idea was rejected. Personality should not play a part in the team's choice of route – but it inevitably will, so team choice, rather than dispassionate expert choice, is a high-risk tactic. Try to minimise the risk by emphasising the project success criteria and asking for votes for which route will best reach these.

Clashes in communication styles and inabilities to understand the pressures which others are under require team development sessions. Role play, especially reversing the roles, can be simple but often useful. Depending upon the severity of the situation and how long the team members have known each other, a short meeting where you ask them to act it out for you while sat in their chairs might be enough. Take care that your intervention is not seen as heavy pressure or attributing blame and, if necessary, be prepared to abandon the idea and call in further help. On other occasions you may need to organise a formal training session with some kind of external help.

Clashes about what is 'fair' can be particularly difficult to handle because, when challenged, the 'injured' party can feel their entire value system is being undermined: *'I got you coffee so obviously you should get me coffee next time because I am generous and friendly and we are all equal round here.'* Pointing out the contradictions in that will not help you win the day! Team members may even perceive their real grievance as too embarrassing to voice because they are admitting to personal needs for affirmation of worth – and that can lead to all sorts of diversionary (and ultimately project-time-wasting) accusations. Rather than attack the problem head-on, try a more subtle approach such as asking each; *'What one little thing would help you feel that you are appreciated as part of the team by [person X]?'* Try to build a series of little steps over time to rebuild the trust. Again, the dispassionate involvement of your HR department can be very helpful in these situations.

There are, of course, times when conflict is so great that it is no longer a project team management issue but a disciplinary one. If the parties still retain line-reporting roles with their original departments, then you will have to involve their managers – and probably the HR department as well, if you have one. If one or more of the parties belongs to another organisation, the matter needs referring urgently to the steering committee/project board rather than directly to the relevant line manager(s). In considering disciplinary routes, remember that questions will almost certainly be asked about the project management that allowed the situation to arise in the first place. This does not mean you should not do it: just prepare your answers carefully and have some suggestions for a solution at the ready.

7.10 Your student project

If you are a student with much knowledge of your IS/IT subject but little experience of employment, this chapter may have considered much that you have, so far, been able to relegate to a lesser role. However, there are immediate parallels between an academic project, completed largely on your own, and a 'real-world' project, completed by a large team.

Consider, first of all, the academic equivalents of a project champion and a project board: you can think of your supervisor as your project champion, who has to convince the Faculty examination committee (project board) that your project meets its regulations. Just like a project board, the examination committee will want to know that your project meets their predefined success criteria including timescales and report formats.

In pursuing your project you will probably need to provide interim reports for your supervisor and these should show good use of resources – although 'financial reporting' is likely to be replaced by 'academic reporting' – the sources which you have used. Remember: your 'project board' is an academic one!

You should think also about the skillsets you need to use and how you are going to develop and present them.

Activity 7.16

Transforming your academic project to the real world

Imagine your project has access to unlimited experts: which specialists do you need, when – and *why*?

Make a list.

7.11 Summary

This chapter should have clarified not only that 'people factors' are key to any successful project – but that there are many aspects to these people factors.

You have to select an appropriate team – blending *technical* skillsets with *project-behaviour* skillsets

Myriad external influences will need to be factored in, including:

- Other stakeholders
- Reporting structures
- Legal and ethical issues.

7.12 Review questions

 Question 7.1

Why do you need to factor training and development into project teamwork?

 Question 7.2

What are the two key sets of lists you should consider when forming a project team?

 Question 7.3

What is the role of the project champion?

 Question 7.4

What project behaviours differentiate a project leader from a project manager?

 Question 7.5

Give two external factors and one internal factor that have an influence on project team selection.

 Question 7.6

Who owns any software created by the project?

Question 7.7

What is the key to managing different preferences for communication styles?

7.13 Feedback on activities

Activity 7.1: Project success criteria

Comfort is concerned with the ability of the client and the project team to communicate easily and openly with each other and to trust each other; also comfort concerns from the client viewpoint, acceptance of the product as being of high quality and pleasant to work with. Comfort from the project team's viewpoint is not having tight deadlines or overly challenging tasks to complete.

Competence is required in the human interaction and in the technical and management skills at all stages of the project.

Commitment is required by the project team to work hard and deliver the project on time and within budget. There must be commitment to designing a design solution that meets all the requirements. There must also be project team commitment to ensuring the design solution as delivered actually meets the requirements – that means building in quality and carrying out thorough testing.

Communication is required to negotiate and agree all the project success criteria. Communication is especially needed to determine what the client's views are on the system's acceptability as the software is developed; also to continuously monitor whether the requirements or the business situation have changed.

Activity 7.2: Team values

No feedback

Activity 7.3: Personal team skills

No feedback

Activity 7.4: Project constraints

Common constraints	Impact on project team-working
Set budgets	Depends on how restrictive. **Negative,** if too tight
Phasing of payments	**Positive.** Will encourage the team to get on with the work
Restrictions on number of personnel and/or their time availability	**Negative.** Will create pressure
Set deadlines and sign-off dates	**Positive.** Will encourage the team to get on with the work. If too tight, then **negative**
Existing technology to be used	**Negative.** Will the technical staff wanted to use new technology **Positive** in the sense that staff don't have to learn new technology – unless there is a shortage of skills availability for the existing technology – that would increase pressure, especially if technology is ageing as no one would be keen to invest time in learning such skills
Assigned office space	Depends on the quality of the office space. Might cause problems if not a sensible layout. Very unusual for people to choose where they sit in an office!
Employment legislation (which may vary from country to country) and working hours	**Positive** generally as staff would not be working antisocial hours. Could cause pressure if overtime became essential
Mandated quality control system(s)	**Positive** – unless they were draconian
Multilingual project documentation	**Negative** – pressure of getting materials translated and having to get screen designs and error messages translated. Also might introduce multi-site working which could cause pressure of working abroad

Activity 7.5: Organisational culture

- **Language:** a supermarket system can be friendly and use colloquial language. The tax department would be more formal and use standard English. It would also provide other language versions

- **Use of symbols:** both would want consistency in the use of any symbols

- **Ceremonies:** supermarkets might strive to make their reward systems seem important. The tax department would promote their tax deadlines!

- **Customs:** the tax department would be very correct in welcoming and signing off users; also in giving any required legal information

- **Methods of problem solving:** the tax department would put more effort into problem solving and give more information to users. There would be easy routes to communicate with tax department staff

- **Use of tools and technology:** both very similar

- **Design of work settings:** the tax department would have a simpler interface. It would be less busy with no distractions. The supermarket would have advertisements and would be trying to present a 'fun' image. Its aim would be to keep you using the site for as long as possible and to keep you buying items or identifying items you might like to purchase. The tax department would want the user to answer questions as quickly as possible or to be provided with relevant information as soon as possible.

Activity 7.6: It's not just the end result

There are many factors that come into this. Perhaps Student A read the rules on description of methodology and criticism of methodology while Student B failed to criticise their methodology at all and under that heading just wrote 'It worked!'   Reading the marking criteria and other constraints can help ensure that your project addresses the key concerns.

Activity 7.7: Making compromises

Your answer will depend partly on the sector in which you work but here are some guidelines.

- When assembling the team, you will always need to manage f). If your first choice is not available, then your assigned resources become your second (or third…) choice. If you are managing the team, your internal and external customers will both judge your professionalism by your success in this area

- d) and e) are rarely negotiable so should not be your first choices

- c) is sometimes negotiable – but the customer may choose to reduce the time or the budget as a trade-off

- You may be able to trade between a) and b) without visible impact if, say, your second choice worker is more expensive but quicker – but you then have to think why that person was not your first choice (see 'Influence of team dynamics').

Activity 7.8: Team roles

No feedback

Activity 7.9: Quick wins

Any of the *agile methods* or *evolutionary delivery* would address rapid delivery and so quick wins.

Waterfall or *Incremental phased delivery* would not achieve this.

Activity 7.10: CRM in action

No feedback

Activity 7.11: Working with the team

These suggestions are only indicative and you may encounter many others but, however they manifest themselves, the reactions are unprofessional and need to be challenged (see 'Working as a team').

- Where one individual has spent many years honing their skills in a way that gains them recognition (e.g. hands-on practice) and someone has little actual experience but has, say, researched a paper on the subject, the practitioner is likely to resent the 'shortcut' to team recognition of the academic

- Simple dislike of a person's non-work-related hobbies, tastes in food or dress

- Belief that people of that tribe/gender/country/religion 'should not' do that job.

Activity 7.12: Paying a bonus

1. A month's extra pay is a substantial amount and you may not wish to jeopardise morale for the forthcoming stages, especially if they are also likely to be difficult. However, to pay a bonus when the deadline is clearly missed is sending out a message that deadlines are flexible. Misleading the accountant is never acceptable as it affects business governance and external company reporting. One way out of the dilemma is to discuss the issue with the accountant and gain agreement to pay the bonus after a team-meeting explaining the decision. The team meeting should then be backed up by a confirmatory e-mail or letter explaining that this is a one-off decision.

2. This needs referring to the steering committee with, if appropriate, a team recommendation that the other national project team members remain the same because it was a team failure to deliver precisely on time.

Activity 7.13: IPR

It is possible that the contract anticipates this eventuality and, in any case, you need to read it carefully. Your answer will be a business decision.

- You may be able to charge the customer extra for such exclusive code

- You may be able to license the code from the customer for use in other applications. Because of customer confidentiality, you may not be able to ask another of your company's teams to design the generic code first and then have your team adapt it

- You may also find that ideas created within a project belong to the customer – although proving where an idea came from can be difficult.

Activity 7.14: Getting to know you

Some people retain very strong links to their roots all their lives and may define themselves as 'working-class, Northern, Protestant' even when they are living in a large house in London and earning well above the national average. Others will more readily describe themselves by their profession, and 'web designers' or 'software project managers' may find that the specialist nature of what they do partly excludes them from the people with whom they grew up – while simultaneously creating a sense of community with other professionals.

Activity 7.15: Your personality style

Your answers will give you some insight, if you did not have some already, into your own needs for interaction with people and your need (or lack of need) for structure. It's worth discussing your feelings on each of these issues with colleagues or fellow students, just to appreciate how (presumably!) different people would react to different requirements.

Activity 7.15: Transforming your academic project to the real world

No feedback

7.14 References

Belbin R.M., (1981), *Management Teams: Why they Succeed or Fail*, Butterworth-Heinemann

Handy, C., (1978), *Understanding Organisations*, Penguin.

Hofstede G., (2005), *Cultures Consequences: International Differences in Work-Related Values* (Abridged) Sage Publications.

Markus, M.L., (2000), Toward an Integrative Theory of Risk Control, in Richard Baskerville, Jan Stage, and Janice I. DeGross (Eds). *Organizational and Social Perspectives on Information Technology*, Boston, MA: Kluywer Academic Publishers.

Markus, M.L., and Cornelis T., (2000), The Enterprise Systems Experience – From Adoption to Success. In R.W. Zmud (Ed.) *Framing the Domains of IT Research: Glimpsing the Future Through the Past*, Cincinnati, OH: Pinnaflex Educational Resources, Inc.

Melymuka, K., (1997), Top Guns, *Computerworld*, October 20, reproduced in *Project Management 1* readings by ACS.

Nguyen, Ogunlana and Xuan Lan, (2004), A Study on Project Success Factors in Large Construction Projects in Vietnam in *Engineering, Construction and Architectural Management* Volume 11, Issue 6, Emerald Group Publishing Limited.

Schein E., (1980), *Organizational Psychology*. Englewood Cliffs, NJ: Prentice Hall Inc.

Schein E., (2004), *Organizational Culture and Leadership*, 3rd ed. New York: Wiley Publishers.

Scholtes P., (1996), *The Team Handbook*, Pfeiffer Wiley.

Standish Group (2004), *Chaos Report* **www.standishgroup.com/sample_research/ chaos_1994_1.php**

Thompson K., (2006), Nature's four teamwork systems in *The Bumble Bee Bioteams Features*, January 16 2006, **www.bioteams.com**

Trompenaars F., and Hampden-Turner C., (1997), *Riding the Waves of Culture* Nicholas Brealey Publishing Ltd.

U.S. Army Handbook (1973), Military Leadership.

Yardley D (2002), *Successful IT Project Delivery: Learning the Lessons of Project Failure* Addison-Wesley Professional.

CHAPTER 8

Project quality management

OVERVIEW

This chapter focuses on the principles and techniques of project quality management. Quality management has been a major concern for IT organisations over the last thirty or so years, with drives to comply with quality standards (such as the International Organisation for Standardisation (ISO), ISO 9000 series), to improve business processes, and to ensure conformance to requirements. Above that, the need to meet customer expectations has increasingly been recognised as an aim for quality management.

Given the number of project problems and failures being experienced, it would seem that implementation of project quality management still has some way to go. However, quality management has already had a significant effect in improving the quality of projects and has been a major influence on project management.

Moreover, within an organisation, the need for quality improvement is a major driver for initiating projects. In other words, the key changes that a project has to bring about are mostly quality-driven.

Quality management must therefore be seen as an integral part of project management.

Learning outcomes	At the end of this chapter you should be able to:

- Understand the importance of quality management

- Describe the main processes of project quality management and understand how they relate to projects

- Describe several quality control techniques

- Understand the contribution of the major quality experts to quality management

- Discuss quality standards and models.

8.1 Introduction

The aim of this chapter is to introduce the main elements of project quality management, and give an appreciation of the contribution of *quality* to project management.

Project quality management is discussed under four main topics:

- Definitions of quality and project quality management
- Quality control techniques
- The people who have made significant contribution to the theory of quality
- Quality standards and models.

8.2 What is quality?

What is quality? Once again we find ourselves with a term that is difficult to define and can mean different things to different people. Quality is important when we talk about products. No doubt you are trying to produce a quality report that will summarise your project. Your final working product may also be judged in terms of its quality. So how do we define quality?

Let's consider an example: suppose you were to walk into an exclusive shop and order a quality table. What would you expect?

You would expect such a shop to offer you first-class products, probably at a premium price. You may also expect to be able to order a product to be designed and tailormade to your specifications – but this is likely to make it extremely expensive. You will probably expect the salesperson to be pleasant and polite.

You would expect the resulting product to be a solid table that would last a long time. You may also expect your table to be constructed of the best materials and show good standards of craftsmanship. Maybe it would be designed by a famous designer and made by a named craftsman. You would expect continuing good service, and for the delivery person to be very careful when they delivered your new, solid and probably very heavy table, to you.

Now what is it that determines the quality of your table? Is it the craftsmanship? The standards of work? The name of the craftsman on the table? The materials? The exclusive shop? The salesperson? The price? The hype?

The answer is probably *all* of the above – and no single one in particular. You are told that this is a quality table and you accept it as it comes from a reputable shop. You can also see that it feels strong and smells like solid wood.   Furthermore, the guarantee that comes with the name of the craftsman adds a certain aura of respectability and an expectation that the product will stand up to the name stamped on it.

Many organisations now view quality not simply as a product, but as a service. The shop may, therefore, be interested in you as a customer and try to make sure that you are satisfied with the product and the service so that you will come back to the same shop, and tell your friends and relations to try it as well.

In the same way, however, you could go to a branch of IKEA or any other mass-producer of furniture and buy a table. How would you define quality in that situation? Or, to take a different example, how would you define quality in the context of a meal at a fast-food restaurant, such as McDonald's, and in an exclusive and very expensive restaurant?

Definition of quality

So how should 'quality' be defined? Juran (who we shall discuss in more detail later in this chapter), distinguished 'quality of design' and 'quality of conformance' as two of his five attributes of 'fitness for use' (the other attributes being availability, safety and field use) (Juran 1988).

- **'Quality of design'** introduces the concept of designers proactively deciding the level of quality that they consider is required. The level of quality therefore defines the characteristics specified by the designers, such as the type and grade of materials and their tolerances and the performance specifications
- **'Quality of conformance'** refers to the degree to which the design specifications are followed during manufacturing (Pressman 2005). Many other definitions of quality simply focus on 'conformance to requirements', which means that the project's processes and products meet the specified requirements
- **'Fitness for purpose'** means that a product can be used for the purpose it was intended. This is typically seen as being more rigorous than 'fitness for use'.

  To give an example, a Jaguar, or a Rolls-Royce may be perceived to be the highest-quality car available, but does it provide 'fitness for purpose' for a typical family?   It is not your typical family car and cannot be viewed as cheap to run. If you are looking for a new car to enable you to take the children to school and to leave it in the middle of a city, you may need a smaller family run-around car that can fit into the small parking spaces outside the school. You may also decide that investing in expensive leather upholstery that does not clean easily is a waste of money when the children insist on eating sandwiches and chocolate bars in the car. 'Fitness for purpose' is therefore important in defining whether a product addresses customer needs adequately.

The key thing that all these definitions have in common is that they move 'quality' away from its popular definition as being associated with high quality: the emphasis is on meeting whatever requirements were specified. Under these definitions, a supermarket's plastic bag could be declared a quality item so long as it meets its intended requirements.

More recently, many people emphasise that the customer defines quality. The Kodak organisation defines quality as 'those products or services that are perceived to meet or exceed the needs and expectations of the customer at a cost that represents outstanding value' (Kerzner 2003). The interesting point to note with this definition is how the customer viewpoint impacts on a project: a project must take great care that it accurately defines the customers' needs and expectations, and ultimate power about deciding on quality is given to the customers. So with this definition, conformance to requirements is not necessarily sufficient – the customer must be satisfied with the resulting product or service. Consider the current trend for large organisations to have call centres and automated telephone response systems; is 'quality' or 'conformance to requirements' in this case something which addresses the organisation's needs – or the needs of its telephoning customers?

Further, in order to maintain the satisfaction of customers and their loyalty, products need to be revised and adjusted to reflect shifting needs and expectations (as well as market trends and the competition). So maintaining quality becomes a continuous process of product improvement.

Different views of quality

Over the years, several different views of quality have been employed. We have just seen a number of the perspectives, so let's briefly identify and explore some of them:

- **Quality as a product-based quantity**: this is the traditional view of quality. The assumption is that quality is related to the content of the product

- **Quality as a user-based view**: quality is based on the values of the users. Such a view will, therefore, encompass the user's ideas through the notion of fitness for purpose and conformance to requirements. Initially this was viewed as a static value that had to be extracted prior to embarking on the process of development

- **Quality as a specification**: this view is derived from the manufacturing industries. The assumption is that a clear (technical) specification of the product exists or can be obtained. Quality can, therefore, be determined as conformance to this formal specification

- **Quality as a value-based approach**: the value-based perspective acts as a composite of the last two views. Quality is assumed to equate to what the user wants at an acceptable price and while conforming to an exact specification at an acceptable cost. Quality can thus be equated with value to the user (justified in terms of manufacturing costs)

- **Quality as a transcendent property**: quality can be equated with some kind of innate excellence. The exact parameters cannot be defined precisely. It is also difficult to impose tests to ascertain achievement as quality is felt rather than measured

- **Quality as a continuous property**: the modern approach views quality as the evolving satisfaction level of the users. The view is that change will force adjustments and that all aspects of the system, including quality, must be considered dynamic.

Activity 8.1

Basic quality measures

Assume that you are developing a computer program for a user. Define what each of the following would mean (write a sentence for each item):

- Fitness for use

- Meet the requirements specification

- Fitness for purpose

- User satisfaction.

Now do the same for a product that you are planning to develop (say, for your student project) and try to determine what level of quality you are offering.

8.3 The cost of quality

Cost of quality factors

Cost of quality (COQ) includes all the costs associated with carrying out quality-related processes. These quality costs can be classified into categories as follows:

- **Prevention costs** include quality planning, technical reviews, test equipment and training
- **Appraisal costs** include inspection and testing
- **Failure costs** include:

- **Internal failure costs**: rework
- **External failure costs**: helpline support and fixing customer fault reports (bugs).

The cost of quality (COQ) is the price of conformance (POC) and the price of non-conformance (PONC) added together (Crosby 1980).

- **POC** is the 'costs in making certain that things are done right the first time'. This is the sum of the prevention costs and appraisal costs

- **PONC** is the failure costs (the sum of the internal and external failure costs). This is the cost of not doing things 'right the first time'. It includes rework, which is an important consideration in software development.

Crosby (1980) promoted the concept that 'quality is free'. He quotes Geneen that 'quality is not only right, it is free. And it is not only free, it is the most profitable product line we have'. Crosby argued that it was the cost of not doing things 'right the first time' (that is, PONC) that really costs and, therefore, one of the major aims of quality management must be to eliminate PONC.

<table>
<tr><td>Activity 8.2</td><td>

Considering the cost of quality

Look at the three main types of cost listed in Section 8.3, *'The cost of quality'*, and consider how these costs would apply to your student project. What impact are they likely to have on your student project?

</td></tr>
</table>

The timing of quality activities

Capture defects early: Having considered the costs involved in fixing errors, we should now talk about the impact of timing. The relative cost of correcting errors in software is a function dependent on the phase in which they are corrected. That is, the later an error is detected, the more it costs to fix (see Figure 8.1). This makes sense, as the later the mistake is discovered, the more backtracking it requires. It therefore pays off to invest in finding and correcting the errors during the earlier stages, rather than waiting to find the error during operation, and having to spend, say, a 100 times as much resources to correct it.

To illustrate this, let us take the example of a car designer, who has some incorrect requirements.

Our designer is fond of drawing his preliminary drawings on a white board. If you were to walk in today and point out a minor mistake in the basic architecture, he would be able to correct it by rubbing it out and re-drawing the right section. Once the design has been signed-off, it will become increasingly more difficult to find and resolve the error. It is still possible to correct, but the costs will now start to increase.

When the first prototype is ready, it is possible to correct the error if it were to be discovered, but much of the design would have to be re-done.

However, once, the cars have been shipped out, it is no longer a question of simply rubbing off a line and re-drawing. First, there is a complete recall of all cars (which will cost the company in financial terms as well as in reputation). There is also a need to modify the design. If, say, the chassis no longer fits, we may be looking at a serious problem.

You now see how costs could range from a single monetary unit to millions, depending on the error and when the error is detected. Software projects also begin with a requirements phase and the cost of correcting defects escalates according to how long it takes to discover the defect (see Figure 8.1).

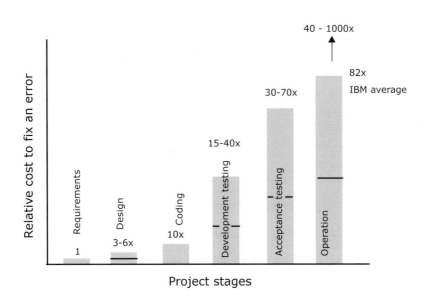

Figure 8.1: How cost escalates as you move towards field use. From an analysis of 63 projects cited by Boehm (1981) quoted in Gilb and Graham (1993).

Student projects are very similar. If you discover a critical error in a data flow diagram, you could use a pencil and rubber and correct it. If you were to discover the same error during the design stage, you may need to spend longer on re-doing parts of the requirements analysis and design stages. If you discover the same error three weeks before the project is due in, you may need to make some extensive changes. If, however, you only discover the error once the project has been submitted, it may become impossible to correct. The phase and the timing can, therefore, become crucial to making corrections and will determine the cost of the rework and the feasibility of finalising the product.

Of course, there is an alternative: at an even earlier stage of a project, steps could be taken to try to *ensure the errors are less likely to occur.* Prevention is better than cure!

8.4 Project quality management

Project quality management involves three main processes (*PMBOK Guide* 2004):

- **Quality planning**
- **Quality assurance**
- **Quality control.**

Quality planning

Quality planning involves identifying which specific quality procedures and standards are relevant to a specific project, and determining how the project will meet those standards. It is important to design quality into both the product/system produced by a project and into the project processes.

There will often be an existing set of organisational procedures and standards, as well as industry standards, which a project will have to conform to. The aims of such standards are to ensure best practice is communicated and adopted throughout an organisation. Also to support continuous process improvement: the organisational procedures and standards will be updated as better practices are identified. In addition to considering how to apply these industry standards, and organisational procedures and standards, a project has to consider any additional specific needs that it might have (for example, higher security requirements).

Quality planning for a project relies upon the availability of appropriate and clearly defined requirements. The requirements will be agreed between clients and developers to guarantee that they refer to real needs, which must be satisfied. Hopefully, the process will also involve the actual users to ensure that the system is acceptable to them.

In order to be able to prove that the basic requirement has been met, you will need to plan a demonstration or a set of tests to ascertain achievement. This means that you will have to avoid vague requirements and be as clear and precise in terms of the definition to ensure that the tests will cover the right aspects of the system.

Acceptance criteria documents are being included in contracts as standard practice. Developers can then utilise the test definition and ensure that their work is aimed towards achieving the defined tests. One use of the quality plan or the acceptance criteria will therefore be, just prior to delivery, to ensure achievement. A project needs to build in a demonstration or a way of measuring and proving that it has conformed to the client's acceptance criteria.

Quality assurance

This is the process of carrying out the planned quality activities. So this is actually carrying out the reviews, inspections, testing, etc. These quality activities help ensure the project delivers the appropriate levels of quality.

Quality control

Quality control involves *monitoring project results* to ensure they meet the relevant quality standards. It also includes identifying ways to eliminate the causes of unsatisfactory project results. A variety of statistical monitoring techniques are used for quality control. Their main outputs are as follows:

- **Quality control status reports**: these state whether or not the product/system is meeting its required quality levels
- **Rework**: the activities required to fix the product/system to meet the required standards
- **Process improvements**: these alter the current processes to address the causes of the quality problems so they will not recur.

Let's now look at some methods used for quality control.

8.5 Quality control methods

Methods and techniques used for quality control include:

- **Management reviews**
- **Testing**
- **Pareto analysis**
- **Control charts**
- **Walkthroughs**
- **Inspections.**

We have already discussed 'Management reviews' and 'Testing' in Chapter 4. So here we shall look at the remaining quality control methods.

It is worth, however, just mentioning that whenever using any of these methods, thought needs to be given to how representative any chosen sample actually is to the issue under consideration. For example in some cases, *sample size* should be considered, and perhaps calculated, to ensure a sample is sufficiently representative of the population of interest.

Pareto analysis

Pareto analysis can be used to identify the main quality problems in a system. It is sometimes known as the 80-20 rule; in this case, referring to the fact that 80 per cent of the problems are often due to 20 per cent of the causes. Pareto diagrams are histograms. Figure 8.2 is an example of a Pareto diagram.

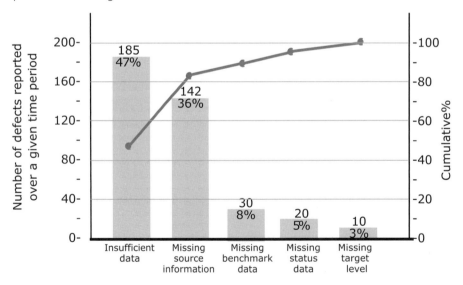

Figure 8.2: An example of a Pareto diagram (percentages rounded down)

It shows that 47% (of the total of 387 defects) are caused by 'insufficient qualifier data', and 36% are caused by 'missing source information'. So (47 + 36 =) 83% of the defects are being caused by just two types of problem. Of course, the value to the organisation of the different types of problem needs to be determined in order to decide which types of problem to fix first. The problem type that is costing the organisation the most would be the one to look at first – it might not be the one, which is occurring most often.

Control charts

Control charts enable you to determine whether a process is in control (stable) or out of control (unstable).

A control chart (see Figure 8.3) provides a picture of how a specific process is behaving over time. Its main use is to prevent defects, rather than to detect them. Every control chart has a centre line with control limits on either side. The centre line represents the observed average of the data and the control limits set a measure of the data variability. The control limits are usually set up at ± 3 sigma (3s) where s represents the population standard deviation. This provides 0.001 probability limits (that is, **chance causes** have only a one in a thousand chance of being above the upper control limit and only a one in a thousand chance of being below the lower control limit). Any variation outside these control limits can therefore be considered due to **special causes** (also known as **assignable causes** or **sporadic causes**). Special causes can be controlled at the local or operational level. Eliminating special causes means that the process returns to its controlled state.

Variation due to **common causes** (also known as **endemic causes** or **chronic causes**) is considered inherent in the process, and such variation will remain stable and exhibit a consistent pattern over time. Only if management decide to change the basic process will common causes be addressed.

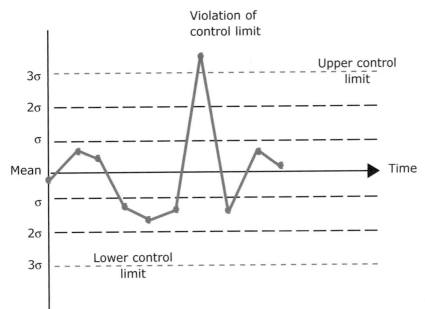

Figure 8.3: An example of a control chart

To determine whether a process is in a state of statistical control, the control chart has to be examined for patterns that can suggest non-random behaviour. Several different criteria have been proposed; for example, Zultner suggests:

1. A single value lies outside the control limits
2. Two out of three successive values lie more than two standard deviations away from the mean
3. Four out of five successive values lie more than one standard deviation away from the mean
4. Eight consecutive values lie on one side of the mean.

   (Zultner 1999 quoted in Pressman 5th Edition 2000)

If special causes exist, then corrective action needs to be taken. Control charts can be used to monitor such things as defects in documents, and cost and schedule variances. To give an example, control charts are often used in manufacturing, and when a process starts exhibiting special causes, it means some problem has occurred, such as some part of the equipment has developed a fault, which needs fixing.

Walkthroughs

A walkthrough can be defined as a type of peer group review of a technical product. It is a direct descendant of the informal and casually conducted round-robin peer review. They generally have the product author (presenter) describing the structure and logic of the reviewed material to an audience of colleagues. As the presenter is familiar with the material and has prepared it for the session, there is a lesser need for other team members to spend large amounts of time in preparation. The purpose of walkthroughs is to enforce standards, detect errors and improve development visibility and overall system quality.

A walkthrough is led by a co-ordinator who plans and organises the session and distributes the material beforehand. The walkthrough meetings are scheduled and conducted in an informal atmosphere. Typical walkthroughs take between 1 and 1½ hours. User representatives may supplement the team to ensure that products conform to their requirements. The session results in an action list containing problems and questions. The ultimate outcome is a decision on whether to accept the product as it stands, to make revisions, or to make revisions and follow up with another walkthrough.

Walkthroughs are easy to implement as they do not require any special tools or equipment and may be applied at any phase regardless of the project type and size. They can focus on documentation rather than code.

The main advantages of walkthroughs include:

- Early identification of analysis and design errors
- Reduced number of errors in product/system
- Improved team communication
- Sharing of new methods, approaches and best practice.

Inspections

Inspections are essentially a more formal review mechanism than walkthroughs. Inspections are carried out on written documents and involve checking them against their source documents and standards aiming to detect major defects.

Originally, Michael Fagan developed the inspection method at IBM for use on source code as a systematic procedure for defect detection and removal. More recently, Tom Gilb has moved the inspection process upstream to requirements specifications, contracts and even technical drawings, and introduced the concept of sampling. The method has moved to being a mechanism for determining quality levels, rather than fixing defects. The rationale behind this is that if the quality level is too low it is better to completely rewrite the specification rather than to try to fix it. At IBM, Robert Mays has pioneered extending inspection to support continuous process improvement by using it to identify opportunities for defect prevention – the root causes of defects are brainstormed and fed into the process improvement team. (Gilb and Graham 1993)

See Figure 8.4. The first meeting of the team is the kick-off meeting where the team members are assigned roles, given documentation and instructed on what checking to carry out.

Checking rates are also discussed because they are crucial for optimum defect detection.

Team members then separately read and check the documentation and produce lists of any 'issues' found. Checking consists of the main specification document being cross-checked against its source documents and against the standards that apply to it. Checklists of the key points to check are used to assist the process and guide the checker to finding the major defects.

A formal logging meeting is then conducted and the issues are logged. The logging meeting should last a maximum of two hours. After the logging meeting and a brief break, a process meeting can be held for about 30 minutes to establish some possible root causes for a small sample of the issues (defects) found.

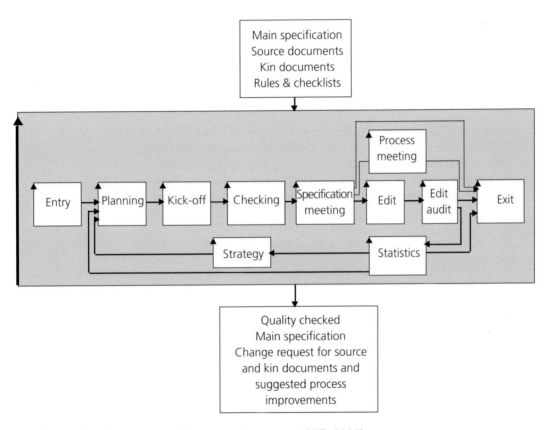

Figure 8.4: An overview of the inspection process (Gilb 2005).

The logged issues are handed to the editor, usually the author, for correction. If sampling is being used and the defect density level is sufficiently low, then maybe no action needs to be taken – the document can simply successfully exit. If inspection has been abandoned because too many errors where found, then the team members' lists might well simply be handed over to the editor.

Inspection must be economic otherwise it should be dropped. Inspection has an excellent track record of reducing downstream error correction costs. As we have discussed earlier in this chapter (see earlier Figure 8.1), the cost of fixing errors increases as a product moves towards field use.

Inspection and testing are complementary techniques. Inspection does not replace testing.

Inspection can be carried out at an earlier stage than testing, and it is probably true to say that errors detected early by inspection that would have been later caught by testing, are fixed at lower cost. However, both methods perform some unique functions and neither can replace the other.

8.6 Quality metrics

We discussed in Chapter 2 the role of success criteria for a project and the idea that the success criteria should be picked up as the project objectives. Doran's SMART method was also introduced as a way of ensuring objectives were more precise.

We also considered quality requirements in Chapter 4. If quality is defined as meeting the requirements, then *all* the different types of requirement have to be met, not just the quality requirements – 'quality' as discussed in this chapter is a somewhat wider issue. However, it is also true that the quality requirements play the most important role in helping define what is quality for a product/system. The quality requirements express the different quality attributes of interest (such as availability, usability and security) and, further, they capture the information about the benchmark and target values, which express the levels of quality.

In Section 8.4, under 'Quality planning', it was stated that it was important to design quality into both the product/system being produced by the project and the project processes. This implies two different sets of metrics: product/system metrics and project process metrics. System developers are interested in both sets of metrics. However, if you are taking the customer viewpoint, then remember it is the product/system metrics that are the main interest.

Activity 8.3

Quality process metrics for your student project

It is likely when defining your objectives for your student project that you focused on the *product/system* metrics.

However, considering what you have learned in this chapter, can you now state some *process metrics* for your student project?

8.7 Key contributors to the quality movement

In this section, we shall discuss some of the key contributors who helped develop the concepts of modern quality management. In order to successfully apply the principles, methods and techniques of quality management, it is very useful to understand the background to the different approaches.

The key contributors include:

- **Walter Shewhart**
- **W. Edwards Deming**
- **Joseph Juran**
- **Philip Crosby**
- **Kaoru Ishikawa.**

Note that several textbooks discuss these key contributors. See Schwalbe 2006; Kerzner 2003; Marchewka 2006; Truscott 2003. The information here is mainly drawn from these sources.

Walter Shewhart

In 1924, while working at Western Electric Company, which manufactured telephone equipment for Bell Telephone, Walter Shewhart developed the **control chart** as a tool for understanding variation. His aim was to allow managers to think about problem prevention and process improvement, rather than simply being concerned with the inspection of finished products (Marchewka 2006). (Here the term 'inspection' is used in the sense of manufacturing inspection. It is not the same thing as the inspection method described earlier in this chapter!)

Shewhart also devised the Plan/Do/Check/Act cycle for process improvement (Deming 1986).

W. Edwards Deming

Deming was influenced by the work on statistical theory carried out by Shewhart. The two men met while working at Bell Laboratories in the 1930s. Shewhart's cycle for improvement (see Figure 8.5) is often referred to as the Deming cycle as Deming was responsible for popularising it and its widespread use!

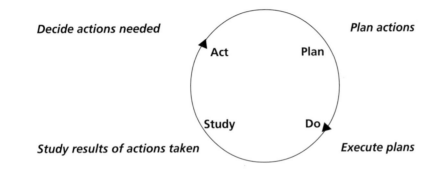

Figure 8.5: The Shewhart or Deming Cycle. Deming preferred to use 'Study' rather than 'Check'. See (Gilb 2005).

In the 1950s, Deming was sent to help the Japanese improve the quality of their manufacturing products. He lectured on statistical control and insisted that higher quality meant greater productivity and lower costs. The Japanese applied the principles very thoroughly and the result was a complete turnaround in the quality of Japanese manufacturing goods. At this point, the USA 'woke up' to what Deming was teaching, and companies such as the Ford Motor Company adopted Deming's methods.

Deming (1986) realised that quality was a management issue: common causes were often beyond the ability of the workers to fix and so required management action. He developed his '14 Obligations of Management', also known as '14 Points for Management'.

Joseph Juran

Like Deming, Juran was also an engineer in the 1920s, and he too lectured in Japan in the 1950s. Juran (1988) wrote the *Quality Control Handbook*, which was first published in 1951. His message was that quality must be planned. He developed his '10 Steps to Quality Improvement' as well as the 'Juran Trilogy':

- Quality planning
- Quality improvement
- Quality control.

Juran stressed that while a manufacturer's view of quality was conformance to specification, a customer's view was 'fitness for use' (discussed previously in Section 8.2, 'Definition of quality').

Philip Crosby

We have already discussed COQ earlier in this chapter. Philip B. Crosby is best known for suggesting that organisations should aim to achieve zero defects, and should carry out 'cost of quality' calculations.

Cost of Quality **(COQ)** =

Price of Conformance **(POC)** + Price of Non-conformance **(PONC)**

Crosby developed his '14 Steps to Quality Improvement' as well as his 'Four Absolutes of Quality Management':

- Quality is defined as conformance to requirements
- Quality comes from prevention
- Quality sets the performance standard at 'zero defects'
- Quality is measured by the cost of non-conformance.

Kaoru Ishikawa

Ishikawa (1985) developed the concept of quality circles and also, 'cause and effect' diagrams, which are often called fishbone or Ishikawa diagrams (see Figure 8.6). He also worked for a while with Deming.

Quality circles are teams within organisations (say, a department or a business process – they can be cross-divisional or even involve people from different organisations) that volunteer to work as a group to improve their work processes. A quality circle (a team) holds meetings on a regular basis (say, once a week or once a month), to address specific quality problems, which they select to work on. The team discusses root causes and potential solutions and decides appropriate corrective actions. The corrective actions are then carried out and the results reported back to the team. Further corrective actions are decided and taken as appropriate. Regular meetings are held until the team decides to disband.

'Cause and effect' diagrams aim to identify the root causes of quality problems. The diagram is usually drawn up using brainstorming techniques as follows:

1. First, the problem, called the 'effect', is documented in the furthest right-hand box.
2. Then the main 'causes' contributing to the problem are brainstormed. The different categories that could give rise to one or more causes are considered in turn to see if any causes of that type can be identified. These categories include machine, method, material, measurement, personnel and environment.
3. Next the sub-causes are brainstormed. What defects lead to the cause?
4. Finally, the causes and sub-causes are analysed and solutions, also known as 'corrective actions', are recommended.

Look at Figure 8.6. Here the problem or effect is 'Software not delivered on time'. Under the category of 'personnel', the cause of 'Inexperienced project team' was identified. Sub-causes or defects thought to contribute to the cause were considered to be 'Insufficient prior project experience' and 'Poor training'. Corrective actions (not shown in Figure 8.6) could be 'Improve training course', 'Additional training course', 'Hire more experienced staff' and 'Ensure any lessons learned or good practices are documented and communicated within the project team'.

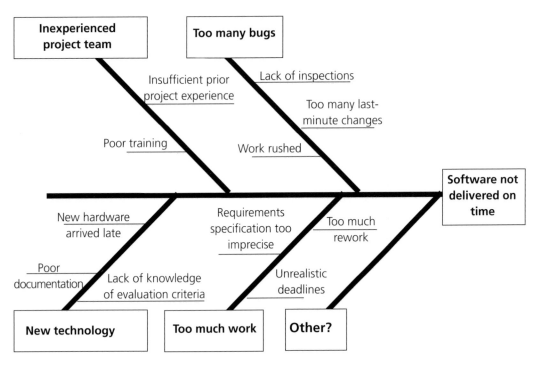

Figure 8.6: An Ishikawa diagram. Also known as a 'cause and effect' or 'fishbone' diagram

Draw a fishbone diagram

Look again at the Ishikawa diagram in Figure 8.6. Draw such a diagram to capture the 'causes' that could explain the 'effect' of a student receiving a poor grade for a piece of coursework. Also recommend some solutions.

Use the process outlined in the text:

1. **Identify the problem or effect.** Draw the main backbone of the fish and the right-hand box.

2. **Brainstorm the causes.** The categories under which to think about causes include: machine, method, material, measurement, personnel or environment. For each cause, draw a fishbone line with a box off the main backbone.

3. Next, for each cause, **think of some sub-causes** (that is some defects) that would lead to the cause. Draw in the sub-causes as fishbones connecting to the appropriate main cause fishbone.

4. Finally, can you **think of some solutions or corrective actions** that would address the sub-causes?

8.8 Continuous improvement

'Continuous improvement' represents a concentrated effort and investment by organisations to *continuously* improve their capabilities by learning from earlier feedback and improving processes to take account of the new knowledge. This means continuously striving to produce better products and to improve processes. Quality is thus seen as a long-term investment and the aim is to drive up the quality standards on an ongoing basis by improving on the existing baseline.

An organisation continually seeks to identify and try out improvements and learn from the experience (think back to earlier discussion in this chapter on PDSA cycles). The entire product lifecycle is examined. One key requirement for continuous improvement is that an organisation has 'stable' processes; in other words, that the processes are sufficiently predictable that an organisation can detect the impact of any change (think back to the earlier discussion in this chapter about control charts).

Given the scale of the changes, it is hardly surprising that there can be problems in adopting such quality initiatives. These problems include:

- Long-term justification is often ignored
- Excessive focus on current product
- Lack of management commitment
- Lack of employee involvement
- Diffused efforts when too many problems are tackled at once
- Amorphous quality management plans.

Continuous improvement initiatives have to address all these problems if they are to succeed.

In this section we shall describe Six Sigma, which is currently the best-known quality approach being adopted by many large organisations, most notably Motorola and General Electric Company (GE).

Note: you may find reference in the literature to total quality management (TQM), which is an earlier approach to organisational quality.

Six Sigma

'Six Sigma' is a holistic approach to quality: it is an organisation-wide approach that is customer-focused, and aims to raise quality to breakthrough levels. The work of many of the quality experts (such as Deming, Juran and Crosby) has contributed towards the Six Sigma principles and methods.

A Six Sigma organisation sets high goals and uses a continuous improvement process. Originally a five-step, DMAIC improvement process was proposed. (DMAIC stands for *Define, Measure, Analyse, Implement* and *Control*.) However, three additional steps of *Identify, Develop* and *Communicate* have since been added to this, so the process has become as follows (Truscott 2003):

- **Identify** the project: find a project that matches the criteria as being suitable for Six Sigma (see later)
- **Define** the project: define the problem/opportunity, process and customer requirements, including Voice of the Customer (VOC) data. Examples of VOC data are customer complaints and customer comments. Specifically, define customer satisfaction goals and sub-goals as

these provide a baseline or benchmark for the process improvement (for example, reduce cycle time, reduce costs and reduce defects)

- **Measure** current process performance: define and collect relevant measures to support the goals
- **Analyse**/probe the problem: use the data obtained from the measuring and look for patterns and trends (statistical analysis allows for testing out hypotheses and modelling). Look for process improvement opportunities. Try to prove the suspected root causes – use Ishikawa diagrams
- **Develop** the improved process – pilot and verify: generate improvements for solving the problem/seizing the opportunity. Run a pilot test to check out the improvements work as expected
- **Implement** the changes: implement the improvements that have been developed; achieve breakthrough in performance. (*Note this step is often called 'Improve' in other texts.*)
- **Control** – measure and hold the gains: track and verify the improvements – use control charts. Put in place control methods to maintain the achieved new quality levels
- **Communicate** – exploit the achievement in other areas: ensure the new knowledge gained is communicated. Transfer the improvement on to similar areas.

The name 'Six Sigma' refers to the high-quality level that is set as the target: no more than 3.4 defects, errors or mistakes per million opportunities. It is the repeated use of the disciplined approach on project after project that drives up the quality levels. Project selection is singled out as being of prime importance: an ideal Six Sigma project must have a quality problem or gap that requires solving, it must not have a clearly defined problem, and it must not have a predetermined solution.

8.9 Industry quality standards

Industry standards assist organisations that do business with one another: there is a common understanding of the standard of the work, and also compatibility issues can be addressed.

ISO Standards

The International Organization for Standardization (ISO) is (as the name implies) an international organisation, independent of any national government. The group of ISO 9000 standards focus on quality management with respect to improved customer satisfaction and continuous improvement. These standards were revised in 2000 and called ISO 9000:2000.

ISO 9000:2000 focuses on eight quality management principles:

1. **Customer focus**
2. **Leadership**
3. **Involvement of people**
4. **Process approach**
5. **System approach to management**
6. **Continual improvement**
7. **Factual approach to decision making**
8. **Mutually beneficial supplier relationships.**

These principles form the basis of the ISO 9000 series. Go to the ISO website (**www.iso.org**), search for ISO 9000:2000, and under that you will find an online description of each of the principles.

TickIT

The TickIT initiative began in 1991 when a report on software quality by the UK Department of Trade and Industry suggested that many software organisations were reluctant to adopt the ISO 9000 standards because they believed them to be 'too general and difficult to interpret'. The British Computer Society (BCS) were asked by the British Government to provide a method for registering software organisations under ISO 9000 standards, and the result was the TickIT project (Marchewka 2006).

TickIT provides support for organisations to obtain certification under the ISO 9001:2000 framework. This framework applies to all kinds of information system development. According to the *TickIT Guide* (2001), the principal aim of TickIT is to encourage software system developers to think about:

- What quality is in the context of the processes of software development
- How quality may be achieved
- How quality management systems may be continuously improved.

A further major objective was to provide industry with a practical framework for the management of software development quality by developing more effective quality management system certification procedures. These involved:

- Publishing guidance material to assist software organisations interpret the requirements of ISO 9001
- Training, selecting and registering auditors with IT experience and competence
- Introducing rules for the accreditation of certification bodies practising in the software sector.

Although certification is a contractual requirement for software suppliers in certain market areas, it should be a by-product of the more fundamental aims of quality achievement and improvement and the delivery of customer satisfaction.

TickIT registration is achieved by audit. An external independent auditor, who has been trained by the International Register of Certified Auditors, which is supported by the BCS, carries out an ISO 9001:2000 audit. After a successful audit, an organisation receives its certificate of compliance with ISO 9001:2000 and is allowed to use the TickIT logo.

Look on the TickIT website (**www.tickit.org**) for further information, such as the scope of TickIT, and which organisations have TickIT certification.

8.10 Maturity models

Maturity models provide frameworks for organisations to enable them to assess their overall capability. Their principal aim is to help organisations understand what they need to do to achieve process improvement or to enhance organisational capability.

In this section, we shall discuss the Capability Maturity Model Integration (CMMI), and the organisational project management maturity model (OPM3).

Capability Maturity Model Integration (CMMI)

The Software Engineering Institute (SEI) at Carnegie Mellon University (see **www.sei.cmu.edu**) was established to improve the capabilities of the US software industry. The initial result was the SEI Software Capability Maturity Model (CMM), which put in place a framework for process improvement. Other models followed, produced by other organisations as well as by the SEI. The SEI then decided to produce an integrated model to integrate all the models. Two different instantiations were produced:

- **Staged CMMI** assesses an organisation's process capability at one of five maturity levels
- **Continuous CMMI** assesses individually the maturity levels of different process areas across an organisation, so a set of different maturity readings results.

Given that organisations tend to operate different processes at different levels of maturity, the continuous model better reflects reality, and allows organisations to have additional flexibility over their process improvement. The staged CMMI in contrast requires organisations to focus on each maturity level in turn across the entire organisation.

The model operates by setting out specific goals for each process area within an organisation. An organisation is assessed according to how far it meets these goals.

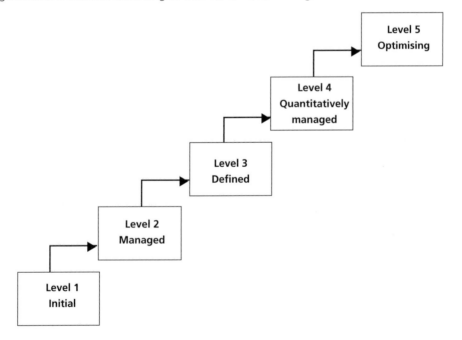

Figure 8.7: The CMMI staged model.

We'll give a brief outline of how the CMMI levels progress, but see **www.sei.cmu.edu/cmmi** and, specifically, **www.sei.cmu.edu/publications/documents/02.reports/02tr002.html** for further details.

- **At Maturity Level 1**: *Initial:* processes are ad hoc and chaotic
- **At Maturity Level 2**: *Managed:* the projects of the organisation have ensured that requirements are managed and that processes are planned, performed, measured and controlled. The status of work products and the delivery of services are visible to management at defined points (for example, major milestones). Work products are reviewed with stakeholders and are controlled

- **At Maturity Level 3**: *Defined:* processes are well characterised and understood. They are described in standards, procedures, tools and methods. The organisation's set of standard processes is established and improved over time. Projects establish their defined processes by tailoring the organisation's set of standard processes according to tailoring guidelines. Process objectives are set and addressed. Processes are qualitatively predictable

- **At Maturity Level 4**: *Quantitatively Managed:* quantitative objectives for quality and process performance are established and used as criteria in managing processes. Quantitative objectives are based on the needs of the customer, end-users, organisation, and process implementers. Quality and process performance is understood in statistical terms and these are managed throughout the life of the processes. Processes are quantitatively predictable

- **At Maturity Level 5**: *Optimising:* the focus is on continually improving process performance through both incremental and innovative technological improvements. Whereas Level 4 was concerned with addressing special causes, Level 5 is concerned with addressing common causes of process variation and changing the process to improve process performance.

Project management maturity models

In the late 1990s, several organisations developed project management maturity models loosely based on the SEI CMM. The aim was to improve and standardise project management processes. The Project Management Institute (PMI) produced an Organizational Project Management Maturity Model (OPM3). (For further information see; Project Management Institute, *Organizational Project Management Maturity Model: Knowledge Foundation*, 2003).

OPM3 builds on the *PMBOK Guide* project management processes introduced in Chapter 1 of this book: initiating processes, planning processes, executing processes, monitoring and controlling processes, and closing processes.

OPM3 extends these processes into the domains of programme management and portfolio management (Remember programme management and portfolio management were discussed in Chapter 2). The aim of OPM3 is to facilitate the systematic management of projects, programmes and portfolios to achieve an organisation's strategic goals. So there is an implied notion that, by working across all three domains, impact can be made at a strategic level.

OPM3 builds what it calls a 'model context' by putting these processes in the three domains (project management, programme management and portfolio management) into a framework for continuous process improvement. The stages of process improvement are **S**tandardise, **M**easure, **C**ontrol and Continuously **I**mprove.

OPM3 describes how to assess the maturity levels of an organisation's processes and how to improve these processes. It does this by establishing a model that includes:

- Best practices
- Capabilities necessary to support the best practices
- Observable outcomes proving that a capability exists
- Key performance indicators (KPIs) for measuring outcomes
- Pathways showing how capabilities map to best practices and the dependencies among them all.

  (PMI OPM3 2003)

8.11 Addressing quality issues in student projects

If you have carried out Activities 8.1-3 in this chapter with care, then you will have gone some way towards considering quality in your student project. In Activity 8.1, you considered the level of quality you were planning to offer, in Activity 8.2 you considered the cost of quality for your project and in Activity 8.3 you thought about quality process metrics.

Hopefully, you have realised that you have to build quality into your student project, and the activities have shown you some ways to go about doing this. At all times, the requirements of your customers (client and supervisor) need to be checked and you should plan to obtain feedback from them. Additional quality costs resources so, given limited resources, you always have to be determining the 'right balance'.

8.12 Summary

This chapter has introduced the main current ideas on project quality management. It has also discussed the key people who have helped over the years to shape quality management.

If you think about early versions of the systems development lifecycle, you will see that quality was largely an afterthought. Quality was initially viewed as a measurable attribute only existing in the final product. Over the years we have learned that quality cannot be engineered into the last stages of the process: it needs to be designed in from the beginning.

Engineering quality into a system takes forethought and careful planning. It also consumes time and resources. However, quality is not just about errors and their elimination: it is also about prevention. Further, it is a dynamic concept.

Modern project quality management emphasises the usefulness and acceptability of a product to its users: the satisfaction levels that the project solutions offer to clients and users are used as the measures for project success.

8.13 Review questions

 Question 8.1

Think of an organisation that you recognise as having a customer-focused approach to quality. What makes you think of this organisation as opposed to others?

 Question 8.2

When is prevention not better than cure? Can you think of anyone with a vested interest in cure?

 Question 8.3

Think of a quality problem you have experienced (for example, a new product that you bought not working properly, or a computer application with insufficient user documentation). Can you work out the time very roughly that the problem cost to sort out? Could there be any other costs involved?

 Question 8.4

When considering quality costs, what is the key difference between prevention of errors and appraisal?

 Question 8.5

As quality improves, what is likely to happen to the cost of prevention?

 Question 8.6

If you were investigating a quality problem, what would be one of the first things you would want to establish?

 Question 8.7

Think about V & V as defined by Boehm (1981) (discussed in Chapter 4):

Verification: Build it right?

Validation: Build the right thing?

How does Juran's definition of quality as 'fitness for use' relate to this?

 Question 8.8

If a contract specifies acceptance criteria, whose responsibility is it to ensure the acceptance criteria are met?

Question 8.9

Can you produce a rough timeline covering the work of the quality gurus discussed in this chapter? How did they influence each other?

Question 8.10

What CMMI level(s) are the systems development processes that you are using, or planning to use, in your student projects?

8.14 Feedback on activities

Activity 8.1: Basic quality measures

- **Fitness for use** would mean that your program does not crash and provides basic facilities needed

- **Meeting the specification** would suggest that your program was produced according to the written specification

- **Fitness for purpose** means that your program covers the basic needs of your client. Not only can your client use the program, but also it provides exactly the functionality features the client needs

- **User satisfaction** means that the customer is actually satisfied (happy?) with the product and how it covers their basic needs.

In terms of your product for your student project, you should at the very least make sure that it is fit for use and does not collapse. As you are working on a specific problem, you probably also have a client and should, therefore, expect to find 'fitness for purpose'. This should really be the absolute minimum for all final-year projects.

If your project is not too large, it would be good practice to ensure that you can prove conformance to your customer requirements specification. This assumes that you have a clear and unambiguous definition of the requirements.

It would be nice if you could ascertain the degree of customer satisfaction with the actual product or a prototype of it.

Activity 8.2: Considering the cost of quality

You would need to consider costs in the areas of prevention, appraisal and internal failure. Cost of external failure is less of an issue as you will not be able to make any corrections following the submission of your report. However, if your student project 'went live' in the field with use by customers then there would likely be external costs incurred.

In terms of prevention of errors, you will need to figure out how you are going to carry it out. What amount of time are you going to allocate for quality planning? What technical reviews are you going to have?

You also need to think about how you will perform appraisal. What testing are you planning? Are you going to use inspection or some alternative?

Once you have decided about the different categories, you can plan for implementation. The main implication is going to be in terms of time allocated for the task of appraisal and additional time allocated for the correction of errors. Allocations of time will need feeding into your scheduling. You will need to ensure that sufficient time has been allocated!

Activity 8.3: Quality process metrics for your student project

Quality process metrics for a project are used to monitor how good the project processes being used to create the product/system actually are. In the case of your student project, these are the project processes you are utilising.

The standards you have to conform to come from two sources:

- **Your module/course:** you will have been given information about the requirements for the project and its evaluation criteria. Maybe you have been given a proforma of the contents expected and guidelines about project activities

- **Your client/industry:** depending on your chosen project, there could be industry standards that you have to conform to. In addition, your client could impose their standards.

If you have been given no information on standards, you should always ask if any apply!

Such standards form the basis of thinking about your process quality metrics. All the following – likely to be set out in student/customer documentation – reflect on the quality of your project processes:

- Attendance at lectures/seminars

- Conformance to project deadlines

- Conformance to content demanded in evaluation criteria

- Feedback/marks for mandatory work handed in

- Conformance to client documentation standards.

To this you can add measures in the following areas:

- Holding review meetings with customers

- Project progress to plan

- Bugs/feedback errors reported.

Think about what you would recognise or would want as a quality improvement in your project processes and try to capture it as a measure. Arriving on time to seminars might be a goal for some!

Activity 8.4: Draw a fishbone diagram

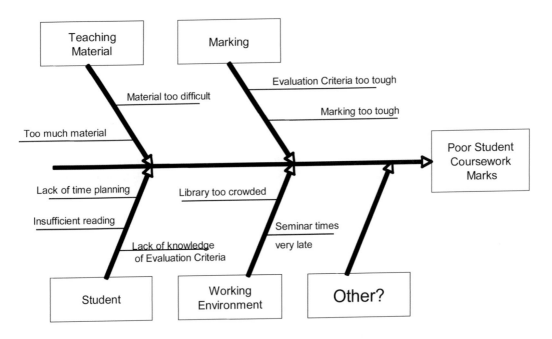

Figure 8.8: An Ishikawa diagram showing a possible solution to Activity 8.4

Potential corrective actions (in other words, potential solutions) could include:

- Ensuring students understand evaluation criteria

- Altering the seminar times

- Reducing the amount of module material.

8.15 References

Boehm, B. W., (1981), *Software Engineering Economics*, Englewood Cliffs, NJ: Prentice Hall, ISBN 0 13 822122 7

Crosby, P. B., (1980), Quality *is Free*, Mentor, ISBN 0 451 62585 4

Deming, W. E., (1986), *Out of Crisis*, MIT Center for Advanced Engineering Study (CAES), ISBN 0 91137901 0

Gilb, T., (2005), *Competitive Engineering: A Handbook for Systems Engineering, Requirements Engineering and Software Engineering using Planguage*, Elsevier Butterworth-Heinemann, ISBN 0 75066507 6

Gilb, T. and Graham, D., (1993) *Software Inspection*, Addison-Wesley, ISBN 0 201 63181 4

Ishikawa, K., (1985), *What is Total Quality Control? The Japanese Way*, Prentice Hall, ISBN 0 13952433 9

Juran, J., (1988), *Quality Control Handbook* (4th Edition), McGraw-Hill Education, ISBN 0 07033176 6

Kerzner, H., (2003), *Project management: a systems approach to planning, scheduling and controlling* (8th edition), Wiley, ISBN 0 471 22577 0

Marchewka, J. T., (2006), *Information Technology Project Management: Providing Measurable Organizational Value* (2nd edition), Wiley, ISBN 0 47171539 5

Pressman, R. S., (2005), *Software Engineering: A Practitioner's Approach* (6th edition), McGraw-Hill, ISBN 0 07 123840 9. (5th Edition published in 2000 is also referenced, ISBN 0 07 709677 0)

Project Management Institute, (2004), *A Guide to the Project Management Body of Knowledge* (3rd edition) (PMBOK Guide), ISBN 1 93069945 X, ISBN13 978 193069945 8. **www.pmi.org/** [Last accessed: November 2006].

Project Management Institute, (2003), *Organizational Project Management Maturity Model: Knowledge Foundation*, PMI, ISBN 1 930699 08 5

Schwalbe, K., (2006), *Information Technology Project Management* (4th edition), Thomson Course Technology, ISBN 0 619 21528 3

The TickIT Guide: Executive overview, Issue 5.0, January 2001. **www.tickit.org**

Trustcott, W., (2003), *Six Sigma: Continuous Improvement for Businesses*, Butterworth Heinemann, ISBN 0 7506 5765 0

CHAPTER 9

Project risk management

OVERVIEW

The aim of projects is to bring about change, and therefore they have a high level of uncertainty and innovation. Risk management is the discipline that enables project managers to make informed decisions and manage their projects in the face of such change, uncertainty and unpredictability.

Risk management is an area of increasing interest and is definitely on the corporate and project 'agenda'. It is viewed as a key skill in a world struggling with uncertainty and risk – indeed, most surveys place it at the top of the skills needed to cope with the realities of modern business and technical development. As organisations look for new proactive approaches, a systematic approach to risk (and opportunity) management is taking central stage. So risk management is a skill worth developing. If you look at project management job advertisements, you will discover that many now expect some familiarity with the approaches and techniques of risk management. This chapter will endeavour to provide you with an introduction to risk management, and enable you to assess some of the risks in your student project.

Note that this chapter is concerned with project risk management rather than general IT risk management that would include wider issues for IT security (such as data security). So whenever the terms, 'risk' and 'risk management' are used in this chapter, interpret them as meaning 'project risk' and 'project risk management'.

Learning outcomes	At the end of this chapter you should be able to:

- Define risk

- Define risk management

- Identify and evaluate risks

- Utilise checklists and other generic lists to determine project risks

- Categorise and prioritise action lists for risks

- Discuss strategies for dealing with project risks.

9.1 Introduction

This chapter defines 'risk' and describes how projects carry out risk management.

The structure of the chapter is as follows:

- Attitudes towards risk are considered and a definition of risk is given
- Risk management is defined and a risk management process is discussed
- The benefits of evolutionary systems development to risk management are considered
- An approach to dealing with deadline pressure is suggested
- A generic checklist of risks for student projects is given.

9.2 Attitudes towards risk

Let's first consider how people talk about risk and their attitudes towards risk.

Popular perspective of risk

We hear the term 'risk' on an almost daily basis. It would appear that most current debates invoke risk at some stage. Some examples:

- Is it safe to use mobile phones because of radiation?
- Do mobile phones masts affect the growth of children? Is their radiation level acceptable?
- Should we consume genetically modified food? What do we do about genetic mutations?
- Is our drinking water safe? From aluminium? From microbes?
- Is it safe to eat fish from a contaminated sea?
- Is it safe to fly due to deep-vein thrombosis?
- Is climate change threatening our coastline?
- Will a large asteroid strike our planet?
- Was the most recent train accident predictable? Could it have been stopped?

You could be excused for wondering if it is safe to get up in the morning!

Activity 9.1

Risk identified in newspapers

Open a daily newspaper of your choice and look through the headlines. Can you identify five stories that involve some kind of risk? Find stories about IT projects and risk: look in the IT press.

Risk appears to dominate the headlines in the newspapers. We know that risk affects many facets of our life. It is probably safe to assume that you have used the term 'risk' in some context. But do we really understand risk? Before we proceed, it is time to see what risk means to you.

What does 'risk' mean to you?

Think about the term *risk*. What does it mean? Can you define it? What does it mean when someone says, 'You are taking a risk'?

Objective and subjective risks

A lot of the time we think we understand risks. However, it is useful to make a distinction between objective and subjective risks.

- **Objective risk** represents *what actually exists*: the true magnitude of a given risk

- **Subjective risk** is what the analyst, manager or the observer *believes to be the risk*.

In most situations we are not dealing with objective risks, as we do not have the facts. Many risk scientists argue that we never do and we only deal with perceptions of risk and opinions as they are expressed in the newspapers. It is useful therefore to remember that normally we will not find common agreements about, or accurate definitions of, specific risks. Most of the time we work with values and perceptions!

Tolerance towards risks

Risk tolerances vary. Different individuals and organisations have different attitudes towards taking risks. Three preferences for risk are as follows:

- **Risk-averse**
- **Risk-neutral**
- **Risk-seeking.**

A risk-averse person or organisation gains less satisfaction and becomes more uncomfortable, when more is at stake. A risk-neutral person or organisation has a balance between accepting payoff and risk. However, a risk-seeking person or organisation gains more satisfaction when they can see the opportunity for a bigger payoff: they have a higher tolerance for risk.

9.3 Definition of risk

Basic definitions of risk

A basic dictionary definition of risk is the 'chance of bad consequences' (Pocket Oxford Dictionary, Revised Fourth Edition with corrections, 1961). This fits with the everyday approach to risk as discussed earlier. However, for project risk we need a definition that is more practical and that can be used in a quantitative way.

The Project Management Institute (PMI) *A Guide to the Project Management Body of Knowledge* (PMBOK Guide) defines project risk as:

'An uncertain event or condition that, if it occurs, has a positive or negative effect on a project's objectives'. (*PMBOK Guide*, 2004)

Notice the reference here to the possibility of a positive effect, and also the concern about the impact on the project objectives.

Alternatively, Kerzner (2003) gives the following definition:

'Risk is a measure of the probability and consequence of not achieving a defined project goal.'

This definition focuses more on the negative effect of risk. It usefully highlights the concept of risk involving 'probabilities' and 'consequences'.

In both these definitions, for a given event, there are two main components of risk:

- **Probability or likelihood** of the event occurring
- **Impact** if the event occurs (what is at stake?).

As either probability or impact increases, so does the risk (see Figure 9.1).

As we shall see later in tl
exposure'.

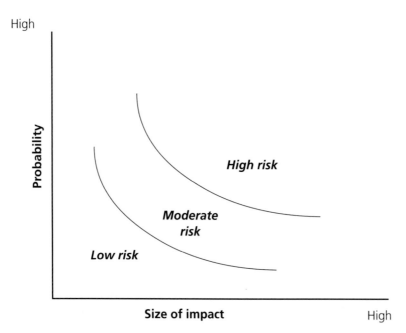

Figure 9.1: Risk is a function of *probability* and *impact*.

(Adapted from Kerzner 2003, Figure 17-1).

Kerzner makes the point that risk is also a function of hazard and safeguard. As he points out, a hole in the road is a much greater danger to the driver who is not aware it exists: a driver who knows about the hole can take action to avoid it. A hazard is the *source* of a risk (so the cause of a risk is here seen as a fundamental element of risk). Safeguards are means of overcoming, or partially overcoming, hazards. Risk increases with hazards, but decreases with safeguards.

So if hazards can be identified, then maybe safeguards are available, or can be developed, to tackle the hazards and help reduce the risk.

Good risk management is about identifying the potential hazards and taking action to have appropriate safeguards against them. This of course needs to be driven by the probabilities and consequences of the risks.

In other words, events may or may not happen. Your knowledge will not make a difference to the likelihood of the event happening. However, it can make a difference to your preparedness and ability to respond.

These varying definitions of risk seem to explain why we refer to a risk in several different ways:

- **As a probability:** for example, 'the risk that this will happen is 10%'
- **As an impact:** for example, 'the risk is that a car accident will happen', or 'we will lose 100 monetary units'
- **By its source:** 'lack of user involvement' or 'lack of adequate testing'.

Costs and benefits associated with risk

We can look at risks in terms of impact: costs and benefits. On the cost side, there are a number of factors associated with risks as follows:

Costs:

- (Unexpected) losses
- The cost of uncertainty itself:
  - strain – both physical and mental (e.g. stress and panic)
  - less than optimal performance including improper use of resources, timing problems, oversupply, undersupply, and degraded decision quality.

The costs involved in a risk include the obvious losses that are feared (sometimes termed unexpected losses). They also include the associated stress, panic and strain, which can be physical or mental that result from facing a risk (or an uncertain situation).

Alternatively, on the benefits side:

Benefits:

- Performance: the only way to achieve anything is by taking risks
- Potential for opening up creative chances.

The potential for gains drives us to take risks. With the potential for gain also comes the opportunity to take greater benefit from new emerging situations, for example by being the first organisation to provide a certain type of service on the Internet or from specialising in selling a new service or product before the opposition does. Creative chances and opportunities can lead to developing a serious advantage over the competition. Risk can thus be said to be the only source for innovation. Indeed, economists maintain that greater economic performance can only be achieved through greater uncertainty and the taking of risks (just think about all the major entrepreneurs and how they got there).

Choices and decisions

At the most basic level, risk implies a choice. That is, a decision has to be made on how to react to risk where there is a set of different potential outcomes; that is, different risk possibilities exist each associated with a different potential outcome.

Project managers have to decide which options to take. Some decisions will have crucial impacts. Some risks are negative and imply potential harm, but others may give opportunities and potential gains (after all, that is why we take chances).

The need to manage risks

Pressman (2005) describes some project managers as belonging to what he calls the 'Indiana Jones School of Risk Management'. Whenever faced with an apparently impossible situation, the eponymous hero simply observed, 'Never mind, I will think of something'. Sadly, as Pressman says, the average project manager is no match for Indiana Jones (a charismatic adventurer): too many project teams rely extensively on reactive risk strategies. In other words, too many projects do not practise risk management.

Risk management implies the ability to identify, quantify and control risks accurately. Project managers, who are normally involved in operating in unique and new conditions, are prime examples of professionals, who are asked to balance potential gains and new strategic opportunities with the elimination of harmful risks. They should be proactive towards risk management.

Approach to handling risks

We may feel uncomfortable with risk and uncertainty, all too often we try to reduce them by using resources in an attempt to eliminate the likelihood or reduce the expected impact of a given risk. However, there is also the potential benefit and the potential for new and strategic gains to be considered.

The starting position for managing risk should be the recognition that *total elimination of risks is impossible* (and may even be undesirable). Human beings rely on experience to reduce risks and uncertainty in a given situation. The more you know about your risks, the less uncertain you are about their potential impacts. The tendency to eliminate risks must be balanced with the knowledge that reducing one risk may increase others, and introduce new unknown risks in new, and as yet unexplored, situations.

There is also the question of time. The increasing pace of change and the rate of innovation mean that there simply is not time to cater for all risks, and in many cases there is insufficient experience to fully know in advance the probability of risks occurring.

It is important to remember that we are dealing with events that may or may not happen and that the decisions about risk management have to be made in advance.

9.4 The risk management process

Process overview

The Project Management Institute (PMI) *A Guide to the Project Management Body of Knowledge* (PMBOK Guide) defines project risk management as:

'The processes concerned with conducting risk management planning, identification, analysis, responses, and monitoring and control on a project. The objectives of Project Risk Management are to increase the probability and impact of positive events and decrease the probability and impact of events adverse to project objectives.'

(PMBOK Guide, 2004)

In outline, risk management involves:

- Continuously assessing risks
- Determining what risks need dealing with
- Implementing strategies to deal with those risks.

Risk management requires effective mechanisms for identifying and addressing risks. In other words, we need a process for dealing with risks.

It is very important to realise that risk management is an *ongoing activity* – throughout the life of a project. It is not enough to carry out an exercise at the project planning phase and leave it at that, thinking you have done all that is reasonable to do, to minimise the consequences of risks.

It is also important to understand that risk management must be *fully integrated* into the work of the project team; it is not a task to be carried out completely in parallel to the other project activities.

The risk management process we propose in this chapter is as follows:

Risk management process:

- Risk policy
- Organisational context
- Risk identification
- Risk assessment
- Risk evaluation
- Risk planning
- Risk control (execution)
- Risk monitoring
- Reflection and communication.

This risk management process consists of nine steps, where many textbooks have only four steps. The intention here is that the separate sub-processes are emphasised more distinctly.

A reason the risk management process given in this chapter differs from those normally given in project management and software engineering books is because it starts at an earlier stage in the project lifecycle and ends later – indeed, it encompasses the entire project lifecycle. The aim is to provide a more comprehensive coverage of risk in the systems development and management processes. The process begins before project inception (to ensure the project is feasible) and progresses until the completion of the project and beyond (to make sure knowledge retention and sharing take place).

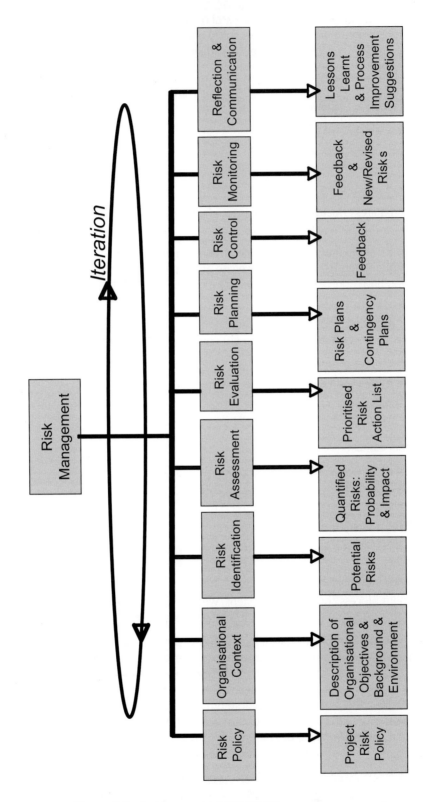

Figure 9.2. A risk management process

This risk management process is continuous and iterative, thereby reflecting the nature of risk.

Before exploring each step within the process in more detail, we will try to give you a flavour of the steps so that you can see how they work together.

- **Risk policy** involves deciding how the project should approach risk. What is the organisational risk policy, what is the risk tolerance of the sponsors of this project, and what is at stake with this project?

  Organisational context is not directly concerned with risk, but rather with what the organisation (as opposed to the project) is trying to achieve: that is, the organisational context in which the project exists, which includes investigating such things as the organisational objectives, the background to the project being initiated, and other current projects
- **Risk identification** involves determining which risks are likely to affect a project. It involves looking for the obstacles and potential obstacles in the path to achievement, and asking what has the potential to stop the project from completing successfully
- **Risk assessment** attempts to characterise, qualify and quantify these threats (and opportunities) to enable effective decision making
- **Risk evaluation** looks at potential options for overcoming the effects of risk, culminating in the selection of the most suitable strategies
- **Risk planning** plans the implementation of the strategies to deal with the risk prior to the risks adversely affecting the project's progress
- **Risk control** is the actual execution of the selected risk management strategies
- **Risk monitoring** tracks the project and the success of the selected strategies and tactics in dealing with the effects of identified risks, while also monitoring for new or revised risks (threats and opportunities)
- **Reflection and communication** mark the attempt to learn the lessons from the present to improve organisational (and personal) ability to address risks in the future.

Technical development teams are likely to be involved in the risk planning, control and monitoring steps. Systems analysts and/or risk analysts will probably lead the earlier steps. The project manager, however, is concerned with the full range of risk management activities and their impact on the project.

Each of the steps will now be explored in turn.

Risk policy

Risk policy decides how the project is going to approach risk. Any organisational policies and templates for risk handling need to be identified and considered, and then the specific policy for the project needs determining. How risk-tolerant are the stakeholders, and specifically the project sponsors? How ambitious is this project: what level of risk does it need to take? What methods for risk management is the project going to adopt and who is going to take main responsibility for risk management? What level of contingency planning, and contingency resources should exist?

Organisational context

This is not a traditional step in risk management and is added to the sequence to emphasise the fact that life does not begin with project inception. Every organisation is likely to have plans, desires and history, and their impact on any given project cannot be overemphasised.

Project managers will normally be familiar with an organisation's mission statement, organisational objectives and strategic plans. Some discipline-specific plans are also likely to exist: for example, IS plans or security plans. Project managers will study all these plans to understand how they relate to their projects. One main purpose of studying the IS plan is to understand how any other projects are likely to impact the project in question. For example, many projects have been launched as an attempt to resolve a specific problem only to discover that some other initiative is addressing the same area. Alternatively, there could be infrastructure projects that impose design constraints on the project.

It is also very important to establish additional context information. The context is crucial to identifying any relevant factors within the environment. Relevant factors can range from physical layout of the organisation, to competitive information that may support (or hinder) the project. The 'background' gives the historical context: what specific problems did similar projects encounter in the past (such as user resistance, management obstacles, problems with the unions).

In short, the project manager is concerned with looking for any piece of organisational information that may impinge on the proposed project.

Risk identification

Risk identification is concerned with identifying, categorising and characterising the risks. The main questions the project manager needs to ask at this stage are 'What are the risks?' and 'What kinds of risk are they?' Identification is reasonably straightforward.

The main outputs of the identification process are risk events for the project, and risk symptoms. Risk events are specific things that may occur and negatively impact the project (for example, significant scope change, a performance failure of a product, and supply shortages). Risk symptoms are indicators of actual risk events (for example, defective products may be a symptom of a low-quality supplier).

Useful means of identifying risks include:

- Using checklists (identifying generic risks)
- Using critical success/failure lists (highlighting generic problems or issues)
- Examining task decomposition (your WBS can reveal specific problems)
- Investigating decisions, rationales and assumptions already made on the project
- Detailed reading of activity plans (with a particular emphasis on the critical path and events close to being on the critical path, as well as making sure that events off the path are not likely to be exposed to major problems)
- Examining project specifications to uncover other problems
- Interviewing people with recent experience on similar projects
- Asking a panel of experts (Delphi technique).

Let's look at some of these methods in slightly more detail:

Checklists:

There are a number of generic risks associated with all projects; a list of some of these is given below.

Generic risks include:

- Personnel shortfalls: for example, loss of key staff; difficulty in recruiting specialists
- Unrealistic budgets and schedules: for example, aggressive targeting with little regard to reality

- Continuing stream of requirements changes: for example, users who were denied adequate consultation at the outset of the project
- Use of unproven technologies: for example, component-based development in an organisation only familiar with procedural languages, such as C.

It is very useful if you can find a list of generic risks that tells you where to look for the common problems that apply to most projects. Risk management applications can be a source of such checklists and questionnaires (Though note that such applications can be more centred on IT security, rather than specific project risks).

Additionally, there will be risks specific to a particular project. These 'project-specific risks' will be less easy to identify and will only be found by examining the project documentation.

Critical success factor lists:

Success factors try to predict what is needed in order to succeed in a project. While the lack of a success factor does not guarantee a failure, it can be viewed as a risk to the project (being unable to reach the best outcome. Try to imagine what would happen to a project if any of the following were missing.

- Typical critical success factors (in no particular order):
  - user involvement
  - clear statement of requirements
  - proper planning
  - realistic expectations
  - smaller project milestones
  - competent staff
  - ownership
  - clear vision and objectives
  - hard-working, focused staff
  - technical feasibility.

Failure factor lists:

Now, take a look at the list of failure factors below. Failure factors explain why projects who have these symptoms tend to fail. Many of the factors can be viewed as generic failure causes, and hence viewed as risks:

- Typical failure factors (in no particular order):
  - user involvement
  - changes to requirements
  - unrealistic deadlines
  - inaccurate estimation
  - ignored risks
  - weak design
  - lack of motivation
  - poor progress tracking due to lack of visibility
  - inexperienced management
  - insufficient or late testing
  - failure of suppliers
  - new technology.

- Risks can be categorised into risk types, such as:
  - user involvement
  - personnel
  - organisational
  - environment
  - process
  - technology
  - tools and equipment
  - costings, measurement and schedules.

Classify by project risk type

Here is a list of some typical risks that a project manager might worry about:

- Theft of laptop from project team member travelling between work and home
- Loss of key project staff through illness and/or leaving organisation
- Incorrect objectives due to lack of access to strategy documents
- Reliance on unknown 'off-the-shelf' application package that has to be tailored by the project
- Delay in availability of customer premises, which will house the system produced by the project (building work is still in progress and is already delayed)
- Delay in hardware development (some hardware required by the project is still under development and doesn't exist as yet)
- Inadequate requirements specification
- Access to key client staff proving difficult – they are busy with other work
- Not meeting major customer deadline
- Time estimates are unrealistic – too ambitious
- Sign-off of requirements is likely to be delayed because of requirement conflict
- Insufficient knowledge within the project of customer business
- Lack of experienced project staff
- Project team have not worked together before
- Failure to get additional funding agreed at project review board
- Possibility of cutback in project budget next year
- Lack of a project champion within the customer base
- Customer staff do not have sufficient experience of using this technology
- Fire at project premises
- Hardware failures
- Theft at project premises
- Software failures.

Classify each of these risks using the following risk types:

- Personnel
- Environment
- Technology
- Costings, measurement and schedules.
- Organisational
- Process
- Tools and equipment

Activity 9.4

Identify user prototype trial risks

Think back to Activity 4.1: *Trialling a prototype*, where the basic question asked then was as follows:

Imagine you are working on a project team and have developed a prototype user interface. You want some users to try it out for you. Consider how you would go about arranging for this to take place and how you would conduct the user testing.

Now, for this activity, write down a list of the potential risks that you think might apply. Try to identify at least one potential risk for each of the different risk types as follows:

- Personnel
- Organisational
- Environment
- Process
- Technology
- Tools and equipment
- Costings, measurement and schedules.

Risk assessment

Risk assessment is concerned with quantifying and assessing the impact and sensitivity of risks.

After identifying the risks, the next step is to prioritise them, as it is unlikely the project will have the resources to eliminate (or even to reduce the effects significantly) of all the risks. Choices have to be made. Prioritising implies that we have the ability to determine how critical the risks are (that is, have some idea about how to measure the risks).

One approach is to estimate a parameter, 'risk exposure', for at least the main risks (by 'main risks' we mean the risks that are considered likely to be significant. For example, it is not worth spending too much time on very low risks).

Risk exposure (RE) is defined as the product of the probability of the risk materialising and the size (impact) of the consequential loss, or the cost to the project should the risk occur.

RE = Probability (of a risk) x **Impact** (Loss as a result of the risk materialising)

Think back to the definition of risk given at the start of Section 9.3, 'Definition of risk'. The definition involved both 'probability' and 'impact'.

For example, let us suppose that there is a 50% chance that a key technical specialist will leave the development team after the conclusion of the project initiation phase: they are known to be unhappy and seeking alternative employment. The direct cost of recruitment of a replacement is estimated by the human resources department as 3,000 monetary units and typically such posts remain vacant for at least two months following the departure of a holder. However, it might be possible to outsource the work to a subcontractor or else the project may have to be slowed down, resulting in a new risk of not delivering the product at the agreed time. If this happens, the company will be liable to pay penalties.

In this case, the risk exposure must be calculated for the two possible outcomes. In one case the consequential loss consists not only of the direct recruitment cost, but also the subcontracting cost. In the other, the consequential loss equals the direct cost plus the risk exposure of having to make penalty payouts. Remember, having to make penalty payouts is not a certainty even though the probability of having to do so is high. See Figure 9.3, which captures this information as a decision tree. Decision trees are used to provide a visual view of the various decisions and their possible outcomes. In Figure 9.3, there is only one decision that he project manager has control to make, assuming the technical specialist does leave.

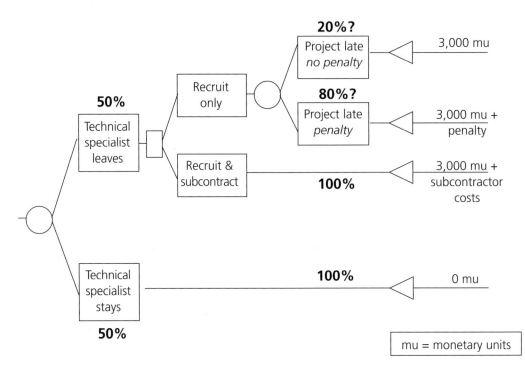

Figure 9 3. A decision tree for the technical specialist example

This process may seem straightforward and if one knew the probabilities and sizes of the consequential losses it would be a simple matter in a mathematical sense. However, in practice one is faced with having to estimate both parameters (probabilities and consequential losses).

Consider another situation: let us now suppose we have estimates of the risk exposure for a number of risks and furthermore they are all in a narrow range of values. We are faced then with prioritising when the information we have about the risks is at best partial, if not inaccurate. Ranking by size of risk exposure might seem the way ahead, but let us consider a not uncommon scenario.

Say we have two risks with approximately equal risk exposures. However, one of these is an extremely unlikely risk with a huge consequential loss, the size of which would destroy the business. The other is a much more likely risk with a modest loss. This is a classic dilemma. Should we do everything possible to minimise the chances of disaster, or are the scarce resources better used reducing either the likelihood and/or the consequential loss of the more modest risk?

Despite such reservations, many organisations do prioritise risks on the basis of risk exposure. (Note that some organisations also produce a list of the most critical risks; say, the top ten chart, which is used to keep track of the risks viewed to be the most serious.) After all, this is better than the more traditional focus on the loss alone, or the isolated view that emphasises frequency (or probability) as the only critical factor. Judging the relative merit associated with a risk at least measures the two essential aspects related to the risk.

When you think about project risks, one suggestion is to compile a list in order of probability and impact on the project. This can help you to estimate the relative values of probabilities of risks and the impact (consequential loss) of each of them. To calculate the probabilities you can also use a qualitative probability scale that has the values *impossible*, *improbable*, *probable* and *frequent*, and then you can associate a mathematical probability with each qualitative value (for example, 0.2 for improbable, 0.8 for frequent, etc.).

Alternatively, some project managers plot percentage probability against impact so they can more easily identify the risks with both high probability and high impact (see Figure 9.1).

Risk evaluation

Risk evaluation is concerned with the selection of the most suitable resolution strategies and tactics, and confirmation that the solutions conform to organisational norms and project objectives.

The four basic risk strategies are avoidance, acceptance, transference and reduction.

- **Risk avoidance** involves eliminating a specific threat or risk, usually by removing its causes or taking an alternative course of action. As we have seen, most risks cannot be completely eliminated, but specific risk events can be. Altering the requirements or changing the design would be ways of avoiding a risk
- **Risk acceptance** or assumption means accepting the consequences if a risk should occur. Nothing is done to avoid the risk – it may, or may not, occur, but at any case no specific action will be taken
- **Risk transference** or transfer is shifting, partially or totally, the consequence of a risk and responsibility for its management to a third party – for example, taking out an insurance policy to cover the event of hardware faults or employing a specialist contractor (such an electrician or a qualified engineer) to address a specific risk
- **Risk reduction**, mitigation or control involves reducing the impact of a risk event by reducing the probability of its occurrence or by limiting the loss impact. You will recall that the exposure to risk is a product of the probability and the loss: reducing either aspect would lead to an expected reduction in the exposure to risk. For example, ensuring a project has a good project manager is likely to reduce the occurrence of problems.

For each risk, the different risk strategies have to be considered and the potential tactics for handling any threats or enhancing any opportunities have to be defined. Identification of potential responses to a particular risk could benefit from using creativity-enhancing techniques such as brainstorming to generate new approaches to handling risks. Each of these responses needs to be evaluated in terms of organisational objectives to make sure that the solution does not create new problems and does not clash with other projects or solutions or duplicate other solutions.

Before a decision is made, the risk is also looked at in terms of its acceptability to determine if the project/organisation is better off addressing the risk or ignoring it. If it is decided to address a particular risk, comparison of different solutions can done by using the risk reduction leverage (RRL) approach which looks at the obtained reduction against the cost of facilitating that reduction:

RRL = Reduction / Cost

(where the reduction is measured as, RE (before the solution) – RE (after))

Working through an example could be helpful at this point:

Activity 9.5

Risk reduction leverage (RRL) calculation

Note that the figures are from a real project and that you are given all the values needed for the calculations.

A software project has an interface problem related to recovery from errors. Experience tells us that the probability of this error occurring is 30% and the resulting loss would be £1,000K. As the risk is significant, the project manager has investigated the situation and discovered that there are two possible approaches for solving the problem.

Approach 1 uses an interface checker during the requirements stage at a cost of £20K reducing the risk to a new probability of 10%.

Approach 2 means additional testing and will cost £150K, reducing the original probability to 5%.

First of all suggest the best option based on your gut reaction. Then do the RRL calculation to see which approach is more effective at solving the problem.

Once each risk has been considered individually, then the risks have to be considered collectively in the overall context of the project.

Many project managers utilise network diagrams as part of the decision-making process in an attempt to assess the impact of different solutions. Risk evaluation culminates in the making of clear decisions regarding which risks will be tackled and how.

Risk planning

The purpose of risk planning is to prepare for the task of dealing with the risks.

Planning begins with a clear definition of the tactics required to address each risk obtained from the risk evaluation. The individual tactics are combined to form an integrated list of solutions, which provides a final opportunity to ensure that solutions do not clash with one another and do not duplicate.

Some risks will need to be planned for immediate response; others will have a contingency response planned (that is, in the event of the risk materialising then plans will be in place to tackle it).

Risks that you know you are going to deal with (immediate response) will need resources allocated 'upfront'. Risks that are only going to be dealt with if they materialise will need to have contingency resources planned and held in reserve.

Once the overall plan is complete, the project manager will list the requirements for monitoring the results. Monitoring must be planned and the mechanisms required for monitoring the effectiveness are therefore listed during the planning stage.

Risk control

Risk planning is followed by risk control, also known as risk resolution, execution or implementation. The purpose of this step is to carry out the agreed actions in accordance with the plans. At this stage the project manager will therefore be following the agreed risk tactics (for example, prototyping, using contractors or using alternative tools).

Risk monitoring

Risk monitoring ensures that the risk tactics are being effective, that no new risks have emerged and that the results of the project are still compatible with the organisational and the project objectives.

The focus is on observation of the results, and the actions meant to ensure the top risk items are being controlled. Part of this process entails comparison of the actual results with the expected risks, and comparison of actual results with the original objectives. The perceived effectiveness of mitigating tactics determines whether to continue with the same approach to reducing the risks, whether to adjust them in accordance with the emerging results, or whether to respond to new threats and opportunities.

Reflection and communication

Reflection and communication together with learning take place in the remainder of the process. At the end of the project they are formulated (often during the post-implementation review stage). Most risk lifecycles leave off prior to this stage, but this step is essential to the development of the project team members and to the growth of organisational knowledge, skills and capability.

Knowledge from the risk management process can be utilised for future estimates of risks and costs. It can be used to calibrate and adjust models on the basis of past results. In addition, it may also help in obtaining effectiveness measures with respect to certain solutions and approaches. More importantly, it can be used to obtain a degree of confidence in the assessments related to both the solution approaches and the process.

9.5 Evolutionary systems development

It has already been emphasised that risk management must be an on going process throughout the life of a project and that it should not be a parallel activity but fully integrated into the other project activities.

Let's now discuss how evolutionary approaches to systems development address risk management because they do provide an extremely proactive risk management mechanism.

The benefits of evolutionary approaches to risk management include:

- **Small evolutionary steps mean that only a small amount of the total time and effort allocated for the project duration is at stake** – typically only 2% to 5%: this means that if things go badly wrong then the problems are detected early and retreat is possible. Other strategies can be considered as there is still time left to explore other alternatives. Also little time has been lost.

  For example, carrying out work to improve the 'time taken to get data onto a corporate website' from '4 hours on average' to 'less than 1 hour on average' (the ultimate goal) can be done in small weekly increments. Each increment could reduce the time taken to load the data in turn down from 4 hours to 3.8 hours, to 3.6 hours... to 1.2 hours, to 1.0 hour (target reached). If any single 2% step fails to deliver the improvements expected, then we can try other strategies, or improve on the strategy we tried. But we cannot lose more than a 2% of total time/effort before we realise we have a 'loser' to deal with. The risk of wasting our entire budget on things that don't work as expected is sharply reduced (Tom Gilb, *personal communication*).

- **Measurement of progress occurs at the end of each evolutionary step, so the project gets an early chance of feedback and can take any necessary corrective actions:** the project finds out how good it is at predicting the outcomes, and how well their development processes are working.

  For example, if after one Evo cycle, the projected improvement of a reduction to 3.8 hours for the time to get data onto a website does not occur. Say the result were in fact only a reduction from 4.0 to 3.9 hours, then we have an instant, real-time message that our change strategies are not delivering the expected results. We immediately have the opportunity to analyse why. It could be that the strategies are incapable of ever doing so. It could be that good strategies are just poorly implemented (like failing to train and support people in using them). So we have an opportunity to change strategy, or improve its implementation, and see if we then actually get the improvements we expect. We have reduced the risk of betting too much (a whole project) on a bad strategy or bad strategy implementation (Tom Gilb, *personal communication*).

- **The project gets early feedback from the users so it knows if the outcomes are off-track and are not what the users actually require:** the requirements and strategies can be adjusted as needed to meet the user needs

- **The steps are prioritised so that the users get the high-value steps delivered earliest:** this means that the project builds up a record of early deliverables and early success. The users bank early benefits

- **The project team also has the ability to try out high-risk steps early and find out just how much of a problem they are:** better to find out at an early stage that something is too ambitious before too much time, effort and money has been expended

- **Smaller steps are easier to control,** so there is less risk involved.

One of the main benefits of all this proactive handling of risk is that greater risks can actually be taken. When there is less at stake, it is much easier to take more radical steps knowing that retreat is possible. Also, assuming the project has already delivered some success to the users, there will be no loss of face – everyone will understand exactly what is being attempted. In addition, a forward-planning project manager might well have alternative steps lined up ready for delivery to cover his or her project team in the event of any problems occurring with a step.

9.6 Dealing with deadline pressure

Deadline pressure is one of the persistent project risks. Let's look in this section at some strategies to attack such risks – you might find them helpful for your student projects.

Tom Gilb (1986) wrote an excellent paper, '*Deadline Pressure: How to cope with short deadlines, low budgets and insufficient staffing levels.*' In it, he provides ten suggestions on how to cope with such situations.

Note that actually all these elements, tight deadlines, small budgets and insufficient staff, could be viewed as risks.

Gilb's 'ten suggestions' are as follows:

- Re-think the deadline given – is it for real?
- Re-think the solution – is it compatible with the deadline?
- What is the client's point of view on this problem? Does that help you understand their real needs?
- Don't accept 'expert' opinions blindly. Insist on evidence that something will work – has it worked before now?
- Determine which requirements must be delivered by the deadline. Some requirements will be crucial, but your client probably doesn't need everything by then
- Don't cave in and accept impossible deadlines, even as a last resort
- Change the solution to meet the deadline
- Make maximum use of existing systems and known technology
- Break the project into earlier and smaller deliverables. Remember to think about the results that you want to deliver, not the technology
- Don't forget to take credit for the success.

These suggestions capture many of the pitfalls that projects can inadvertently stumble into. For example, some deadlines are absolutely fixed, such as the date that a new law comes into force, but many are arbitrary and could be negotiated. What does the client actually want? Many projects suffer because they lose focus on the results that the client wants: somehow the project manager's or the systems analysts' additional requirements overtake the requirements as specified by the client. Also, there are often key requirements that the client needs, but they get buried in the detail of all the requirements that the client has specified. So by separating out and focusing solely on the key requirements, a project can often speed up its delivery.

There are two main themes in Gilb's paper:

- To 'think smarter' about what really matters to your client
- To use evolutionary delivery to ensure you deliver early.

Both will relieve deadline pressure, and make for a better project relationship with the client.

Activity 9.6

Dealing with 'deadline pressure'

Do any of the deadline pressures (short deadlines, low budgets and insufficient staffing levels) apply to your student project? Gilb proposes several strategies to deal with deadline pressure (see Gilb's 'ten suggestions'). Assess them against your student project. Which strategies could be relevant?

9.7 Dealing with risk in student projects

Common pitfalls for student projects – a generic list of potential risks

Some of the most useful things to know about individual projects are the common pitfalls. Many of these points have been mentioned before, so the following can be used as a partial checklist. Here are some of the common causes of failure:

- **Choosing/starting the project too late:** submit your project proposal on time and start the project as soon as you can. The longer you leave it, the harder it is to get motivated, especially when all your friends seem to be flying ahead

- **Allowing too little time for writing the report:** you should try to produce as much of your report as you can as you go along, even though you don't know in advance its exact structure. The last two weeks of the project should be dedicated to pulling together the material you have accumulated and producing a polished final product. You can spend time improving any implementation after you have submitted the report

- **Failing to meet your supervisor regularly:** if you arrange a meeting with your supervisor, turn up at the agreed time. If you are stuck for any reason and you have no meeting arranged, contact him or her immediately. You gain no sympathy from anyone if you lose contact with your supervisor and produce a poor project as a result. Your supervisor will be happy to help you, but they can do nothing if they are unaware that you are having trouble

- **Trying to satisfy an external customer at the expense of your grades:** do not let any outside interests interfere with your work. The guidance for your project should come from your supervisor, not your current or prospective employer

- **Over-/under-ambition:** try to be realistic about what you can achieve in the time available: A good project requires a lot of input from you and should prove to be technically challenging throughout. At the same time, however, it is better to do a small job well than it is to fail to do a big job at all. Your supervisor will advise you on his or her expectations of the project and this will help you to set your sights accordingly

- **Failing to plan a fallback position if the planned work is not completed on time:** try to plan your project in stages so that if things go wrong in a later stage you have a completed stage to fall back on

- **Lack of clear explanation of your reasons for making decisions during the course of the project:** decisions, in particular, ones involving selection of methods and choices need to be justified

- **Lack of clear statement of objectives:** objectives need to be clearly stated in an early chapter and revisited in the conclusion section. Remember there can be project objectives and product objectives

- **An inadequate literature review:** the literature review ought to include a minimum of 15 references (the references should be given in the references section, and be correctly cited, using the required format, for example using the Harvard referencing format). References should cover both the IT theory and the relevant business area. The literature review (using your references) should demonstrate you have an understanding of the current state-of-the-art and show how your project fits into it

- **Deliverables by magic:** on opening a report, the immediate impression is of a large volume of code or analysis/design documentation with no idea of its source. Try to make sure you explain the methods by which the work was produced; explain design decisions; include a road map to guide the reader, etc. You also need to clarify the context relating to any practical project. In general, when you are writing, consider the storyline and let it guide the writing process

- **Deliverables of unknown quality:** the work appears sound but there is no evidence of its validity. Include test results (summarised), relevant reports of meetings, walkthroughs, inspections and workshops, with a commentary on their relevance. If the main output is intellectual, try to justify your position and support your argument

- **Deliverables of unknown origin:** in some cases, the work seems to be of good quality but seems too extensive to have been done as a project. If work existed before the start of the project, define what existed, its status and who was responsible for its production

- **Blind assertions of fact/lack of source of information:** the assertion of facts, often as a list (e.g. the critical success factors are… OR it is known that…). Everything in your report has either an external source or is a result of your work. Either way, you should make the source clear. It should be clear whether the assertion was derived through logical argument, practical evidence and results or evidence from the literature. Only repeat an external source list if you intend to discuss every point

- **Complex diagrams with no source(s) acknowledged:** a diagram is supplied without a source. Give the source. If you have adapted several sources, make clear the contribution of each

- **A large number of small annoying errors,** which could have easily been corrected through proofreading and careful use of a spell-checker

- **Lack of definitions** of terms or acronyms, which spoils readability

- **Perfectionism:** try to avoid the tendency to perfect every task: remember, a 'good enough' project finished on time is better than the promise of unfinished 'perfection' (see over-ambition on the previous page).

Plagiarism

Once again, remember that the work you submit must be your own.

- Acknowledge any quotations you use from published or unpublished sources
- Do not copy the work of fellow students or project reports completed in previous years. Such unacknowledged quoting or copying (plagiarism) will constitute an examination offence and will be treated as cheating.

Deliberate damage to, or misuse of, computer systems or the work of others or acts in contravention of normal legal and ethical requirements may lead to outright failure.

Final note

Finally, you will need to keep monitoring your risks on a continuous basis. It is a good idea to remind yourself of the pitfalls at regular intervals and to make sure you are not about to slip into one of them.

Identifying the major risks for your student project

Try to identify the major risks to your student project. Use the list of common pitfalls for student projects as your checklist. Re-read the section on 'Risk identification' for additional ideas on what to consider.

Dealing with stress

You may have experienced some stress (a sign of risk) related to either previous coursework or your student project.

Project stress comes from inability to interact with deadlines and other constraints.

Major sources of stress include:

- Lack of planning
- Ambiguity about the project goal and objectives
- Imposed deadlines
- Slippage
- Lack of communication
- Lack of feedback
- Lack of visibility of progress
- Conflicting priorities
- Inability to deal with change.

If you have any worries about your student project, you should make a point of discussing them with your tutor as soon as possible.

9.8 Summary

Risk management – where do we stand?

The risk management process helps managers to make more informed decisions and so enables organisations to respond effectively to potential risks. It also provides a means of recognising opportunities before the competition.

Most managers believe they are managing risk. However, all too often they are simply managing costs and schedules. Very few projects manage risk in a systematic way. Approaches tend to be ad hoc, undocumented and incomplete.

While risk management used to be an optional extra, it is now becoming part of mainstream software engineering and project management. Many projects (including government projects in most countries) now require the use of structured and controlled risk management, and often also use a specified risk management process. Risk management needs to be integrated into the project process (systems development lifecycle) and beyond, to ensure that organisations are attuned to the area of risk and opportunity.

9.9 Review questions

 Question 9.1

Think about how you would categorise yourself with regards to risk tolerance. How would you categorise your client for your student project?

 Question 9.2

Can you think of three different ways that you have heard people express risk with regard to IT systems?

 Question 9.3

Is avoiding risk ever a possible strategy?

 Question 9.4

Do the same risks apply to all IT projects?

 Question 9.5

How would organisational policy impact on risk evaluation?

 Question 9.6

Is there cost incurred in carrying out risk management?

Question 9.7

If evolutionary project delivery reduces risk by enabling the following:

- Small amount of project time and effort at stake
- Chance of early feedback about project systems development processes
- Chance of early feedback from users
- Early delivery of high-value deliverables to users
- Possibilities of trying out high-risk steps early
- Increased control over the systems development process due to smaller steps...

... what does this imply with regard to the traditional waterfall method – how does it compare?

9.10 Feedback on activities

Activity 9.1: Risk identified in newspapers

It will be extremely difficult not to find some stories involving an element of risk. It could be related to any of the questions just posed as examples, to some form of accident, to the threat of terrorist strikes, to the possibility of a war between two countries, to a new storm or floods, the use of drugs such as ecstasy tablets, and so on…

Activity 9.2: What does 'risk' mean to you?

You are likely to have come up with one or two specific words when trying to define risk: 'danger' or 'hazard'. In fact, most people would tend to select a word implying some potential harm.

A second possible set of words you might have decided on includes 'gamble', 'taking a chance' and may even begin to touch on issues such as 'probability' and 'likelihood'.

There is also a third grouping that is sometimes mentioned, which includes words such as 'gain', 'potential' and 'opportunity'. This does not come up very often, but some people do associate risk with potential gain. In the context of projects, there is increasing recognition of opportunity being delivered by risk.

The type of headlines we read in the newspapers equates risk with harm (that is, a danger or a hazard), and leads to the traditional negative view of risk. A useful informal definition of a risk that encapsulates this perspective is, 'an accident waiting to happen'. This definition is good at capturing the challenging nature of risk, but it is not sufficient (as is shown later in the chapter).

Activity 9.3: Classify by project risk type

Some risks are difficult to classify without having a specific context – in these cases, more than one risk type has been given in the table below.

Note, 'Organisational' has been used here for any risk caused by issues interfacing with the customer organisation.

Risk	Risk Type
Fire at project premises	Environment
Theft at project premises	Environment
Theft of laptop from project team member travelling between work and home	Environment
Loss of key project staff through illness and/or leaving organisation	Personnel
Incorrect objectives due to lack of access to strategy documents	Organisational/Process
Hardware failures	Tools and equipment
Software failures	Technology

Reliance on unknown 'off-the-shelf' application package that has to be tailored by the project	Technology
Delay in availability of customer premises, which will house the system produced by the project (building work is still in progress and is already delayed)	Environment
Delay in hardware development (some hardware required by the project is still under development and doesn't exist as yet)	Technology/Tools and equipment
Inadequate requirements specification	Process
Access to key client staff proving difficult – they are busy with other work	Organisational
Not meeting major customer deadline at end of January	Costings, measurement and schedules
Time estimates are unrealistic – too ambitious	Costings, measurement and schedules
Sign-off of requirements is likely to be delayed because of requirement conflict	Process/Organisational
Insufficient knowledge within the project of customer business	Personnel
Lack of experienced project staff	Personnel
Project team have not worked together before	Personnel
Failure to get additional funding agreed at project review board	Process/Organisational
Possibility of cutback in project budget next year	Environment
Lack of a project champion within the customer base	Organisational
Customer staff do not have sufficient experience of using this technology	Organisational

Activity 9.4: Identify user prototype trial risks

Your list of potential risks could include (in no particular order):

- Some users might be too busy to take part in the trial – they might not be willing to give up sufficient time for testing

- A key user might not be available

- Certain required user stakeholder types might not be available

- The prototype might not have the correct scope for the users

- The prototype might not be ready on time

- A key member of the project team might be unavailable to help with the trial

- The hardware on the user site might not work

- Software could fail during the trial

- It might not be possible to 'reset' the software after failure

- The users might not understand what was required of them/might not have prepared any test data

- The user test data might not be compatible with the prototype software

- There might be some loss of image if the prototype is not sufficiently impressive

- Performing the trial might take too long for the users, and they don't complete all the tests you planned

- You might not manage to capture all the feedback.

You probably have thought of other risks as well!

Activity 9.5: Risk reduction leverage (RRL) calculation

The risk reduction leverage formula should help you to determine the best choice of approach for this risk:

RRL = Reduction / Cost
(where reduction is measured as RE (before the solution) – RE (after))

RE = Probability (of a risk) **x Loss** (as a result of the risk materialising)

Let us start by looking at the interface checker solution.

The exposure before any measures are tried can be given as RE (before) which is the product of the probability and the loss.

RE (before) = 0.3 x 1,000K

RE (after) for the interface is reduced. Note that while the probability is reduced, the loss stays the same: there is as much at stake, only it is less likely to happen. Generally, solutions tend to reduce either the probability OR the loss. We can now calculate the RE (after).

RE (after) = 0.1 x 1,000K

Having obtained the risk exposure before and after, we need the cost of introducing the measure, which is given in the problem. We can now use the RRL formula to calculate the reduction leverage we get for our money.

$$RRL_{Interface} = \frac{(0.3 \times 1{,}000K - 0.1 \times 1{,}000K)}{20K} = \frac{(300K - 100K)}{20K} = \frac{200}{20} = 10$$

We can use a similar method to calculate the reduction leverage of a testing solution. Note that the reduction before is identical as we are dealing with the same risk. So,

$$RRL_{Testing} = \frac{(0.3 \times 1{,}000K - 0.05 \times 1{,}000K)}{150K} = \frac{(300K - 50K)}{150K} = \frac{250K}{150K} = 1.67$$

Our results show that the interface checker produces a higher reduction per cost ratio. A decision based on RRL would suggest that using an interface checker would be more effective by a factor of six. (However, there may be other considerations that need to be taken into account, for example the safety-criticality of the application or an acceptable probability, which may require alternative ways of determining the most suitable option.)

If you think about the result, what we have proved here is that early verification and validation is more cost-effective than catching the same errors further downstream during testing. (You can find out more about this in Chapter 8, 'Project quality management'.)

Activity 9.6: Dealing with 'deadline pressure'

Regarding deadline pressures, the student project deadlines are certainly fixed and fairly tight. Budget and staffing levels are dictated by the fact that this is a student project – this doesn't stop them being challenging though. Certainly, excellent utilisation of scarce resources is called for.

Picking up on some of Gilb's suggestions:

- Re-think the deadline given – is it for real?: the deadline given to you for your student project is all too real!

- Re-think the solution – is it compatible with the deadline?:

Do you need to re-visit the scope?

Determine which parts of the scope are absolutely necessary. Don't look for any extras at this stage. Delivering a working project would be a good start.

- Change the solution to meet the deadline: it is almost always acceptable to deliver a partial working product, explain the difficulties, explain why you encountered them, explain what that has taught you, and make suggestions for future work

- Make maximum use of existing systems and known technology: it depends on your student project objectives, but building on something that already exists, rather than starting from scratch, enables you to deliver faster something that works. Using technology that you are already familiar with reduces risk – you can pay attention to addressing the problem, rather than learning about the technology. Consider limiting the use of technology that is new to you to one specific area of your project. This limits the risk to your project: it helps ensure you can deliver something even if the unfamiliar technology doesn't work out as you planned

- Break the project down into earlier and smaller deliverables. Results, not technology: by breaking the project down into earlier and smaller deliverables, you will be able to assess progress and determine whether you need to make any adjustments to the scope of your project. Also – an extremely important point – by focusing early on delivering results, you are far more likely to deliver something. So aim to deliver an early result and 'bank' it. The stress and strains of project work will become much more bearable once you know you have achieved and delivered some good work.

Think – what is the smallest thing you could deliver early that your user would value and could use? For example, students developing website applications could think about putting a subset of the data online at the earliest possible time so that customers could access it to gain basic information. If that cuts down the number of telephone calls asking for this information, and provides out-of-hours information, then you have already achieved something for your client.

Activity 9.7: Identifying the major risks for your student project

It is normally a good idea to start by identifying the generic risks. These are likely to be identified by using checklists (in this case the common pitfalls for student projects), and critical success/failure factors.

You can then take a look at your WBS and try to identify any vulnerable work packages. You should also look at your decisions and at the critical events (and those close to being critical), and try to determine if there are any possible delays that affect them.

9.11 References

- Gilb, T., (1986), Deadline Pressure: How to cope with short deadlines, low budgets and insufficient staffing levels, *Information Processing*, pp. 293-299
- Kerzner, H., (2003), *Project management: a systems approach to planning, scheduling and controlling* (8th edition), Wiley, ISBN 0 471 22577 0
- Marchewka, J. T., (2003), *Information Technology Project Management: Providing Measurable Organizational Value*, Wiley, ISBN 0 471 39203 0
- Pressman, R. S., (2005), *Software Engineering: A Practitioner's Approach* (6th edition), McGraw-Hill, ISBN 0 07 123840 9. Note (5th edition published in 2000 is also referenced, ISBN 0 07 709677 0)
- Project Management Institute, (2004), *A Guide to the Project Management Body of Knowledge* (3rd edition) (PMBOK Guide), ISBN 1 93069945 X, ISBN13 978 193069945 8. **www.pmi.org/** [Last accessed: November 2006].

CHAPTER 10

Project review and reflection

OVERVIEW

The chapters in this book have taken you through the steps required to select, manage and report on a project. Throughout this book you have encountered a variety of methods and approaches for conducting research, planning your project, managing the project implementation processes, dealing with quality, and so on. The methods provide the tools you need to guide you through the management tasks in order to achieve the best project results. However, the management process does not end with the delivery of a working product: a post-delivery review provides the opportunity to reflect and consolidate any lessons learned during the course of the project, and relevant project information should be captured in a project report.

Learning outcomes   At the end of this chapter you should be able to:

- Understand how to carry out an end-of-project evaluation

- Reflect on project events, problems and deliverables

- Adopt a professional attitude to continuous improvement and personal development in project work.

10.1 Introduction

You are likely to already have encountered a variety of problems while working on your student projects. In order to overcome them, you will have devised approaches and methods that specifically addressed the problems. But how do you avoid repeating the very same mistakes in the future? And what should you take away with you to your next project?

This chapter discusses the need to improve professional practice by learning from projects and then taking those experiences on to subsequent projects. The chapter also provides various checklists to propose ways of evaluating the performance of products and project processes.

10.2 Project closing activities

In Chapter 1 we stated that project management activities can be categorised into process groups as follows (*PMBOK Guide* 2004):

- **Initiating processes**
- **Planning processes**
- **Executing processes**
- **Monitoring and controlling processes**
- **Closing processes.**

This chapter is concerned with the *closing processes* activities. We define 'Closing' as follows:

- Formalising the acceptance of the project or phase, and ensuring all relevant documentation is put in place.

Note the use of the words, 'or phase', which indicates that closing activities should occur at the end of *each* phase throughout the life of a project.

Projects terminate for many reasons. As we have discussed previously, not all projects are successful. However, it is important that for whatever reason a project terminates, that there is an orderly closedown and that any lessons are captured and learned. In this chapter, we shall be mainly concerned with two aspects of the *closing processes* activities:

- **Post-delivery reviews**
- **Project reports.**

10.3 Post-delivery review (PDR)

Many textbooks tend to overlook the topic of project reflection. However, the importance of learning from past projects is given increasing recognition by many organisations. Understanding why past projects were successful or failed is a key part of a learning process and leads the way to process improvement. Organisations wanting to enhance their project management capabilities should always conduct post-delivery reviews.

This section makes the case for carrying out a post-delivery review and describes what such a review should include.

The impact of the lack of a learning process

Many organisations transfer their staff to the next project as soon as handover has taken place: it is the natural temptation to move on and start the next task once the technical work has been completed. After all, the *completion of development activities* will have been properly planned to allow for a direct handover to users, all *documentation* (including user manuals) will have been finished, and *specific training* organised to enable users to make full use of their new facilities will have been carried out.

The problem is that transferring staff immediately deprives them of an opportunity for reflection and learning, and condemns them to repetition of any similar mistakes that may have been made. Further, the organisation as a whole loses out, in terms of knowledge that is not acquired and shared.

One solution to these problems is to introduce a post-delivery review for each project. Post-delivery reviews should be an opportunity to facilitate learning through the sharing of knowledge across projects: every project contains a variety of relevant lessons that the project manager and the team can use in future projects.

Conducting a post-delivery review process

A post-delivery review (PDR), also known as post-completion review (PCR) or post-implementation review (PIR) entails a 'post-mortem' analysis of the activities that took place and the results they delivered. The review reveals to the entire organisation, which patterns and activities should be repeated (and which should not), and what actions are likely to work in specific circumstances. Such knowledge can be built into training and apprenticeship programmes within the organisation and become part of the available organisational knowledge used to enhance performance and improve working practices. The feedback resulting from reviews of completed projects reinforces good behaviour, while also identifying what does not work. We have briefly covered the topic of reviews in Chapter 4 'Managing progress and change'. In contrast to quality-checking reviews, post-project reviews are more informal. They are typically conducted at a fairly high level of detail, focusing on specific trends and issues.

The best sources to support a PDR are in the actual project documentation. In particular, look for the aim and objectives definitions, the WBS, the Gantt chart, the critical path, the risk management documents and the reports from earlier review meetings. Another excellent source of information is the members of the original project team, as they can provide the rationale behind the decisions that were made.

A PDR should not be used as an occasion for disciplining and punishment. Such a review is not meant to be a personal vendetta against any member of the team, nor should it be viewed as a negative search for a culprit. The main objective of a PDR is to facilitate learning and improvement. Improving performance depends on learning lessons from every opportunity: learning grounded in practice is always more instructive.

Scope of a post-delivery review

The specific aspects for a PDR to consider include:

- The success of the product produced (delivered value/actual benefit)
- How the project is delivered with regard to the project triangle factors (financial budget, schedule and scope) and the specified quality objectives
- The project process including the quality of the project documentation and the project plans
- The team-working.

As well as looking at the team-working, an individual performance review should be carried out for each member of the project team.

Who carries out a PDR?

A project PDR is carried out by the project manager with the rest of the project team; the project manager would carry out the individual performance reviews by holding separate reviews with each individual.

In addition to a PDR carried out by the project team, an independent PDR (sometimes known as a project audit) can also be carried out. This is conducted by people external to the project and its purpose is to get independent opinion. The aim would be to gain some further insights.

Checklists

The following checklists provide sets of questions to initiate reflection about a project.

The *project/product* checklist

- Was the main project aim achieved?
- Was it achieved within the schedule/financial budget projections?
- Were the project objectives clearly defined?
- Were all aspects of the work completed?
- Are there any aspects that remain undone? (Note in your student project reports, this would give you scope for discussion in the last part of your report when you talk about problems and future plans.)
- Did the project give the client what was promised?
- Are the users happy with the result?
- Is it what they needed?
- Were their needs correctly identified?
- Did their needs change during the course of the project?
- Were all stakeholders identified from the outset?

The *project triangle* checklist

- How accurate was the financial budget?
- Was the planned budget exceeded? If so, why?
- What problems caused the escalation?
- Could they have been predicted?
- Could they have been avoided?

- How accurate was the schedule?
- Was the planned schedule exceeded?   If so, why?
- What problems caused the escalation?
- Could they have been predicted?
- Could they have been avoided?
- Was it just one problem that delayed all other activities or were all activities mis-estimated?

- Was the original scope achieved?
- Were there any changes to scope during the duration of the project?
- Why were they approved (or why were they needed)?
- Did they lead to any escalation in either budget or schedule?

- Was the overall quality acceptable?
- Were the test plans adequate?
- Did they pick up all the errors that you know about?

The *process* checklist

- What process was used to manage the project?
- What parts of the process worked well?
- What parts of the process would be done differently if you had a second chance?
- Were milestones observed? If not, why not?
- What were the reasons for misapplying them?

The *team* checklist

- Was the team effective?
- Did the team work together and support each other?
- Would you define the entire project as a success? Why/why not?
- Was the project organised effectively?

Dealing with problems checklist

If you have identified any major events that have taken place, ask yourself:
- Was this event positive or negative in terms of impact on the project?
- Was it predictable?
- Was it avoidable?
- When was it identified?
- Were the actions effective from that stage on?
- Was the communication chain effective?

The *project reflection* checklist

- What where the main strengths of the project?
- What were the major weaknesses?
- What changes would you recommend for the next project?
- Did you learn anything from this project?
- Do you think the project was effectively managed?
- Was the overall communication process effective?
- Where did it break down? Did this happen often?
- Did any of the methods work particularly well?

- What would you change in the management of the project?
- Describe one thing that you could have done personally to improve the outcome of the project.

What do you do with the lessons learned?

It is not sufficient to produce detailed documents emphasising the findings and the lessons from the review (however, this is better than simply ignoring them). The following list identifies some of the key actions:

- **Lessons need to be shared:** distribute lessons to all participants so that they take something away from the project
- **Revisit working practices:** if you have guides and procedures, update them as a result of lessons
- **Use lessons to facilitate training:** use the updates to train new team members
- **Maintain a repository of key lessons:** this could be used as a basis for detailed risk assessment. It can also be used to calibrate methods and produce detailed checklists
- **Ensure project managers access the resource prior to embarking on a new project:** knowledge from relevant projects can be utilised in kick-off meetings for new projects. For example, build it into the project management process that a project manager should try out and report on at least one 'new lesson learned' in each project.

Becoming a professional

Making effective decisions and assessing potential options is grounded in experience. Becoming a professional means developing the skills required to be able to make reasonable decisions as part of everyday practice.

The professional engineering and computing societies look for evidence of this ability to reflect upon and critically evaluate events and actions. The true mark of a professional is not in always making the correct decisions (with the benefit of hindsight), but rather in the ability to identify and use learning and improvement opportunities.

Professionalism grows incrementally through the amassing of experience. Reviewing and challenging the results from every project provides the key steps in a journey to continuous professional improvement.

Activity 10.1

Using checklists to conduct a post-delivery review

Ideally, a PDR is conducted immediately after delivery to ensure events are still fresh in people's minds! However, select a memorable project you have worked on in the past (maybe a piece of coursework) which you found difficult – or maybe your experience during the course of preparing and delivering your project. Use the checklists provided earlier in this chapter to evaluate your experience. Identify one key lesson.

10.4 Project reports

We first discussed the nature of project reports in Chapter 4 'Managing progress and change'. Let's now return to the subject, and first discuss the purposes of an end-of-project report, and then look ahead and consider specifically what project evaluation will mean for your student project reports. Writing to achieve set criteria is always a useful skill to acquire.

Purposes of project reports

The final report written for a project has several purposes:

- Informing stakeholders that project work has finished
- Describing the delivered project/product
- Setting out the achievements of the project
- Documenting all the artefacts/products produced by the project
- Handing over the product
- Requesting product sign-off
- Releasing resources
- Stating additional work that is still needed
- Thanking people for their help and their effort.

Contents of project reports

Marchewka (2006) suggests that as a minimum, the final project report should include and discuss the following:

- **Project summary**
  - project description
  - project measurable organisational value
  - scope, schedule, budget, and quality objectives
- **Comparison of planned versus actual**
  - original scope and history of any approved changes
  - original scheduled deadline versus actual completion date
  - original budget versus actual cost of completing the project
  - test plans and test results
- **Outstanding issues**
  - itemised list and expected completion
  - any ongoing support required and duration
- **Project documentation list**
  - systems documentation
  - user manuals
  - training materials
  - maintenance documentation.

Note that this list fails to explicitly ensure that reflection is captured; it is more about project progress and handover (as Marchewka discusses post-mortem reviews separately). It is also more industrial in its approach; it does not satisfy academic requirements for a student project report – see below.

It is important that there is formal handover of products and documentation. Otherwise, once the project team disperses, it becomes increasingly difficult to track down the artefacts, and there is little chance of further product documentation being carried out.

10.5 Reflecting on, and checking, your student project report

In Chapter 4, the document layout and the document structure for a student project report were discussed. Let's now turn our attention to the evaluation of the contents of your student project reports. For the purposes of such a review, you can view the report as a specific product that has very clearly defined 'user acceptance criteria' – the marking criteria!

Check the marking criteria against which your work will be assessed. This should help with your reflection process as well as your review. Your clients (that is, the academic staff) have provided you with a clear set of guidelines that reflects what is expected at each stage and how much work is required to obtain each level of 'user satisfaction'.

For example, a missing abstract may lead to a *fail* grade in that component, while to obtain an *excellent* assessment in this element you will probably be required to develop an abstract which clearly defines the subject area including the main aim, approach and conclusions.

The first level of assessment – already covered in Chapter 4 – should be to simply ensure that you have covered all the aspects.

Are all the following included in your report?

- **Abstract**
- **Introduction**
- **Problem definition**
- **Analysis/design**
- **Results/product**
- **Evaluation**
- **Conclusion.**

Now compare each of these items against the criteria for assessment given in Table 10.1 (and the standards used in your own institution). It would be a good idea for you to aim high and try to address these requirements.

Abstract checklist

- Clearly defines subject?
- Includes aims?
- Includes approach?
- Includes conclusions?

Assessment criteria for a student project

Abstract: Clearly defines subject. Includes aims, approach and conclusions.

Introduction: Precise description and explanation of all project objectives. Concise, clear, sets scene and presents summary for rest of document.

Problem definition: Excellent interpretation and conceptual grasp. The problem definition and its context is fully presented to a knowledgeable reader. Scope is appropriate. Almost all significant points covered.

Analysis, design and method: Analysis and design is explicit. All problems addressed. Similar justification of the choice (and range) of methods and tools.

Results/product: Results/product offer a notable original feature, quality or purpose. Pathway indicated for further development. Findings are original and could be applied in other projects and appear superior to the usual alternatives, OR software released is of high quality, OR outputs are of particular importance. Documentation includes advanced issues. Deep understanding of assumptions and trade-offs.

Evaluation (of both process and results): Reflective and insightful evaluation of the project and associated conclusions. Assessment of both process and outcome. Choices of approaches and methods revisited in light of outcomes. Objectives fully reviewed. Clear understanding of potential and limitations. Appropriate and realistic recommendations consistent with results.

Conclusion (section): Accurately identifies and summarises key points/issues and outcomes with reference to the original problem. Critical, reflective conclusions.

Use and citation of literature: Excellent use of evidence to support arguments/points. Substantial evidence of good use of a wide range of sources. Use of up-to-date information and relevant sources. Material used includes different types of evidence including contradictions and challenging information. Appropriate balance between classical and recent academic references.

Research & concepts: The research undertaken is relevant, sourced and critically reviewed in a synoptic fashion. The relevant concepts are understood and are explicitly articulated within the report and well applied. Exposition of relevant issues. Good awareness of nuances and complexities. Insightful and well informed.

Presentation: The report is well constructed. A convincing case is made. A clear storyline forming a coherent case with aims, arguments and conclusions fully compatible. Chapters are well organised and fit together. Very effective use of

English. Clear, concise and easy to read. Impartial academic style. Very high standard in terms of spelling, grammar and syntax. Negligible errors. Carefully organised and well presented. Interesting to read and visually appealing. Good use of relevant tables, examples, figures and data to break up text. References accurately cited and listed.

Student competence: Outstanding understanding of the project. Able to identify and implement novel aspects. (In addition to the use of standard techniques, novel approaches have been developed.)

Student management of the project: Clear evidence of motivation and management throughout the project. High-level planning and organisational skills. Able to overcome obstacles. All supervisor-set (or agreed) deadlines met, and plans made to ensure they are met, and contingencies made in case of possible delays. Responsive to changes.

Table 10.1: Assessment criteria for a student project

Introduction checklist

- Precise description and explanation of objectives?
- All objectives included?
- Concise?
- Clear?
- Sets scene?
- Presents summary for the rest of the document?

The two checklists cover the first two items in the assessment criteria. Can you see how each item was composed from the definitions?

Activity 10.2

Writing a project report to meet the marking criteria

Look at the assessment criteria in the Table 10.1. Draw up a checklist for 'Evaluation (of both process and results)' in the same manner as shown above for the 'Abstract' and 'Introduction' sections.

Now for each of your checklist items, decide what you would have to do to ensure you met it. For example, the Abstract checklist has an item, 'Includes conclusions'. To ensure you met it, you would need to:

1 Reach one or more conclusions about the results of your project

2 Ensure that these conclusions were summarised in the Abstract section.

Remember, your own institution will have a document that specifies their expectations in terms of projects and their key components. It may be useful at this point to compare these requirements with the items discussed in this section and to check if there are any further areas that you need to be focusing on.

10.6 Summary

This chapter should have given you some ideas and help about how to reflect on project experiences in a mature and professional manner. You will be required to do this for the purpose of your student project report. You will also find if you try to become a chartered member of a professional society that they too are interested in your ability to reflect on your experiences and to identify the important lessons.

One of the main aims of this book was to introduce you to current project management ideas and terminology. By now you should be able to pick up any of the textbooks on information technology project management and make some sense of its chapter structure. You should also have an understanding of the tasks of project management and how they differ from technical systems engineering tasks. If you have mastered the basics of this book's 'theory', you should find that when you go out into industry and start working in a project team, that you have a much better understanding of what is going on.

Remember, project management is likely to impact in some way on the rest of your professional life.

10.7 Review questions

 Question 10.1

To what extent have you designed quality into your project?

 Question 10.2

In which chapter of this book have we discussed in some detail, how to deal with possible 'problems'?

 Question 10.3

Can you name one quality control method that uses checklists?

 Question 10.4

Which should come first – the project report or the PDR?

10.8 Feedback on activities

Activity 10.1: Using checklists to conduct a post-delivery review

Work your way through the different checklists. Try to answer as many questions as possible. Some of the questions (such as those related to the financial budget) may not be relevant to your 'project', but try to imagine what would have happened. You should focus mainly on the schedule and scope elements of the project. If you were forced during the project to revise either, this should start a reflection on what happened – and why.

As well as focusing on the product, you should take a careful look at the process as any improvements can be taken to the next project (and provide a scope for learning, reflection and discussion).

If you can't answer a checklist question – ask yourself why? Is it because you didn't collect this type of information while you were working on the project? Should you have done so?

Overall, are you happy with your performance? What lessons do you need to learn for 'next time'?

Remember: every project has a lesson that can be used in your next project.

Activity 10.2: Writing a project report to meet the marking criteria

As this chapter is focusing on review, reflection and evaluation, it is useful to take another look at the criteria for 'Evaluation (of both *process* and *results*)'. The criteria are very explicit about what is required for an excellent evaluation.

Evaluation (of both *product* and *process*)

- Reflective and insightful evaluation of the project and associated conclusions

- Assessment of both process and outcome

- Choices of approaches and methods revisited in light of outcomes

- Objectives fully reviewed

- Clear understanding of potential and limitations

- Appropriate and realistic recommendations consistent with results.

One key point is that you are required to evaluate both product and process.

You should convert each item into one or more specific checklist items, and read each item very carefully, focusing on every word and trying to ensure that you have developed checklist items that fully meet the expected criteria.

You should look back at the checklists given in the earlier part of this chapter. They will provide some potential questions to help answer these points, but not all.

It is always a good idea to look at what is expected from an excellent product (even if you know that your report may not be viewed as such this time around).

An additional tactic is to specifically review the negative marking criteria (things that you will lose marks for if you do them) – ensure you have appropriately catered for both the positive and negative criteria.

The aim of this activity is to start you thinking about some of the things you need to do to strengthen your evaluation, such as identifying and logging the problems you encounter (when you identify any such problems, think about why they came about, and what could have been done differently).

By being proactive early, there is still time to do something.

By preparing in advance to ensure you capture the information you need to write up your report, you should make your writing up a much more straightforward process. By taking this approach, you will be extremely likely to save time over the course of your project – for example, you will know exactly the minimum information you must capture, and there will be no last-minute hunting for required information.

Note, however, that you can't achieve absolutely everything in advance. For example, when finally writing up, you will have to assess your final results against your initial targets and objectives. Only at this point can you see if the original targets were achieved. You can then reflect and try to see how any problems impacted and stopped you from achieving the targets.

This activity reflects the learning outcome about taking a professional approach in the sense that it shows the importance of carrying out preparation in advance rather than simply starting writing. However, there is much more to taking a 'professional approach', including considering the ethics of a situation.

10.9 References

Marchewka, J. T., (2006), *Information Technology Project Management: Providing Measurable Organizational Value* (2nd Edition), Wiley, ISBN 0 47171539 5.

Project Management Institute, (2004), *A Guide to the Project Management Body of Knowledge* (3rd edition) (PMBOK Guide), ISBN 1 93069945 X. **www.pmi.org/** [Last accessed: November 2006.]

Answers to review questions

Answer to review questions, Chapter 1

Question 1.1

The need for some change has to be recognised and championed by at least one stakeholder. To implement the change must require some new work being carried out that requires additional resources.

If sponsorship to fund the project can be obtained, a project manager is appointed and given the task to set up and run the project.

Question 1.2

Project management is more demanding because it is dealing with the introduction of change and is concerned with a one-off endeavour. Due to the uncertainties, the level of risk involved is much higher.

Question 1.3

This question should give you cause to reflect on how software projects appear in the public domain and what is at stake; also to consider how the success criteria discussed in this chapter translate into what was reported.

Question 1.4

- Waterfall model: not iterative, maybe some feedback between successive stages

- Incremental phased delivery: not iterative, maybe some feedback between the phases

- Evolutionary delivery (Evo): iterative, uses stakeholder feedback to help determine what to do next

- Spiral model: uses iterative prototypes

- Dynamic systems development method (DSDM): the last three phases of the development lifecycle are iterative, uses feedback from prototypes

- Rational unified process (RUP): iterative within phases, can use feedback from prototypes in the Elaboration phase

- Extreme programming (XP): iterative, uses customer feedback

When product delivery occurs is a key differentiator.

Answers to review questions, Chapter 2

Question 2.1

Your project proposal is the nearest equivalent to a feasibility study for your project. If you look at the student project proposal form, the following sections correspond:

	Student project: Proposal section	Feasibility study section
1	Title	Title
2	Keywords	-
3	Problem definition	Perceived need for change of the organisation/product/system
	-	Alignment with organisational strategy/objectives
4	Aims	Aim of the proposed project
5	Objectives	Objectives for the proposed project
6	Evidence of requirement	-
7	Context description	Analysis of the external environment Product/system scope Overview of current business processes and planned changes Overview of current product/systems and planned changes Product/system interfaces
	-	List of stakeholders Potential benefits and costs of the proposed solution(s)
8	Research methods	-
9	Brief product description	Proposed solution(s) Technology considerations Staff availability Dependencies, issues, assumptions and risks
10	Deliverables	-
11	Outcome/product evaluation approach	*For 'Outcome', see project success criteria within 'Objectives for the proposed project'*
12	Resources	*See 'Potential benefits and costs of the proposed solution(s)', 'Technology considerations' and 'Staff availability'*
13	Bibliography	-
14	Project plan	Outline project plan
	-	Summary of financial information
	-	Recommendations
15	Supervisor's name and signature	-

Your seminar tutor will ultimately decide if your proposal is suitable. However, you too have a say, as you select your own topic.

Question 2.2

Extensions to the scope are likely to mean additional implementation costs and pose a threat to the agreed deadlines.

However, if the 'scope creep' concerns real requirements, it can't be such a bad thing. Maybe additional resources and revised deadlines need negotiating, rather than refusal to alter scope. Contracts will tend to be written to allow for a certain amount of flexibility and negotiation.

Question 2.3

Evolutionary approaches break systems development into small steps or cycles, and deliver systems to the users incrementally in order to deliver value and gain feedback. As the next step is only decided on the basis of the feedback from the last step, it is fairly easy to extend the scope. Additional steps can be added as required to add additional functionality, or to improve system performance even further, or to extend the system to a new user area. Understanding the costs incurred by altering the scope is much easier in an evolutionary environment when you can readily determine the extra work.

As evolutionary steps get delivered to the users early and on a regular basis, there is no sense of incurring additional delays to system delivery (as there would be under the Waterfall model).

Question 2.4

The proposed product/system benefits justify the costs of the planned work. If the benefits are insufficient, then it is likely the project will be scrapped.

Question 2.5

The major benefit of a SMART (Specific, Measurable, Assignable, Realistic and Time-related) objective is that it is much more likely to be met. It is also possible to prove it has been met as it is measurable.

Answers to review questions, Chapter 3

Question 3.1

Research methodologies you would be unlikely to use include:

- Grounded theory

- Action research

- Ethnography.

Question 3.2

Two research methodologies typically used in quantitative research are *survey* and *experiment*.

Question 3.3

The advantages of *interviews* over *questionnaires* include:

- Allow for more flexible questions

- Allow the interview to broach new topics that the researcher hadn't anticipated.

- Foster a positive relationship between interviewer and interviewee.

Answers to review questions, Chapter 4

Question 4.1

It depends on the systems development lifecycle model being used: an evolutionary approach will have reviews at the end of each delivery cycle, which will track project progress and status.

There certainly will need to be regular meetings with your tutor and they will require a form of management reporting.

Management meetings with your client management will also be needed at key points where decisions have to be agreed.

Regular written reports to your client management ought to be considered to keep them informed of your progress.

Question 4.2

There are several benefits. The main one is that you know what information you are expected to include in your report.

Your readers also know exactly what to expect and where specific information is likely to be found in the report. For example, if they are expert in a specific subject area, then maybe there is a specific section of the report that they will read with greater care. Also, comparison of content across several reports becomes easier.

Question 4.3

Using a Waterfall model, testing is delayed until the testing phase. Also there is no delivery to the customer until the end of the Waterfall process.

With an evolutionary systems development lifecycle, delivery occurs more frequently and the systems development cycles are far smaller. This tends to reduce the risk in testing as early feedback is obtained and because smaller-scale development and testing is easier to control. The testing workload is spread throughout the life of the project rather than occurring mainly in one specific testing phase. Also because the delivered software is being used, there is confidence that it is 'what the customer wanted' and the software performance levels are known.

Question 4.4

You are probably already using your own informal filename naming standards. You are possibly also keeping a log of changes made.

Question 4.5

Given it's a user interface prototype that's being tested, the systems development lifecycle model being used is most likely to be the dynamic systems development method (DSDM).

Answers to review questions, Chapter 5

Question 5.1

While there are standard tasks for most software engineering projects, such as requirements analysis, system design, and implementation, identifying the project tasks is not always a straightforward task. Some tasks may only become apparent later on, after the initial planning. For example, during the requirements capture phase, it may become apparent that significant user training will be necessary.

Question 5.2

Gantt charts are beneficial for managing projects for several reasons:

- They provide a visual representation of the necessary tasks and the timing of those tasks
- They are simple to understand
- They are easy to construct

Question 5.3

Not only is MS Project easy to use, Gantt charts can be made quickly because MS Project automatically enters some of the information, and changes to the Gantt chart can be made easily. MS Project allows you different views of your project. For example, you can 'hide' the subtasks, providing you with a simple overview of the main tasks that need to be completed.

Question 5.4

Although you will calculate expected end dates for each task, which in itself gives you something to aim for, milestones provide larger goals to work towards. This is especially important for large project teams, where it is important not just to ensure that individual teams are meeting their task deadlines, but also that the team as a whole is on track.

Question 5.5

It is true that you do not have to use the 'linking' facility that MS Project provides to order dependent tasks. Instead, having developed your AoN diagram, you could use the information from that to manually adjust the start dates for each task, so that if task B is dependent on the completion of task A, task B's start date is set for after the finish date of task A. However, the benefit of linking the tasks is that if you realise that task A is going to take longer than expected, you can adjust its duration and then MS Project will automatically update the start date for task B and reflect any other necessary date changes.

Question 5.6

The main benefit of AoA diagrams is in visualising the sequencing of activities and their durations. The fact that the duration is placed on the arrow helps distinguish the duration from the other data.

Question 5.7

Identifying your project's critical path allows you to determine which tasks must be completed on time for the project as a whole to be completed on time.

Question 5.8

A critical path is concerned only with the time schedule of a project. It does not need to include all the critical activities.

Question 5.9

Ultimately the project manager has the last word. However, the project manager should discuss and agree these details with the project members concerned

Answers to review questions, Chapter 6

Question 6.1

Different people might respond differently to an absence of cost management. Some people might want to increase the amount they get paid, while decreasing the amount of personal effort they put in. Others are happy to take on extra work, provided they get paid for it. Lack of concern for costs may free software designers to build higher levels of functionality and quality into a solution. This can lead to highly engineered solutions, which might be regarded as over-engineered.

'Throwing money' at a problem sometimes allows it to be solved more quickly. But sometimes it simply generates complexity and confusion, and things can actually take longer. When software is produced for a mass market (think Microsoft or Google), the most important consideration is achieving the greatest utility for the greatest number of potential users. Cost management is still practised, but it is not a dominant factor.

Question 6.2

If a project manager is not concerned about user operating costs or maintenance costs, then he or she may try to shift costs from developers onto users (and will certainly resist shifting costs onto developers).

Such shifting of cost will tend to happen even if a software project is within an organisation – even though it increases the total software cost for the organisation. Where the software project is carried out by a separate organisation, the project manager typically is given no incentive to save the client money. This highlights the importance of identifying all the different kinds of cost (even if there are no cost estimates as yet) early in a project and actively and transparently managing them to avoid unpleasant surprises. A combination of contractual agreement and requirements specification can be used to capture and assign responsibilities for costs – but this is by no means straightforward to achieve!

Question 6.3

Developers who are rewarded for quantity will produce quantity – possibly at the expense of quality/relevance. It is tempting and very easy for a programmer to write surplus lines of code – which add nothing to the functioning of the software, and may add to future maintenance costs. This distorts the accuracy and usefulness of size metrics.

Question 6.4

Counting lines consistently aids comparison within the project and also between one project and another. It also allows feedback adjustments to be made to the figures. For example, if one code module has taken twice as long as estimated and there is another module of similar code to be written, then as long as the counting was done in the same way, correcting the estimate for the second module, by doubling it, is reasonable.

Question 6.5

The increased visibility of project progress and the improved predictability that it brings could make the contractors somewhat uneasy. If work was not progressing well, then the actual cost (AC) would be higher than the earned value (EV). Also if work was progressing faster, then questions would be asked about why that was and the customer might wonder why they were paying so much.

Question 6.6

Your costs would increase exponentially and you would no longer be able to estimate the cost. It is very important to appreciate how even one extremely challenging requirement can completely derail your cost estimation.

Answers to review questions, Chapter 7

Question 7.1

Firstly, the organisation needs to be seen to allow development if it is to be able to recruit. Secondly, if you wish to be able recruit people to future projects of yours, you need to be seen to be willing to let people develop. Moreover, the organisation needs to think about the balance (and availability) of skills and capabilities that might be required for future projects.

Question 7.2

Specialist skill sets and standard team roles as described, for example, by Belbin.

Question 7.3

To promote and defend the project .

Question 7.4

The leader provides vision and inspiration. The manager controls by collating data for reports and highlighting discrepancies from project plans.

Question 7.5

External factors include: organisational culture; business sector(s) in which the project is taking place; regulation compliance; desired secondary outcomes. Internal factors include leadership style, available resources and anticipated team dynamics.

Question 7.6

You may not know! Within the organisation, the organisation is almost certainly the owner – not the writer. In inter-organisational projects or customer projects, you need to read the contract but, again, it is unlikely the writer is the owner.

Question 7.7

Discussion. You can use a variety of tools to facilitate this but the key is to talk to each other. Very simple to say; possibly quite hard to achieve?

Answers to review questions, Chapter 8

Question 8.1

Advertising is likely to be a key factor deciding which organisation you thought of. Many companies base their advertisements around how quality is inbuilt into their products. For example, think of car adverts describing how they design and test their cars, or supermarket adverts describing how they source their products.

However, some companies do have more customer focus as they ask for feedback on their products and services. Other companies invest in ensuring their staff know more about the products they are selling with a view to giving the customer better advice.

Question 8.2

Organisations that make money from fixing faults would suffer if prevention activities reduced the number of errors occurring. However, working on solving problems that could have been prevented does seem rather a waste of effort – especially if the same problem occurs numerous times and/or recurs.

Question 8.3

Very often it is only when you stop and think about such problems, do you realise how much time they waste.

Cost of quality (COQ) includes all the costs associated with carrying out quality-related processes (POC + PONC). These quality costs can be classified into categories as follows:

- **Prevention costs** include quality planning, technical reviews, test equipment and training

- **Appraisal costs** include in-process and inter-process inspection, equipment calibration and maintenance, and testing

- **Failure costs**

  - **internal failure costs** include rework, repair and failure mode analysis

  - **external failure costs** include complaint resolution, product return and replacement, helpline support and warranty work.

Prevention costs and appraisal costs are POC, whereas failure costs are PONC. Crosby argued that it is the PONC that costs by far the most. Let's assume you bought a mobile phone that didn't work. First of all let's consider the PONC. There would be the time you spent establishing that there was indeed a problem and that it was not just your unfamiliarity with the phone. Maybe you asked the shop where you bought it for help, maybe you had to phone a helpline or send an e-mail asking for further information. There would be the additional cost of the time of whoever helped you. Then there would be any time you spent filling in forms and collecting together all the components and packaging to return the product. Then if you returned it to a shop, the sales assistant's time establishing the fault occurs, completing the required paperwork and labelling up the product for return.

Hopefully, then the sales assistant could hand you another mobile phone to replace the returned one. But if they couldn't because of being out of stock or because you had to wait for the phone to be repaired and returned, then that would most likely mean another trip to the shop. Then there is the cost of whoever receives the returned phone, and the cost of its repair or the losses incurred if it has to be scrapped. The failure costs mount up, but I suspect it would be optimistic to say under two hours for the combined time of your efforts, the retail staff, and the manufacturing staff. Of course, to the mobile phone manufacturer, in the short term, it is the staff costs, the waste product costs and the loss of product sale value that impact the 'bottom line' (the profit).

However, there is also the long-term issue: the matter for the manufacturer and the shop of the loss of image. People aware of faulty products are less likely to choose to buy similar models. If the product got a bad product rating, then this would result in loss of sales, increased stock, and maybe even the need to discount the phone to encourage sales.

The POC would be any costs associated with testing the phone components or the finished phone in the factory or in the shop, prior to its being sold. Also the quality of the components used would have some bearing on product quality and costs.

Question 8.4

'Prevention of errors' occurs before the errors are committed, 'appraisal' occurs after the errors have occurred.

Question 8.5

Most likely, the cost of prevention will increase as more effort is expended on preventing errors. For instance, a high-quality restaurant will spend more on staff, food ingredients and fixtures and fittings to ensure that the restaurant maintains its image. Extra staff and/or more highly trained staff will be utilised to ensure more checks are carried out on things like the presentation of tables, the level of attention given its customers, and extra checks on the presentation of dishes prior to serving.

Question 8.6

You would want to establish the scale of the problem (how often it occurred, and the cost of the failure when it happened). There would be little value in spending vast sums on finding a solution to something that was trivial and happened very infrequently. When resources are restricted, it is important to prioritise what actions to take.

Question 8.7

Juran's definition of 'fitness for use' relates to Boehm's definition of 'validation'. Both are concerned with how the product/system actually satisfies the user. In contrast, 'verification' is concerned with whether the product meets its build specification – conforms to the requirements specification. From a developer's perspective, ensuring 'fitness for use' is more challenging than building to a specification (though of course, it does depend on how unambiguously the specification is written as to how easy it is for the developer to know there is conformance to specification).

Question 8.8

The contract will specify who is responsible. It will depend on the size and complexity of the system. In some cases, the developers and the users will work together in situ at the various user sites carrying out the acceptance testing. It is the responsibility of the project management to ensure the acceptance criteria is defined and understood. Testing specification ought to be carried out alongside requirements specification. Testing is not something that should be left until the end of the project before being considered.

Question 8.9

Your timeline should run from Shewhart (control charts in the 1920s) to Deming (quality control, build quality into the product, train and empower workers – from 1950s onwards) and Juran (quality management and 'fitness for use' – from 1950s onwards) and Ishikawa (fishbone diagrams, and also quality circles – about 1949) to Crosby ('quality is free' – in the 1980s.

Shewhart influenced Deming, who taught Ishikawa.

Question 8.10

Most likely they are at Level 1, unless you are using defined processes that have been assessed as being at a higher level. Level 2 has clear process areas that need to be formally addressed. Nonetheless, the definition of Level 2 provides some thing to aim at and a target that you can use to improve your current approaches.

At Maturity Level 1: Initial: Processes are ad hoc and chaotic.

At Maturity Level 2: Managed: The projects of the organisation have ensured that requirements are managed and that processes are planned, performed, measured and controlled. The status of work products and the delivery of services are visible to management at defined points (for example, major milestones). Work products are reviewed with stakeholders and are controlled.

If you have worked in industry, you possibly have experience of higher levels and may have copied or utilised certain aspects or procedures from that environment. See the references given in Section 8.10, 'Maturity models' for further information and for details on which aspects need to be improved to progress to Level 2.

Answers to review questions, Chapter 9

Question 9.1

Think about your attitude towards risk in your personal and academic life: do you plan carefully to be on time for meetings? Do you plan your university work to avoid last-minute work to beat deadlines?

You probably know *your* risk tolerance, but do you know your client's?

Only if there is conflict over risk tolerance between you and your client is there a problem. You need to be aware of your client's views and take them into account when designing potential solutions. Don't be surprised if a risk-averse client seems not too impressed with your highly ambitious design!

Question 9.2

For example:

- A milestone slippage by a month

- The requested user documents not yet supplied

- At least, 10% over budget.

Question 9.3

Total risk avoidance would not work for the vast majority of IT projects, as the main rationale for projects is to introduce innovation and change. Change always introduces risk.

However, there are risk avoidance strategies that need at least to be considered. For example, consider the situation where a project team decides to use known technology – it is avoiding the risk of encountering problems and delays: that is, the project team knows how to use the technology and knows it can be used to achieve the required tasks. This is an excellent, albeit short-term, risk avoidance strategy. Can you think what new risks this project team might be introducing with this decision?

Question 9.4

Each IT project will have its unique set of risks. This is the reason that understanding the risk management process is so important. However, generic checklists of the risks likely to impact IT projects are a useful starting point to ensure all the likely risks have been considered.

Capers Jones found that patterns of risk are different across different types of IT projects (Marchewka (2006) page 180-1, quoting Jones, T. C., *Assessment and Control of Software Risks*, Yourdon Press/Prentice Hall, 1994).

Question 9.5

Risk evaluation would be directed by the overall organisational policy, which would reflect the organisational attitude towards risk. Consider the differing attitudes of a bank, NASA (space agency), and a school website towards risk. Maybe the choice of project manager would be influenced by how well a project manager's attitude towards risk matched that of an organisation?

Question 9.6

Yes, risk management is an investment – there are costs associated with it. The nature of the project dictates how much resource a project is willing to expend on it. The benefits of avoiding or mitigating a potential risk have to be weighed against the costs.

Evolutionary approaches to systems development can help with risk management (see Section 9.5).

Question 9.7

Using the waterfall model, project delivery occurs only towards the end of the development process.

- So almost all the project time and money has been used prior to delivery occurring

- There is feedback if the various systems development stages are not meeting their deadline dates, but little can be done with the information because Waterfall is a sequential process (all the requirements specification is done, then all the systems design, then all the coding, etc.), so the feedback is of limited value

- Likewise, any feedback from the users comes too late to do anything

- Nothing is delivered early to the users so no early value is gained

- Likewise, there is no possibility of trying out high-risk parts of the system early

- There is no concept of breaking down the workload into small deliverable steps. There is the concept of the various stages of systems development, but if anything the specific skills (such as requirements specification, systems design, implementation) are required all at the same time rather than being spread throughout the project duration as in evolutionary delivery.

Answers to review questions, Chapter 10

Question 10.1

Quality has been described in a variety of ways including 'fitness for purpose', 'conformance to requirements' and 'customer satisfaction'. Any steps that you have taken to ensure that you correctly understand how the customer intends to use the product, that you have accurately captured the requirements, that you will monitor your project results, and that you will track customer feedback, can be used as evidence that you are designing to produce a quality product.

Question 10.2

Chapter 9, 'Project risk management', should spring to mind! Possible problems can be linked to risk, so ideally you can identify the risks and build in checks to try to mitigate these risks.

Question 10.3

Inspection. In fact, can you see how you could use inspection to determine the level of conformance of your project report to the stated requirements?

Question 10.4

The answer is the project report and some iteration! You will need a first draft project report to assist your PDR, and then ideally you will feed the key results of your PDR into your project report. Reflection should be a key part of an academic project report.

PRINCE2

We saved discussion of the PRINCE2 project management method until last. If you have already read through the rest of this book you should find much in this description of PRINCE2 that you are familiar with!

Note the PRINCE2 website at **www.prince2.org.uk** contains case studies and a glossary of terms in several languages.

Note also that *Practical PRINCE2* (3rd revised edition), by Colin Bentley and published by The Stationery Office is the main source of much of the following description of PRINCE2.

A.1 Introduction

PRINCE2 is a project management method developed as a UK Government standard for project management. It is currently the UK's 'de facto' standard. PRINCE2 has become increasingly popular and is now widely used in both the private and public sectors – for both IT and non-IT projects – and is growing in importance internationally, particularly in Europe.

PRINCE2 is a 'structured method' for project management. PRINCE stands for PRojects IN a Controlled Environment. The method offers process-based control of projects, combined with recognised good practice. It provides a comprehensive repository of standards, processes and techniques that cover many major project management issues; for example, risk analysis and risk management are incorporated into the PRINCE2 processes. It is highly tailorable and scaleable, and should be customised by an adopting organisation for a successful implementation.

It should be noted that PRINCE2 also has its detractors, who argue it is too bureaucratic and overly prescriptive. Certainly PRINCE2 sits uncomfortably alongside the demands of agile methods for 'light' documentation. PRINCE2 did originate in the environment of large projects using Waterfall or incremental systems development lifecycles and that should be borne in mind when considering the various elements of PRINCE2.

Background

First established in 1989 by the UK government's CCTA (Central Computer and Telecommunications Agency), PRINCE was developed from PROMPT, a method devised in 1975 by Simpact Systems Ltd. PROMPT II followed in 1979 as a standard method for all government information systems (IS) projects, and PRINCE superseded this in 1989. The CCTA became the OGC (Office of Government Commerce, part of the UK Treasury) who continued to develop the method. The most recent version, known as PRINCE2, was launched in 1996. It is based on accumulated experience, with the explicit intention of extending beyond IT projects and providing improved guidance on all projects. PRINCE2 is Crown Copyright, but anybody may use the method without payment of fees or royalties.

Basic functionality of PRINCE2

PRINCE2 covers the core aspects of the project management lifecycle, but it does not claim to cover all aspects of project management. It sits beneath any higher, more strategic activities (such as strategic information systems planning or programme management), and above any techniques required to create technical products within the project (such as the systems development processes – requirements specification, coding and testing, etc).

Some IT project management methods 'know about' the systems development method being used to develop the product and thus help in integrating management actions with the technical processes. The PRINCE method, for example, was initially closely related to the Structured Systems Analysis and Design Methodology (SSADM) systems development method. Such a close relationship facilitates the tracking of both project progress and the specific products (deliverables). This enables joint focus on management products and technical deliverables.

The PRINCE2 project management lifecycle covers the project management processes, from starting up the project, planning, initiating the project, controlling and monitoring project progress and products (directing the project), through to the final completion of the project. Under PRINCE2, a project is conducted in stages (see Figure A.1). (Note: compare this to the PMI's project management lifecycle discussed in Chapter 1.)

There are only two mandatory stages in PRINCE; each project must have an Initiation stage and a minimum of at least one Doing stage. At the end of each Doing stage there is a formal end of stage assessment to ensure stage completion (conformance to the required quality criteria) and to get project board authorisation for the next stage (see later).

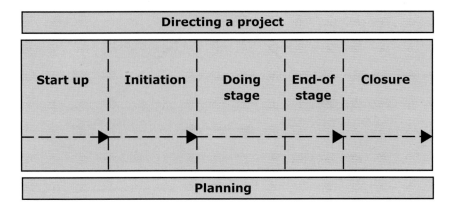

Figure A.1: The PRINCE2 project management lifecycle processes. There can be one or more Doing stages each followed by an End of stage assessment

PRINCE2 assumptions

It is assumed by PRINCE2 that projects have the following characteristics:

- A finite and defined lifecycle with defined and measurable business products
- A corresponding set of technical activities to produce these products (note a systems development method such as SSADM or Dynamic Systems Development Method (DSDM) is required to develop the product)
- A defined set of resources
- That those responsible for a project may not have experience of working together in the past to produce a similar set of results for the same customer
- That co-ordination of those working on the project will need to be well organised; the responsibilities need to be clearly defined and to be shared among those sponsoring the work, those managing it, and those who carry the development work out.

A.2 Main elements of PRINCE2

PRINCE2 consists of three main elements, summarised in Figure A.2:

- **Processes:** the PRINCE2 project management processes used by a project manager to manage a project
- **Components:** several project management components that need to be given specific attention during a project
- **Techniques:** practical techniques that can be applied to help manage the project.

We shall discuss each of these elements in more detail in this appendix.

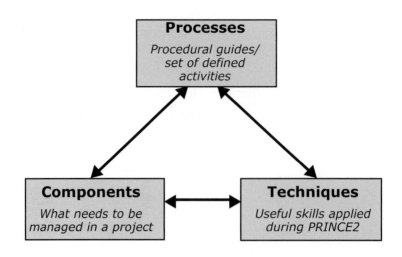

Figure A.2: The major elements of PRINCE2

Processes

PRINCE2 has 45 sub-processes, organised into 8 processes. The 8 processes are as follows (see figure A.3 for their inter-relationships):

- **Starting up a project (SU):** this process covers the appointment of the project board (the decision-making team) and the project manager, and the pre-project preparation: establishing the project brief and objectives, constructing an initial business case, identifying the project tolerances and initial risks, and deciding the overall approach of the project. The work to set up the project contract between customer and supplier is also planned

- **Initiating a project (IP)** consists of constructing a more detailed business case (the justification for the project), and producing detailed definitions and the project plans. The approaches to project controls and quality are decided. The project risks are re-examined. The project initiation document (PID) is produced. This is a mandatory definition of as much of the project as is visible at the time before commencement of the 'doing' stages to construct the deliverables. It forms a baseline against which to measure project progress. All the decision-makers have to agree on the PID

- **Directing a project (DP)** focuses on the work of the project board members throughout the project and the management decisions at key points, which include authorising:
  - initiating the project
  - starting the development of the deliverables (authorising the project)
  - closing the project
  - other key stages during the project
  - any changes to the products
  - any exception plans.

Liaison with the senior executives and with the project manager is also involved. The interests of both the customer and the supplier have to be looked after. This process basically provides the overall control for the project.

- **Controlling a stage (CS)** focuses on the day-to-day work of the project manager in managing a stage, that is in managing the project work carried out between formal assessments by the project board. The project manager has to produce regular highlight reports for the project board and also any required exception reports if project tolerances are exceeded. Work is allocated in work packages

- **Managing project delivery (MP)** is concerned with controlling how teams agree their allocated work with the project manager, and also report progress on carrying the work out to the project manager, between formal assessments by the project board. Checkpoint reports will be produced for the project manager. The process is also concerned with establishing approval for the finished work

- **Managing stage boundaries (SB)** prepares a stage plan for the next stage; updates the project plan with the actual costs and schedule of the current stage and the estimated costs and schedule for the next stage; reviews the business case in preparation for a formal assessment by the project board on whether to authorise the next stage; updates the risk log and produces an end of stage report. If required, exception reports can also be raised. Any lessons learned must also be captured

- **Closing a project (CP)** ensures a smooth, orderly closure, handover, shut down and post-project review. All the required products (deliverables) must have been produced and accepted, any issues must have been resolved, lessons learnt and required corrective actions must be recorded, and plans for measuring the benefits of the project deliverables must be put in place. The recommendation is made to the project board to closedown the project

- **Planning (PL)** defines the planning tools and methods used to construct the plans used throughout project and states the level of plans required. The products (deliverables) are identified, the activities required to produce the deliverables are established together with their dependencies, estimates of the effort involved to carry out the activities are made, the schedule is produced and the risks involved in the plans are analysed.

Two of the processes, **DP** and **PL**, are relevant throughout the project lifecycle.

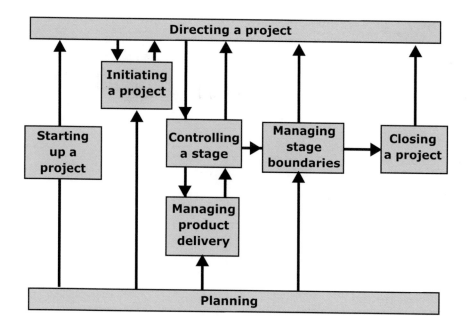

Figure A.3: The PRINCE2 process model

To give an example of the sub-processes, *Starting Up a Project* (SU) consists of the following sub-processes:

- **SU1: Appointing the executive and project manager**
- **SU2: Designing a project management team**
- **SU3: Appointing a project management team**
- **SU4: Preparing a project brief**
- **SU5: Defining project approach**
- **SU6: Planning an initiation stage.**

Likewise, all the other seven main processes can also be decomposed into their sub-processes.

A project run under PRINCE2 will typically include each of these main processes. However, it is important that, before a project starts work on producing the products (the deliverables), it tailors the process model to its needs, and determines how extensively each of these processes will be applied.

Components

The eight PRINCE2 components are shown in Figure A.4.

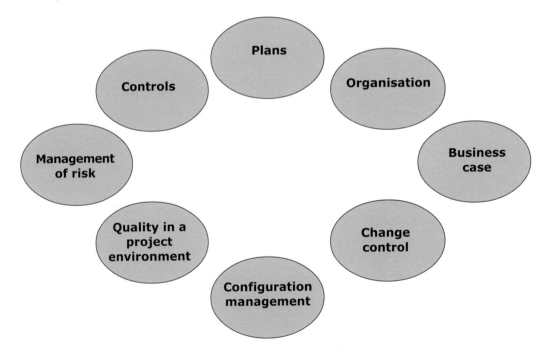

Figure A.4: PRINCE2 components

- **Business case:** it describes the justification or reasons for setting up, continuing or changing the project and is the basis for all management decisions
- **Organisation** defines the management structure, and the roles and responsibilities of the people involved in the project
- **Plans** hold details of the products required and the schedules of the activities needed to construct them. PRINCE2 involves product-based planning

- **Controls** provide the mechanisms that allow the project to be governed
- **Quality in a project environment** involves capturing the user expectations and ensuring that the project meets them
- **Management of risk** describes the current understanding of potential problems and their appropriate risk responses, and control of any threats
- **Change control** defines how project issues and change requests are progressed
- **Configuration management** allows the tracking of different versions or copies of products (deliverables) and prepares for future audits.

The PRINCE2 components cover the key aspects of project management that need to be given specific consideration. It is up to each individual organisation to determine which components it should include (in many cases there will be organisational guidelines or procedures that must be followed) and this will change from project to project. Components must be tailored to fit an organisational environment and the needs of each project.

Most organisations (and projects) will have used some or all of these components before - although maybe not in such a formal approach.

Let's now look at three of these components in more detail:

- **Organisation**
- **Plans**
- **Controls**.

Organisation

'Role' and 'project board' are the key organisational concepts in PRINCE2. A role is a part that is played in the project that is identified by its functionality. All the project's activities can be assigned to the different project roles. Examples of project roles are sponsor, customer, user, project manager, quality assurance manager, team manager and project support (see later).

One or more roles can be assigned to an individual and an individual might be working full-time or part-time for the project. A role can be shared but then care has to be taken over responsibility for the role: if a decision has to be made do all the people assigned to the role have to be asked? What happens if there is conflict?

PRINCE2 places specific importance on identifying the customer and supplier roles and establishing who is responsible for them. The customer is the person or group that expects to obtain benefit from the project's product(s). The customers that fund the project are termed 'sponsors'.

Suppliers on the other hand provide products for the project to use. Sometimes the project will subcontract project work out to third-party suppliers. Often this occurs because specialist skills are required that the project team does not possess and does not wish to acquire. Alternatively it could be that extra staff resources are needed, which are not available within the organisation.

PRINCE2 identifies an organisational structure consisting of four management levels as follows:

- **The senior executives**
- **The project board**
- **The project manager**
- **The team managers.**

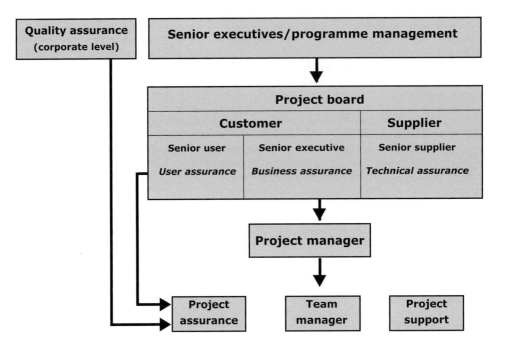

Figure A.5: The PRINCE2 management structure. This is a modified version of figure 11.2 in (Bentley 2005)

The senior executives set up the project board. Representatives of the senior executives, the customers and the suppliers are typically found on the project board. The project board agrees all the major project decisions and allocates project funding. It also has responsibility for the quality assurance of the project. The senior customer representative will be responsible for *user assurance* (including user's requirements, acceptance criteria and quality reviews); the senior representative of the senior executives, for the *business assurance* (including feasibility and business impact of changes); and the senior representative of the suppliers, for the *technical assurance* (including quality criteria and methods and standards for quality assurance). Given the seniority of the representatives, the project assurance roles are often delegated to the project assurance group.

The project manager reports to the project board; the team managers report to the project manager. Team managers are responsible for teams which have been set up to work on discrete parts of the project (to carry out work packages) that are considered to warrant such control; for example, the project may be sufficiently large, or maybe a work package is specialised and would benefit from a team manager who has the appropriate skills to better understand the work involved.

Figure A.5 also shows two additional organisational units: *project assurance* and *project support*. The project assurance unit reports in to the project board, it is responsible for carrying out the quality checks to ensure the project's products meet their required quality criteria. This project assurance unit might well also report in to the corporate quality assurance unit, which is responsible for quality at an organisational level. There might be organisational quality standards that have to be complied with as well as the project standards.

Project support is a technical specialist unit that provides the project team (the project manager as well as the other project team members) with assistance concerning the use of project management applications and guidance on the PRINCE2 project documentation requirements.

A particular project might not have all of these management levels – but there will always be a project manager. If there are no team managers, for example, then the project team members will report directly to the project manager.

Note that a project can be part of a programme, in which case the project manager will most likely report to the programme manager. For very large projects there might be a separate project board as well, but control might well be at programme-level.

Plans

There are four main types of PRINCE2 plan as follows:

- **Project plan:** the project plan is mandatory and gives the overview plan for the entire project. It has to state the project schedule with timescales, the products (deliverables), the staff and other resources, and the financial costs
- **Stage plan:** the stage plan is a more detailed plan for a stage; it is produced just before the previous stage finishes
- **Team plan:** team plans are optional and detail the plans for subsets of the project that are working on work packages in discrete teams with a team manager
- **Exception plan:** exception plans are produced on an ad hoc basis as needed, typically when an existing plan (that is a project, stage or team plan) goes wrong and a change of plan is needed to try to correct the situation.

Plans always have to be authorised by the appropriate level of authority. Typically, the project manager authorises *team plans* and the project board authorises the *project plan* and the *stage plans*.

Controls

There are several project control mechanisms. These include:

- **Stages**
- **Tolerances**
- **Management structure**
- **Logs.**

Controls can only operate within a framework of plans. There has to be a *schedule* in place to monitor against, and there have to be *assigned authorities* in place carrying out the monitoring, taking responsibility and deciding what actions are required when any problems are identified. The initiation stage of a project is the key stage where the high-level requirements for the project are negotiated and agreed.

- **Stages:** PRINCE2 projects are authorised, one stage at a time, by the project board. At the end of each stage there is a formal decision, taken by the project board, whether to continue the project or close it down. The project board makes its decisions by considering the business case, the progress against the project plan, the products (deliverables) produced and the detailed plan for the next stage

- **Tolerances:** tolerances can be set for time, cost, scope, risk, benefits and quality. They give the degree of flexibility associated with each particular constraint to enable the project manager to make intelligent tradeoffs. It is important to note that some of these areas are interlinked and an acceptable delay to the project (in terms of schedule) may lead to an unacceptable cost increase (when there is no tolerance for adjustments to the budget). Typically there will be organisational standards setting out the permitted ranges of tolerances in the different areas. The project board will delegate authority, together with some tolerances, to the project manager. If there are no relevant standards, then the project manager will have to set the tolerances within which the different management levels can operate with sufficient flexibility to make decisions. If the tolerances seem inadequate, the project manger will need to return to the project board and present a case for exceeding them, which will either be approved or denied by the board

- **Management structure:** we have already discussed the four management levels: senior executives, project board, project manager and team manager. The senior executives will be closely involved in setting the vision for the project and then will delegate authority for controlling the project to the project board. The senior executives will only take action if the project board reports problems for their attention.

  The project board will authorise the project and authorise each stage. They will delegate the day-to-day running of the project to the project manager. They will agree each of the stage plans with the project manager as the project progresses.

  The project board will expect only to be involved at the end of each stage, in authorising the next stage plan. They will, however, expect the project manager to provide highlight reports at regular intervals. The highlight reports will detail (for the current reporting period) the products completed, the products expected to be completed in the next reporting period, and any problems. The project board will also be asked to authorise any change requests, and any exception plans recommended by the project manager. As discussed earlier, the project board will also take responsibility for quality assurance of the project's products.

  At the end of a project, the project board will be asked to authorise project closure. Some time after project closure, a post-project review will be carried out, instigated by the senior executive on the project board. The project manager will have set out the plan for how the post-project review is carried out.

  As mentioned earlier, the project manager has day-to-day control of the project – specifically the current stage of the project. The project manager may decide to break the project work down into work packages and delegate responsibility for them to team managers. The project manager agrees the team plans with the team managers, who will send the project manager checkpoint reports at regular intervals detailing how the work package is progressing. The checkpoint reports form the basis of the highlight reports to the project board

- **Logs:** in addition to the highlight and checkpoint reports, several logs – daily, risk, issue and quality – are also maintained. These are project management products (deliverables):

  - **daily log:** the project manager should keep a daily log to record what has happened and what people have promised. Each week the project manager should also inspect the stage plan, the risk log, the issue log and the quality file to establish progress and what is coming up in the next week or so. The daily log will be set up immediately the project manager is appointed and information will be kept on a stage-by-stage basis

- **risk log:** this holds (or acts as a repository for) information about the risks, their countermeasures, and current status in the project. The risk log is initially created during *Preparing a Project Brief* (SU4), which is part of the *Starting Up a Project* (SU) process. Some risks will be identified during initiation and then further risks will be identified throughout the project. The risks are reviewed (as a minimum) at the end of every stage. The risk log is updated as the risks are identified, assessed and reviewed – and also as countermeasures are considered, put in place and evaluated
- **issue log:** this keeps track of the project's problems and change requests. It is set up in *Set up Project Files* (IP5), which is part of *Initiating a Project* (IP)
- **quality log:** this keeps a record of all the quality checks and tests that are planned or have taken place. It is also set up in *Set up Project Files* (IP5). Entries are added when the stage plans are created. The entries are updated as the checks and tests take place. They are completed when all the corrective actions identified by the check/test are signed off as successfully carried out.

Techniques

Having discussed processes and components, let's now discuss the third main element of PRINCE2, the PRINCE2 techniques. PRINCE2's intention is that individual organisations should integrate their existing organisational practices with PRINCE2, and adapt PRINCE2 according to the circumstances of the project. So PRINCE2 offers only a limited coverage of techniques. This consists of the following three techniques:

- **Product-based planning (PBP)** is the most important of these. PBP results in hierarchical families of deliverables being created and captures the logical relationships amongst these deliverables (PRINCE2 covers the 'traditional' techniques of planning, such as network diagrams, Gantt charts and critical path analysis). PBP also enables quality criteria to be input for each deliverable. The purpose of carrying out PBP is to enable later activity planning
- **Change control** enables change requests to be handled in a dynamic environment. Note project issues are handled in a similar fashion
- **Quality review** supports the final quality review of products (deliverables). It is a technique for reviewing completed deliverables to ensure they meet the previously agreed quality criteria.

A.3 Product-based planning (PBP)

Let's now look in more detail at PRINCE2's product-based planning (PBP). Although PRINCE2 has a process-based approach to project management, it also provides a product-based framework that can be applied to any project. Product-based planning occurs early on in the planning process – we need to agree where we are going prior to starting the journey! Planning the products that are required is a stepping stone to completing the more traditional activity-based plans such as Gantt charts and network diagrams and, of course, the overall project and stage plans.

PBP focuses on the products first (rather than the activities) and ensures all products are identified, whether there are products external to the project, and involves both *specialist products* (the subject of the development including the software and the user manual) and *management products* (project management and quality management deliverables such as reports and plans).

Using the alternative activity-based planning, some activities may be overlooked and it may be difficult to accommodate extra activities into the project plan at a later date – leading to delays and 'surprises' later in the project! If all products required are identified first, then products are less likely to be overlooked. It also allows users and suppliers (called specialists or technical staff) to communicate using a common language. Lastly, the project is complete only when all the defined products are complete.

PBP is a valuable technique in the real world, and can be used to help define what is achievable and reduce the risks associated with product delivery. Product breakdowns identify the set of products that are required. Product descriptions detail how they should look (from a quality review perspective); product flow diagrams (PFDs) identify the dependencies between products and the sequence in which they must be developed.

Then there is a firm foundation to move into activity analysis and produce our overall project and detailed stage plans.

Let's now give an example to illustrate some of the points we have just discussed. See Figure A.6, which sets out the simple kitchen scenario that we shall use.

My new kitchen scenario

My old kitchen desperately needs replacing.

The project is to dismantle the existing kitchen, and assemble a new kitchen in its place.

The old kitchen has some materials that may be re-used. In dismantling the kitchen the specialist (builder) must decide which materials are to be disposed of and which may be re-used, albeit after some further restoration. Replacement materials must then be identified and ordered from the kitchen company.

New units and appliances will also be needed, and a list of required materials and required units and appliances is to be made as the kitchen is dismantled.

The kitchen site must also be prepared before the new kitchen can be assembled.

Figure A.6: Simple kitchen scenario

Product breakdown structure (PBS)

The first step in PBP involves identifying all products required and breaking them down into their constituent sub-products. This aids the later identification of all the necessary work activities involved in the creation of these products.

The products are placed into a hierarchical structure. At the top of the structure is a single box which summarises the overall finished work or final product. Each product making up the final outcome is then decomposed, until an appropriate level of detail for the plan has been reached, as shown in Figure A.7.

- The lowest-level products are known as **simple products** (because they cannot be further broken down)
- Products on higher levels are known as **intermediate products** and represent major products or product groups.

A numbering system indicates each product's level in the hierarchy and its parent. 'External products' are identified by using a different symbol (an ellipse). This basically means that the project manager is not responsible for, and has no control over, their provision. 'Old kitchen' is an external product because it has to exist before the project starts.

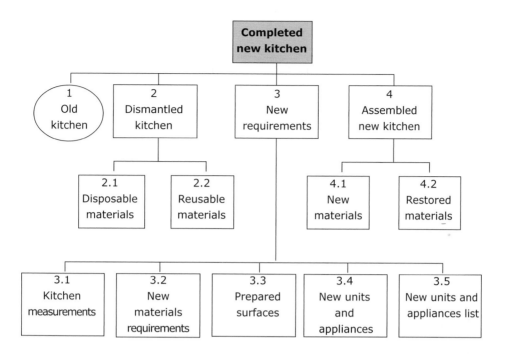

Figure A.7: Product breakdown structure for kitchen scenario

A clear and unambiguous description of products is a tremendous aid to their successful creation. A product description (see section A.4 for a template) is written for each significant product to ensure it is understood and to define its quality criteria. It is written soon after the need for the product has been identified and then updated in an iterative manner. It may be more prudent to write the detailed product descriptions last, when you are sure that all the products identified are correct and needed.

This exercise could cost a lot of resource (in terms of people as well as their resulting cost) – some projects have been known to have in excess of 12,500 products! Whenever a product is baselined or completed, the associated product description should always be baselined as well.

Product flow diagram (PFD)

A product flow diagram is derived from the PBS and identifies the logical relationships and dependencies between all the products specified; see Figure A.8. Every product in the PBS should be in the PFD (so just some of the higher-level boxes of the PBS will be missing). External products remain as ellipses and the text and numbering in the PBS boxes should stay the same.

The PFD is an essential aid in revealing parallel and sequential work. It enables the project team to see the big picture before detailed planning begins.

The PFD represents the flow or order – *not* the time taken/due to be taken. Time flows in one direction only (in this case, top to bottom).

Both the PBS and the PFD diagrams are completed *before* we start to think about, and identify, the activities involved in producing the products. The PFD shows the sequence of product development and its dependencies. Again this is an iterative process; amendments and enhancements will be made to both diagrams as new products are identified.

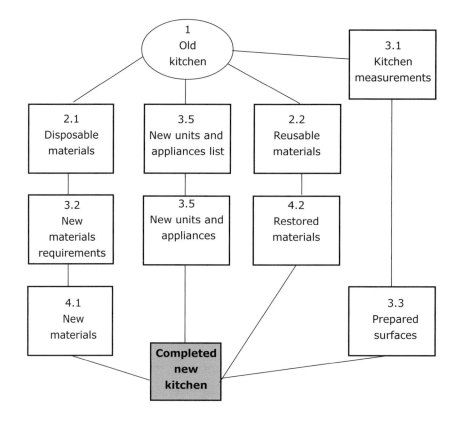

Figure A.8: Specialist PFD for my new kitchen

The product checklist can then be created, containing all the products required together with planned and actual dates. Planned dates are added when *Planning* (PL) has completed scheduling. The project manager adds the actual dates as they are achieved (and identified in the highlight report).

A.4 PRINCE2 documentation

Finally, let's consider PRINCE2 documentation. We have already discussed many of the PRINCE2 project management products in this appendix. Table A.1 provides an overview of the complete set of the PRINCE2 project documentation. Remember that PRINCE2 is intended to be tailored to your project – a given project might not need to maintain *all* this documentation.

We have discussed many of these documents already in this appendix and many will be familiar to you. A few are new and need some further explanation:

- A **project mandate** is the initial request for a project supplied by the senior executives – after further work, it becomes the project brief
- A **communication plan** is a formal description of the exchange of information. It describes which roles in the project are to be given which information – and exactly when the information is to be given
- A **configuration management plan** identifies how the project's products will be controlled and who has responsibility for them
- A **configuration item record** details the status information that needs to be stored about a product (a deliverable) such as its owner, its status, its location and its latest version number.

PRINCE2 project documentation	Product description	Form (template)	Project filing
Project mandate	Y		P
Project brief	Y	Y	P
Project initiation document	Y		P
Project approach	Y		P
Organisation and job descriptions			P & S
Project quality plan	Y		Q
• Acceptance criteria	Y		Q
• Customer's quality expectations	Y		Q
• Configuration management plan	Y		Q
Project plan	Y		P
• Product breakdown structure (PBS)	Y		P
• Product flow diagram (PFD)	Y		P
Exception plan	Y		P
Communication plan	Y		P
Business case	Y	Y	P
Risk log	Y		P
Configuration item record (CIR)	Y		Q
• Product description	Y		Q
• Product status account	Y		Q
Quality log	Y		Q
Issue log	Y		Q
• Project issue	Y	Y	Q
Stage plan	Y	Y	P
Stage approval			P
Product checklist	Y		S
Daily log	Y		S
Correspondence			S
Highlight report	Y	Y	S
Exception report	Y	Y	S
End stage report	Y	Y	S
Team plan			S
Work package authorisation			S
Work package	Y		S
Checkpoint report	Y	Y	S
Lessons learned log	Y		P & S
Lessons learned report	Y		P & S
Post-project review plan	Y		P
Follow-on action recommendations	Y		P
End project report	Y	Y	P

Key: P = Project file   S = Stage file   Q = Quality file   Y = Yes

Table A.1: PRINCE2 project documentation. Derived from information in (Bentley 2005), the table shows which project management products have product descriptions and which have templates. It also shows in which part of the project's filing the documentation will be found – the main categories being *project*, *stage* and *quality*.

It is beyond the scope of this appendix to discuss all the PRINCE2 documentation in detail. However let's look at two examples of PRINCE2's standard templates.

Product description template

Given that we looked at PBP earlier in this appendix, we shall first look at the template for product descriptions. The purpose of a product description is to understand the nature of each product, to describe the required appearance or functionality and the level of quality required, and also to enable the activities required to be identified together with the people and skills needed to develop the product. See the product description template in Table A.2.

Identifier	Unique key: used later for configuration management
Title	Standard product name
Purpose	Definition of purpose helps to understand functionality, size, quality, complexity, etc.
Composition	A list of the parts, which go to make up the product. This information can be derived from the product breakdown structure (PBS).
Derivation	What are the source products from which this product is derived? This information can be derived from the product flow diagram (PFD)
Format and presentation	There may be a standard appearance to which the product has to conform
Allocated to	The person/group/skill type that will be required for the development
Quality criteria	The quality specification or criteria that the finished product must meet, including the quality exit criteria that will be used for inspections; may reference common standards
Quality method	How the quality checking will be carried out to test/check/review the quality or functionality of finished product
Quality check skills required	Indication of skills required to perform quality check. Specific individuals could also be identified, but this will typically only be done when the stage in which the quality check is to take place has been planned in detail (as more will then be known about resource availability)

Table A.2: Template for a product description

Risk log template

The other template we shall look at is for the risk log, as shown in Table A.3.

Risk Identifier	Unique identifier
Description	Brief description of risk
Risk category	Category of risk (for example commercial, legal and technical.)
Impact	❏ High ❏ Medium ❏ Low *Likely effect on the project if risk were to occur*
Probability	❏ High ❏ Medium ❏ Low *Estimate of the likelihood of risk occurring*
Proximity	❏ Long term ❏ Medium term ❏ Short term *How close (in time) is the risk likely to occur?*
Countermeasure(s)	❏ Prevention ❏ Reduction ❏ Transference ❏ Acceptance ❏ Contingency *The actions that will be taken to counteract this risk. Not all types of countermeasure will be appropriate, although it is possible that several possible countermeasures will be identified and selected.*
Owner	The person or role who is appointed to keep an eye on the risk
Author	The person/role who initially identified and submitted the risk
Date identified	The date the risk was first identified
Date updated	The date the risk was last updated or the status of the risk was checked
Current status	The current status of the risk (for example reducing, increasing, no change and no longer relevant)

Table A.3: Template for a risk log entry

A.5 Summary

This appendix has described the main elements of the PRINCE2 project management method. Hopefully, you can see the parallels between the chapters of this book and the various components of PRINCE2. These parallels include:

- Having separate project management and systems development lifecycles (Chapter 1)
- Establishing a business case (Chapter 2)
- Ensuring the project's continuing business relevance (business reviews (Chapter 4)
- Putting in place configuration management and change control (Chapter 4)
- Establishing the project products (deliverables, Chapter 4)
- Producing project reports (Chapter 4)
- Creating a product breakdown structure (as opposed to a work breakdown structure (WBS) (Chapter 5)
- Producing project plans, which include schedules and financial costs (Chapters 5 and 6)
- Carrying out the project manager role and reporting to a project board (Chapter 7)
- Handling of quality assurance (user, business and technical assurance) (Chapter 8)
- Using quality plans including quality acceptance criteria (Chapter 8)
- Use of PRINCE2 as applying an industry standard (Chapter 8)
- Handling of risk, including the various logs (Chapter 9)
- Carrying out a post-project review and reporting the findings (post-delivery review, Chapter 10).

A.6 References

Bentley, C. (2005), *Practical PRINCE2* (3rd revised edition), TSO (The Stationery Office), ISBN: 0 11 703544 0.

Office of Government Commerce (2005), *Managing Successful Projects with PRINCE2* (5th revised edition), TSO (The Stationery Office), ISBN: 0 113 30946 5.

*entries in **bold** signify main treatments*